THE CAMBRIDGE COMPANION TO
EXISTENTIALISM

Existentialism exerts a continuing fascination on students of philosophy and general readers. As a philosophical phenomenon, though, it is often poorly understood as a form of radical subjectivism that turns its back on reason and argumentation and possesses all the liabilities of philosophical idealism but without any idealistic conceptual clarity. In this volume of original essays, the first to be devoted exclusively to existentialism in over forty years, a team of distinguished commentators discusses the ideas of Kierkegaard, Nietzsche, Heidegger, Sartre, Merleau-Ponty, and Beauvoir and shows how their focus on existence provides a compelling perspective on contemporary issues in moral psychology and philosophy of mind, language, and history. A further sequence of chapters examines the influence of existential ideas beyond philosophy, in literature, religion, politics, and psychiatry. The volume offers a rich and comprehensive assessment of the continuing vitality of existentialism as a philosophical movement and a cultural phenomenon.

STEVEN CROWELL is Joseph and Joanna Nazro Mullen Professor at Rice University. He is the author of *Husserl, Heidegger, and the Space of Meaning* (2001), and the editor of *The Prism of the Self: Philosophical Essays in Honor of Maurice Natanson* (1995), and, with Jeff Malpas, of *Transcendental Heidegger* (2007).

OTHER VOLUMES IN THE SERIES OF CAMBRIDGE COMPANIONS

ABELARD *Edited by* JEFFREY E. BROWER *and* KEVIN GUILFOY
ADORNO *Edited by* THOMAS HUHN
ANCIENT SCEPTICISM *Edited by* RICHARD BETT
ANSELM *Edited by* BRIAN DAVIES *and* BRIAN LEFTOW
AQUINAS *Edited by* NORMAN KRETZMANN *and* ELEONORE STUMP
ARABIC PHILOSOPHY *Edited by* PETER ADAMSON *and* RICHARD C. TAYLOR
HANNAH ARENDT *Edited by* DANA VILLA
ARISTOTLE *Edited by* JONATHAN BARNES
ATHEISM *Edited by* MICHAEL MARTIN
AUGUSTINE *Edited by* ELEONORE STUMP *and* NORMAN KRETZMANN
BACON *Edited by* MARKKU PELTONEN
BERKELEY *Edited by* KENNETH P. WINKLER
BOETHIUS *Edited by* JOHN MARENBOM
BRENTANO *Edited by* DALE JACQUETTE
CARNAP *Edited by* MICHAEL FRIEDMAN
CONSTANT *Edited by* HELENA ROSENBLATT
CRITICAL THEORY *Edited by* FRED RUSH
DARWIN 2nd edition *Edited by* JONATHAN HODGE *and* GREGORY RADICK
SIMONE DE BEAUVOIR *Edited by* CLAUDIA CARD
DESCARTES *Edited by* JOHN COTTINGHAM
DEWEY *Edited by* MOLLY COCHRAN
DUNS SCOTUS *Edited by* THOMAS WILLIAMS
EARLY GREEK PHILOSOPHY *Edited by* A. A. LONG
EARLY MODERN PHILOSOPHY *Edited by* DONALD RUTHERFORD
EPICUREANISM *Edited by* JAMES WARREN
EXISTENTIALISM *Edited by* STEVEN CROWELL
FEMINISM IN PHILOSOPHY *Edited by* MIRANDA FRICKER *and* JENNIFER HORNSBY
FOUCAULT 2nd edition *Edited by* GARY GUTTING
FREGE *Edited by* THOMAS RICKETTS *and* MICHAEL POTTER
FREUD *Edited by* JEROME NEU

Continued at the back of the book

The Cambridge Companion to EXISTENTIALISM

Edited by

Steven Crowell
Rice University

CAMBRIDGE
UNIVERSITY PRESS

CAMBRIDGE
UNIVERSITY PRESS

University Printing House, Cambridge CB2 8BS, United Kingdom

Cambridge University Press is part of the University of Cambridge.

It furthers the University's mission by disseminating knowledge in the pursuit of education, learning and research at the highest international levels of excellence.

www.cambridge.org
Information on this title: www.cambridge.org/9780521732789

First published 2012
Reprinted 2012

A catalogue record for this publication is available from the British Library

Library of Congress Cataloguing in Publication data
The Cambridge companion to existentialism / edited by Steven Crowell, Rice University, Houston.
pages cm. – (Cambridge companions to philosophy)
Includes bibliographical references and index.
ISBN 978-0-521-51334-0 (hardback) – ISBN 978-0-521-73278-9 (paperback)
1. Existentialism. I. Crowell, Steven Galt, editor of compilation.
B819.C28 2012
142′.78–dc23
2011044362

ISBN 978-0-521-73278-9 Paperback

CONTENTS

CONTRIBUTORS

KRISTANA ARP is Professor of Philosophy at Long Island University, Brooklyn, and the author of *The Bonds of Freedom: Simone de Beauvoir's Existentialist Ethics* (2001).

ROBERT BERNASCONI is Edwin Erle Sparks Professor of Philosophy at Pennsylvania State University. He is the author of two books on Heidegger and of *How to Read Sartre* (2006). He is co-editor with Simon Critchley of *The Cambridge Companion to Emmanuel Levinas* (2002) and with Jonathan Judaken of the forthcoming *Situating Existentialism: Key Texts in Context*. He is also the author of numerous articles in the critical philosophy of race and in nineteenth- and twentieth-century European philosophy.

WILLIAM BLATTNER is Professor of Philosophy at Georgetown University and the author of *Heidegger's Being and Time: A Reader's Guide* (2006) and *Heidegger's Temporal Idealism* (1999).

MATTHEW BROOME is Associate Clinical Professor of Psychiatry at the University of Warwick and Consultant Psychiatrist, Coventry and Warwickshire Partnership Trust, UK. He is also Chair of the Philosophy Special Interest Group at the Royal College of Psychiatrists. Together with Lisa Bortolotti, Broome edited *Psychiatry as Cognitive Neuroscience: Philosophical Perspectives* (2009) and is currently co-editing *The Maudsley Reader in Phenomenological Psychiatry* with colleagues from the Maudsley Philosophy Group.

TAYLOR CARMAN is Professor of Philosophy at Barnard College, Columbia University. He is co-editor of *The Cambridge Companion to Merleau-Ponty* (2004) and author of *Heidegger's Analytic* (2003) and *Merleau-Ponty* (2008).

DAVID E. COOPER is Professor of Philosophy Emeritus at Durham University, UK. His many books include *Existentialism: A Reconstruction* (1990, 1999); *World Philosophies: An Historical Introduction* (1995, 2002); and *The Measure of Things: Humanism, Humility and Mystery* (2003). He is co-editor of *Philosophy: The Classic Readings* (2009).

STEVEN CROWELL is Joseph and Joanna Nazro Mullen Professor of Philosophy at Rice University. He is the author of *Husserl, Heidegger, and the Space of Meaning: Paths toward Transcendental Phenomenology* (2001), and editor, with Jeff Malpas, of *Transcendental Heidegger* (2007). Crowell authored the article on "Existentialism" for *The Stanford Encyclopedia of Philosophy* and has served as Executive Co-Director of the Society for Phenomenology and Existential Philosophy. Currently he is editor of *Husserl Studies.*

HUBERT L. DREYFUS is Professor of Philosophy in the Graduate School at the University of California at Berkeley. His publications include: *What Computers (Still) Can't Do* (1992); *Being-in-the-World: A Commentary on Division I of Heidegger's Being and Time* (1991); *Mind over Machine: The Power of Human Intuition and Expertise in the Era of the Computer* (with Stuart Dreyfus,1986); *On the Internet* (2001, 2009); and most recently, with Sean Dorrance Kelly, *All Things Shining: Reading the Western Classics to Find Meaning in a Secular Age* (2011). Dreyfus has been a Guggenheim Fellow and is a Fellow of the American Academy of Arts and Sciences.

THOMAS R. FLYNN is Samuel Candler Dobbs Professor of Philosophy at Emory University. He is the author of *Sartre and Marxist Existentialism: The Test Case of Collective Responsibility* (1984); *Sartre, Foucault, and Historical Reason*, vol. I, *Toward an Existentialist Theory of History*, vol. II, *A Poststructuralist Mapping of History* (1997); and *Existentialism: A Very Short Introduction* (2006).

ALASTAIR HANNAY is Emeritus Professor of Philosophy at the University of Oslo. He has been Visiting Professor at the University of California (Berkeley and San Diego) and the University of Stockholm. He was for many years editor of *Inquiry* and is author of *Mental Images – A Defence* (1971, 2002); *Kierkegaard* (1982, 1999); *Human Consciousness* (1990); *Kierkegaard: A Biography* (2001); *Kierkegaard and Philosophy* (2003); and *On the Public* (2006). He has translated several of Kierkegaard's works and is a Fellow of the Royal Society of Edinburgh as well a Member of both the Royal Norwegian Scientific Society of Science and Letters and the Norwegian Academy of Science and Letters.

KARSTEN HARRIES is the Brooks and Suzanne Ragen Professor of Philosophy at Yale University. He is the author of many books, including *The Meaning of Modern Art* (1968); *The Bavarian Rococo Church: Between Faith and Aestheticism* (1983); *The Ethical Function of Architecture* (1997); *Infinity and Perspective* (2001); *Art Matters: A Critical Commentary on Martin Heidegger's "The Origin of the Work of Art"* (2009); *Between Nihilism and Faith: A Commentary on Either/Or* (2010); and the forthcoming *Wahrheit: Die Architektur der Welt.*

LAWRENCE J. HATAB is Louis I. Jaffe Professor of Philosophy at Old Dominion University. His books include *A Nietzschean Defense of Democracy* (1995); *Ethics and Finitude: Heideggerian Contributions to Moral Philosophy* (2000); *Nietzsche's Life Sentence: Coming to Terms with Eternal Recurrence* (2005); and *Nietzsche's On the Genealogy of Morality: An Introduction* (2008).

WILLIAM MCBRIDE is Arthur G. Hansen Distinguished Professor of Philosophy at Purdue University, and Director of its interdisciplinary Ph.D. program in philosophy. He is currently President of the International Federation of Philosophical Societies (FISP) and was co-founder and first director of the North American Sartre Society, past president of the North American Society for Social Philosophy and of the Société Américaine de Philosophie de Langue Française.

He has written, edited, or co-edited nineteen books, including *Sartre's Political Theory* (1991) and the eight-volume edited essay collection entitled *Sartre and Existentialism* (1997).

JEFF MALPAS is Professor of Philosophy at the University of Tasmania, Hobart, and Distinguished Visiting Professor at La Trobe University, Melbourne. Among many other works, he is the author of *Place and Experience* (1999) and *Heidegger's Topology* (2006), and is the editor of *Dialogues with Davidson* (2011).

MATTHEW RATCLIFFE is Professor of Philosophy at Durham University, UK. He is author of *Rethinking Commonsense Psychology: A Critique of Folk Psychology* (2008); *Theory of Mind and Simulation* (2007); and *Feelings of Being: Phenomenology, Psychiatry and the Sense of Reality* (2008).

RICHARD SCHACHT is Professor of Philosophy and Jubilee Professor of Liberal Arts and Sciences (Emeritus) at the University of Illinois. He has written extensively on Nietzsche and other figures and developments in the post-Kantian interpretive tradition. His books include *Nietzsche* (1983); *Making Sense of Nietzsche* (1995); *Hegel and After* (1975); *Alienation* (1970); *The Future of Alienation* (1994); and *Finding an Ending: Reflections on Wagner's Ring* (2004, with Philip Kitcher). He has also edited several volumes on Nietzsche, including *Nietzsche's Postmoralism* (2000) and *Nietzsche, Genealogy, Morality* (1994).

MEROLD WESTPHAL is Distinguished Professor of Philosophy at Fordham University. He has served as President of the Hegel Society of America and of the Søren Kierkegaard Society and as Executive Co-Director of the Society for Phenomenology and Existential Philosophy. He is the author of many books, including *History and Truth in Hegel's Phenomenology* (1982); *Kierkegaard's Critique of Reason and Society* (1987); *Becoming a Self: A Reading of Kierkegaard's Concluding Unscientific Postscript* (1996); *God, Guilt, and Death: An Existential Phenomenology of Religion* (1984); *Transcendence and Self-Transcendence: An Essay on God and the Soul* (2004); and *Levinas and Kierkegaard in Dialogue* (2008).

1 Introduction

STEVEN CROWELL

I Existentialism and its legacy

In a conversation recorded shortly before his death, Maurice Natanson reports an encounter he had in 1951, when he was lecturing to a philosophical society on Jean-Paul Sartre's *Nausea*. A philosopher stood up and indignantly exclaimed, "I came here with my wife! And whether it's in the regulations [of the Society] or not, I think matters of this kind should not be discussed in front of ladies!"[1] This air of scandal has accompanied existentialism wherever it has appeared: Kierkegaard was the target of a nasty press campaign in nineteenth-century Copenhagen; Nietzsche's first book was vilified by the academic establishment and he had to self-publish several others; Heidegger's early critics called him "death-obsessed"; and Sartre never held an academic position at all, cultivating an oppositional stance to bourgeois values as a matter of principle. This air of scandal – together with an extraordinary cultural reach by way of literature, art, and film – is no doubt largely responsible for the fact that existentialism, almost alone among philosophical "isms," has never disappeared from the public imagination as a stance toward the world. It is hard to imagine "rationalism," say, or "utilitarianism" being revived by each new generation, and by name, as a way of life. But this has been existentialism's fate. David Cooper cites Simone de Beauvoir's recollection that "a set of young people really did ... label themselves 'existentialists,' wear an all-black uniform, frequent the same cafés, and assume an air of *ennui*" – and there have been such ever since.

But this very fact, while certainly emblematic of *one* aspect of existentialism, tends to obscure other aspects. If closer inspection of philosophical movements such as rationalism and utilitarianism shows that they, too, had (and have) their notorious side – that their emergence in their own place and time was hardly the dry academic affair that their entombment in textbooks can make it seem – closer inspection of existential thought reveals that it by no means exhausts itself in being a protest against philosophical business as usual. With other movements in the history of philosophy, students first become familiar with a certain set of ideas in the abstract and are often less familiar with the way such ideas challenged or otherwise engaged with the broader culture: modern rationalism's entanglement with the social and political tensions attendant upon the emergence of Copernican astronomy and Galileo's physics, for example, or the connection between utilitarian ethics and the social implications of an emergent economic liberalism. In the case of existentialism, however, it is the reverse: the cultural attitude is what is most familiar, while the philosophical content of existential thought is rather less so. Authenticity, commitment, *Angst*, death, alienation, nothingness, the absurd: can these notions, so familiar as slogans, be seen to do any real philosophical work? Is existentialism the repository of an identifiable set of philosophical ideas that might not merely have a history, but also a future? In his contribution to the present volume David Cooper offers a set of such ideas, an existentialist "manifesto" that other chapters will confirm, enhance, and in some cases contest. But more generally, *The Cambridge Companion to Existentialism* has been conceived as an argument for the thesis that existential concepts and ideas have much to teach us as we pursue philosophy in a climate quite removed from the one in which they initially appeared. Existentialism is as much a *legacy* as it is a history.[2]

The legacy of existentialism is widespread, and it shows up in some unlikely places. For example, a central concept of classical existentialism is commitment. Drawing on Kierkegaard's reflections on faith, Heidegger developed the idea more systematically and phenomenologically in his analysis of authenticity as resoluteness (*Entschlossenheit*), and Sartre followed suit with his own concept of *engagement*. Initially both Heidegger and Sartre understood commitment mainly in relation to their own political involvements – with National Socialism in Heidegger's case, and with Marxism in Sartre's. Thus one might expect to find the legacy of this idea in contemporary social and political thought, and one does. It may come as a surprise, however, to find it deployed in philosophy of science and philosophy of mind.

Beginning not with Sartre or Heidegger, but with analytic philosophy and debates over the nature of mental content, John Haugeland argues that "existential commitment" – that is, the "freedom ... to take responsibility for the norms and skills in terms of which one copes with things" – is a necessary condition for all determinate thinking or cognition, including scientific cognition.[3] Scientific truth is possible only where there are social practices that involve norms governing what counts as objects, evidence, and acceptable forms of dispute. Such norms are necessarily general and public, but, as norms, they operate only if I, from my first-person standpoint, embrace them as binding on my thought and behavior. In Haugeland's work, the legacy of existentialism shows up in his demonstration that such normative commitment cannot be parsed into a combination of beliefs and desires but is an irreducible form of self-understanding in which I constitute both myself and my world.[4] At the same time, I do not *create* natural things, and in science everything depends on allowing those things to have the last word ("objectivity"). Here too one finds the legacy of existential thought in Haugeland's analysis, for though the norms of scientific practice are *binding* on me, they are "ungrounded," i.e., their validity is not rationally established. And indeed, for science to be radically beholden to objects, it must be possible for the whole "world," the whole edifice of meaning sustained by my commitments, to collapse. From the first-person perspective this is to experience the *death* of my way of life, and part of my existential self-understanding must involve being prepared to endure the "nothingness" of my commitments.[5]

Haugeland's project holds itself to the standards of analytic philosophy of science, but it flies under the banner of a "new existentialism." That it is "new" reflects another aspect of the legacy of existentialism that the present volume would highlight, namely, the ability to "become what it is" through encounters with more recent developments in philosophy. Reflecting on the classics of existentialism from the vantage point of contemporary thought reveals new dimensions in them, which in turn may suggest further perspectives on contemporary problems. By developing existential themes in dialogue with philosophers such as Daniel Dennett, John

Searle, and John McDowell, for instance, Haugeland is able to read *Heidegger* in a way that reveals more to this thinker's project than he himself might have imagined – or appreciated. The legacy of existentialism is not always identical to the legacy that the canonical authors may have imagined for themselves – a point that they, in turn, often exploited in their own dealings with their historical predecessors. Indeed, the very idea that Kierkegaard and Nietzsche – or Pascal or Augustine or Montaigne or even Socrates – belong to an extended tradition of "existentialism" is something of an artifact of how these figures were interpreted by Heidegger, Sartre, Marcel, Jaspers, and other canonical existentialists. Whatever suspicions this might engender from a purely historical point of view, it is unobjectionable as philosophy – especially *existential* philosophy, with its insistence that thinking is always a free, creative response to its own history.

Today this phenomenon – using existential concepts to address contemporary questions, thereby revealing new dimensions in existentialism's founding texts – can clearly be seen in the field of ethics. Each of the major existentialists represented in this volume (with the notable exception of Simone de Beauvoir) has been accused either of lacking an ethics or else of paying insufficient attention to the distinction between ethics and politics. One might expect, then, that the legacy of existentialism would contain little of importance for contemporary ethical debates. But the matter is a good deal more complicated. Writing in the 1970s, as the heyday of existentialism's social and intellectual impact was waning and in an effort to hasten its demise, Karl-Otto Apel noted that in the ideological landscape of the West (primarily Western Europe, England, and the United States), positivism and existentialism – commonly thought to be profoundly antagonistic – actually constituted a complementary "division of labor."[6] As understood at the time, both existentialism and positivism agreed that the realm of objectivity – of cognitive validity, or truth – is exhausted by the individual empirical and formal sciences, while the realm of "value" (ethics, politics, aesthetics) is a matter of subjective conviction or decision. Thus the classical existential idea that ethics is ultimately political and relative to rationally ungrounded contingencies of history found its correlate in the ethical "emotivism" that arose from positivism's preferred approach to value – namely, the rejection of first-order investigation of ethical phenomena in favor of "meta-ethics," a second-order analysis of ethical *language*. But the actual *legacy* of existential ideas – for instance, the constitutive significance of choice and commitment, the potential conflict between meaning and virtue, the priority of self-responsibility over rational grounding, and the refusal to define "human being" as "rational animal" – rendered this division of labor obsolete. If Thomas Kuhn's critique of positivist philosophy of science opened a space for a "new existentialism" in that field, the collapse of positivism also brought with it a new estimation of the domain of value and meaning – which in turn enabled a more nuanced appropriation of existential ideas than could be found within the scope of the "division of labor."

Nowhere is this more apparent than in the emergence of "moral psychology" as a vibrant field of inquiry – one that did not so much as exist when Apel described the division of labor – and the resurgence of normative ethics on its basis. Without making reductive claims for historical causality – and the full story would certainly have to take into account the rise of feminism, a topic that is also not unconnected with the legacy of existentialism[7] – much of the most interesting work being done in ethics today draws on themes that will be quite familiar to readers of the classical existential philosophers. When Bernard Williams reflects on tensions that exist between the issues at stake in ethical inquiry and the "impartial standpoint" demanded by traditional philosophical analysis – between "experience" and "theory," as it were – he ranges widely over the history of philosophy.[8] But the tension itself was first sharply formulated by existential thinkers such as Kierkegaard and Nietzsche. And the texture of Williams's own philosophical approach – keen argument supported by fine-grained descriptions of concrete moral life – is very much in line with the existentialists' embrace of the descriptive phenomenological method.[9] In turn, Williams's acute moral-psychological analysis of the distinction between what is meaningful and what is rationally groundable allows us to see more clearly what is at stake in Heidegger's notion of authenticity or Camus's notion of the absurd.

Similar points can be made regarding Harry Frankfurt's deployment of the concept of "care" in discussions of moral obligation and responsibility; Richard Moran's treatment of first-person authority in terms of "avowal"; Charles Taylor's appeal to a kind of "strong evaluation" that undergirds anything that can be contested rationally; Stephen Darwall's argument that moral philosophy must take the authority of the other person into account in the phenomena of address and claim; and many others.[10] The contrast between such work and the dominant trends in ethics even forty years ago could not be greater. The charge made against philosophical ethics at that time by Iris Murdoch in her untimely book, *The Sovereignty of Good* (1970)[11] – namely, that it was in full flight from any of the *real* ethical and political issues facing human beings – could never be made today. And be the "official" stance toward existentialism taken by these and other thinkers what it may, the change itself belongs in part to the legacy of the existential approach to ethics and value.

One particularly influential example is Christine Korsgaard's inquiry into the sources of moral normativity. If one places the emphasis on Kant's rationalism – his insistence that moral obligation derives from pure reason and is strictly universal – then one can find a stark contrast between Kantian ethics and the existentialist emphasis on choice "in situation," an ethical stance that seems to align better with the Aristotelian tradition of *phronesis*.[12] And it is certainly true that Kantian ethics was a prime target for many existential thinkers. Nevertheless, Kant's rationalism was inseparable from doctrines of freedom and self-determination – the "primacy of *practical* reason" – that have genuine affinities with those notions as they appear in the writings of canonical existential philosophers. Exploiting such connections, Korsgaard agreed with Thomas Nagel's assessment of her work as "rather existentialist."[13] What makes it so?

Above all, it is the idea that the self is not something simply given – as substance or even as "subject" – but is something *made* or constituted through my choices and commitments. My inclinations and instincts, for instance, are not brute facts but part of my "facticity," i.e., are present in my experience ever only as opportunities or challenges that take on meaning – become *mine* – through my identification with or refusal of them.[14] Korsgaard's concept of practical identity ("a description under which you value yourself,"[15] the source of practical reasons) – tracks Haugeland's idea of "self-understanding" because both of them channel the existentialist idea of commitment, where commitment is not an act of consciousness, a mental process or disposition, but my fundamental stance, or "being," in the world. Korsgaard's employment of the notion, in turn, allows for a deeper understanding of *Kant*. One can now better appreciate how the "anthropological" features of his view (emphasizing the contingent psychological and situational factors in *human* life, in contrast to the life of a purely rational agent) are essential to his moral psychology, rather than being inconsistent appendages. Kant is more existential than we knew!

At the same time, the existentialists are more Kantian than we knew. Where Kant emphasizes self-*legislation* as the key to morality, Korsgaard alters the emphasis. It is *self*-legislation that counts; my valuing myself under a certain description, my practical identity, is what gives normative force to anything that purports to bind me morally. In Sartre's terms, the "exigency" of the alarm clock, its power to influence my behavior, is bestowed on it by me precisely in the act of getting up.[16] For Sartre, once I begin to *reflect* on whether to get up, I confront my vertiginous freedom. Korsgaard makes a similar point: when I reflect, my inclinations are inevitably "distanced" from me, called into question, and I must decide whether to take them as reasons to act.[17] Such reasons are provided by my practical identity: because I value myself as a teacher, I have a reason to resist my inclination to stay in bed and a motivating reason to get up and do my job. But this Kantian appeal to reasons may give out: is there a reason for me to value myself as a teacher? For Sartre, I ultimately choose such identities "without justification and without excuse."[18] Korsgaard, in contrast, claims that there is a practical identity that you *must* value, if you value anything at all – "your own humanity"[19] – one which therefore provides you with ultimately justifying reasons. The hypothetical character of this "must" leads straight to the existential problem of suicide, however, and the question of the meaning of life.[20] Must I value anything at all?

Another example of the legacy of existentialism is found in the work of Richard Rorty, the title of whose *Contingency, Irony, and Solidarity* could practically serve as the teaser for a course in existentialism. The idea that the self is "contingent" – that existence precedes essence, that human nature is self-making – is central to classical existential thought. This legacy of existentialism is both challenged and advanced when Rorty argues that self-making is more akin to poetic imagination than to instrumental deliberation.

If earlier existentialists like Sartre and Heidegger pictured the self in its social, natural, and historical situation as a heroic originator of "worlds," Rorty – drawing on Wilfrid Sellars's critique of the Myth of the Given and on Donald Davidson's coherentist philosophy of language – deflates this heroic individualism by redescribing self-making as the permanent possibility of "redescribing" things in ways that make them more one's own. Contingent selfhood thus entails dependence on linguistic material that is shared with others, together with a refusal of the idea that there is One True Description.[21]

But if there is no One True Description what remains of philosophy, which since Plato has sought precisely the Truth? Rorty's concept of "irony" is meant to address this question, and here too he advances the legacy of existentialism. On the one hand, Rorty follows the existentialist critique of traditional philosophy ("metaphysics") found above all in Nietzsche and Heidegger. Philosophy is not an abstract theory of ultimate reality carried out from some God's-eye view but the passionate struggle to express one's understanding of the world precisely from *within* one's contingent, historical, first-person situation. In contrast to existentialists like Heidegger and Sartre, however, who treat such expressions as having something of the cognitive force of traditional philosophy, Rorty argues that the construction of "final vocabularies" is *authentic* only if pursued with a certain irony. In crafting a "final" vocabulary within a contingent historical situation, I must realize that there can be no such finality and so I stand, or ought to stand, at a certain ironic distance from my project – doubt about the possibility of such a project being endemic to the project itself. It follows – in contrast to the hopes of traditional philosophy and some existential thought as well – that no final vocabulary can be called upon to *justify* what we do. In Rorty's hands, then, the legacy of existentialism entails a radical public/private split, where irony – "play" with one's final vocabularies, the pursuit of the big picture – belongs to the private sphere, while "hope" – but not rational justification – supports one's political commitments in public.[22]

On Rorty's view, practical social and political problems do not call for philosophical analysis but for expanding our sense of *solidarity* with others, and this is best achieved through literature, since the imaginative encounter with diverse possibilities of the human condition found there enhances our capacities for empathy and identification. This, in turn, ought to make us "ironists" amenable to abandoning the desire for what philosophy cannot provide: ultimately grounded answers to questions like "Why not be cruel? Why be kind?" In both this appeal to solidarity and in the idea that solidarity is to be fostered through the literary imagination, Rorty's pragmatism exemplifies a critical appropriation of existentialism similar to what we found in the areas of philosophy of science, mind, and ethics.

The legacy of existentialism, and the way that the overt or covert appropriation of existentialist ideas reveals new dimensions in the work of canonical existential philosophers, is evident in recent continental European philosophy as well. One might have expected this to be the case – after all, the major existentialists were themselves "Continental" philosophers – but here too the legacy is complicated. If at the time of its first appearance existentialism was almost universally ignored in American and British philosophy departments, one or another version of it had been an important feature of European philosophy since the 1920s, and by the early 1960s Sartre and existentialism had achieved such prominence in the public mind that the next two decades of European thought might be seen, without too much exaggeration, as a series of attempts to kill the existentialist beast through a conspiracy of silence.[23] Nevertheless, the ideas had staying power and have recently re-emerged in a form that allows us to read the work of their originators with new appreciation.

As examples, one need only consider Michel Foucault and Jacques Derrida. Both thinkers began their careers well versed in the phenomenological tradition that gave rise to modern existentialism, and both were entirely conversant with the themes of the Hegelianized existential version of phenomenology that had displaced Edmund Husserl's original project for a "rigorous science" of philosophy: the emphasis on contingency, historicity, the "nothingness" of the self, the critique of rationalism, the meaning-constituting role of moods such as *Angst*, and so on. In their early work, however, neither Foucault nor Derrida developed these themes phenomenologically, drawing instead on a certain *structuralism*. Why? One obvious answer is that this enabled them to escape the "atmosphere" of existentialism by proclaiming the "end," or philosophical irrelevance, of the concept of individual subjectivity. Structuralism's basic idea – that the subject is not a ground but an effect or function of codes, norms, and relationships within a system (of mythemes, signifiers, "power," etc.) – dominates these early works.

In books such as *The Order of Things* (original French edition, 1966) and *The Archaeology of Knowledge* (original French edition, 1969), for instance, Foucault combined a structuralist approach to language and representation with an aspect of Nietzsche's thought – "genealogy" – that had not played a large role in the latter's reception as an existentialist. His aim was to undermine the idea, found in both Sartre and Heidegger, that the human being is the locus of the constitution of meaning. Instead, "man" appears here as something like a character in a novel, constituted by the "anthropological" discourses of the eighteenth and nineteenth centuries – thus, "a recent invention" that is "perhaps nearing its end."[24] And in early works like *Of Grammatology* (original French edition, 1967) and *Writing and Difference* (original French edition, 1967), Derrida, too, took aim at existentialism's so-called "humanism." Echoing Foucault's criticism of the modern idea of man as an "empirico-transcendental doublet,"[25] Derrida's essay, "The Ends of Man" (a lecture from 1968), suggested that existentialism's basic terms – Sartre's "for-itself," Heidegger's "Dasein," Husserl's "transcendental consciousness" – are unstable (yet necessary) amalgams that entail the perpetual *deferral*, rather than the phenomenological recovery, of what philosophy seeks: clarification of the meaning of being.[26] If Derrida was more willing than Foucault to admit that a simple escape from this philosophical fantasy was not in the cards, they both dismissed what to them appeared to be the naïvety and "nostalgia" of phenomenologically inflected existentialism.

In later works, however, both returned to recognizably existential themes – not in the form of a regressive repetition but nevertheless with enough fidelity to allow us to see the legacy of existentialism at work. In his three-volume *History of Sexuality* (French edition, 1976–84), for instance, Foucault employs the genealogical method not to demolish the modern concept of the self but to recover a premodern experience of selfhood whose features contrast in important ways with the self as formed by the technological and disciplinary imperatives of modern social systems. In so doing, however, his interests are not antiquarian but concern present possibilities. This is made plain in his late essay, "What is Enlightenment?" If

Foucault's earlier writings pictured a system of power in which individual freedom could scarcely be imagined, this essay invokes "work carried out by ourselves upon ourselves as free beings," precisely in the name of a "practical critique that takes the form of a possible transgression." Here we cannot but note a legacy of the existentialist imperative of self-making and the commitment to liberation. And Foucault also rejoins existentialism via ancient Greek philosophy when he insists that philosophy so conceived is not an abstract play with concepts but "an attitude, an *ethos*, a philosophical life."[27] In works such as *The Gift of Death* (French edition, 1992), Derrida also returns to existential themes – in this case, the *Ur*-existential topics of choice and responsibility – revisiting Kierkegaard's account of the story of Abraham through the eyes of the phenomenologist Jan Patočka's "heretical" philosophy of history. By focusing on the "aporia" of responsibility – a responsible choice (one that is rationally justified) is not a choice, while choosing without rational grounds is irresponsible – Derrida recovers the existential themes of inwardness, "secrecy," and the weight of ethical commitment; furthermore, he does so in a philosophical register that is far closer to the existential mood of *Angst* than it is to the *jouissance* of his earlier work.

Finally, European feminist thought developed by means of a complicated relation to existentialism and has provided important resources for rereading the existentialist canon in a productive way. This is most obvious in the case of Simone de Beauvoir, but more recent thinkers such as Julia Kristeva and Luce Irigaray also contribute, often in spite of themselves, to the legacy we are tracing. Irigaray, for instance, draws upon psychoanalysis and post-structuralist philosophy to identify serious lacunae in existential theories of subjectivity. To her, Merleau-Ponty's concept of "flesh" is a kind of intrauterine fantasy, while his major insight into the origin of reflection in *tactile* experience is ultimately subordinated to the traditional (and masculinist) priority of vision. On her view this "cancels the most powerful components" of Merleau-Ponty's insights into embodiment, but when Irigaray then begins to recover these insights by reflection on the female body and the experiences of maternity, she remains in the draft of a certain existentialism nonetheless.[28]

A different aspect of the legacy of existentialism can be found in the work of the American philosopher Judith Butler, who draws upon the tradition of European feminism while criticizing its gender-essentialism. Against the idea that there is a fundamental female identity, Butler, like Foucault, insists that the rigid distinction between male and female rests on the operation of contingent social codes and regimes of power, and that one's gender identity is thus a construct – whether a neurotic and anxious accommodation to the dominant codes, or a more subversive, transgressive one that plays with this very contingency. But this insistence on the *performative* character of gender identity exhibits the same intimate relation to the existential legacy of Nietzsche and Sartre that we found in the later Foucault.[29]

Several *Cambridge Companion* authors have, in their own work, contributed to this legacy, and some evidence of that will appear in the chapters they have provided. However, the present volume does not pretend to pursue these legacies in any detail. Its goal is to provide reliable, informative, and philosophically provocative reflections on the primary sources of this intellectual tradition which will allow the reader to appreciate its ongoing potential and perhaps be moved to carry on that legacy in their own work.

******

Unlike most other volumes in the series, *The Cambridge Companion to Existentialism* is not devoted to the work of just one philosopher, and this has imposed some unique editorial challenges. Regarding the structure of the volume, and the selection of figures and topics to include, two principles have governed. First, it is meant for *students*. Authors were asked to provide readers with the means to appreciate the importance of the topic or figure in question, rather than to pursue the kind of argument that only specialists could follow. The hope, nevertheless, is that students (and general readers) at every level will find something of value in the chapters. At the same time – and this is the second guiding principle – each chapter aims to develop an independent stand on some philosophically pertinent aspect of the position under discussion. In this way, the volume is meant performatively to demonstrate the vitality of existential thought. Whether their origin is acknowledged or not, existential themes and concepts are not the "scandalous" tropes they once were but are common currency in contemporary philosophy – though they still have the power to provoke!

The first principle – that the volume be useful to students – has governed the selection of figures and topics. The term "existentialism" covers a very large and heterogeneous set of authors, artists, intellectuals, and cultural producers, and a comprehensive guide to existentialism in this sense would certainly be useful. The present volume, however, is restricted to *philosophical* existentialism, and, within this rubric, to those figures and problems that are most frequently taught in courses on existentialism in philosophy departments. To this extent, the volume does not try to alter the prevailing picture of who or what is central to existential philosophy.

The stage is set in Part II by two chapters that provide something of an overview of existentialism in historical perspective. Drawing upon main currents of nineteenth- and twentieth-century European thought, David Cooper argues that "existentialism" names a distinctive, and systematically coherent, picture of the world shared by a "family" of thinkers. Typically, existentialists assert the *uniqueness* of the human situation in the world (i.e., they reject a theoretically reductive philosophical naturalism). This situation is characterized by ambiguity and estrangement, but also by a sense of freedom and responsibility for meaning. As Cooper suggests, one philosophical benefit of this way of thinking (contrary to what many hold to be the radical subjectivism of existentialism) is precisely that it avoids an absolute division between a scientistic "objectivity" and a merely "subjective" world of meaning and value. William McBride places philosophical existentialism in the broader cultural milieu of mid-twentieth-century Europe. Identifying the emergence of theistic and atheistic versions of existentialism at the "French epicenter" of the movement, McBride traces the shifting alliances and political involvements of the main players in this drama and describes the post-war climate in which existential ideas were globally disseminated. As McBride shows, this climate led to a great many artists, writers, filmmakers and even musicians being "associated" with existentialism – a term that reminds us that while important intellectual movements often influence cultural practices directly, they just as often draw the interpretation of other, not so directly related, works into their orbit.

The impact of philosophical existentialism in areas beyond philosophy is explored in the four chapters of Part IV. One of the most prominent of these areas is literature. Jeff Malpas deals with the problem alluded to at the end of the previous paragraph by distinguishing between the "existential" (that is, a general concern with existence) and "existentialist" (that is, having to do with the historical movement, existentialism) – and he argues that existentialism is as much a "literary genre or style" as it is a "philosophical attitude." He supports this with readings of existentialist "precursors" – Kafka, Dostoevsky, Tolstoy – and the literary output of Sartre, Beauvoir, and Camus. But the reach of existentialism in literature is wider, as Malpas shows by tracing connections between existentialism and such very different writers as Samuel Beckett, Hermann Hesse, Milan Kundera, Ernest Hemingway, and Allen Ginsburg.[30] Merold Westphal then analyzes the encounter between existentialism and religion in the writings of Kierkegaard, Nietzsche, Sartre, and Marcel. Understanding existential thought as involving risk, passion, choice, and urgency – right up to the question of what I might be willing to die for – Westphal insists on Kierkegaard's point that faith, my trust in God, can indeed go against reason's dictates *and* that there is no guarantee that such trust is not misplaced. "Atheistic" existentialism fares no better, however. With the death of God, as Nietzsche understood, we also lose our ability to place confidence in our reason, science, and morality; while for Sartre, radical freedom means that norms have no binding force beyond my commitment to them and that my relations with others are, in essence, sado-masochistic. Without invoking God directly, Marcel's existentialism responds to this Sartrean conundrum with the idea that to be a self is to "make room" for the other in myself, to belong to the other.[31]

Existential thought has been important in the development of critical race theory and post-colonial political philosophy, and, as Robert Bernasconi argues, one of its significant contributions is the idea that racism is not primarily an attitude (something "in the mind") but a system (built into institutions, often invisible to those who inhabit them). Bernasconi traces the emergence of this idea in the mutually critical, and mutually instructive, relation between Jean-Paul Sartre and Franz Fanon. If Fanon's experience of racism as a system was initially given expression through the language of Sartre's existentialism, Sartre's later move toward a more structural and Marxist account of how attitudes are constituted drew heavily upon Fanon's "rich account of Black experience."[32] Finally,

Matthew Ratcliffe and Matthew Broome show how existential phenomenology provides a framework for exploring psychopathology in a clinical setting. Following the lead of earlier existential psychotherapists – Karl Jaspers, Medard Boss, Ludwig Binswanger, and R. D. Laing, among others – Ratcliffe and Broome analyze one existential category ("possibility") and provide an account of a case history of schizophrenia which exemplifies the existential notion of "death of possibilities." What is all too often taken to be a matter solely for psychopharmacology is thereby reinserted into the communicative texture of the human experience that plays out between therapist and patient.[33]

Framed by these two sections, Part III contains substantial chapters devoted to the individual philosophers who are most frequently associated with existentialism and whose influence within philosophy has been, and continues to be, greatest. The aim has been to provide some account of the main ideas and influence of the thinker in question – to the extent that such ideas involve connections to existentialism – but from the point of view of a particular philosophical, critical engagement. In cases where two chapters are devoted to a single philosopher, the aim has been to explore two different aspects of their relation to existentialism. One central characteristic of existential thinking, for instance, is concern with its own form of expression, often accompanied by experimentation with philosophically non-traditional strategies. Thus, Alastair Hannay's contribution on Kierkegaard explores that author's project of "indirect communication," while Lawrence Hatab reflects on the relations between Nietzsche's ideas and his experimentation with language and personae. Hannay lays out some of the puzzles involved in the Dane's repeated suggestion that thoughtful attention to "existing" requires a way of gaining access to singularity – to the "single individual," whether oneself or another – and so requires a kind of communication that concerns itself not only with the content of what is said but also the relation between the speaker and hearer. Do these notions have a significance beyond Kierkegaard's quite specific project as a religious "missionary," as many subsequent existentialists have assumed? Hannay's nuanced treatment of such questions is not the only place in this volume where a thinker's belonging to the existentialist canon is questioned.[34] A different sort of problem of communication is raised by Nietzsche's texts. On the basis of a certain kind of naturalism, in which the evolution of consciousness and the emergence of language as a tool for the generalization and simplification (falsification) of experience go hand in hand, Nietzsche confronts the problem of how to express that kind of singularity (or existence) that is the target of his exhortation to "transvalue" all traditional values. In his examination of Nietzsche's "stylistic choices" – aphorism, exhortation, metaphor, fictional historical narrative, and the like – Hatab introduces us to strategies of creativity, performativity, and address that became very much a part of the legacy of existentialism.[35]

Two further chapters on Kierkegaard and Nietzsche take up a different set of issues. Hubert Dreyfus is concerned not so much with how existential ideas are communicated as with how they are *appropriated*. Focusing on the concept of self in Kierkegaard's meditation on sin, *The Sickness unto Death*, Dreyfus situates it in the Western tradition's oscillation between a "detached" way of understanding the self and its appropriate way of life (generally associated with Plato and traditional philosophy) and the more "involved, concrete, committed" conception that derives from the ancient Hebrew tradition. Kierkegaard's approach to what Pascal discovered as the "contradictory" self involves the paradoxical idea of realizing the eternal in time, in the *Augenblick* ("moment"), by way of an unconditional commitment to something finite. Does it matter what the content of that commitment is? Kierkegaard seems to hold that only the God-man, Jesus Christ, can serve that role in faith; Dreyfus, in contrast – and here he develops the legacy of existentialism in his own way – argues that it is the structure of the commitment itself that counts.[36] Richard Schacht, in turn, challenges the very idea that Nietzsche should be included among the existentialists. His argument depends on drawing careful distinctions between existentialism, existential philosophy, and *Existenz*-philosophy. If twentieth-century existentialism is something of an amalgam between *Existenz*-philosophy (of which Kierkegaard is a prime example) and Husserl's phenomenology, then much that is distinctive in Nietzsche's thought stands in sharp contrast to both sources of existentialism – for instance, to Kierkegaard's emphasis on the individual and to Husserl's Cartesian emphasis on consciousness. Still, as Schacht's naturalistic reconstruction of Nietzsche's iconically existentialist idea of the death of God makes plain, it is not hard to see how Nietzsche was something of a necessary "catalyst" for the emergence of twentieth-century existentialism.[37]

The two chapters each devoted to Heidegger and to Sartre also form something of a dyad. The first major systematic treatise devoted to the concept of "existence" in the specifically existentialist sense was Heidegger's *Being and Time* (1927). William Blattner's account of this text begins by contrasting Heidegger's project with traditional metaphysical ways of construing existence, essence, substance, and subject. As Blattner shows, the first half of *Being and Time* presents a picture of the self as being-in-the-world – that is, as inseparably limited in a certain way by its natural and historical context, but always equally in such a way that that context is there as the self's "own" possibility. What this "being one's own" amounts to, then, is the topic of Blattner's analysis of the second half of the book, where the key concepts of Heidegger's existentialism are lucidly explained: anxiety, death, guilt, conscience, and resoluteness.[38] Karsten Harries, in turn, focuses on "The Letter on Humanism" (1947), a seminal text in which Heidegger discusses Sartre and existentialism explicitly while announcing the so-called "turn" (*Kehre*) in his own thinking. Identifying existentialism with a kind of "humanism" that is linked to the "metaphysical" origins of the "homelessness" that prevails in the twentieth century, Heidegger denies his connection to it and proposes in its stead the "thinking of Being." Harries relates this argument to Heidegger's political involvement with National Socialism, and to his underlying struggle with the nihilism of the modern world, thus drawing out what is at stake in Heidegger's turn: a heroic freedom and commitment, in the manner of Sartre, is a symptom of nihilism, not its overcoming. Any position, such as existentialism, that begins with the "individual in situation" will fail to recognize the genuine philosophical task: to attune ourselves to – and so to think – that which "*calls* us into the situation."[39]

A similar "turn" can be found in Sartre's work as well. According to Steven Crowell's analysis, the key to understanding the central text of Sartre's existentialism, *Being and Nothingness*, lies in phenomenology – in the non-representational theory of intentional consciousness first advanced by Edmund Husserl and the novel approach to meaning it made possible. Sartre's critical appropriation of Husserl in early works such as *The Transcendence of the*

Ego engenders the idea that a "non-positional" self-consciousness belongs to the essence of consciousness, which in turn underwrites the ontological duality of the *en-soi* (in-itself) and *pour-soi* (for-itself) that structures Sartre's famous accounts of freedom, anguish, negation, and bad faith.[40] It also underwrites a picture of social relations as the site of irreconcilable conflict – "Hell is other people!" – which comes in for significant revision in Sartre's later work, as Thomas Flynn shows in his contribution on Sartre's political existentialism. Tracing Sartre's political thought and involvement throughout his career, Flynn brings out how, through that very involvement, Sartre came to hold that his earlier existential concept of individual freedom was one-sided and paid insufficient attention to the relative autonomy of economic, social, and historical factors. Nevertheless, as Flynn also insists, while Sartre's "turn" toward Marxism demanded revisions in the ontology of *Being and Nothingness*, it also retained and highlighted an element of Sartre's thought that was there from the beginning: the liberating function of the *imagination.* Thus we might speak of a "political imaginary" as itself an important legacy of Sartre's existentialism.[41]

The two final chapters in this section – on Simone de Beauvoir and Maurice Merleau-Ponty – also trace intellectual developments in which existential ideas are both employed and questioned. Carefully unearthing the existential themes that take form in Beauvoir's early fiction and essays, Kristana Arp provides vibrant testimony to the way Beauvoir maintained an independent voice even during the years of her closest intellectual association with Sartre. Indeed, Beauvoir's "ethics of ambiguity" plunges directly into the issues that Sartre failed to address – and perhaps could not address, as many have argued – in *Being and Nothingness.* By the time she wrote *The Second Sex,* however, Beauvoir's existentialism was increasingly leavened with the yeast of Hegel's dialectic. It is this, Arp suggests, that allowed Beauvoir to appreciate what is distinctive about the existential "situation" of woman, so brilliantly analyzed in that text.[42] Finally, by focusing on Merleau-Ponty's most distinctive contribution to the tradition of existential phenomenology – his analysis of the importance of *embodiment* in the constitution of meaningful experience – Taylor Carman provides further evidence that existential thought is not reducible to a fixed system but grows and develops, often in connection with work in other fields. In his early book, *The Phenomenology of Perception*, for instance, Merleau-Ponty began with the Husserlian notion of consciousness and drew on psychological studies to show how the world as it is revealed in perception could be adequately understood only if that consciousness is embodied in ways that neither contemporary science nor traditional philosophy was in a position to clarify. In his later work, however, it was to the visual arts that Merleau-Ponty turned for clues about how to think the nature of embodiment as our imbrication in the "flesh of the world." And as Carman argues, what Merleau-Ponty abandons in this late work is not the stance of existential phenomenology, but only his earlier assumptions about the "primacy of *consciousness*."[43]

Of course, the strategy of giving ample space to the most visible existential philosophers has necessitated some regrettable omissions. Even if one limits oneself to the figures most closely associated with philosophy, there might well have been chapters on Karl Jaspers, Gabriel Marcel, José Ortega y Gasset, Emmanuel Levinas, Martin Buber, and – perhaps above all – Albert Camus. The fact that Camus's thought as a whole, and not merely his literary work, is extensively discussed in the chapter by Jeff Malpas, and that some discussion of Jaspers, Marcel, and Ortega can be found in other chapters, only highlights the self-imposed limits of the volume. But just as there has been no attempt here to provide anything like full coverage of the connections between existential philosophy and the fields of literature, religion, psychology, or politics, so there has been no attempt to do justice to all those who have contributed to the legacy of existentialism in philosophy itself. By focusing in some depth on the major existential philosophers, the hope is that the volume will serve to sustain (or to spark) the reader's interest in the core issues of existential thought, and to that extent encourage the exploration of figures and topics not covered, or not adequately covered, here.

NOTES

1. See Crowell, "A Conversation with Maurice Natanson," pp. 305–6. Throughout this *Companion*, references in notes have been given by author and a short title. Full bibliographical information can be found in the Bibliography. If abbreviations are used for frequently cited texts, they will be introduced in individual chapters by the authors.

2. In addition to the works cited in the individual chapters, the reader may wish to consult the following recent general accounts: Cooper, *Existentialism*; Crowell, "Existentialism"; Flynn, *Existentialism*; Guignon, "Existentialism"; and Reynolds, *Understanding Existentialism*. Additional readings on specific topics will be mentioned in subsequent notes to this Introduction.
3. Haugeland, "Toward a New Existentialism," p. 2; Haugeland, "Truth and Rule Following."
4. Haugeland, "Truth and Finitude."
5. Haugeland, "Letting Be." For a sympathetic, yet critical view of the existential aspect in Haugeland's work, see Rouse, *How Scientific Practices Matter*.
6. Apel, "The Apriori of the Communication Community and the Foundation of Ethics," pp. 233f.
7. This connection cannot be explored here, but one area in which it is particularly perspicuous is in the ethics of "care." See, for instance, Gilligan, *In a Different Voice*; Noddings, *Caring*; and Bartky, *Sympathy and Solidarity*.
8. Williams, *Ethics and the Limits of Philosophy*, pp. 70ff.
9. Though there has not been space to explore this connection in detail here, see Cerbone, *Understanding Phenomenology*; Dreyfus and Wrathall, *A Companion to Phenomenology and Existentialism*; and D. Moran, *Introduction to Phenomenology*.
10. See Frankfurt, *The Importance of What We Care About*; R. Moran, *Authority and Estrangement*; Taylor, *The Sources of the Self*; and Darwall, *The Second-Person Standpoint*.
11. Murdoch, *The Sovereignty of Good*. Interestingly, Murdoch lumped existentialism and analytic philosophy together because both attribute "to the individual an empty lonely freedom" (p. 27).
12. The legacy of existentialism is evident in contemporary Aristotelian and communitarian ethics as well, of course. We have already mentioned Charles Taylor's work, which develops aspects of the "hermeneutic" tradition that arose from Heidegger's early existential phenomenology – for instance in Hans-Georg Gadamer's *Truth and Method*. Notable also is the attempt by Martha Nussbaum – begun in her *The Fragility of Goodness* and developed in later works such as *Cultivating Humanity* and *Hiding from Humanity* – to ground a moral psychology as much in emotion as in reason, and to see literary art as a source of moral intelligence. In these and other ways she shares common ground with existential philosophers.
13. Korsgaard, *Sources of Normativity*, p. 237.
14. These points are developed in detail in Korsgaard, *Self-Constitution*.

15. Korsgaard, *Sources of Normativity*, p. 101.
16. Sartre, *Being and Nothingness*, pp. 75–76.
17. Korsgaard, *Self-Constitution*, pp. 114–17.
18. Sartre, *Being and Nothingness*, p. 78.
19. Korsgaard, *Sources of Normativity*, pp. 122–23.
20. Korsgaard, *Sources of Normativity*, pp. 160–64.
21. Rorty, *Contingency, Irony, and Solidarity*, pp. 23–43.
22. Rorty, *Contingency, Irony, and Solidarity*, pp. 73–95.
23. See Wood, "A Revisionary Account of the Apotheosis and Demise of the Philosophy of the Subject"; and Wood, *Understanding Sartre*.
24. Foucault, *The Order of Things*, pp. 386–87.
25. Foucault, *The Order of Things*, p. 322.
26. Derrida, "The Ends of Man," pp. 109–36.
27. Foucault, "What is Enlightenment?" pp. 32–50.
28. See Irigaray, *An Ethics of Sexual Difference*, pp. 173–75. For recent readings of Kristeva's work that struggle with the existential issues of subjectivity and agency, see Oliver, *Ethics, Politics, and Difference*.
29. See Butler, *Gender Trouble*; and Schrift, "Judith Butler." A classic collection that includes other American feminists with ties to the existential tradition is Allen and Young, *The Thinking Muse*.
30. In addition to the readings mentioned in the notes to Chapter 14, the reader may wish to consult: Keefe, *French Existentialist Fiction*; Kern, *Existential Thought and Fictional Technique*; and Natanson, *The Erotic Bird*.
31. In addition to the readings mentioned in the notes to Chapter 15, the reader may wish to consult: Evans, *Passionate Reason*; Kaufmann, *Existentialism, Religion, and Death*; and Westphal, *God, Guilt, and Death*.
32. In addition to the readings mentioned in the notes to Chapter 16, the reader may wish to consult: Gordon, *Bad Faith and Anti-Black Racism*; Gordon, *Fanon and the Crisis of European Man*; and Judaken, *Race after Sartre*.
33. In addition to the readings mentioned in the notes to Chapter 17, the reader may wish to consult: Broome *et al.*, *The Maudsley Reader*; Kendler and Parnas, *Philosophical Issues in Psychiatry*; May *et al.*, *Existence*; and Sass, *Madness and Modernism*.
34. In addition to the readings mentioned in the notes to Chapter 4, the reader may wish to consult: Mackey, *Kierkegaard*; Mulhall, *Inheritance and Originality*; Schönbaumsfeld, *A Confusion of the Spheres*; and Walsh, *Living Poetically*.
35. In addition to the readings mentioned in the notes to Chapter 7, the reader may wish to consult: Conway, *Nietzsche's Dangerous Game*;

Gillespie and Strong, *Nietzsche's New Seas*; and Gooding-Williams, *Zarathustra's Dionysian Modernism*.

36. In addition to the readings mentioned in the notes to Chapter 5, the reader may wish to consult: Hannay and Marino, *Cambridge Companion to Kierkegaard*; Rée and Chamberlain, *Kierkegaard*; and Westphal, *Becoming a Self*.
37. In addition to the readings mentioned in the notes to Chapter 6, the reader may wish to consult: Danto, *Nietzsche as Philosopher*; Jaspers, *Nietzsche*; Pippin, *Nietzsche, Psychology, and First Philosophy*; Poellner, *Nietzsche and Metaphysics*; Richardson, *Nietzsche's System*; and Schacht, *Nietzsche*.
38. In addition to the readings mentioned in the notes to Chapter 8, the reader may wish to consult: Carman, *Heidegger's Analytic*; Crowell, *Husserl, Heidegger, and the Space of Meaning*; Dreyfus, *Being-in-the-World*; Olafson, *Heidegger and the Philosophy of Mind*; Polt, *Heidegger's Being and Time*; and Raffoul, *Heidegger and the Subject*.
39. In addition to the readings mentioned in the notes to Chapter 9, the reader may wish to consult: Sluga, *Heidegger's Crisis*; Thomson, *Heidegger on Ontotheology*; Zimmerman, *Heidegger's Confrontation with Modernity*; and Dreyfus and Wrathall, *A Companion to Heidegger*.
40. In addition to the readings mentioned in the notes to Chapter 10, the reader may wish to consult: Aronson, *Camus and Sartre*; Busch, *The Power of Consciousness*; Catalano, *A Commentary on Jean-Paul Sartre's Being and Nothingness*; Jensen, *Sartre and the Problem of Morality*; Schilpp, *The Philosophy of Jean-Paul Sartre*; and Solomon, *Dark Feelings, Grim Thoughts*.
41. In addition to the readings mentioned in the notes to Chapter 11, the reader may wish to consult: Aronson, *Sartre's Second Critique*; Drake, *Intellectuals and Politics in Postwar France*; Flynn, *Sartre and Marxist Existentialism*; and McBride, *Sartre's Political Theory*.
42. In addition to the readings mentioned in the notes to Chapter 12, the reader may wish to consult: Arp, *The Bonds of Freedom*; Fallaize, *Simone de Beauvoir*; Heinämaa, *Toward a Phenomenology of Sexual Difference*; Kruks, *Situation and Human Existence*; O'Brien and Embree, *The Existential Phenomenology of Simone de Beauvoir*; and Simons, *Feminist Interpretations of Simone de Beauvoir*.
43. In addition to the readings mentioned in the notes to Chapter 13, the reader may wish to consult: Baldwin, *Reading Merleau-Ponty*; Priest, *Merleau-Ponty*; Stewart, *The Debate between Sartre and Merleau-Ponty*; and Weiss, *Intertwinings*.

II Existentialism in Historical Perspective

DAVID E. COOPER

2 Existentialism as a philosophical movement

2.1 THE EXISTENTIALIST "FAMILY"

Most popular characterizations of existentialism – for example, "the metaphysical expression of the spiritual dishevelment of a post-war age"[1] – apply at best to the cultural movement described in Chapter 3 of this *Companion*. While some of the concerns of existentialist philosophy – such as the significance of death or the scope of individual moral responsibility – may become especially urgent under certain historical conditions, they are perennial ones, without date or place. Still, those popular characterizations have the advantage that no one denies the reality of the cultural phenomenon they describe – one captured on film, in memoirs, and still present in the memories of elderly people who, in their youth, were right there and experienced it. A set of young people really did, as Simone de Beauvoir recalled, label themselves "existentialists," wear an all-black uniform, frequent the same cafés, and assume an air of *ennui*.[2]

The reality of existentialism as a philosophical movement, by contrast, has sometimes been doubted. It has been denied, that is, that there ever was a distinctive philosophical perspective or tendency shared by those thinkers who have been labeled "existentialists." Thus Paul Ricoeur, in the course of repudiating Søren Kierkegaard's reputation as "the father of existentialism," asserts that "the supposed family of 'existentialist' philosophies never really existed," so that there was nothing for Kierkegaard to have fathered.[3] The only reason that Ricoeur gives for this verdict – that the "family" soon "collapsed" – is, however, inconsistent with it. For a family circle to collapse, it must once have been in place. The fact, for example, that Martin Heidegger's thinking had veered away from the position espoused in his *Being and Time* of 1927, or that Jean-Paul Sartre came to embrace Marxist views remote from those proclaimed in his 1946 lecture "Existentialism is a Humanism," cannot contradict the usual perception that, in those writings, the authors were articulating existentialist philosophies.

Ricoeur's verdict would be sounder if he were denying the existence, not of a family, but of a "school" of existentialist philosophers. For while it exaggerates to gloss existentialism as "the refusal to belong to any school of thought,"[4] there never was among existentialist thinkers an agreed program of the kind followed, in the inter-war years, by the Vienna Circle of logical positivists or the Frankfurt group of critical theorists. "Existentialist," certainly, was a name refused by nearly all those to whom it was extended after its initial application, by Gabriel Marcel in 1945, to the emerging ideas of Sartre and Beauvoir. It would be too hasty, however, to treat this refusal as good reason to doubt the reality of a distinctive existentialist tendency. For the refusal is explained by an understandable reluctance to become too closely identified with Sartre's particular position as well as, in Heidegger's case for instance, by the abandonment well before 1945 of the views which had inspired Sartre.

To maintain that there never was an existentialist family or movement is, in effect, to hold that "existentialism" is a mere label – that, as one author suggests, existentialism is "not some essential idea that gets ... expressed ... in the history of philosophy. It just *is* those expressions."[5] On this approach, figures such as Sartre, Heidegger, and Karl Jaspers are existentialists not because of a shared philosophical position but simply because that is what they have been labeled. But this is surely a judgment to accept only if one has failed to identify serious philosophical affinities among at least some of the thinkers familiarly called "existentialists." Since no one suggests withholding the name from Sartre, this means, in effect, failing to find significant affinities between his philosophy and that of these other thinkers. It is clear, in fact, that such affinities are to be found, and that when, for example, it is written that Heidegger and Sartre are "radically opposed in every respect,"[6] this can only be due to wild misrepresentation. Especially persistent is the image of Sartre – which would indeed set him at odds with Heidegger – as a Cartesian dualist. But given his denunciation of the Cartesian self as a fictitious "idol" and his robust denial that a person is "the contingent bringing together of two substances radically distinct"[7] – a mind and a body – it is hard to fathom how such an image could endure.

The denial that there was an existentialist family or movement is therefore implausible. A number of twentieth-century thinkers are reasonably regarded as belonging to just such a family in virtue of their subscribing to a number of philosophical ideas. In what are commonly regarded as classics of existentialism – Sartre's *Being and Nothingness*, Heidegger's *Being and Time*, and Maurice Merleau-Ponty's *Phenomenology of Perception* – but also in works by Jaspers, Marcel, Beauvoir, Martin Buber, and José Ortega y Gasset, there is affinity on each of the following issues. The human predicament that inspires the very enterprise of philosophy; the distinctive character of human existence that distinguishes it from all other types of existence; the intimacy of the relationship between human beings and their world; the radical character of individual human freedom; the tone that a life led in appreciation of this freedom must possess; and the structure of interpersonal relations consonant with this radical, existential freedom.

Affinity with respect to these issues allows, to be sure, for interesting differences among existentialist thinkers. Nevertheless, the affinity is substantial. Each of the writers mentioned in the preceding paragraph would, at some time in their careers, have endorsed the following general statement, a sort of existentialist "manifesto":

> Human beings are prone to experience estrangement from the world in which they live, and it is this sense of estrangement which has long inspired philosophical attempts to locate human existence in relation to the order of things. A sense of estrangement is rooted in the fact that, while human beings are embodied occupants of the world, their powers of reflection, self-interpretation, evaluation, and choice distinguish them from all other occupants of the world – from animals, plants, and mere things. It would be wrong, though, to infer from this distinction that there is no intimate relationship between human beings and the world. Indeed, philosophical reflection on human existence and the world reveals that neither is thinkable in the absence of the other. A main reason for this is that the world of things cannot be understood except by reference to the significance that these things have in relation to human purposes and practices. Once this intimacy is appreciated – and once the sense of estrangement is properly construed – it emerges that each human being is possessed of a radical

freedom and responsibility, not only to choose and to act, but to interpret and evaluate the world. Honest recognition by people of the disturbing degree of freedom that they possess requires cultivating a moral comportment or stance towards themselves and others that honours the reciprocal interdependence of individual lives.

This "manifesto" invites several comments. First, it is only a sketch, which will be elaborated in subsequent sections of this chapter. It is a sketch, moreover, which uses few if any of the terms frequently associated with existentialist writings – "absurdity," "anxiety," "authenticity," "commitment," "bad faith," and so on. This is because these are terms of art, which should not be taken at face value and are best introduced when the sketch is elaborated. Second, the sketch is intentionally rough – inevitably so, if it is to be a manifesto to which all members of the existentialist family, given their differences, could sign up. Third, however, the sketch is sufficiently definite to capture a distinguishable philosophical perspective. It is sufficiently definite, for a start, to exclude certain popular characterizations of existentialism, particularly those which accuse (or extol) existentialists for preaching irrationalism and a rejection of all systematic thought. It is true that existentialist thinkers consider that the power of reason has often been exaggerated – that, for example, reason has wrongly been deemed capable of yielding an entirely objective account of the world, independent of all human perspective. But existentialists have not themselves arrived at the views sketched in the "manifesto" by some alternative to rational reflection – intuition, divination, "thinking with the blood" or whatever – nor do they advocate a life uninformed by rational reflection. Similarly, while limits are put by existentialists on the scope of systematic explanation of human conduct, there is nothing "unsystematic" in the philosophical thinking that led them to espousing this, among many other views. On the contrary: the component views in the "manifesto" are held to be closely integrated, to constitute a coherent direction of thought.

The sketch is sufficiently substantial, as well, to guide judgment on the existentialist credentials of the many writers – including St. Augustine and Shakespeare – to whom the name has been attached. It would be tedious to go through the whole list, but comments on a few figures often included in the existentialist family might be helpful. There is no strong reason to include in the family novelists such as Dostoevsky and Kafka, or poets like Rilke. To be sure, each of them addresses themes that recur in existentialist writings – anxiety and alienation, for example – but none of them locates these themes within a general philosophical perspective of the type sketched in the "manifesto." A harder case is the Nobel-prize-winning novelist, Albert Camus, who features on several shortlists of existentialist authors. We have it from Camus's own mouth that he was not an existentialist, indeed not a philosopher at all. But these denials are not decisive, for it is unclear why Camus reckoned that his *The Myth of Sisyphus* failed to count as philosophical – or indeed why he discounts his novels, given his opinion that "a novel is never anything but a philosophy expressed in images." As for his rejection of the existentialist label, this may have been due to his understanding of existentialism as requiring "a leap of faith," as well as to a reluctance to be too closely associated with Sartre.[8] Nevertheless there is good reason not to describe Camus as an existentialist philosopher. A main ambition of Heidegger, Sartre, Merleau-Ponty, and other existentialists is to establish that human beings are not, in reality, estranged from their world: far from the world being set over against us, it is unimaginable except in relation to us. For Camus, on the other hand, a human being is indeed "an alien, a stranger ... his exile" from the world "without remedy" – a world that maintains a total and "unreasonable silence" in the face of our efforts to understand it.[9]

As later chapters in this *Companion* demonstrate, there is ample justification for considering two great nineteenth-century writers, Kierkegaard and Nietzsche, alongside the existentialist thinkers of the following century. The sense of "exist" that inspired the name "existentialism" was first articulated by Kierkegaard, and Nietzsche was among the first writers to expose the intimate relationship between experience, practice, and the world that came to play a central role in existentialist philosophy. Nevertheless, the familiar description of these two thinkers as "the fathers of existentialism" is more apposite than "the first existentialists" or "the founders of existentialism." For each of them rejects significant aspects of the existentialist "manifesto." Nietzsche, in places at least, rejects the doctrine of radical individual freedom that Kierkegaard helped to bequeath to existentialism, while the Dane, in turn, does not ground this freedom in a conception of the relationship between practice and the world that existentialists inherited, in part, from Nietzsche. And in neither case do we find – as we do in the writings of J. G. Fichte and G. W. F. Hegel – the emphasis on intersubjective relationships that was to become prominent in existentialist writings.

While taxonomy has its value for the historian of ideas, the important issue is not whether this or that thinker is labeled an existentialist. What matters is to appreciate the respects in which their thinking approximates to the position sketched in the "manifesto" I drew up on behalf of the existentialist family. It is in the light of this appreciation that the relatively unimportant decision to call them "close family" or "distant kin" is to be made. It is also, of course, of interest to the historian to explore where a philosophical movement came from, what currents flow into it. But again, the important matter is to identify those origins or currents, not to agonize over the legitimacy of applying the existentialist label to the works – by Kierkegaard, Fichte, Nietzsche, or whomever – in which these are identified.

2.2 ESTRANGEMENT AND EXISTENCE

In the most poetic of existentialist texts, *I and Thou*, Martin Buber wrote that the person who lives in an "I–It" relation to the world lives in "severance and alienation," without a "home, a dwelling in the universe."[10] In another major existentialist text, Maurice Merleau-Ponty maintains that when we "suspend our ordinary preoccupations" the world can appear "hostile and alien ... a resolutely silent other ... which evades us."[11] Such remarks attest to a wider existentialist perception that human beings are prone to a sense of estrangement or alienation from the world, but also to the judgment that this sense is misguided. It is only when we are relating to the world in an unsatisfactory way – or at any rate one that deviates from a more basic one – that the world is experienced as alien. Heidegger speaks for existentialists generally when he claims that, properly regarded, "self and the world belong together ... not two beings, like subject and object," but "the unity of Being-in-the-world."[12]

How our basic relationship to the world is to be properly regarded will emerge in the next section. For the moment, I concentrate on the issue of estrangement, for hostility to those philosophies, like

Descartes's, which dualistically separate human beings from their world, is a striking aspect of existentialist thought. In taking the issue of estrangement as a central one for philosophy to resolve, existentialists engage with one of the great themes of philosophy – one that ran through the history of the subject long before Hegel and Marx made it a topic of explicit attention. Indeed, Hegel himself contended that not only the history of philosophy, but human history as a whole, is a long struggle to overcome the sense of alienation to which we are prey. William Wordsworth put the point well in 1818: "the groundwork of all true philosophy is the full apprehension" of a tension between "an intuition of ... ourselves, as one with the whole" and the thought of "ourselves as separated beings" placed in "antithesis" to the natural world, as subjects are to an object.[13]

If one shares Wordsworth's "apprehension" of this tension, it is not hard to construe many of the main chapters, and much of the rhythm of conflict, in the history of philosophy as attempts to resolve the issue of estrangement. It is tempting, for example, to perceive the recurrent battles between materialist and idealist philosophical systems not as owing to a quest for knowledge of reality for its own sake, but as a reflection of two opposed styles of overcoming the sense of alienation encouraged by dualist pictures. In the one case, human beings are held to be entirely physical and natural creatures and hence no different, in principle, from mere things. In the other case, the world is assimilated to the mind, with objects being treated, for example, as nothing more than sets of actual or possible experiences. It is worth noting that even dualists typically try to soften the alienating impact of their doctrine. Some Cartesians, for example, were anxious to establish that, while mental and physical events are logically quite independent from each other, there nevertheless exists a divinely arranged harmony between them. A sense of separation from the world is too disturbing, it seems, for philosophy to do nothing to dissolve or mitigate it.

A sense of estrangement is not, of course, the product solely of dualist philosophies. Rather, it is the understandable product of a perception of the human condition that perhaps every reflective person has at some time experienced. The perception is of what has been called the "ambiguity" of human beings. From one standpoint, they are obviously embodied beings that are found within the world, subject to the laws and processes that everything else in the world is. At the same time, there are salient features of human beings which seem to set them uniquely apart from all other beings. A person can exercise free will, a moral sense, and an appreciation of beauty, and can reflect on and contemplate matters, his or her own future actions included. In Sartre's terminology, people are necessarily possessed of both "facticity" and "transcendence" – of features that locate them as creatures in the world, but also of a power to distinguish themselves from and "go beyond" any such given features. This ambiguity appears to render us "natural aliens."[14]

People respond differently to this perception of human ambiguity. In some, it may prompt pride and delight in the apparent capacity of human beings to soar, so to speak, above the natural order. In others, it inspires instead a sort of envy of creatures whose nature is fixed and stable, who do not need to agonize about what to do and what to value. These people may agree with Rilke, who writes in the first of his Duino Elegies (line 12) that, unlike animals, "we are not very much at home in this world we've expounded." Most people perhaps veer back and forth between such attitudes in an oscillation that itself makes for an estranged condition.

It is a striking aspect of existentialist writings that, in the attempt to recall us from a sense of estrangement, there is no compromising of the features that distinguish human beings from all other creatures and objects in the world. There is, for example, none of the flirtation with naturalism – with assimilating human thought and practice to natural processes – that is found in Marx's, and even Nietzsche's, attempts to repudiate what the latter called "the whole pose of 'man *against* the world'."[15] This uncompromising stand is manifest in the very notion of existence that makes the name "existentialism" an apt one.

This notion goes back to Kierkegaard, who, for a start, restricts the term "existing" to individual human beings. Individuals, he continues, are "infinitely interested in existing" and "constantly in the process of becoming."[16] Suitably unpacked, these remarks were to become central to the existentialist understanding of human being. Kierkegaard's "interest in existing" is not the desire, shared with other creatures, to stay alive, but a concern – unique to human beings – for the kind of life one lives, the kind of person one is to become. As Heidegger was to put it, a creature with our kind of existence (Dasein) is "distinguished by the fact that, in its very

Being, that Being is an *issue* for it."[17] And when Kierkegaard speaks of individuals being in the process of becoming, he does not mean, simply, that human beings – like other living things – change and develop. His point, rather, is the one Heidegger was to express by saying that a human being is always "ahead-of-itself" – always, as it were, on the way to a future that "awakens the Present."[18] For Heidegger, the etymology of the term "exist" (Latin *ex-stare*, "to stand out from") makes it a suitable one to capture the kind of being that we humans enjoy. For not only do individuals have the capacity to step back from themselves, so as to reflect on the issue that their lives pose, but at any given time they can be understood only by reference to what is beyond their present state, to future possibilities that they are on the way to realizing.

The existentialist notion of existence is condensed in what has become a slogan of the movement – Sartre's declaration that, in the case of human beings, "existence precedes essence."[19] Unlike other things and creatures, what individual human beings are, or are like, at a given time is the outcome, not of their given and fixed nature or "essence," but of the choices that they have made, the ways in which they have tried to resolve the "issue" that their lives present them with, and the future possibilities they are in pursuit of. Ortega y Gasset expressed this idea eloquently: a person "consists not in what it is already, but in what it is not yet ... Existence means, for each of us, the process of realizing ... the aspiration we are."[20]

We shall return to the existentialist understanding of individual existence, but it is already clear that, on this understanding, human beings are indeed unique: their kind of being is distinct from that of anything else in the world. But this uncompromising refusal to assimilate human being to any other kind makes it all the more challenging to resolve the issue of estrangement. How, if we are unique in our being, can we *not* experience ourselves as strangers in the world? The existentialist answer to this question is the subject for the next section.

2.3 THE HUMAN WORLD

Heidegger, we saw, denies that self and world are "two beings, like subject and object"; they can, he adds, be only "provisionally" separated. This means that human existence and the world are not logically independent of one another. It is impossible cogently to conceive of human existence in isolation from the world, and of the world without human existence. It is because of this intimate relationship that, despite the salient differences between human and non-human beings, human existence is not set over against that of the world. There is, after all, no "alienation between the I and the world," as Buber puts it. The point can be made in the form of a rejection of Descartes's dualist separation of two kinds of substance, mental and physical, which, he maintained, could in principle exist independently of each other. Had God so willed, He could have created a purely mental or a purely physical universe. Resolution of the issue of estrangement by rejection of this dualism of substances is common to all existentialists. Sartre, for example, denies that a being "for-itself" – a human consciousness, roughly – is an "autonomous substance," while Ortega recommends that we think of ourselves, not as substances, but as narratives ("dramas") of beings that are, necessarily, in the world.[21]

More difficult to understand is the claim that the world requires human existence – that, in Sartre's words, it is the for-itself "by whom it happens that *there is* a world" at all.[22] The claim is certainly not a traditional idealist one that treats the allegedly external world as existing only "in the mind," as "ideas," "sense-data," and the like. Such a claim would, in effect, reduce one substance to another, rather than dismantle the whole metaphysics of substance. As Merleau-Ponty remarks, while in a sense "the world is wholly inside me," equally there is a sense in which "I am wholly outside myself," out there in the world.[23]

The thought that the world is a human one, since it depends for its being on human existence, might usefully be called a type of *humanism*. This was the term that William James, for example, gave to the view that from any conception of the world "you can't weed out the human contribution."[24] And Sartre, when justifying his description of existentialism as a humanism, invokes the claim that "the only universe that exists is the human one."[25] Existentialist humanism, however, differs from earlier versions of humanism. It differs, for a start, from the version found in Immanuel Kant. For Kant, any world that we can experience and describe is conditioned by forms of human perception and understanding. In itself, reality is not spatial, temporal, or causally governed, since space, time, and causality are only forms of our experience. Most existentialists, however, reject the Kantian distinction between the world of appearances and reality in itself, and the style of their argument for the world's being a human one is very different from his. They do not appeal, as Kant did, to fixed, innate structures of mind in order to explain why any world we could experience is a human one.

The style of their argument owes more to the humanism of Nietzsche and of Henri Bergson and his pragmatist cousins across the Atlantic. "Subtract every human *contribution*" to the world, argued Nietzsche, and nothing is left over to experience: and this is because experience is thoroughly shaped by human purposes, needs, and aims – ones inseparably connected with "the preservation of creatures like ourselves."[26] It is these practical purposes and "physiological" needs that are responsible for the world being experienced and articulated as it is. Creatures with very different needs or purposes from our own would not experience the world as containing horses, leaves, stars, and the like. Bergson and the pragmatists make similar remarks, speaking, for instance, of our "carving out" such objects as leaves or horses in the processes of "constructing" a world that will, as James put it, "suit our human purposes."[27]

The existentialists' debt to this earlier current of humanism is apparent from Sartre's reference to the world as one of "tasks" and of the "instrumentality" of our relationship to it; from Heidegger's proposal that the world is "primordially" encountered as a world of "equipment"; or from Ortega's characterization of the world as "a conjunction of favourable and adverse conditions encountered by man."[28] The thought in each case is that the world may only be conceived of in relation to human purpose and activity. In fact, the existentialist adheres to this thought more faithfully than Nietzsche and some pragmatists, who sometimes tend to construe their humanism naturalistically, as an empirical, scientific thesis about the interaction between the world and biological needs. Existential humanists recognize that, if the world is truly inseparable from human existence, the relationship between them cannot be of the empirical kind investigated by the natural sciences. To understand their account of this relationship – and, indeed, the distinctive character of their argument for its intimacy – another debt must be recorded, this time to Edmund Husserl's phenomenology.

The crucial debt is to Husserl's insight that, just as words refer to things in virtue of what they mean, so experiences also have "the peculiar feature of being related to ... things through their ... posited meaning."[29] As Husserl puts it, in experiencing things we are related to them "intentionally" – not in a causal or physical manner of the kind exposed by, say, biological science. There is, however, a striking difference between Husserl and the existentialists, one that marks the transition from his "pure" phenomenology to what is often described as existential phenomenology. Husserl thinks of the "posited meanings" whereby we can experience things as "essences" grasped through intellectual cognition, through "mental acts." But, as Heidegger argues, cognition "presupposes [human] existence," so that it is at a more "primordial" level of existing – of practical engagement with things in the world – that meaning must emerge. Merleau-Ponty elaborates this point: whereas Husserl had conceived of meaning as "an act of thought ... of a pure 'I'," the "imposition of meaning" is in fact the work of bodily activity. It is "*operative* intentionality," not the performance of "mental acts," that is the source of the significance things have for us.[30] Things in the world, and hence the world itself, show up for us as objects of experience only in virtue of the significance they possess in relation to human projects and purposes. That is why, as we heard Sartre saying, it is through us that it happens that there is a world.

Existentialists are alert to an objection to their humanist thesis. Granted, the objection goes, that objects would never have been experienced in the absence of engaged, purposive activity, why – once they *have* shown up for us – can one not then ascend to an "absolute" account of a world free from any "human contribution"? Why – to take the most popular contemporary version of this objection – can one not coolly stand back from objects as familiarly encountered, look at them in the objective manner of the scientist, and proceed to provide an account of a world that is independent of human perspective? It is, of course, precisely this objective, detached stance towards the world that, according to the remarks of Buber and Merleau-Ponty cited in section 2.2, encourage "severance" from the world, rendering it "hostile and alien." But it is one thing to lament this stance, another to fault it. For a persuasive criticism of the stance, existentialists are again in debt to Husserl, but also to Nietzsche, for both men argued that the sciences, despite their pretension to objectivity, are irredeemably shaped by human purpose, so that the resulting scientific account of the world remains "all-too-human," imbued by human concerns and perspectives. The phenomenologist Max Scheler summarizes the argument when he writes that science is thoroughly "human" since it is inspired by "a will to order the whole of nature" – a point reiterated by Heidegger when he refers to the "fixed ground-plan" that governs both the style of explanation (causal) permitted by the sciences and the kinds of entities (mathematically measurable) that the sciences countenance.[31] None of this entails a rejection of the natural sciences, which have an important role in human life, especially where accurate prediction of events is imperative. What is rejected is the "scientistic" pretension that a scientific account of the world, unlike our everyday, engaged description of it, captures the world as it is in itself, with the human contribution finally weeded out.

With scientism rejected, an important inducement to a sense of estrangement from the world is removed. But for the more positive aspect of the existentialist resolution of the issue of estrangement, we need to recall the idea of an "intentional" relationship between human beings and their world. For what this idea inspires is a vision of the world as a language – with all that this implies by way of an intimate relationship. The vision is expressed when Heidegger speaks of the world as a "referential totality," and as having a "sign-structure" that enables the experience of "any entity whatsoever." It is expressed again when Merleau-Ponty explains that the world is "inseparable" from us since it is a "cradle of meanings."[32] Just as words, and the language they belong to, would not be what they are except in relation to their use in human speech, so things, and the world they belong to, are what they are only in relation to purposive human activity. And just as native speakers of a language, who use and understand it smoothly and effortlessly, are "at home" with it, so people are "at home" in the world they move about in and engage with. It is, after all, *their* world.

That the world matters to and is significant for people engaged with it is not, for existentialists, a contingent matter. It is not that we might have experienced the world in a purely neutral manner and only later attributed value and significance to things. As Heidegger remarks, we do not encounter a "naked" object and then "throw a signification" over it or "stick a value on it." Sartre concurs: values are a condition of our experience of things, for ours is a "world of tasks" in which things and situations are experienced in terms of "lacks" – as calling for action, as failing to be what they *should* be.[33] Evaluation, therefore, is integral to our experience of the world. Existentialism is sometimes accused of promoting a "subjectivist" view of values, but the charge is mistaken. Values do not, to be sure, belong to a world that is independent of human perspective – but then nor does anything else, so there is nothing distinctively "subjective" about values. And if what is meant by the charge is that values are aspects of the world that are imposed on it only *after* it has been experienced and articulated in neutral, objective mode, then – as Heidegger and Sartre's remarks make clear – the charge is entirely unwarranted.

2.4 FREEDOM, *ANGST*, AND AUTHENTICITY

In the account of existentialist humanism given in the previous section, no explicit mention was made of the radical individual freedom which, as we know, is a central, indeed defining, component of existentialist thought. Nothing was said, for example, to warrant Sartre's talk of a human being as someone "who makes himself." Admittedly, a certain sense was lent to Sartre's dictum that "nothing foreign has decided what we are,"[34] since it emerged that our conceptual and evaluative schemes are not determined by the way the world objectively or absolutely is – for there is no such way. But this says little about your or my freedom in particular, since these schemes are embedded in practices that are thoroughly social. Indeed, the picture of human beings as experiencing the world in and through practices they share with others – and not as isolated Cartesian mental substances viewing the world – seems to render problematic the possibility of existential freedom. How, as John Macquarrie pertinently asked, does one "reconcile the fact that existential analysis reveals the fundamentally communal character of existence" with individualism?[35] On the surface, Sartre's claim that a person "chooses" his or her "original relation ... with the world" sits badly with the insistence that we experience a world "always already" interpreted in virtue of a communal engagement with it.[36]

The issue here is not one that existentialists and their predecessors have shirked. On the contrary, a salient theme in their writings is the degree to which, for the most part, individuals live under the sway – the "dictatorship," even – of what Kierkegaard, Nietzsche, and Jaspers respectively call "the public," "the herd," and "mass-existence." An especially acute account of our everyday "absorption in ... publicness" is provided by Heidegger. "We take pleasure as ... *they* take pleasure ... we find shocking what *they* find shocking. The 'They' [*Das Man*], which is nothing definite ... prescribes the kind of Being of everydayness." So complete is this prescription that, for the most part, the "self" or "subject" of thought and action is not the individual person, but "the *they-self*."[37]

Heidegger makes it clear that "absorption in publicness" is not some historical contingency, a feature encountered only in especially conformist or dictatorial societies. Rather, it is a feature of the human condition: only creatures for the most part "absorbed" in public ways and practices can come to experience and understand their world in the first place. But this point makes it all the more urgent to see how the idea of radical existential freedom can be salvaged. Why, if we are so absorbed in publicness, should it be imagined that we possess this freedom? And if this question is successfully answered, another arises: why, if we do possess such freedom, do we seem so ready to let "Them" prescribe our enjoyments, ambitions, and understanding?

The charm of the existentialists' notion of *Angst* is that it offers answers to both questions. For the mood of *Angst* – a term of art best left in German rather than rendered as "anxiety," "anguish," or the like – is at once an intimation of our individual freedom and an explanation of why we typically behave as if we are not free. The concept goes back to Kierkegaard, for whom *Angst* and allied moods attest to the "existing individual's" ability to make an ungrounded "leap of faith," and hence register the "dizziness of freedom."[38] Variations on this idea are found throughout later existentialist writings. Sartre, picking up on Kierkegaard's metaphor, describes *Angst* as "vertigo," akin to the experience of a person who is assailed, not by fear of falling off a cliff, but by the thought that nothing at all prevents jumping off. But this perception of freedom is not confined to the capacity to perform particular actions. More importantly, for Sartre, *Angst* is awareness that one always "exists in ... detachment from what is," and so can always "disengage ... from the world."[39] In effect, it is the mood in which – to recall some earlier terminology – the individual's potential transcendence of facticity becomes salient, and it is therefore a "reflective apprehension" of one's freedom.

Sartre is here reiterating ideas already articulated by Jaspers and Heidegger, especially in the latter's dramatic account of the way that, in the experience of *Angst*, the world becomes "uncanny," things within it losing their ordinary, conventional significance so that, as it were, they "sink away." The effect of the experience is a vivid recognition of one's potential for a distinctive, individual "disclosure" or interpretation of the world: it is in this way that "*Angst* individualizes," freeing a person from the dictatorship of "the They."[40] Jaspers observed that the mood of *Angst* or "metaphysical fear" is especially liable to arise in what he called "boundary [or limit] situations" – critical, personal situations in life where "Their" rules and conventions are of little help, since one must decide for oneself how to respond.[41] The most important of these boundary situations is confrontation with one's mortality. As Heidegger was to elaborate, a person's steady, honest recognition that he or she is going to die – that their "possibilities" will be cut off – serves, as *Angst* does more generally, to individualize. Such recognition induces a sense of a person's life as a limited whole that only he or she – not "They" – can shape into a coherent narrative.

If *Angst* and "resolute anticipation" of death both individualize, so does another mood famously discussed by Sartre – the sense of "absurdity." The absurdity he refers to needs distinguishing from the kind that preoccupied Camus, namely the absurdity of our "longing for reason" in a world that remains resolutely "silent" and inscrutable. Nor is it the absurdity that Simone de Beauvoir hopes to "escape" through integrating the otherwise unconnected, dangling moments of one's life into a "unity."[42] For Sartre – building on Heidegger's reference to the "null basis" on which our lives are finally built – a sense of absurdity, like *Angst* itself, attests to the lack of objective foundations for the choices, values, and interpretations that we adopt. It attests, in effect, to the truth of existentialist humanism. If the idea of absurdity adds anything to that of *Angst*, this is perhaps the sense of an ineliminable tension between serious commitment to choices and "the feeling of [the] unjustifiability" of – the lack of a final basis for – any commitment.[43]

Angst, anticipation of death, and a sense of absurdity are not cheerful states. It is unsurprising, therefore, that people are prone to suppress them and thereby fail to apprehend the freedom that these states attest to. If people generally remain "sunk" or "tranquilized" in the embrace of "the They" – doing, thinking, and interpreting as "They" do – this is not evidence of the *absence* of freedom, but of an understandable *flight* from their freedom. In familiar existentialist terminology, to live "authentically" is a forbidding task – a matter, as Heidegger puts it, of retrieving one's "ownmost possibility" for being from the clutches of "the They" or, in Sartre's words, of a "self-recovery of [one's] being." It calls for stiff "inner resistance," says Jaspers, to the "social configurations" that are imposed on the self.[44] So forbidding is the authentic life sometimes made to sound that one wonders if anyone could want to seek it. But we should recall here a distinction that Heidegger makes between an initial mood of *Angst*, where disturbing feelings like "uncanniness" dominate, and a more mature mood which is one of sober but "unshakable joy" in reclaiming one's "individualized potentiality-for-Being."[45] Authenticity has, after all, its own rewards.

The authentic person – the "existing individual" – is one who acts, chooses and evaluates fully conscious that he or she does so as a free being.

But what, quite, is this to be conscious of? Is it to be aware, as we saw Sartre maintaining, that since nothing foreign decided what one is, this must be the outcome of an entirely free "initial choice" of a relationship to the world and other people? Few existentialists followed Sartre here, and perhaps under the sensible influence of Simone de Beauvoir, it is a view Sartre himself soon abandoned. Most of them agreed with Marcel, that it is a "fatal error" to equate freedom and choice.[46] That I am free does not mean that I chose my current situation, values, emotions, commitments, opinions, or whatever. It means, rather, that – as Merleau-Ponty explains – I am, or can make myself, "open to the world," so that I may exercise a power of "refusal" and a power to "begin something else."[47] While the popular picture of the existentialist hero may be of someone choosing and creating *ex nihilo* – performing *actes gratuits*, in effect – the very different and more considered vision shared by existentialist philosophers is of a person who is resolutely prepared to stand back from his or her situation and commitments, calmly to consider these and the alternatives to them, and only then to take a decision, perhaps to "begin something else," for which responsibility is fully accepted.

2.5 BEING WITH OTHERS

One important debt of existentialist thinkers is less to Kierkegaard and Nietzsche – both of whom focused on the self-cultivation of solitary individuals – than to German idealist philosophers who, at the turn of the eighteenth century, articulated an original account of the relationship of the self to other persons. The debt is important not least because it helps in identifying the characteristic style of existentialist approaches to ethics.

For Fichte and Hegel, subjectivity requires intersubjectivity: as the former puts it, "the human being becomes a human being only among other human beings."[48] The thought here is that a creature can only be a genuine subject or self – and hence a rational human being – if it is self-conscious, and self-consciousness requires recognition of other similar subjects who, in turn, recognize one's own existence as a rational subject. To be a human individual at all, therefore, requires participation in a community of beings that mutually recognize one another's existence. To exist is necessarily to exist *with* others.

This is a thought inherited by twentieth-century existentialists and explains why, for them, there can be no problem of "other minds" – of, that is, satisfying oneself that other people exist. For Heidegger, "*Dasein* is in itself essentially Being-with," since in encountering the world as a world of "equipment," a person is ipso facto encountering those for whom the "work-world" is "destined": other people. For Sartre, too, I do not need to infer the existence of other people since I experience or encounter "the Other" through, originally, "the Look" that he or she directs at me. In becoming uncomfortably aware that I am an object of the Other's Look, "behold now I *am* somebody."[49]

The claim that subjectivity requires intersubjectivity is key to understanding the character of existentialist ethics. For the general idea is that to be an authentic individual entails that one stands in appropriate relationships to other human beings. The task for philosophical ethics is to identify those relationships. Before elaborating on this idea, a few comments are necessary on the very notion of an existentialist ethics – since it has sometimes been denied that there is such a thing. Certainly, existentialism owed some of the excitement it generated to the perception that its attitude towards morality was nihilistic – that it preached the overthrow of "conventional" morality, and its replacement by personal choices or "commitments" that are without any rational support. On this view, the existentialist imperative of authenticity calls on people, not to perform or desist from any particular actions, but only to choose decisively and without illusions. This view of existentialism, however, better captures an attitude of the cultural movement associated with the name than the positions advanced by existentialist philosophers themselves.

That said, there are elements in those positions which, at first glance, might support the nihilistic interpretation. There is, for example, a marked animus against adherence to a morality as a set of rules that govern one's actions. But this animus – inspired in part by Kierkegaard's suspicion that doing things "on principle" is usually a way to "avoid all personal responsibility"[50] – should not be construed as a general rejection of moral concern. Again, existentialist writers agree that there are no objective moral values, if this means values that are part of the given furniture of reality. But it would be wrong to interpret this as a defence of moral subjectivism, of the kind being contemporaneously advanced in the English-speaking philosophical world by, for example, the "Emotivists." If values are not items in a reality independent of human engagement, that is because nothing at all is thus independent. As remarked in section 2.3 above, Heidegger and Sartre explicitly reject the suggestion that values and meanings are subjectively imposed on an otherwise "neutral" world. Finally, some of Sartre's rhetoric, especially in his hastily written popular lecture "Existentialism is a Humanism," might encourage the nihilistic picture. In particular, an example he gives there – of a student faced by a moral dilemma and told by Sartre "You are free, so choose ... invent"[51] – is often cited as proof of existentialism's rejection of any grounds for moral judgment. Carefully read, however, the example is intended to make the quite different point that it can be impossible rationally or impersonally to decide between courses of action for *both* of which good grounds *do* exist. To appreciate what these grounds are, we need to return to the theme of intersubjectivity.

This theme was already ethically invested by Fichte and Hegel. As Fichte explains, the mutual recognition of one another that self-conscious, rational beings must exercise is not merely theoretical. It is recognition, as well, in the sense of honoring one another's status. In Hegel's famous discussion of the master–slave relationship, he establishes that the master cannot, as he had hoped to, achieve a sense of dignity through the recognition afforded him by someone he regards merely as an object, a slave.[52] Such recognition, to be meaningful, must come from people who are themselves respected and accorded human dignity. Both Fichte and Hegel put their point in terms of freedom: for me to have a proper appreciation of my own freedom as a rational being, I must recognize a like freedom in others. Almost all existentialist authors give voice to this same point about reciprocal freedom. For Sartre, "my freedom impl[ies] mutual recognition of others' freedom," while for Jaspers, "man becomes free only insofar as the other becomes free."[53] Translated into the terminology of authenticity, the point is that, in order to live authentically – in full awareness, that is, of my freedom – I must honor the freedom of others and work with them to foster a communion of human beings living in recognition of their reciprocal freedom. To be authentic, as Marcel remarks, is not only to "apprehend" the other as free, but to "collaborate with his freedom," while, in Heidegger's words, people are "authentically bound together" only when each "frees the Other in his freedom for himself."[54]

It is important to appreciate that, according to existentialist thinkers, the ethical challenge posed by our relationships with others is not only to respect the freedom of others, but one's own freedom as well. And this is something which, they agree, people generally fail to do. A main form taken by "bad faith" – Sartre's name for inauthentic comportment – is surrender to the way that one is seen, pigeon-holed, or stereotyped by other people. In the best-selling of all existentialist writings, *The Second Sex*, Simone de Beauvoir's complaint is not only against men for their "objectification" of women, but against women themselves for living up to the male image of how they are "supposed" to be.

The existentialists' consensus on authenticity as requiring an ethics of reciprocal freedom is compatible with significant differences among them over the exact implications for actual moral conduct. Perhaps the most significant of those differences recalls

Sartre's distinction, in *Existentialism is a Humanism*, between a "morality of sympathy, of personal devotion" and "a morality of wider scope" concerned, for instance, with global injustice or tyranny. It was between these two moralities that the student who sought Sartre's advice had to choose, for his dilemma was whether to look after his dependent mother or to join the Free French in the fight against fascism. A rough distinction may be made between those, like Sartre, Merleau-Ponty, and Beauvoir, who emphasized commitment, in the name of freedom, to struggles against anti-Semitism, colonialism, and capitalism, and figures like Buber and Marcel, whose emphasis is instead on the nurturing of personal "I–Thou" relationships. In Marcel's case, for example, it is primarily in and through being "available" to friends that one honors and "collaborates with" the freedom of others and thereby comes fully to know him- or herself "*qua* freedom."[55] The tension between these two styles of ethics is a perennial one, found for instance in the debates between Confucians and Daoists more than two thousand years ago. That such a tension should be found among the existentialist family is not therefore surprising, and certainly not a reason for concluding that there cannot be an existentialist ethics.

2.6 CONCLUDING REMARKS

This chapter has presented existentialism as a distinctive philosophical movement, a set of ideas and perspectives agreement on which united a recognizable "family" of twentieth-century thinkers. The name "existentialism" does not refer only to a post-war cultural fashion or mood, nor is it a mere label arbitrarily pinned on a number of quite disparate writers. The chapter has also indicated that existentialist thought, for all its originality, did not emerge from nowhere. Whether or not one chooses to dub this or that earlier philosopher as an existentialist, it is clear that twentieth-century existentialism develops and combines in a distinctive manner themes found in the writings of, among others, Fichte, Hegel, Kierkegaard, Nietzsche, Bergson, and Husserl.

Finally, the chapter has tried to demonstrate that existentialism not only *is* a philosophical movement but that existentialist thought *has* movement or direction. What unites the existentialist "family" is not a set of discrete, unconnected ideas. Inspired by the issue of estrangement, existentialist thought moves in a coherent direction, from conceptions of the world and human existence to a doctrine of radical human freedom that leads into an ethics of authenticity and reciprocal freedom.

NOTES

1 Harvey, *Oxford Companion to French Literature*, p. 261.
2 Beauvoir, *The Force of Circumstance*, pp. 151–52.
3 Ricoeur, "Philosophy after Kierkegaard," p. 10.
4 Kaufmann, *Existentialism from Dostoyevsky to Sartre*, p. 12.
5 Nivison, *The Ways of Confucianism*, p. 234.
6 Haar, "Sartre and Heidegger," p. 168.
7 Sartre, *Cahiers pour une morale*, p. 497; Sartre, *Being and Nothingness*, p. 409.
8 See Sherman, *Camus*, pp. 3–4.
9 Camus, *The Myth of Sisyphus*, pp. 10, 22, 110.
10 Buber, *I and Thou*, pp. 58, 115.
11 Merleau-Ponty, *Phenomenology of Perception*, p. 376.
12 Heidegger, *Basic Problems of Phenomenology*, p. 297.
13 Wordsworth, *The Friend*, pp. 261–62.
14 Evernden, *The Natural Alien*.
15 Nietzsche, *The Gay Science*, p. 286 (section 346).
16 Kierkegaard, *Concluding Unscientific Postscript*, pp. 253, 78.
17 Heidegger, *Being and Time*, p. 32.
18 Heidegger, *Being and Time*, pp. 236, 378.
19 Sartre, *Existentialism is a Humanism*, p. 20.
20 Ortega, "Man the Technician," pp. 112–13.
21 Sartre, *Being and Nothingness*, p. 786; Ortega, "History as a System," section VII.
22 Sartre, *Being and Nothingness*, p. 707.
23 Merleau-Ponty, *Phenomenology of Perception*, p. 474.
24 James, "Pragmatism and Humanism," p. 455.
25 Sartre, *Existentialism is a Humanism*, p. 52.
26 Nietzsche, *Beyond Good and Evil*, section 11.
27 James, "Pragmatism and Humanism," p. 453.
28 Sartre, *Being and Nothingness*, pp. 272–73; Heidegger, *Being and Time*, sections 15–16; Ortega, "Man the Technician," p. 114.
29 Husserl, *Ideas*, p. 346.
30 Merleau-Ponty, *Phenomenology of Perception*, p. 147.
31 Scheler, *On the Eternal in Man*, p. 97; Heidegger, "The Age of the World Picture," p. 118.

32 Heidegger, *Being and Time*, section 17; Merleau-Ponty, *Phenomenology of Perception*, pp. 499–500.
33 Heidegger, *Being and Time*, p. 190; Sartre, *Being and Nothingness*, Part 2, chapter 1.iii.
34 Sartre, *Being and Nothingness*, p. 708.
35 Macquarrie, *Existentialism*, p. 118.
36 Sartre, *Being and Nothingness*, p. 589.
37 Heidegger, *Being and Time*, section 27.
38 Kierkegaard, *The Concept of Anxiety*, p. 61.
39 Sartre, *Being and Nothingness*, pp. 72, 78.
40 Heidegger, *Being and Time*, section 40.
41 Jaspers, "Introduction."
42 Camus, *The Myth of Sisyphus*, pp. 22ff.; Beauvoir, *The Ethics of Ambiguity*, pp. 26–27.
43 Sartre, *Being and Nothingness*, p. 618.
44 Heidegger, *Being and Time*, p. 68; Sartre, *Being and Nothingness*, p. 116; Jaspers, *Philosophy*, vol. II, p. 30.
45 Heidegger, *Being and Time*, p. 358.
46 Marcel, *The Philosophy of Existence*, p. 58.
47 Merleau-Ponty, *Phenomenology of Perception*, pp. 525, 530.
48 Fichte, *Foundations of Natural Right*, p. 37.
49 Heidegger, *Being and Time*, p. 156; Sartre, *Being and Nothingness*, p. 353.
50 Kierkegaard, *The Present Age*, p. 85.
51 Sartre, *Existentialism is a Humanism*, p. 33.
52 Hegel, *Phenomenology of Spirit*, section B.iv.A.
53 Sartre, *Cahiers pour une morale*, p. 487; Jaspers, "Philosophical Autobiography," p. 85.
54 Marcel, *Being and Having*, p. 107; Heidegger, *Being and Time*, p. 159.
55 Marcel, *Being and Having*, pp. 106–7.

WILLIAM MCBRIDE

3 Existentialism as a cultural movement

3.1 WHO OR WHAT IS AN EXISTENTIALIST?

Few if any other modern Western philosophical movements have had as strong an impact on the general culture as has existentialism. The epicenter of this impact was certainly Paris, especially the Latin Quarter of Paris, and the time of maximum intensity was the period following the end of the Second World War, during which Paris had been under German occupation. But of course there had been existentialist stirrings, at least some of which had had broader cultural influence beyond the world of philosophy, in other places and long before that time, and there would be existentialist waves of extended cultural influence in many other countries for years to come, arguably right up to the present time. It would be impossible to track down and catalogue all of these earlier and later impacts; and any such enterprise would be burdened from the start by disagreements concerning just which cultural tendencies were "really" influenced by existentialism and to what degree, as well as by the question of just which of the various "existentialisms" were of greater importance in such-and-such an instance. After all, both "existentialism" and "culture" are concepts with exceedingly vague edges.

The nature of this difficulty can perhaps most easily be seen if we focus our attention initially on the immediate post-war Paris scene to which I have referred, on the highly diverse currents that were operative even within that comparatively small "epicenter" within just a few years' time. A recounting of the interaction of a few of these currents will at the same time offer insights into just how strongly existentialism influenced the society in question and into something of the nature of that influence. Subsequently I shall consider a few aspects of existentialism's impact on the (increasingly) global culture.

Of course, the term "existentialism" (or "existential philosophy") did not originate with Jean-Paul Sartre or Albert Camus or Simone de Beauvoir – three of the four French writers who must be regarded as most central to existentialism's ascendancy in the late 1940s. There is some reason to attribute the first recognizably systematic use of the word as a technical philosophical concept to the fourth of these, Gabriel Marcel, but already in the 1930s it was being used regularly to refer to the work of Søren Kierkegaard and Martin Heidegger. The Russian exile Leon Shestov's *Kierkegaard and the Existential Philosophy* was published in its French version in Paris in 1936, Karl Jaspers was already writing about "existential philosophy" around the same time, and Jean Wahl published a history of existentialism in 1943. That year, in the middle of the Occupation period, also saw the publication of Sartre's *Being and Nothingness*, which, along with Heidegger's much earlier *Being and Time* (1927), has come to be treated in histories of philosophy as the quintessential systematic existentialist treatise. But at least two shorter, more literary works – Sartre's novel *Nausea* (1938) and Camus's essay *The Myth of Sisyphus* (1942) – had already seen the light of day and had begun to be associated, in the familiar but complex, ambiguous way in which broad intellectual movements come to acquire distinctive labels somewhat independently of the intentions of particular writers, with a new cultural movement, not confined to philosophy strictly speaking, called existentialism.

Camus's *Myth of Sisyphus* well illustrates this ambiguous development. Early in that essay he singles out three authors in particular – Jaspers, Shestov (written "Chestov"), and Kierkegaard – as "existentials," representatives of "the existential attitude," which he deems to be an attitude of philosophical suicide, as epitomized in Kierkegaard's notion of the "leap of faith."[1] As far as Camus is concerned, this leap constitutes an effort to escape – rather than to acknowledge and to live with – "the absurd," by which he meant the insuperable lack of fit between reason's aspirations and the world as we find it. Camus's aim in this seminal work was to establish a very strong line of demarcation between himself, the "absurdist" philosopher, and all existential philosophers "without exception." But he did not succeed in this: almost from the start, Camus himself came to be associated with existentialism in the cultural collective consciousness, despite the objections of purist readers of the text, as well as his own objections.[2]

By contrast Gabriel Marcel, who had already considered himself an existential thinker when those who were later to become his fellow existentialists were still adolescents and who had already encouraged Sartre to further develop some of his philosophical ideas before the outbreak of the war, eventually came to feel such hostility toward the existentialist movement, increasingly identified with Sartre, that he sought to distance himself from it. No matter: the burgeoning secondary literature on existentialism, especially during the late 1940s and the 1950s, typically began to bifurcate it into theistic and non- (or a-) theistic existentialism, assigning Marcel a niche in the former half of the existentialist pantheon along with Kierkegaard. Indeed, Marcel had affirmed just this in a short interview published in the December 1, 1945 issue of *Les Lettres Françaises*, one of a series of interviews on the theme "What Is Existentialism?" There he had said that, while Sartre's existentialism was negative, there was a positive Christian existentialism, of which he himself was a proponent.[3]

As for Sartre and Beauvoir, neither of them began the period in question by coveting the existentialist label. At a colloquium organized by members of the Dominican order, Sartre once declared that he did not know what existentialism was. But both of them very soon came to accept the label as theirs, and both then began defending existentialism against criticisms of it that they considered to be unfair.[4] Sartre's single most famous such defense was his lecture, "Existentialism is a Humanism," delivered to a packed audience in Paris under conditions of near-pandemonium in late October 1945. Beauvoir's most sustained early apologia was her essay on "Existentialism and the Wisdom of Nations," in which she argued that, contrary to critics' claims, typical folk-wisdom (as expressed especially in proverbs and other old sayings) tended toward pessimism, whereas existentialism, with its emphasis on freedom and responsibility, was in fact a very hope-filled worldview. This essay was first published on December 1, 1945, in the journal that Sartre, Beauvoir, Maurice Merleau-Ponty, and others had just launched, *Les Temps Modernes* – the same date as that of the publication of the previously mentioned interview with Marcel in *Les*

Lettres Françaises. An interview with Beauvoir was also published in the same issue of the latter, while one with Sartre had appeared in the previous week's issue.

Thus it seems incontestable both that existentialism had become a familiar term among the educated French public – and not just among philosophers – within roughly a year after the end of the German Occupation, and that its exact meaning was already very much in dispute. The broader public's familiarity with the existentialists whom I have mentioned should be unsurprising when one recalls that all four of them had published in literary genres other than philosophy, and indeed that at least Camus and Beauvoir, and most likely Sartre as well, were probably better known for their more strictly literary works than for their philosophical ones. This is not to suggest, however, that Sartre's long and difficult philosophical magnum opus, *Being and Nothingness*, was not treated seriously as a defining work, even in this early period. On the contrary: most of the initial reviews of it, even the most negative (such as one by Marcel, who did not hesitate to call it diabolical and a debasement of the human), manifest an awareness of its great importance.[5] Nor was this awareness confined to French reviewers. One of the most sympathetic of the latter, Claude-Edmonde Magny, hailed *Being and Nothingness* as a great event both in the history of French thought and for the future development of that thought, precisely, she wrote, because it marked such a sharp break with the insularity to which French thought had been condemned during the war years.[6] In other words, *Being and Nothingness* was part and parcel of the explosion of existentialism on the world stage.

3.2 DISSEMINATING EXISTENTIALISM

Drawing upon early reviews of *Being and Nothingness*, let me cite just three illustrations of the sort of role it played. Writing in the Argentine journal *Sur* in August 1945, Georges Izard claimed that young French people were reading *Being and Nothingness* in large numbers and taking the difficulty of the work as a valuable challenge, given its magic qualities.[7] As may be surmised from that remark, this review was highly favorable. Discussing the book in the then-influential *Partisan Review* in New York, the American philosophy professor William Barrett, who was to be a significant proponent of existentialism in the United States in the years to come, admitted that it had become "the Bible of French existentialism," even though he evinced a quite critical attitude towards it and evaluated almost all of Sartre's other published works more highly.[8] A. J. Ayer – who was already well known and was later to become the dean, so to speak, of the British philosophers of his generation – while also showing a notable lack of enthusiasm for Sartre's philosophy, grudgingly acknowledged the great importance of *Being and Nothingness*, saying that its "metaphysical pessimism," which was very much "in the existentialist tradition," fit in very well with the spirit of the age.[9]

With these three reviews from three different countries, then, we begin to move away from our initial focus on the French epicenter. Already in 1946, Jean Wahl began a public lecture by recounting an anecdote about his leaving a café and being asked, by someone from a group of students, whether he was an existentialist (he said that he was not, because he hated vague generalities). "The subject of existentialism," he continued,

> or philosophy of existence, has begun to receive as much attention in New York as in Paris. Sartre has written an article for *Vogue*; a friend informs me that *Mademoiselle*, a magazine for teen-age young ladies, has featured an article on existentialist literature; and Marvin Farber has written in his periodical that Heidegger constitutes an international menace.[10]

In fact, New York in particular and the United States more generally were early objects of a sort of "existentialist offensive," as it was called, with Sartre and Beauvoir leading the way. Each made tours there, Sartre first as a reporter (designated as such by Camus for the newspaper *Combat*) on a trip sponsored by the United States government, and again soon thereafter as a lecturer, and Beauvoir first as a lecturer at various colleges and universities. It is clear from the accounts of their tours that "existentialism" was already a familiar word to many Americans, who were at the same time eager to become clearer as to just what it was. From *Life* magazine and other popular publications thousands of readers learned about the existentialist *"caves"* (basement bistros) of Paris, where the pace was frenetic, while at the American institutions of higher learning there was a growing awareness that a serious intellectual movement was underway, even though the original texts would for the most part not become available in English translation until 1947–48 at the earliest (Hazel Barnes's English translation of *Being and Nothingness* was first published only in 1956). By the mid 1960s the Society for Phenomenology and Existential Philosophy had become a large and growing concern in the United States.

What was it that gave existentialism its broad cultural appeal? There can be little doubt that the ending of the Second World War, with all the sacrifices and deprivations that it had demanded and the enormous destruction of lives and property that it had brought with it, played an important role. There was at once a new enthusiasm for living, and at the same time a deeper sense of the dark side of life, to both of which attitudes – apparent but not real opposites – the existentialist spirit spoke. Moreover, the facts that Paris had been subjected to the German Occupation and that Camus had participated actively, and Sartre and Beauvoir peripherally, in the Resistance – but also that most of France had not suffered the very severe damage that had befallen Germany and many other European countries – made France seem ideal as the source of new directions in philosophy, literature, and the arts.

There were other, related considerations. The trauma of the war had produced a very widespread feeling, more or less worldwide, that drastic social changes were needed. Old conventions and ways of doing things now seemed untenable – absurd, if you will – to many. It was obvious, and not only to philosophers, that at least the non-theistic existentialists were unconventional individuals, living unconventional lives, whose fictional characters tended also to be unconventional. Roquentin, the leading figure in *Nausea,* is a very strange person whose key experience, the revelation of the superfluousness of everything which comes to him while contemplating the root of a chestnut tree, constitutes a veritable incarnation of absurdity. Stranger still, and presented as such, is Meursault, the central character of Camus's novel *L'Étranger* (one of the first existentialist "classics" to appear in English translation, in 1946, under the titles of *The Outsider* in the United Kingdom and *The Stranger* in the United States). Unconventionality had great appeal, especially to members of the younger post-war generation.

It was this aspect of existentialism – at least of the non-theistic variety of existentialism that had gained the upper hand in the public consciousness – that caused Marcel and a number of other Catholic writers and religious conservatives more generally, first in France and then in the world at large, to denounce it with such vehemence. They recognized the appeal it had for young people and saw it as both contributing to and reflective of their moral decline. To the use by French critics of such epithets as "diabolical," "satanic," and "luciferian" – by Marcel, Jeanne Mercier (whose accusation, that existentialism had forgotten what an infant's smile is like, Sartre cites in *Existentialism is a Humanism*), and Roger Troisfontaines SJ, respectively – may be juxtaposed the outrage of the leading American Kierkegaard scholar of the mid-century, Walter Lowrie, a Protestant. Lowrie vehemently objected to the use of the same label, "existentialist," for both Kierkegaard and Sartre,[11] since he took them to be polar opposites. Existentialism induced feelings of extreme hatred among some on the Right, as could be seen in its most concentrated form in some of the venomous, ultra-sexist reactions that were provoked by the publication of Beauvoir's *The Second Sex*. As Francis and Gontier report: "Few books have aroused such an avalanche of bad faith, hypocrisy, coarseness, indecency. In *Le Figaro Littéraire* François Mauriac waxed indignant: 'We have literally reached the limits of the abject ...'."[12] In a personal note to a member of the staff of *Les Temps Modernes*, Mauriac wrote a sentence about "your boss" that was in effect pornographic – and this from one of the more cultivated "believers"!

Then, of course, there were the reactions of the Left, particularly the Communist Left. In thrall to the dogmatic spirit that characterized Soviet Marxism at the time, writers as intellectually gifted as the French sociologist-philosopher Henri Lefebvre and the Hungarian Georg Lukács published simplistic, extremely polemical attacks on existentialism that condemned it for being a quintessentially "bourgeois" ideology, despite its appearance of unconventionality, and for promoting philosophical idealism, a wrongheaded and obfuscating worldview, in opposition to the truth that was dialectical materialism.[13] Their fears, however outrageously expressed, were well founded from the Communists' point of view, since the existentialism of the 1940s did indeed militate against the dogmatic certainties and insistence on unswerving loyalty to the Party "line" that characterized so-called "orthodox Marxism." Indeed, this early existentialism, as translated to the "street" level of popular understanding, gave the appearance of being highly apolitical, or even anti-political.

3.3 THE CLIMATE OF EXISTENTIALISM

As time passed, this appearance proved to be misleading. Shortly after the celebrations of the Allied victory died down, several new phenomena, all global in their implications, came to dominate people's consciousnesses in various ways, and existentialist thought colored the cultural reactions to all of them: the atomic bomb, the Cold War, and struggles against racism and colonialism. The bomb, of course, had played a role – still disputed, with the question as to just how much of a role remaining unanswerable with precision – in ending the war by inducing the Japanese government to surrender. But its stark broader implications for the future of the human race gradually came into focus, especially as the government of the Soviet Union developed its own nuclear weaponry, and it soon became apparent that the technical knowledge of how to produce bombs with even greater destructive power could not be confined indefinitely within any national boundaries. In this historical context, with awareness of nuclear menace virtually universal, one of the most salient themes of existentialist philosophy – namely, anxiety or *Angst* – took on special relevance. Its principal textual source was in the work of Kierkegaard, and *Angst* had been singled out as a philosophically revelatory mood by Heidegger. Though it did not play such a notable role in Sartre or the other French thinkers,[14] it came to be closely associated with the movement, so that the expression "existential *Angst*" became something of a cliché. The cliché was not always directly associated with the nuclear threat, but the latter was an ineluctable part of the background of everyday life that made it especially resonant.

Of course, the threat was felt to be an imminent and not just long-range threat precisely because the two governments in possession of this weaponry were in fact threatening one another. This was a key part of the so-called "Cold War." The atmosphere of this period is well captured in Beauvoir's novel *The Mandarins*, which portrays the interactions and anxieties of a circle of French intellectuals – some of whom bear remarkable resemblance to actual figures who were involved with *Les Temps Modernes* – as they come to grips with new revelations about the Soviet gulags, the question of what role France and the rest of Europe should play *vis-à-vis* the two "camps" – Soviet and American – and, in the cases of some, their past and present loyalties to the Communist Party. One of the principal characters in the book, Anne, is involved in a transatlantic love affair with an American writer based in Chicago, just as Beauvoir herself was involved with Nelson Algren (to whom she dedicated this novel), and Beauvoir's descriptions of Anne's time in Chicago draw heavily on her personal experiences. The same gloom and pessimism concerning the future, rooted largely in the political situation of the time, characterizes Anne's thinking as she walks through The Loop as it does when she is back on the Left Bank. A label that she applies to herself in passing, "*résistentialiste*,"[15] well captures the increasingly political direction that existentialism was taking.

Nor was the Cold War the only political arena in which existentialist thinkers played a role. The post-war period was also the time of anti-racist and anti-colonial struggles. Sartre's and Beauvoir's travels to the United States had had the effect of intensifying their awareness of the rampant racial discrimination still prevalent there, and they spoke out against it in their writings. One of Sartre's plays, *The Respectful Prostitute*, is set in a Southern town and revolves around racial prejudice. The highly acclaimed African-American author Richard Wright, who claimed to have thought along existentialist lines even before he read Sartre or Camus, befriended the former, along with Beauvoir, and established permanent residence in Paris in 1946 in order to live in a less racially hostile climate. France divested itself of most of its former African colonies soon after the war, eventually managing to maintain relatively amicable relations with many of them despite past history, but the end of colonialism was nevertheless a protracted struggle. In particular, the bloody and ultimately unsuccessful French efforts first to regain control over Indo-china and then to retain Algeria – technically (and ridiculously) considered an integral part of the French national territory – occasioned further existentialist incursions into politics, incursions which had at the same time a specifically cultural dimension. Sartre, in particular, endorsed the "Negritude" movement of the Senegalese poet and statesman Léopold Sédar Senghor, in a preface to an anthology edited by the latter that he entitled

"Black Orpheus."[16] And he later wrote a famous, very militant preface to *The Wretched of the Earth,* the anti-colonialist classic by Frantz Fanon, a philosopher-psychiatrist from Mozambique who spent the last years of his short life in Algeria.[17]

Politics was the most salient factor in the famous "quarrels" of the early 1950s that began increasingly to divide existentialist former friends. Camus, a child of French *colons* who had settled in Algeria, always retained the hope, until his untimely death in an automobile accident in January 1960, that there could be a reconciliation between the French and the Algerians that would leave the special rights of the former intact – an increasingly unrealistic hope as the violence intensified. Camus had been a member of the Communist Party for two years in his youth, but by 1951 (the publication year of his book-length essay *The Rebel*), his increasing antipathy to communism and to the whole idea of political revolution was evident to all. The staff members of *Les Temps Modernes* were in agreement that *The Rebel* must be subjected to a very critical review, though no one was eager to write it. Finally, one of the younger members, Francis Jeanson, took on the task. Camus's reply to this review, addressed in very formal language (*"Cher Monsieur le Directeur"*) to Sartre rather than to Jeanson, showed just how deeply it had offended him, and it signaled a definitive break in their friendship. Sartre's reply to Camus begins: *"Mon cher Camus, Notre amitié n'était pas facile, mais je la regretterai."*[18]

Just a year later a similar rupture took place between Sartre and Merleau-Ponty. The immediate occasion was somewhat less dramatic in nature than the circumstances of the Sartre–Camus break had been – an editorial decision concerning an article to be published in *Les Temps Modernes* that Sartre had made unilaterally while his colleague was on vacation – but the general background was again the Cold War, and, more particularly, the outbreak of actual war in Korea. Merleau-Ponty had initially been more in sympathy with – or at least more eager to understand – the French Communists than had Sartre; indeed, his *Humanisme et terreur: Essai sur le problème communiste*[19] had been seen by some as justifying the Moscow Purge Trials of the 1930s, though it was intended as an effort to comprehend them. However, as Merleau-Ponty was becoming increasingly hostile toward the Communists, Sartre was seeking increasingly to make common cause with them (though he never actually joined the Party). In this context, Merleau-Ponty viewed the North Korean invasion of the South as a straightforward act of Communist aggression, whereas Sartre believed that certain apparently provocative American moves just prior to the invasion had triggered it. Although Sartre and Merleau-Ponty did meet again before the latter's sudden, premature death in 1961, their collaboration effectively came to an end in the spring of 1953.

3.4 ASSOCIATING WITH EXISTENTIALISM

The increasingly political orientation of existentialism, together with the close connection between existential philosophy, literature, and the world of culture in general, is perhaps best epitomized in one of Sartre's most significant essays of the immediate post-war period, *What is Literature?*[20] It includes a long historical review of what Sartre held the function of literature to have been in different epochs, and it raises interesting questions about the relation between politics and ethics, the idea of a classless society, and the reasons for writing at all. In answer to this latter question – "why write?" – the essay offers its most important message: literature today (prose literature; Sartre exempts poetry from this charge) should, must, be *committed* – *"engagée"* – to progressive political goals and must reject the late nineteenth-century ideal of "art for art's sake."

In general, the importance of existentialism for the world of letters beyond philosophy has been both overwhelming and yet difficult to delineate with precision, both chronologically and in terms of deciding how wide to cast the net. Moreover, it would be a serious mistake to think of the influence as simply emanating outward from the best-known existentialist philosophers toward novelists and playwrights; rather, there has been a considerable degree of reciprocity. Heidegger, for example, although unlike many of his French counterparts he never produced strictly literary works, acknowledged many literary influences on his own ideas, the most salient being the nineteenth-century poet Hölderlin. Especially in his later work, he accords a certain priority to poetry, as illustrated by the title, borrowed from a line in one of Hölderlin's poems, of one of his essays from the 1950s: "Poetically Man Dwells." It has become a commonplace to identify Fyodor Dostoevsky as a proto-existentialist novelist; Camus, in particular, was attracted to his work. And both Camus and Sartre, among others, were significantly influenced by the writings of Franz Kafka, who died in 1924. Clearly, it makes sense to speak of an existentialist literature *avant la lettre*, that is, before the word "existentialism" itself entered the cultural vocabulary.

As for literary figures and trends that have been influenced by – or at least shared a common *Weltanschauung* with – existentialist thought,[21] their number is arguably legion. One may begin with the dramatists most closely associated with the so-called "theater of the absurd," notably Eugene Ionesco and Samuel Beckett, and from there span out to include such contemporary playwrights as Jean Genet (of whom Sartre wrote a long and controversial biography, *Saint Genet*), Harold Pinter, and Edward Albee, and novelists such as Walker Percy and Saul Bellow (as well as Richard Wright, already mentioned above). Ernest Hemingway, whose work Sartre admired, is often associated in hindsight with existentialism, even though his literary production began some years before the "existentialist offensive." The Beat movement of the late 1950s has also been treated as similarly "associated." Such associations extended into many different cultural and linguistic milieux.[22]

To appreciate the extent and pervasiveness of this phenomenon that I am calling "association" with existentialism, together with its somewhat paradoxical nature, we may consider the approach taken in two respectable and representative books of the 1980s. The first links Jorge Luis Borges with existentialism, and its author offers the following rationale: "Whether Borges admits it or not, it is inconceivable that existentialism – the most important philosophical development of modern times – would have no reverberations in one of the century's most important writers." But he goes on to admit that "neither the author's work nor the voluminous bibliography about it acknowledges the relevance."[23] The second is from a collection of essays entitled *Existentialism in American Literature*, which, interestingly enough as an indication of existentialism's global scope, was the outcome of a conference that took place in Delhi, India. One of the contributors, who was also the editor, begins her essay by repeating Sartre's caution against applying "the term 'existentialist' so loosely and imprecisely as to render it practically useless,"[24] but then devotes much of her essay to making a pretty good case that existentialist themes pervade two of Eugene O'Neill's last works, *The Iceman Cometh* (1939) and *A Long Day's Journey into Night* (1940). To call Eugene O'Neill a sort of existentialist might be thought to run the risk of violating her initial note of caution, if it does not actually cross the line.

Most of the other arts could claim existentialist associations as well. This is especially true of film, but it is also the case with music and painting. The French film movement known as "la nouvelle vague," or New Wave, which arguably began with Jean-Luc Godard's masterpiece, *À bout de souffle* (Breathless) from 1960, exuded an intensely existentialist atmosphere, a sharp stylistic break with previously dominant cinematic conventions. Strong influences from both non-theistic and theistic forms of existentialism pervade the works of the Swede Ingmar Bergman (*Wild Strawberries, The Seventh Seal,* etc.), of great Italian directors such as Antonioni and de Sica, and of the American Woody Allen. In an appendix to his book *Existentialism,* the American philosopher Thomas Wartenberg, whose recent work has helped to make the philosophy of film an acknowledged sub-specialty, offers a list of roughly seventy films that "present the ideas of Existentialism," while making no claims to completeness.[25] And of course the film medium has allowed for adaptations of works of existentialist theater, such as Sartre's *Condemned of Altona.*

In fact, in one of the more bizarre episodes of his career, Sartre himself, who had always been a great devotee of the cinema, wrote a screenplay, at the invitation of the American director John Huston, about the period of self-doubt and breakthrough ideas in the early life of Sigmund Freud. It was 800 manuscript pages in length, and Sartre knew that it would need to be cut drastically, but the finished product was in his view so seriously compromised that he demanded that his name be removed from the credits. Even Huston was displeased with the end result, because the distributor made still further cuts of which he had not approved. Nevertheless, *Freud, the Secret Passion* was a modest cinematographic success.

As far as music is concerned, connections with twentieth-century existentialism are not as close as in the cases of the other arts.[26] One exception to this generalization, however, is jazz. Sartre, who was an amateur pianist and often played duets with his mother, loved jazz, frequented many Paris jazz clubs, and met famous jazz musicians such as Charlie Parker. The ambivalent ending of his novel *Nausea* involves an American jazz singer whose song, heard on a record, helps the central character, Roquentin, find some possible resolution and future direction to his life. Sartre's very short essay "Nick's Bar, New York City"[27] is an appreciation of jazz as the quintessentially American form of entertainment. Reciprocally, jazz came to be regarded, at least during the period of the "existentialist offensive," as a particularly appropriate existentialist form of music, perhaps in part because of its "contingent," improvisational nature – its refusal to follow a fixed, unalterable score.

Painting is a different matter. Sartre maintained relations with a number of painters and wrote about some of them – notably André Masson, Giacometti, Picasso, and Wols. Merleau-Ponty wrote a noteworthy in-depth study entitled "Le doute de Cézanne."[28] It is generally agreed by art historians that existentialism had a considerable impact on painters especially of the Abstract Expressionist school, of whom Jackson Pollock is probably the best-known figure today. Pollock acknowledged his existentialist inspirations. And the Director of Collections of the Museum of Modern Art, Alfred Barr, wrote an essay in connection with a US-government-funded exhibition that toured Europe called "The New American Painting," in which he very explicitly evoked these inspirations while trying to distance them from radical politics:

> Indeed one often hears Existentialist echoes in [these painters'] words, but their "anxiety," their "commitment," their "dreadful freedom" concern their work primarily. They defiantly reject the conventional values of the society which surrounds them, but they are not politically *engagés* even though their paintings have been praised and condemned as symbolic demonstrations of freedom in a world in which freedom connotes a political attitude.[29]

Other painters in Europe whose names have been associated with the influence of existentialism include Antonin Arnaud, Jean Dubuffet, Henri Michaux, Jean Fautrier, Francis Gruber, Germaine Richier, and Bram van Velde.

Outside the arts, two other important areas of culture on which existentialism exerted significant influence deserve mention: religion and psychoanalysis. Among those most frequently identified as religious existentialists, two Russian writers deserve special mention: Leon (Lev) Shestov, already mentioned at the beginning of this essay as one of the first to write about "existential philosophy," particularly in relation to Kierkegaard; and Nikolai Berdyaev, whose intellectual evolution as a young man took him from Marxism to Christianity – this conversion having originally been inspired in large measure by his reading of Dostoevsky – and, during his years of exile in Paris, to some highly original views of history and creativity. Kierkegaard's thought proved decisive for a great number of twentieth-century theologians. Among the most notable of these was the German Karl Barth, whom some have ranked as among the greatest theologians in the history of Western thought. Other important names in existentialist-oriented German theology from this period are Dietrich Bonhoeffer, who was executed for his role in a plot to assassinate Hitler, and Rudolph Bultmann. Paul Tillich, a German philosopher-theologian of Heidegger's generation who emigrated to the United States in the 1930s and lived there for the remainder of his life, wrote both a work of systematic theology and more popular books in which the existentialist component is obvious. Among his more popular works, *The Courage to Be*,[30] which includes a striking analysis of anxiety in the modern world, was particularly widely read and no doubt played a role in making existentialism better known to a segment of the American reading public that might not have been familiar with either more exclusively philosophical or literary existentialist works. Another prominent American theologian who incorporated existentialist motifs – particularly the themes of anxiety and human freedom – into his own thought was Reinhold Niebuhr. Paul Ricoeur, one of the most prolific and best-known French philosophers of the late twentieth century, whose own roots were in the immediate pre-war movement known as "personalism," wrote many religiously themed works which strive to come to grips with the leading existentialist thinkers. Also on the border between philosophy and theology – though based in a different religious tradition from the broad Protestant one common to Barth, Bonhoeffer, Bultmann, Tillich, Niebuhr, and Ricoeur – was the Jewish existentialist Martin Buber. His work *I and Thou*, first published in German in 1922 and then in English translation in 1958, is considered by many to be a classic of existentialism because of its distinctive approach to the relationship between the human being and God.

As for psychoanalysis, I have already mentioned Sartre's film scenario on a period in the life of Freud. In fact, Sartre's fundamental disagreements with aspects of Freud's systematic thought led him to propose, toward the end of *Being and Nothingness*, the development of an "existential psychoanalysis" that would presumably be superior, both in theory and in practice, to Freudian psychoanalysis. There are those who have taken up Sartre's suggestion, but in fact it is Heidegger's thought that has made more impact than Sartre's on this field.[31] Among Europeans, Ludwig Binswanger – who gave the Heidegger-inspired name *Daseinsanalyse* to his theory and techniques – and Medard Boss loom especially large in this context. Binswanger was in turn very influential on the thought of a prominent and popular American psychoanalyst and writer on psychoanalysis, Rollo May.

3.5 CONCLUSION

By way of concluding this brief survey of existentialism as a cultural movement, I would like to cite two books by anglophone writers – one that was first published in 1956 and one that was published fifty-two years later – to illustrate the extremely wide net that existentialism has cast and continues to cast. Colin Wilson, a product of a working-class British family, was in his mid twenties when his first book, *The Outsider* – its title obviously implying a reference to the principal character of Camus's *L'Étranger* – became a great overnight success. Wilson's work is not outstanding by virtue of its accuracy. For example, at the end of the first chapter, which begins by referring to a novel by Henri Barbusse entitled *L'Enfer* and migrates to an extended comparison between Sartre's *Nausea* and works by H. G. Wells, he writes: "Sartre and Wells have decided that man is never free; he is simply too stupid to recognize this."[32] Nor does it place much emphasis on the *word* "existentialism," which Wilson identifies with the "metaphysical" approach to the phenomenon of the Outsider that he finds in Sartre and Camus – though near the end of the book he does apply the label to Kierkegaard, to whom he is very sympathetic, and to some others. His range of references – mainly but not exclusively literary – is very wide indeed: Hemingway, T. S. Eliot, Hermann Hesse, D. H. Lawrence, Vincent Van Gogh, Dostoevsky, Nietzsche, George Bernard Shaw, and so on. And his conclusion – which looks to the possible dawning of a "new religious age" that would be tolerant enough to include all of these "Outsider" thinkers, however religiously unorthodox many of them were – has the effect of leaving Sartre the philosopher (as distinguished from the novelist) and probably some of the others who are regarded as core existentialist thinkers outside the pale. Nevertheless, particularly in light of this book's great celebrity at the time it was published, it is a useful indicator of just how much of a cultural force existentialism had become. It would not be too much of an exaggeration to say that in the minds of many the term had become nearly synonymous with unconventionality and with protest against the root assumptions of the established, scientific-technical order as such.

Does this remain the case today? Certainly not to the same extent. But the title and content of a recent work by an American philosopher – a modest work, not destined to become a best seller like *The Outsider* – bears witness, it seems to me, to existentialism's ongoing influence. It is Bernard Murchland's *The Arrow That Flies by Day: Existential Images of the Human Condition from Socrates to Hannah Arendt: A Philosophy for Dark Times.* As is immediately evident from the first subtitle, Murchland finds an existentialist thrust in thinkers with whom the term is infrequently identified, including the distinguished philosopher, Hannah Arendt, whose early reporting of the immediate postwar scene in Paris to an American reading public made it evident that, though relatively sympathetic to it, she did not consider herself to be part of the existentialist movement.[33] Other "outliers" to whom Murchland devotes special attention, in addition to the more customary figures of Kierkegaard, Nietzsche, Sartre, Camus, and Marcel, are the Stoics, Augustine, Rousseau, Thoreau, and

William James. Whatever its philosophical merits, the existence of such a book – with the contemporary resonance that sounds in its second subtitle – testifies to the fact that even today existentialism remains evocative of a cultural mood that is not to be limited to the post-war period. In philosophy, literature, the arts, and other areas of culture and society, the *"espèce d'existentialiste"* (existentialist type) lives on.

NOTES

1. Camus, *Le Mythe de Sisyphe*, pp. 50–57; *The Myth of Sisyphus*, pp. 24–28.
2. A good illustration of this is a short article written by Hannah Arendt and published in the February 23, 1946 issue of *The Nation*, entitled "French Existentialism." Arendt writes: "The name of the new movement is 'Existentialism,' and its chief exponents are Jean-Paul Sartre and Albert Camus, but the term Existentialism has given rise to so many misunderstandings that Camus has already stated publicly why he is 'not an existentialist.'" But in the remainder of the article she simply discusses Sartre and Camus as the two leading French existentialist writers. See Arendt, "French Existentialism," p. 2. For more on Camus and Absurdism, see Chapter 14 of this *Companion*.
3. Reported in Contat and Rybalka, *Les Écrits de Sartre*, p. 129.
4. Reported by Francis and Gontier, *Simone de Beauvoir*, p. 241.
5. See McBride, "Les premiers comptes rendus de *L'Être et le néant*."
6. Magny, *Littérature et critique*, p. 59. This is a collection of her essays; the original review appeared in *Esprit* in 1945.
7. Izard, "Jean-Paul Sartre o una nueva etapa de la fenomenología," p. 53.
8. Barrett, "Talent and Career of Jean-Paul Sartre," p. 239.
9. Ayer, "Novelist-Philosophers. v – Jean-Paul Sartre," p. 18.
10. Wahl, *A Short History of Existentialism*, p. 1. The periodical in question was *Philosophy and Phenomenological Research*.
11. Lowrie's essay, "Existence as Understood by Kierkegaard and/or Sartre," which appeared in the Summer 1950 issue of the *Sewanee Review*, was the focus of a thoughtful refutation, "Existence and Communication," by Robert Cumming.
12. Francis and Gontier, *Simone de Beauvoir*, pp. 275–76. The translation is mine.
13. Lefebvre, *L'Existentialisme*; Lukács, *Existentialisme ou Marxisme?*

14. In fact, in the interviews with Benny Lévy that were published just prior to his death, Sartre claimed never to have experienced it himself, even though he had made considerable use of it. See Sartre and Lévy, *Hope Now*, p. 55.
15. Beauvoir, *Les Mandarins*, p. 392.
16. Sartre, "Orphée noir."
17. Sartre, "*Les Damnés de la Terre*."
18. Sartre, "Réponse à Albert Camus," p. 90. Sartre says that their friendship was not an easy one, but that he will miss it. This reply was originally published in *Les Temps Modernes* 82, August 1952.
19. Merleau-Ponty, *Humanism and Terror*.
20. Sartre, "Qu'est-ce que la littérature?" was originally published piecemeal over several issues of *Les Temps Modernes* in 1947. English translation, *What is Literature?*
21. This more open-ended way of putting it is suggested by L. A. C. Dobrez in the introduction to his *The Existential and its Exits*, p. 2.
22. See, for instance, Roberts, *Temas existenciales en la novela española de postguerra*. For further discussion of existentialism in literature, see Chapter 14 of this *Companion*.
23. Agheanu, *The Prose of Jorge Luis Borges*, pp. x, 1.
24. Chatterji, "Existentialist Approach to Modern American Drama," p. 82.
25. Wartenberg, *Existentialism*, pp. 188–90.
26. If, as many claim and some deny, Friedrich Nietzsche may be regarded as a nineteenth-century proto-existentialist (and there is no doubt, at any rate, that he strongly influenced both Heidegger and Sartre), then we have in him an example of someone in this tradition for whom music was extremely important – from the title of his first major work, *The Birth of Tragedy out of the Spirit of Music*, through his association with, and later denunciation of, Richard Wagner. But even in this case, it cannot be said that Nietzsche's existentialism had much if any impact on the music "scene" itself.
27. Sartre, "I Discovered Jazz in America." Of course, that was not Sartre's own title (that would have been "Nick's Bar, New York City," or "Au Nick's Bar à New York") but the title given to it by the translator when it was published in the *Saturday Review*. Nor does the title of the translation convey the truth.
28. Merleau-Ponty, "Le Doute de Cézanne" (1945). English translation, "Cezanne's Doubt."
29. Barr, "Introduction," *The New American Painting*. See also Jachec, *The Philosophy and Politics of Abstract Expressionism*, p. 199. Jachec's

book strongly emphasizes the apparent political strategy behind this exhibit and others of the time, which was to counter more radical currents in Europe and to appeal to the moderate Left there by showing that such "unconventional" artistic endeavors were able to flourish in the United States despite its profoundly anti-communist political climate during the 1950s.

30. Tillich, *The Courage to Be* (1952).
31. For more on both, see Chapter 17 of this *Companion*.
32. Wilson, *The Outsider*, p. 26.
33. See n. 2, above.

III Major Existentialist Philosophers

ALASTAIR HANNAY

4 Kierkegaard's single individual and the point of indirect communication

4.1 THE SINGLE INDIVIDUAL

Kierkegaard once wrote that any historical importance attached to his writings would derive from his "category of the single individual." Many will acknowledge the cultural debt to Kierkegaard in just those terms. Yet his category is a special one, and those apprised of its features may prefer to talk of Kierkegaard's example rather than his legacy. Others may even regret that Kierkegaard's category might seem to mark the road back toward Augustinian theology rather than onward, say, to Karl Barth and Paul Tillich. But the spaces among whose coordinates Kierkegaard's cultural position can be plotted are diverse. So much so that any account that draws on just one of them runs the risk not only of overhasty dismissal but of failure to penetrate the rich existential core of Kierkegaard's thinking, not least in its religious respect.

In claiming the category as "his," Kierkegaard meant it was his own discovery. More than that, he had discovered it in a way other than that in which a zoologist might discover a new species, that is, by collecting and comparing evidence. Nor was it in the way that a mathematician or a philosopher might find a place for a new category in a deductive system. Kierkegaard's discovery was "his" in the special sense that it was the fruit of his own personal experience.

Judging fairly its originator's expectations or hopes, for both it and himself, calls for clarity concerning the origins, content, structure, and not least intended role of this "category of the single individual." It was in fact only after four and a half years of intensive writing, ending with *Concluding Unscientific Postscript*, that Kierkegaard started to ascribe the status of a category to the "single individual." In the pseudonymous writings the single individual was from the start linked to a notion of exceptionality, which one associates less with belonging to a category than with failing to do so. The figure of Abraham in *Fear and Trembling*, a father committed to carrying out God's command to sacrifice his son Isaac, puts the dilemma of exceptionality in especially sharp focus. Abraham's intention is discussed in terms of a "suspension of the ethical" but also of a failure to "realize the universal." The latter topic was first raised by the ethicist, Assessor Wilhelm, of Part Two of *Either/Or*, the work that launched the pseudonymous series. In everyday terms a person failing to realize the universal is one who finds him- or herself, for reasons that may at first seem beyond their control, unable to fulfill normal ethical requirements. As the pseudonymous works develop, we find the exception placed in a narrative in which it becomes clear that higher demands can be made on the individual than those of conventional ethics, and with correspondingly more profound choices to be made, these indicating that the reasons for the failure to realize the universal only appear to be beyond our control. At the close of *Either/Or* the position of the exception even seems privileged, confronting the individual as it does with the true nature of human being and, correspondingly, with an understanding of what it takes to seek and to acquire fulfillment. But it seems to have taken Kierkegaard some time to see the implications of Assessor Wilhelm's closing remarks and to begin describing the single individual in terms of a category.

Once he had done so, however, Kierkegaard was eager to see the category of the single individual at work in all that he had written before.[1] It was his conviction that this was indeed so that enabled him to think of his production, focused in this way upon a notion both potent and unifying, as enough to earn him a place in history.

It is beyond doubt that Kierkegaard's focus on the individual had autobiographical origins. The topic of exceptionality was generated by events surrounding the breaking off of his engagement to Regine Olsen. This gives scope to the psychologizer. Once the biographical background is known, it is easy to read the early pseudonymous works as an extended reflection upon that event, one that Kierkegaard exploits partly to give rein to his considerable literary gifts but also as a personal working-out of the ramifications, perhaps even in search of what would count as an excuse, or could provide a framework that accommodates a justification for his own failure to "realize the universal." From this point of view, the emerging religious aspect can easily appear in the guise of a device, more evidently so to us who live in a secularized culture than to Kierkegaard, in whose Christian and Lutheran background this expedient lay ready to hand, not least in the thought that the purpose of his authorship was revealed to him by a guiding force that had been steering him from the start.[2]

Opinion is divided on how to read Kierkegaard's later, sometimes fraught, account of his earlier intentions, as well as his later claim always to have had a religious purpose.[3] Skeptics have rejected the latter as an attempt to stage-manage his own future,[4] yet the texts can easily be read as supporting Kierkegaard's own interpretation, the contrary view relying on the resolute adoption of a hermeneutics of suspicion. For our own purposes, judgment may be left to the reader, a basic principle which even exponents of a hermeneutics of suspicion must surely accept.

The accuracy of some of Kierkegaard's self-referential comments is beyond doubt. Thus in the journal entry claiming that it was through "Guidance" that he began to see how the various parts of his production hung together, Kierkegaard notes that the person referred to as "*my* reader"[5] in the dedication to the very first two edifying discourses (from May 1843, the same date as *Either/Or*, but under his own name) was an actual individual, namely his former fiancée. He notes that the book "contained a little hint to her, and then for the time being it was especially true personally for me that I sought only one single reader." However, this idea of a single reader turns up again in the final pages of the *Postscript*[6] inside a framework that can be described as "systematic" even though it is to the *reader* that singularity is ascribed.

The clearly autobiographical reference in the preface to the edifying discourses is emulated in the pseudonymous *Fear and Trembling*, *Repetition*, and *Stages on Life's Way*, which followed *Either/Or*. These refocus the notion of exclusion from "the universal" in a variety of staged contexts. The pseudonymity blocks off the autobiographical source of the writings, allowing them to live lives of their own. Also, since that single reader for whom the discourses were written remained unidentified at the time, and could therefore be generalized, these "edifying" (and the later "Christian") discourses published in Kierkegaard's own name became his religious voice, speaking to the established church and its clients one by one.

The pseudonymous works, ironical in their literary mode,[7] make their appeal to a reading public. Kierkegaard later writes: "As an aesthetic author I have gone out, as it were, to get a hold on the public."[8] As he puts it himself, his purpose was to foster a sense of a need that he experienced in himself, a need to *become* a singular individual. One might therefore say that his aim here was to scatter this public, in the sense of indicating to its members that they too should be, as the later *A Literary Review* puts it in connection with "the crowd," individually and inwardly "separated out."[9] However, to prevent the public from receiving any hint of his own experience of this need, Kierkegaard had kept up a façade as an idler, a matter which he would later explain was dictated by a corresponding need for the imparting of such a sense to take the form of an "indirect communication."

Just prior to publication of the *Postscript*, the work with which he had intended to conclude his authorship, Kierkegaard had deliberately provoked a feud with a satirical periodical, *The Corsair*, inviting it to include him among its targets.[10] The effect of its retaliatory ridicule of Kierkegaard's person lingered long after the six months or so of the periodical's actual campaign. His cover as a flippant man-about-town no longer sustainable, Kierkegaard was pressed, one might say all the more openly, into the solitude of his own singularity.[11] The journal entries testify that this bitter experience gave him a clear conception of something he had previously only envisaged from the security of his desk. Formerly, from a freely chosen form of seclusion, he could indulge his literary talents without interruption and at the same time speak, perhaps even self-servingly, and with the plaudits of a reading public, on behalf of the exception that his celebrated transgression of local morals had made him. But now Kierkegaard was an open target of public abuse while – or so he complained – his erstwhile applauders stood by and watched or simply turned their backs.[12]

Already in the final pages of the ethicist's second letter in Part Two of *Either/Or* we read of an exceptionality that accepts its fate but buys its accommodation at a high price. For exceptionality to be more than a ruse it must be lived through in full awareness of the fact that there is no redress. In terms of a now popular example, this can be understood as saying that we should not seek to forgive a Gauguin for deserting his family just because the sacrifice enabled him to produce great art. Truly to remain an exception is to accept an irremediable failure, one for which no amount of service on behalf of the universal or of public celebrity can compensate. The ethicist, Assessor Wilhelm, nevertheless glimpses a way out, though without seeing himself equipped to pursue it. He says that the only way to achieve an accommodation would be through a personal choice that transforms a finite particular into (that is to say, treats it *as*) the universal.[13] As Kierkegaard's spokesman at the time for what might count as realizing the universal, Wilhelm describes this "noble" form of exceptionality as a "purgatory."[14]

It was in this post-*Postscript* period of self-induced solitude that Kierkegaard began to see his project as one that a divine hand, rather like Socrates' daimon, had helped him to launch. By having him bring this suffering down upon himself, it had shown him what it means and costs to be the single individual. The notion of martyrdom for truth arose in his mind, though again accompanied by those doubts about such claims to exceptionality being a mere ruse. Was his own suffering enough to prove that it was not that? Be that as it may, Kierkegaard was now inclined to see his entire production, from *Either/Or* to date, thus including all that he called his "aesthetic" production, as a continuous and progressively *religious* campaign. Kierkegaard now saw himself as engaged upon a mission.

Those final pages of the ethicist's second letter in *Either/Or*, which Kierkegaard himself cites,[15] can be read as supporting his claim to continuity without any need to cite a guiding hand. Read closely, they can be grasped as a platform (still within the ethical sphere) from which, in the authorship beyond *Postscript*, the topic of singularity as a significantly positive notion later emerged in all its peculiarity and richness. There is, after all, a kind of narrative logic in a progression that starts with a program of self-exculpation invoking religion, and then merges effortlessly into a critique designed to sharpen a sense of the actual demands of a religion then routinely subscribed to, and finally developing into a mission to save mankind, not least from the "presumptuous" forms of Christianity that prevail in what Kierkegaard referred to disparagingly as "Christendom."[16]

In short, although one may choose to read the whole of *Either/Or, Fear and Trembling, Repetition*, and *Stages on Life's Way* as nothing but expansive attempts to assure "*my* reader" that exceptions to realizing the universal are intelligible, to be expected, and in some way even admirable, to readers innocent of the biographical details – an innocence that the conventions of pseudonymity at the time presumed even if the author's identity was common knowledge – the texts readily present themselves as a many-sided and graphically presented portrayal of a dilemma whose possibility was at the time, and is perhaps even today, not at all exceptional.

4.2 INDIRECT COMMUNICATION

The pseudonymity can be a source of confusion. One view long held was that it was a cover behind which the true author lurked as a ghostly manipulator of his many fictitious personae. An alternative, just as plausible, takes pseudonymity to be a device that licenses more self-revelation than convention otherwise permits, offering a way of fictionalizing fact that avoids the constraints and distracting implications of actual autobiography. In this light one can appreciate how the distance of pseudonymity might enable Kierkegaard actually to use himself as an example, but in a way that insulates his literary figures from the details of his own life.

Pseudonymity can lead to misconception. The fact that the pseudonymous series culminates in the work of a "humorist" has led scholars into taking *Concluding Unscientific Postscript* to be a skilful parody or a form of extended joke.[17] However, the humor deployed in that work is among the many central notions that its author is at pains to explain in the work itself, and without any obvious sign of unseriousness. With that explanation in hand the reader should have no difficulty in appreciating Kierkegaard's own comment that the "reason why *Concluding Postscript* is made to appear comical is precisely that it is serious."[18]

The pseudonymity is linked, if less clearly than might first appear, to a notion already referred to. Early in the *Postscript* we are introduced to a notion of "indirect communication." Its position there indicates its importance for the topic alongside which it is introduced, namely subjective thinking. We might assume initially then that these two belong together, which is to say that wherever we have subjective thinking and an intention to communicate it, the mode of communication should be indirect. But two questions arise. First, does Kierkegaard mean us to identify subjective thinking *only* with thinking that has becoming a Christian (the overall topic of the *Postscript*) as its aim, or can we take what he says about indirect communication to apply to something we might like to refer to more generally as "existential" thinking? Second, what about the *Postscript* itself? Is it too an example of indirect communication, or does it speak to us directly among other things about indirect communication?

The answer to the second question will depend partly on how we answer the first. Let us therefore begin by asking what Climacus says about communication both direct and indirect.

It is clear that by communication of any kind he does not mean the simple passing along of information. While waiting to meet a friend at the railway station someone comes up to me and asks me the time, I glance at my watch and say, three minutes to three, and then continue looking out for my friend. Here there is minimal input from my side, no desire to impart something that is peculiarly my own. In Kierkegaard's vocabulary it would fail to be a case even of direct communication. The context for both direct and indirect communication is one in which someone has something to impart to another. The Danish "*meddelelse*" has this sense of sharing, or of giving something of oneself. Ordinary life, however, passes in what the *Postscript* refers to as "immediacy," and ordinary communication – that is, direct communication – is similarly immediate.[19]

Kierkegaard points to certain features of the life of immediacy. It is what makes normal life possible, and direct communication makes it easier. Immediacy is rooted in a mutual dependence,[20] and direct communication is the means by which we inform one another of our beliefs and concerns. It is how we express our own beliefs and concerns and respond to what others say about theirs. However, immediacy and its concerns also divert attention from the "eternal" in oneself, preventing that separating out that is needed if one is to become the single individual. This might be to say that direct communication is the mode in which we impart knowledge to one another of the world "out there." Some philosophers of language have been concerned to distinguish matters of fact in this strict sense (or the corresponding propositions) from the attitudes people take toward them. However, direct communication as Climacus explains it is not confined to the communication of facts independently of the attitudes that people have toward them. Our having the attitudes we do have is included in the kind of knowledge we can all share, whatever skeptical doubts philosophers raise about "other minds." Our "immediate" language practices assume that we all know what we mean when we say that we are sad, overjoyed, angry, or pleased.

We can look for a clue here in a parallel with what Heidegger says about human life, as we find it, being essentially "concerned." If what makes communication *indirect* is something bound up with the subject or person, it must be in virtue not only of something other than the world being, as Wittgenstein's *Tractatus* has it, "all that is the case,"[21] but also in virtue of something more than a prevailing Heideggerian *Sorge* ("care"). Climacus leads us to suppose that indirect communication is called for when we transcend the bounds of what can intelligibly be said in the language with which we share our beliefs and concerns and through which we merely add to each other's body of knowledge of facts of the world.

The *Postscript* brings two aspects of indirect communication together in a reference to Socrates.

> Think! Socrates was a teacher in the ethical, but he took note of the fact that there is no direct relation between the teacher and the learner, because inwardness is truth, and because inwardness in the two is precisely the path away from each other.[22]

Instead of teacher and taught coming together as in an instance of direct communication, in indirect communication they must move apart. This is because the lesson, or message, or intimation, is one that must take root spontaneously in the one taught; it has to be appropriated as something whose truth is a matter quite independent of the fact that the teacher also believes it. However, the separation of teacher and learner here is not simply a matter of pedagogy; the need to be individually separated out is also *part* of what is being taught. In order to confront themselves in their spiritual dimension, people need to be single individuals in a radical sense implying that they have no teacher or teaching, or any outside authority, to lean on.

It can be tempting to read Kierkegaard anachronistically through the eyes of Heidegger's *Daseinsanalyse* ("analysis of Dasein"). It can sound as though, while people generally live in a state of *Das Man*, each acting as an "everyone" and their concerns being of this conventional type, the concern that calls for an indirect communication is of a type that lifts you out of immediacy and into some form of synoptic perspective within which an "authentic" acceptance of the finite limitations of human life ("living towards death") is made possible. But Heidegger has himself said of his account of the "structures of Dasein" that it "proposes no covert theology and has in principle nothing to do with theology."[23] With its topic of how to become a Christian the *Postscript* has, however, a clear theological reference. Unless we can find reason *not* to link that reference with indirect communication, the analogy with Heidegger will not work.

Kierkegaard's reference to Socrates needs some unraveling. He admires Socrates for seeing that teaching is a matter of bringing something out in the pupil, hence the need for distance; and also for recognizing that ethics is not the same as conformity with the accepted mores of a society – hence the need to cultivate inwardness. But to Climacus, Socrates is also a precursor of Aristotelian metaphysics and thus, ultimately, of Hegel's speculative idealism. Adverting to Plato's notion of *anamnesis*, he sees Socrates as dedicated to the idea that truth is recoverable in a form of recollection. Having the truth "behind" him, the famous maieutic method is designed to elicit this same truth in his pupil, as demonstrated in the example of the slave boy in the *Meno*. However, since metaphysics was the tradition that Heidegger saw it as the aim of his *Daseinsanalyse* to overcome, it may appear at first glance that the project of becoming a Christian is nothing but the pursuit of metaphysical ends by other, even if more appropriate, means. Seen in this light, Kierkegaard's theological framework appears to fail to infringe the limits set by Heidegger's analysis of the human situation. Whether that is indeed the light in which to see it is a question we may fruitfully leave open. For present purposes we may simply note both an un-Socratic and an un-Heideggerian element in Climacus' project. In his presentation of the truth of Christianity, that truth is not something pre-established in God's mind; it lies in the future, a future in which the individual's becoming a single individual plays a constitutive part.

To uncover the un-Heideggerian aspect we need to ask whether indirect communication, as the communicative means for subjective thinking, is confined to this theologically framed conception of becoming. If not, there may still be something to the proposed analogy with Heidegger's distinction between common cares and something larger or higher. The preliminary answer is less clear than we might wish. It is that, in general, indirect communication is required when "inwardness" is to be communicated. That leaves us asking what "inwardness" means.

To illustrate its meaning Climacus, typically in Kierkegaard, appeals to the analogy of love. He says that the lover who is essentially concerned to "appropriate" love's inwardness has "no result";[24] so long as love is love, it has nowhere to stop. Climacus hints that this is the reason why communicating love cannot occur in a direct form. The lover's state (or perhaps we should rather say ongoing condition) of mind is one he or she cannot express in words directly. We may ask, why not? After all there is no lack of poems with that theme. Yes, but poems do not *describe* reality, they emerge *from* it. Climacus suggests that communication is in any case not the lover's concern; what looks like communication here is really a kind of incontinence, a bursting to give expression. A poem may indeed, in a way, be an indirect form of communication, but it is not intentionally so; or rather it is not part of anything like a Socratic strategy for setting things in motion.

Kierkegaard says that for him indirect communication had been "instinctive."[25] He connects this with the fact that from early on he had felt something higher "brewing" in him. Uncertain of its genuineness, however, or where it might lead, he also had the sense of his own activity as a whole being open-ended and ongoing. It thus differed profoundly from that, say, of a mathematician who has a proof and wants to present it, or of a scientist like Newton who decides to publish precisely the *results* of his calculations and reflections on gravitation. Kierkegaard doesn't even know whether what is brewing in him is some *truth* (it can be an illusion, have a psychological explanation, etc.); he has no such *result*. But the same must be true of the *recipient* of an indirect communication. Here, too, if the communication has taken place, there is no result, and that there should be none is once again part of the communication, perhaps one might call it its performative aspect, the method being the very message, though it may take time for the one taught to realize what that method, and therefore the message, is.

On this interpretation indirect communication and subjective thinking are appropriate only to the cultivation of a sense of an aspiration higher than any belonging to immediacy and finite therefore in the sense of having readily definable and identifiable ends. Concerned as it is with subjective thinking, indirect communication is appropriate for goals of a kind that the subjective thinker must first have, and if not, be made to acquire a sense for. Becoming a Christian in Climacus' terms is one such goal. Existentialists claim there are other ways of seeking "authentic" selfhood; some will claim, though it may be rashly, that Climacus' way does envisage a result, in the "hereafter."

The much-discussed "stages," or "spheres of existence," presented pseudonymously in the works mentioned above and summarized in the *Postscript*, ascend from the aesthetic, through the ethical, to the religious, arriving finally at the paradox or absurdity of religiousness B. One could say that they gravitate towards that religiousness, which Climacus identifies as Christianity, or the doctrine of the God-man, though he is careful to call it not a doctrine (suggesting a set of rules for achieving some result) but an existence-communication.[26] The metaphor of gravitation is not one that Climacus uses here, but we may exploit it on the basis of remarks Kierkegaard makes in his first (and signed) publication, *From the Papers of One Still Living*.[27] In that early work, a review of a novel by Hans Christian Andersen, Kierkegaard had maintained that novels need centers of gravity, and that these are provided by a life-view, which Andersen's works lacked. By extrapolation we might say that the pseudonymous works also lack centers of gravity, but deliberately and in a special way. They have one center, and it lies ahead of them. That they gravitate progressively towards the uniquely saving paradoxical religiousness B would conform with Kierkegaard's later appraisal of his earlier work as already encompassing a religious life-view.

Alternatively we might say that the whole point of the pseudonymity is that the works indeed have their own centers of gravity, and precisely lack any *common* such center, this being precisely what gives them their autonomy as texts and the reader his or her freedom to read them without reference to one another or to their author. Although the present writer inclines strongly to the former reading, which of these models best captures the role of subjective thinking and indirect communication can once again be left to Kierkegaard's reader to decide.

The second alternative is consistent with a reading made fashionable by Alasdair MacIntyre.[28] It says that the life-views on show are to be selected in a radical choice. This is also an interpretation favored by contemporary literary theorists, although it is open to the criticism that here the notion of choice is strained beyond recognition. The argument is that to choose something requires some principle of selection and, strictly speaking, this cannot be chosen in the same act of choice. Making it so is to reduce choosing to mere picking.

Similarly, indirect communication in Kierkegaard is sometimes interpreted as communication entirely freed from its communicator. In his dissertation, *On the Concept of Irony,* Kierkegaard does in fact suggest something like this; he says there that to "master" irony is to so infuse a work with it that, with no non-ironical holds left, the work frees itself from the author and the author from it. For that reason the work will tell us nothing about the author, who for all we know may be a complete reprobate as much as a practicing Christian. To find out which, we would need to go into the kind of (biographical) details "that don't usually concern us."[29] Allied to a claim that the pseudonymous works have their *own* centers of gravity, this lends support to the idea of an author absenting himself from his works once they are put into circulation.

There is a decisive argument against this. Apart from taking us back, paradoxically, to the situation of sheerly direct communication in which there is no input at all from the side of the communicator, here there would no longer be, strictly speaking, any reason to describe the communication as even "indirect."[30] If what the author may have had in mind to impart becomes a redundant feature in the communication, then the author does not figure in the relationship at all, *a fortiori* not even indirectly. Later, however, Kierkegaard himself goes so far as to say that indirect communication *demands* a communicator.[31] Or more precisely, he says that any communication concerning *existing* requires a communicator. We must ask, then, what the relationship of the real author is to what he communicates indirectly about existing. Is the author, though absent, still present in some way in the text?

In notes prepared for a lecture series on "The Dialectic of Ethical and the Religio-Ethical Communication" that he never gave, Kierkegaard lists the elements involved. "Four things come to mind," he says: the object, the imparter, the recipient, and what is imparted.[32] The text itself is conspicuously absent. By "object" he means "subject matter," some topic about which something is said and which may become an object of knowledge (if what is said about it is true and appropriated by the recipient). He also says that the topic *drops out* where what is imparted is some ability (*Kunnens Meddelelse*), and he also claims a correlation between the absence of a topic and the need for the communication to be indirect. Thus, in the case of the existing subject's way of grasping a goal of selfhood "higher" than those that can be described in the finite terms of immediacy, there is no common reference at which directly to point, no "topic" to place on an agenda.[33]

It seems then that indirectly communicating texts are properly identified only when a sense of where the author intended them to go has been evoked in the reader. The indirect communicator has some subjectively appropriated idea of where to look for the truth, and also of the ways in which, if found, it should manifest itself. It is only insofar as we could say that this idea *is* potentially embodied in the text – which is to say that it forms an essential part of it – that a text is included. But then it is already included by implication in the four components that are mentioned. That means that in the case of indirect communication, as Kierkegaard employs this notion, there must be an input on the communicator's part, some vision of truth that may be "brewing" and which the author thinks worth sharing with the recipient. Climacus writes:

> Double reflection is implicit in the very idea of conveying something, that the subject existing in the isolation of his inwardness (who wants through this inwardness to express the life of eternity, in which sociality and all community are unthinkable because the existential category of movement cannot be thought here, and along with all essential communication, too, since everyone must be assumed essentially in possession of everything) nevertheless wishes to convey something personal, and hence wants to have his thinking in the inwardness of his subjective existence and at the same time convey it to others. This contradiction cannot possibly (except for thoughtlessness, for which all things are indeed possible) find expression in a direct form.[34]

We can of course allow that communication can be indirect in other ways, not least and perhaps especially in "immediate" contexts. Much of ordinary communication is indirect, from the "signals" sent by politicians in their voting strategies and carefully scripted press releases to utterances of the kind we call "snide," along with innuendos, insinuations, concealed warnings, and everyday irony. To decipher these, however, all you need is a shared language and an appreciation of the situation. When it comes to expressing what Climacus calls the "life of eternity," however, since this is not something that can be put in "immediate" terms, no shared language is available (or so the reconstructed argument goes). If one nevertheless tries to clothe the life of eternity in such a language, it becomes presumptuous and a fake.

We may now at least see more clearly what *pseudonymity* has to do with Climacus' form of indirect communication. Kierkegaard says that his pseudonyms "represent" indirect communication.[35] That suggests that it is the pseudonymous authors themselves who communicate indirectly and not Kierkegaard who communicates indirectly by virtue of pseudonymity. That of course does not prevent our reading the pseudonymous works as indirectly conveying the meaning and importance that Søren Kierkegaard attaches to them, but the indirectness that concerns him is not that of pseudonymity. It is true that Kierkegaard remarks in one place that *The Sickness unto Death*, by a later (and his last) pseudonym "Anti-Climacus," was not indirect since he had himself written a preface to the work. This seems to imply that it was only because the cover of pseudonymity had been broken that the work failed the test of indirectness.[36] However, in connection with "the religious" (a more accurate term for Kierkegaard than "religion") he also claims to have abandoned indirect communication after the *Postscript*.[37] This means that neither *The Sickness unto Death* nor *Practice in Christianity* is an indirect communication in spite of being (in the former case with the qualification mentioned) pseudonymous. That in turn implies that pseudonymity in itself, although it may achieve some form of indirect communication, is not enough to account for the kind of maieutic role that indirect communication plays (and is "represented") in the works of Kierkegaard's "aesthetic" pseudonyms.

But what about the *Postscript*? Is it also a case of indirect communication? Just prior to the "declaration" appended to it in Kierkegaard's own name, acknowledging himself as author ("as people say")[38] of the pseudonymous works, Climacus revokes the work. Encouraged by the pseudonym's name, commentators have sought to explain this by analogy with Wittgenstein's ladder metaphor at the close of his *Tractatus Logico-Philosophicus*. The suggestion is that, as with Wittgenstein's ladder, what Climacus writes, too, is to be thrown away once the reader has absorbed the elevation it provides. Armed with its vision, the reader can now enter earnestly upon the task ("becoming a Christian") upon whose nature the author has thrown a merely humorous light. It is significant that the distance created by Climacus is that of humor, not of maieutic assistance. The latter, although dependent on a measure of gentle irony, is a matter of prompting a new start in the hearer. But Kierkegaard remarks in his journals that indirect communication also means "taking away."[39] Climacus wants us to see comedy in what he calls "presumptuous forms of religiousness."[40] Readers can see themselves in the role of Socrates' companions as he makes mincemeat of a passer-by's unreflective response to a "What is ...?" question. Humor can have the preparatory role, remarked by Wittgenstein, of ridding us of those false pictures by which we are "held captive."[41]

Whatever we conclude here, Climacus seems to occupy a position not unlike that of a television talk-show host, disengaged enough to have his audience laugh at Christianity (since in common-sense terms its defining narrative is, after all, absurd) but set chiefly on having it laugh at those who are comical because they *fail* to laugh at it, thinking they have conquered its absurdity through reason. Climacus says in one place that humor revokes existence.[42] The point of throwing away the ladder, then, can be to revoke the humor in order to return the reader to existence.

4.3 THE RELIGIOUS RESPECT

We traced a refocusing from singularity as a situation to be excused, though at a cost and repentantly, to singularity held up as an independent category. We indicated that Kierkegaard saw his personal access to this "category" as having been vouchsafed to him, and his importance as depending on his having given an adequate account of this "discovery." If only, he says, "this was the right category, if what was said about it was in order, if I perceived it correctly and understood properly that this was my task ... then I stand and my writings with me."[43]

The passage's opening remark has a prophetic ring: "'The single individual' is the category through which, in a religious respect, this age, history, the human race must pass." If we omit "in a religious respect" this leaves us with a passable motto for existentialism. True, there are religious existentialists such as Gabriel Marcel and Miguel de Unamuno, and religious thinkers like Barth and Tillich, all of whom are indebted to Kierkegaard. In theory, therefore, it might seem that Kierkegaard could be linked with these, even placed at their head, along perhaps (in Unamuno's case certainly) with Pascal, a writer Kierkegaard also refers to.[44]

It is not clear, however, that Kierkegaard would wish to be remembered either as an existential philosopher or as an existentialist theologian. As hinted, the word "missionary" comes more vividly to mind. The term "category" should not mislead us. For Kierkegaard it is not the technical term that it is for Aristotle or Kant. He had formerly used it to refer to the general concepts according to which people live and rationalize: "Many people think in quite other kinds of category than those in which they live."[45] He had been suspicious of the notion: "The categories are the modern age's shewbread, only digestible by priests."[46] Later, however, noting a bias in the priests' "categories" ("They have become so erudite, talk all the time of the whole of world history, and then perhaps a little about the individual in his singularity, but [only] in conclusion"),[47] he began exploiting the notion himself. Looking back at *Either/Or*, he says that it contains the category "'for you' (subjectivity, inwardness)."[48] Finally, he goes so far as to see his own activity in the light of a category: "The category for my activity is to make people attentive to what is Christian."[49]

If we accept this view of his own work, the question of Kierkegaard's place in cultural time and space more generally becomes acute. We may ask, as Jean-Paul Sartre did, how far and in what respects Kierkegaard can still appear as a contemporary. In his essay "The Singular Universal," Sartre concludes that whatever is still alive for us in Kierkegaard, "we cannot revive the martyr of inwardness."[50] For Sartre, what lives on is that writer who, with a contagious "potency" and "virulence," addressed personal themes, including as it happens religious ones (anxiety, doubt and faith, guilt and immortality), existentially. That Kierkegaard did so in a framework now considered alien by many is something that makes him an example rather than a legacy. Still, even as an example Kierkegaard must have something beyond the specifically religious mission and its message that we can all share with him. Sartre's proposal is that Kierkegaard presciently "revealed [that] each man is all mankind as the singular universal."[51]

The claim is worth examining. It posits an abstract level – if you like, a "category" – within which humankind, all history, etc. can be placed. Its terms of reference are the limitations that characterize finite human being, specifically the inherent limitations of perspective owing to a confinement to time. These terms exclude, or are at any rate prior to and independent of, truths thought to be available to metaphysical speculation or religious teaching. It is these limitations that leave us, as Heidegger noted, to face the question of our own nature.[52] It is because Kierkegaard's religious perspective exceeds such limitations that the martyr of inwardness has no place in a singularity that applies everywhere. The hyper-reflective Danish thinker and writer who, flexing his literary muscles on a personal theme, ended up including himself and all humankind in the category of the single individual "in a religious respect" offers just one narrative version among others of universal singularity.

There is a certain ambiguity in Sartre's claim. The implication seems to be that singular universality pertains only to individuals once the "contingencies" of whatever stand they take on the issue of their own nature have been filtered away. But in that case, Sartre's atheism could itself be just another case history with its details to be filed away for universal singularity "in itself" to stand revealed in his person. Yet Sartre appears to claim for his atheism an "authentic" version of such singularity, one that, unlike Kierkegaard's, actually coincides with the noted limitations and requirements.

Might we not choose, though, to read Kierkegaard's "category" as an actual application of Sartre's "singular universal," anticipating it in actual use? It just so happens that the role of analyst of the basic human situation is not the one Kierkegaard chose, the application being for him more important than the analysis. There is certainly enough existential ontology in the *Postscript* and elsewhere to be going on with,[53] and the fact that it is applied in a situation that evokes a sense of what *religiosity* means in the search for a significant life may even be considered a valid amendment to a singularity otherwise too abstractly conceived. That Climacus talks of religiousness rather than religion may not be unimportant.[54] Yes, Christianity is indeed a religion, and we must acknowledge such claims by Kierkegaard himself as that particularity (*det Particulaire*) is "true" only in a "primitive God-relationship," and that Christianity alone is able to justify the elevation of the individual above the universal.[55] But the main focus, especially in the pen of Climacus, is first and foremost on the ability of the God-man idea to change our attitudes and encourage a spirituality or inwardness capable of informing our notions of fulfilled human being.

Hubert Dreyfus has extended the God-man motif beyond the Christian framework by suggesting that this too is an exemplary notion and not confined to the Christian framework. The God-man signifies the general possibility of an all-risks-taken commitment to "something finite."[56] This recalls Assessor Wilhelm's thought that the only way for the noble exception to solve the problem of realizing the universal would be through a personal choice that actually transformed a finite particular into the universal.[57] Assessor Wilhelm was unable to envisage the possibility, but that is just what Climacus' account of religiousness B assumes is possible, though in the face of absurdity. The Christian believer believes in something finite that makes itself out to be the eternal and, via that route, the universal.

The advantage of Dreyfus's generalization of the God-man motif is that it relieves us of the absurdity. On the other hand, without the "offense" to reason, most of what Climacus and Anti-Climacus say falls flat.[58] Also the link between faith and the message of love (derived from the God-man figure) is reduced to contingency. That may not seem problematic for a view that correlates inwardness with uncertainty; in theory one more contingency could actually help. However, to those who see Kierkegaard's signed *Works of Love* as central to the opus this will seem a contingency too far.

The ambiguity of Sartre's "singular universal" has its counterpart in Heidegger, though in reverse. In introducing the notion of human completeness that he calls "authenticity," Heidegger himself appears to have placed at least half a foot outside the perimeter of Dasein as such. As Stephen Mulhall says:

> Kierkegaard's philosophical pseudonym, Johannes Climacus, shares the Heideggerian view that human beings continuously confront the question of how they should live, and so must locate some standard or value in relation to which that choice might meaningfully be made. Moreover, insofar as that standard is intended to govern every such moment of choice, it confers significance on the whole life that those moments make up ... Climacus thus presents the question of how best to live as a question about what gives meaning to one's life as a whole, making exactly the conjunction between authenticity and wholeness that Heidegger deploys.[59]

Accordingly, before drawing the conclusion, against Kierkegaard's hopes, that his category of the single individual has turned out *not* to be the "right" one, we may pause to consider some reasons for postponement. We noted that Heidegger's *Daseinsanalyse* was designed to preclude access via metaphysics and religion to basic truths about what gives a human being significance. In the *Postscript*, a work that Kierkegaard describes as the "turning point"[60] in his authorship, he has his pseudonym similarly deny such access. Instead, there has to be a constantly renewed and fundamental decision against reason and in the absence of doctrinal authority. But what is there to decide? Existentialism typically extols the virtue of authenticity, but on what basis is a goal of authenticity to be established? If authenticity means recognizing that we are confined to "immediacy," and authentic living simply means keeping that fact in focus, we may ask, "Why should we do that?" Are we not better off just getting along with our immediacies, even if at times we dream that this may not be all there is? To face our finitude is in any case disturbing, it gives us a sense of alienation, and no ulterior goal is offered for keeping it in view.

Kierkegaard mentions but passes over the usual reasons for focusing on his topic of subjective thinking – for instance that scientific approaches "omit" subjectivity.[61] Even when rescued from the cognitive cold, subjectivity is just whatever it is. Clear-headedness about the nature of human being needs some further justification if it is to be declared essential to the good life, at least in any but an "immediate" context, or self-beggingly in terms of "facing the truth." Found within immediacy, any such justification is likely to be pragmatic, a matter of prudence, and the *Postscript* tells us that if we are trying to think ethically, our motive for finding out what it is prudent to do is to be able *not* to do it.[62] Again, Climacus reminds us that the human being is the only "animal species in which the specimen is more than the species,"[63] but this observation too remains a mere matter of "structure." In order to have a foothold for believing that there is something we ought to become rather than just be, we need some teleology, a part of Aristotelian metaphysics that won't so easily go away.

According to Sartre, the scenario from which Kierkegaard's figure of the martyr of inwardness emerges blinds him to the many possible worlds we live in. Certainly, in the familiar "doctrine" of the aesthetic, ethical, and religious stages, Kierkegaard has proved his awareness of perspectival change, but he has been too quick to turn a parochial story into the only authentically human one: "Kierkegaard shows historiality, but misses history."[64] Sartre describes Kierkegaard as "my adventure,"[65] by which he apparently means that he can be read in the way we read and are inspired by stories from the past.

But here again, just to restore the balance, we may take a page from Sartre's own book. Sartre claimed that we *make* our own worlds. A challenge to this is to be found in a thought that never seems to have left Kierkegaard. Near the end of the dissertation which he defended just before starting on that four-and-a-half-year stint of signed and pseudonymous writing he describes the world as a gift and a task that comes to us.[66]

NOTES

1. "'This matter of the single individual appears in every one of the pseudonymous works – yes absolutely, in this way among others, that the pseudonyms' computations respecting the universal, the single individual, the special individual [added in the margin: "the exception"], turn on it, so as to identify the special individual in his suffering and in his extraordinariness ... This was already posed by the Assessor in *Either/Or* re. being excepted from marrying ... Then came *Fear and Trembling – Repetition*, the psychological experiment ["'Guilty?' – 'Not Guilty?'" in *Stages on Life's Way*], all commentaries on the category of the single individual ... But also the pseudonyms as books make the category of the single individual applicable in respect of a reading public.'" *Kierkegaard's Journals and Papers*, vol. v, NB10:62, 61a. Henceforth cited as KJN, with volume number.
2. KJN v, NB10:185.

3. See Kierkegaard, *The Point of View for My Work as an Author*, p. 37.
4. See Garff, *Søren Kierkegaard.*
5. Kierkegaard, *Eighteen Upbuilding Discourses*, p. 5.
6. Kierkegaard, *Concluding Unscientific Postscript*, p. 523.
7. Irony in this sense is not an intermittently applied rhetorical device but pervades a whole work.
8. KJN VI, NB13:27.
9. Kierkegaard, *A Literary Review* (Two Ages), p. 55.
10. See, e.g., Hannay, *Kierkegaard*, pp. 317ff.
11. In describing the movement of his authorship (see the journal entry referred to above, n. 8) as one from the public to the private individual, Kierkegaard says (as it happens wrongly): "and so it ends consistently in me, myself the single individual, living in country solitude in a parsonage."
12. For an analogy with a snapping dog (of literary contempt), see *A Literary Review*, pp. 84–85.
13. Kierkegaard, *Either/Or*, p. 587.
14. Kierkegaard, *Either/Or*, p. 589. On the noble exception Wilhelm adds (in a sentence deserving some scrutiny) that in seeing himself as a "task," such a person "perceives that in a sense everyone is an exception, and that it is equally true that everyone is the universally human and at the same time an exception." *Either/Or*, p. 589.
15. KJN VII, NB19:61, 61a.
16. The expression is that of the "humorist," Johannes Climacus, pseudonymous author of *Postscript*. See p. 437.
17. See, e.g., Allison, "Christianity and Nonsense"; Conant, "Kierkegaard, Wittgenstein, and Nonsense," and Conant, "Putting Two and Two Together."
18. KJN VI, NB13:61.
19. Kierkegaard, *Postscript*, p. 63.
20. KJN VII, NB20:152; KJN IX NB27:59; and *Søren Kierkegaards Papirer*, vol. X, 6, B 145, p. 205. Henceforth cited as Pap., with volume number.
21. Supposing, as Wittgenstein seems to assume, that what is the case excludes our interest in what is the case.
22. Kierkegaard, *Postscript*, p. 207; cf. Kierkegaard, *Practice in Christianity*, p. 142.
23. Heidegger, *History of the Concept of Time*, p. 283. In this lecture series from 1925, an early version of *Being and Time* (1927), Heidegger says of those theological factors (original sin, etc.) that can lead to talk of "fallenness," and thus also to the possibility of a return to authenticity, that his "pure consideration of structures ... *precedes* all such consideration," not (we note) that it precludes them.

24. Kierkegaard, *Postscript*, p. 62, fn.a.
25. KJN VII, NB20:152.
26. See Kierkegaard, *Postscript*, pp. 312n., 318, 468, 471, 478–80, 486, 510, and 512.
27. Kierkegaard, *From the Papers of One Still Living*, p. 81: "A life-view [in the novel] ... is its deeper unity, which makes [it] have its center of gravity in itself."
28. See MacIntyre, *After Virtue*, p. 41.
29. Kierkegaard, *The Concept of Irony*, p. 324.
30. In *Practice in Christianity* Anti-Climacus distinguishes two forms of indirect communication, one in which the communicator withdraws in order to let the communication disconcert and the other where the communicator is "dialectically" present and he or she is the disconcerting factor. See *Practice*, p. 134; cf. pp. 141–42 for yet another analogy with love.
31. Kierkegaard, *Practice*, p. 137, though he also says (p. 134) that communication cannot be direct if the communicator *exists* in the communication. See the previous note.
32. *Gjenstanden, Meddeleren, Modtageren, Meddelelsen*. Pap. VIII, 2, B 83 and B 89.
33. In the case of imparting practical knowledge, Kierkegaard distinguishes between ethical knowledge, in imparting which the imparter as it were steps aside, and religious knowledge, to impart which implies authority and thus reintroduces an "object" of knowledge.
34. Kierkegaard, *Postscript*, p. 62n.
35. Pap. X, 6, B 145, p. 203.
36. KJN VI, NB:13.
37. KJN VI, NB11:33c.
38. Kierkegaard, *Postscript*, p. 527.
39. Pap. VI, B 52.
40. Kierkegaard, *Postscript*, p. 437.
41. Wittgenstein, *Philosophical Investigations*, section 115, p. 48.
42. Kierkegaard, *Postscript*, p. 507.
43. KJN IV, NB3:77.
44. See Dreyfus, "Kierkegaard on the Self," p. 11: "Kierkegaard's existential thinking clearly has its roots in the *Pensées* of Pascal." We note, however, that the journal entries on the *Pensées* are dated after the *Postscript*.
45. KJN IV, NB:103: "They speak in the categories of religion and live in those of the sensate, the categories of immediate well-being."
46. KJN II, JJ 146. Interestingly, as himself a kind of poet, he notes that poets live in quite other categories than their works (KJN III, NB 9:11).

47. KJN II, JJ 21. The "erratic nature of ecclesiastical discourse" is put down to the Old Testament having "entirely different categories" from those of the New Testament (1843).
48. KJN III, NB3:61. It is the category "with which *Either/Or* concluded. ('Only the truth that edifies is truth for you')."
49. KJN VI, NB14:3, italic removed; cf. KJN VI, NB12:62: "Mine is the only Christian category, to grasp that one cannot grasp it" (1849).
50. Sartre, "The Singular Universal," p. 231.
51. Sartre, "The Singular Universal," p. 263.
52. See Heidegger, *Being and Time*, p. 67.
53. See Kierkegaard, *Postscript*, Part Two, ch. 3.
54. See Hannay, "Kierkegaard en het einde van de religie" (Kierkegaard and the End of Religions).
55. KJN VI, NB11:183.
56. See Dreyfus, "Kierkegaard on the Self," p. 17.
57. See n. 13, above.
58. According to Anti-Climacus (*Practice*, p. 140), without the offense there would be no basis for using indirect communication (at least with regard to Christianity).
59. Mulhall, *Heidegger and* Being and Time, p. 122.
60. Kierkegaard, *Point of View*, p. 55.
61. "[E]very human being who gives heed to himself knows what no science knows, since he knows who he himself is." Kierkegaard, *The Concept of Anxiety*, pp. 78–9. The translation here is my own.
62. Kierkegaard, *Postscript*, p. 476.
63. KJN X, NB33:15. He says "potentially more."
64. Sartre, "The Singular Universal," pp. 262, 264.
65. Sartre, "The Singular Universal," p. 262.
66. Kierkegaard, *On the Concept of Irony*, p. 235.

HUBERT L. DREYFUS

5 "What a monster then is man": Pascal and Kierkegaard on being a contradictory self and what to do about it

In *The Sickness unto Death*, Kierkegaard summed up everything he had to say about the self in one dense description. Needless to say, the passage needs a lot of unpacking.

> The human being is spirit. But what is spirit? Spirit is the self. But what is the self? The self is a relation which relates to itself, or that in the relation which is its relating to itself. The self is not the relation but the relation's relating to itself. A human being is a synthesis of the infinite and the finite, of possibility and necessity, of the eternal and the temporal. In short a synthesis. A synthesis is a relation between the two terms. Looked at in this way a human being is not yet a self.
>
> In a relation between two things the relation is the third term in the form of a negative unity, and the two relate to the relation, and in the relation to that relation; this is what it is from the point of view of soul for soul and body to be in relation. If, on the other hand, the relation relates to itself, then this relation is the positive third, and this is the self.
>
> Such a relation, which relates to itself, a self, must either have established itself or been established by something else.
>
> If the relation which relates to itself has been established by something else, then of course the relation is the third term, but then this relation, the third term, is a relation which relates in turn to that which has established the whole relation.
>
> Such a derived, established relation is the human self, a relation which relates to itself, and in relating to itself relates to something else.[1]

I wish to thank Jane Rubin, who, over the many years we have studied Kierkegaard together, has helped develop and refine the interpretation presented here.

5.1 THE OPPOSED UNDERSTANDINGS OF BEING AND OF THE SELF IN OUR TRADITION

Kierkegaard's understanding of the self, its despair, and how to overcome it, is a response to two and half millennia of contradictory understandings of the self in the West. Our culture embodies a tension between an abstract, universal, detached way of understanding the self and its appropriate way of life – an understanding that we inherit from the Greeks, especially Plato – and an involved, concrete, committed way of experiencing ourselves that we inherit from the Hebrews.

Plato saw that disinterested reflection enabled the thinker to discover universal truths that are true for all time and all people. He concluded that there is no truth in perception, skilled know-how, intuition, emotion, body, folk wisdom, and tradition. They just get in the way of reflection. To live in the truth, the self must leave the cave of embodied perception and action and seek fulfillment in the detached contemplation of the unchanging forms of which everyday experience gives us only pale copies.

The Hebrews had an opposed view. They didn't think in philosophical terms but, if they had, they would have said that they understood truth as commitment – that they had to remain true to their particular covenant with God. Their truth wasn't universal and for all people for all time; it was just for the Hebrews at a certain time at a certain place, preserved in their tradition. For the self to live in the truth requires not total detachment but total commitment.

Greek metaphysics tells us that the objects of theory are timeless, abstract, conceptual structures and that they are, therefore, the most real. Nothing important happens in time; there cannot be anything radically new, just endless repetition of the cosmos and the events in the world. Therefore, according to Plato, you can live the best life if you cultivate a theoretical, detached frame of mind and die to your temporal embodied self. Indeed, when your rational soul merges with the rational structure of reality you will become a "friend of god," and so become eternal.

In the Hebrew/Christian view, however, everything important happens in time: the world is created, God makes a covenant at a moment in history, gives the Ten Commandments at another, and finally, according to the Christians, God becomes man at yet another moment in history. After God's Incarnation, people live in a new and different world. For the Greeks nothing is radically new. People as they grow realize their potential, like a tree growing from a seed. For the Christians, on the other hand, radical transformation of the self is possible. People can be reborn; they can become new beings.

The Greek and Hebrew views of truth and reality lead to opposed understandings of the self. On the Greek account, the self has two independent aspects: the detached soul and the involved body. Possible ways of life can be seen as ways of relating these opposed sets of factors. If they were equally essential, the self would be in hopeless self-contradiction. The more one expressed in one's life one set of factors – the soul, say – the less one would be able to express the other set. The self could not satisfy its embodied, finite, temporal needs while at the same time exercising its intellectual, infinite, eternal capacities. If, however, the factors were merely *combined*, and only one set of factors was essential, one could live a good life by rejecting the inessential factors and acting only on the essential ones.

On this view, the self begins with these component factors in conflict, but once one realizes that only one set of factors is essential – that one is essentially an eternal soul, merely stuck with a material body as Plato contended, or a material soul with religious imaginings as Lucretius, for example, held – the conflict and instability would be overcome. Life is thus a voyage from confusion to clarity, from conflict to harmony. All one has to do is realize the self's essential nature, find and satisfy its one set of essential factors, and one will experience peace and fulfillment.

5.2 PASCAL DISCOVERS THE ESSENTIALLY CONTRADICTORY SELF

For a long time, thinkers argued over which set of factors was essential. Stoics, Augustinians, Cartesians, and idealists claimed that the soul was the essential self; Epicureans, Hobbes, and other sorts of materialists took sides with the body. But finally Pascal saw that there were two conflicting traditions in the West. He saw that "the God of Abraham and Isaac was not the God of the philosophers"[2] and that the Greek tradition of detachment could never decide which factors were the essential ones, while according to the Judeo-Christian tradition *both* sets of factors were essential. The self was not a combination but a synthesis, and it was therefore an agonized contradiction. As he put it: "What a monster then is man! What a novelty, what a portent, what a chaos, what a contradiction, what a prodigy!"[3]

According to Pascal, a person's highest achievement was not to overcome this contradiction by getting rid of one or the other set of factors but to live in such a way as to fully express the tension between them. Thus: "We do not display greatness by going to one extreme, but in touching both extremes at once, and filling all the intervening space."[4]

Kierkegaard makes explicit Pascal's sense that, according to the Judeo-Christian tradition, the self is a contradictory synthesis between two sets of factors; that *each set is essential* and requires the other. Kierkegaard calls this a dialectical relation. That means that both sets of factors are aspects of one whole. Yet it is impossible on one's own to satisfy both sets of factors at once. One could only satisfy one set of factors by repressing the other, contradictory one. Thus, according to Kierkegaard, the self is in despair even when the despairing self doesn't know it.

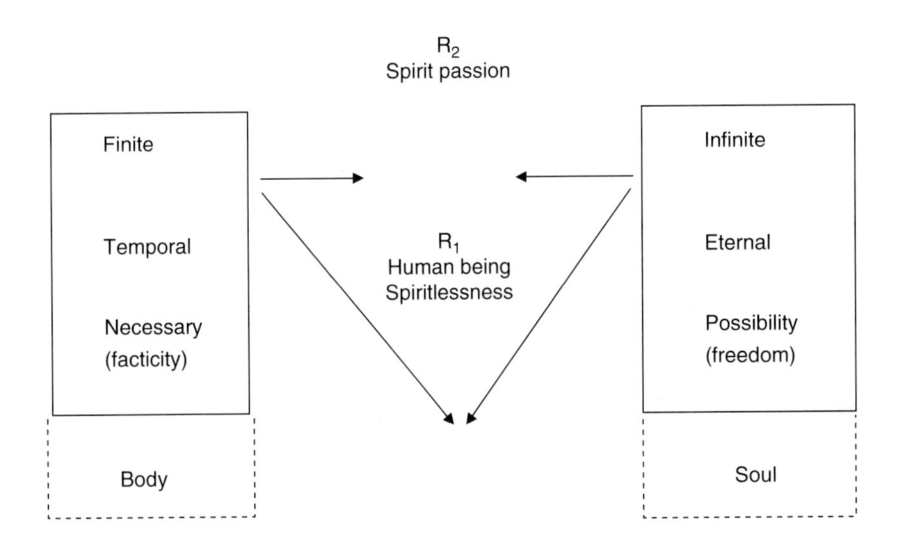

Figure 5.1 Kierkegaard's definition of the self

5.3 DESPAIRING WAYS OF ATTEMPTING TO BE A SELF

As Kierkegaard sums up the situation:

Despair is a sickness of the spirit, of the self, and so can have three forms: being unconscious of the despair of having a self (inauthentic despair), desperately not willing to be oneself, and despairingly willing to be oneself. (*SD*, p. 43)[5]

Spiritlessness. The self can cover up its despair. This is what Kierkegaard calls spiritlessness. One has a sense that the self is a contradiction that has to be faced, but one lives in what Pascal called diversion so that one never has to take a stand in thought or action as to how to get the factors together. Pascal gives as examples of diversion billiards, hunting, dancing, playing squash, or sitting alone in one's room sweating over a problem in algebra.[6]

Kierkegaard thought the most important diversion in his time was the public sphere, where one could discuss events and people without ever having to take responsibility for one's views. One could debate, on the basis of principles, how the world should be run, without running the risk of testing these principles in action. Kierkegaard blamed the press, which we would now call the media. This form of diversion is now consummated in blogs, but of course there are ever-new ways to avoid facing the contradictory nature of the self.

If a human being acts only as a combination of factors, he or she is not yet a self. To be a self, the relation must relate itself to itself through its actions, by taking a stand on both sets of factors. The stand must manifest that some aspect of the self is essential by making something in its life absolute. This can take a negative or a positive form.

The Negative Relation. Kierkegaard notes, as we have seen above:

In a relation between two things the relation is the third term in the form of a negative unity, and the two relate to the relation, and in the relation to that relation; this is what it is from the point of view of soul for soul and body to be in relation. (*SD*, p. 43)

That is, when the relation is a negative unity, the relation relates to itself in the Greek way, denying one of the sets of factors and acting as if only the other set of factors were the essential one. One can, for example, take the soul to be eternal and the body merely to be its tomb, as Plato did, or do the opposite and treat religious experiences as merely psychological phenomena, as did Lucretius.

The Positive Relation. Some selves try on their own to express fully both sets of factors in thought and action, but this turns out to be impossible. For example, if one makes possibility absolute and lives constantly open to new possibilities, one is in what Kierkegaard calls the aesthetic sphere of existence – Kierkegaard's anticipation of Nietzsche and the postmoderns – but that gives no expression to the stable and necessary. So one has no continuity in one's life and so loses one's self. Or, if one tries to make the infinite and the eternal absolute, one loses the finite and the temporal. As Kierkegaard puts it, such mystical types cannot bring their God-relationship together with a decision whether or not to take a walk in the park.

In his account of what he calls the aesthetic, ethical, and mystical/religious spheres of existence, Kierkegaard claims to have shown that "the self cannot by itself arrive at or remain in equilibrium and rest" (*SD*, p. 44). His Pascalian view is that the self is a hopeless tension unable to resolve its internal contradictions.

5.4 DESPAIR: THE SICKNESS UNTO DEATH

In *The Sickness unto Death*, Kierkegaard tries to show that every possible negative attempt to combine the factors defining the self by essentializing one of each pair of factors and repressing the other leads to despair, as does every way of trying to do justice to both. And, according to Kierkegaard, anyone who has not managed to perform the impossible task of getting his or her self together in a stable, meaningful life is in despair.

A person might well think that this claim is utterly unconvincing, since he or she is not in despair. Indeed, one may feel that one is having a great time enjoying all one's possibilities, or that one is living a fulfilling life doing one's duty, taking care of one's family, etc., or that one's life is worth living because one is working to eliminate suffering in the world, and so forth – in general, that one is fulfilling one's capacities and everything is working out well.

Kierkegaard would say that even if you think you are living a life worth living, in fact you are in despair. What right does he have to say this? His answer is in his description of despair:

Despair differs dialectically from what one usually calls sickness, because it is a sickness of the spirit. And this dialectical aspect, properly understood, brings further thousands under the category of despair. If at any time a physician is convinced that so and so is in good health, and then later that person becomes ill, then the physician may well be right about his *having been* well at the time but now being sick. Not so with despair. Once despair appears, what is apparent is that the person was in despair. In fact, it's never possible at any time to decide anything about a person who is not saved through having been in despair. For when whatever causes a person to despair occurs, it is immediately evident that he has been in despair his whole life. (*SD*, p. 54)

Kierkegaard is pointing out that despair is not like sadness, regret, disappointment, depression, etc. Rather, unlike these downers, despair exhibits what Kierkegaard calls "the dialectic of eternity." If you are sad, you know that it is temporary. Even if something so terrible happens to you that you feel that you were happy once but that whatever has happened makes it impossible for you ever to be happy again, that is certainly misery, but it is not despair. Despair is the feeling that life isn't working for you and, given the kind of person you are, it is impossible for things to work for you; that a life worth living is, in your case, literally impossible.

That means that once a person experiences despair, "it will be evident that his [previous] success was an illusion" (*SD*, p. 51) – i.e., that all that person's past joys *must have been self-deceptions*. That, in turn, means that if you ever experience despair, you realize that you have always been in despair and you always will be. So Kierkegaard concludes that, since the self is a contradiction, even though you now feel that things are going well for you, you must right now be in despair and not know it. Only if you have faced your despair – the sickness unto death – and somehow overcome the contradiction that you are, can you be sure you are not now in despair. Thus, given the contradictory nature of the self, all of us, with the exception of those who have faced despair and been somehow healed, must right now be in despair.

The ultimate despair, Kierkegaard contends, is denying that one is in despair by denying the demand that one manifest the two sets of factors in one's life in a way that enables them to reinforce each other. This is not the diversion of the present age, where one represses the call to be a self. Rather, someone in this ultimate form of despair sees that in our religious tradition the self has, indeed, been constituted as having two sets of essential but incompatible factors, but, like Richard Rorty, claims that this is merely a traditional, essentialist view that we can and should give up. Since the traditional Judeo-Christian understanding of the self leads people to despair, we should simply opt out of it and adopt a vocabulary and practices that are healthier and more useful to us.

How can we decide who is right here – Kierkegaard or the Rortian pragmatist? Kierkegaard thinks that this is a question we can only approach existentially. Therefore, in *The Sickness unto Death*, he tries to show that the Christian claim that the self is a contradiction is confirmed by an exhaustive categorization of all the ways of relating the self to itself and how each fails.

5.5 HOW IN AN UNCONDITIONAL COMMITMENT THE FACTORS REINFORCE EACH OTHER

If Kierkegaard is right, not Greek detachment but only the committed Judeo-Christian way of life offers a way out of despair. That is, not being in despair must mean having been somehow cured of it for good. Kierkegaard says: "The possibility of this sickness is man's advantage over the beast; to be aware of this sickness is the Christian's advantage over natural man; to be cured of this sickness is the Christian's blessedness" (*SD*, p. 45). Consequently, Kierkegaard proposed to preface *The Sickness unto Death* with a prayer to Jesus as Savior: "O Lord Jesus Christ, who didst come to earth to heal them that suffer from this sickness ... help Thou us in this sickness to hold fast to Thee, to the end that we may be healed of it."[7]

According to Kierkegaard, Jesus is "God in time as an individual human being,"[8] but how that enables Him to cure us of despair is a rather long story. As we have seen, Kierkegaard tells us that the self can only succeed in relating itself to itself by "relating to something outside himself" (*P*, p. 470). In *Sickness unto Death* he elaborates:

> The self cannot by itself arrive at or remain in equilibrium and rest by itself, but only in relating to itself by relating to that which has established the whole relation ... This then is the formula which describes the state of the self when despair is completely eradicated: in relating to itself and in willing to be itself, the self is grounded transparently in the power that established it. (*SD*, p. 44)

Kierkegaard contends that whether one can get the two sets of factors into equilibrium or whether they remain a contradiction depends on how one defines them. Or, to put it another way, the Greeks found that if you define the factors from the point of view of detachment, you can't get them together. Kierkegaard tries to show that only if you define the factors in terms of an involvement so total that it gives you your identity can you achieve a positive synthesis.

This claim is illustrated in *Fear and Trembling*. The story starts with Abraham the Father of the faith who believed he would be "blessed in his kin, eternally remembered in Isaac."[9] Isaac was obviously essential to Abraham's identity. To illustrate what is at stake in having an identity Kierkegaard draws on the chivalric romances. The example, on which he says "everything turns", is the case of "a young lad [who] falls in love with a princess, [so that] the whole content of his life lies in this love" (*FT*, p. 70). Kierkegaard adds in a footnote, that "any other interest whatever in which an individual concentrates the whole of life's reality" would do as well (*FT*, p. 71).

The lad who loves the princess relates himself to himself by way of this relation. Thanks to it, he knows who he is and what is relevant and important in his world. Any such unconditional commitment to some specific individual, cause, or vocation whereby a person gets an identity and a sense of reality would do to make the point Kierkegaard is trying to make. In such a case the person becomes an individual defined by his or her relation to the object that draws him or her into an unconditional commitment. Kierkegaard's model for such a commitment is the knight whose life gets its meaning by his devotion to his lady. The lad is the lover of the princess; Martin Luther King Jr. is the one who will bring justice to the American blacks; Steve Jobs identifies himself with Apple; and so on.

According to Kierkegaard, if and only if you let yourself be drawn into a defining commitment can you achieve that which, while you were in despair, looked impossible, that is, that the two sets of factors reinforce each other so that the more you manifest one the more you manifest the other. By responding to the call of such an unconditional commitment and thereby getting an identity, a person becomes reborn as what Kierkegaard, following the Bible, calls "a new creation" (*FT*, p. 70). Thus, Jesus gave those who were saved from despair by being unconditionally committed to him new names, and they called Him their Savior.

The saved self can be described by describing its way of relating itself to each of the factors.

The temporal and the eternal: for one to live fully in time, some moment must be absolutely important and make other moments significant relative to it. The moment when one is reborn is obviously such a moment. Kierkegaard, drawing on the Biblical saying that we shall be changed in the twinkling of an eye, calls this moment the *Augenblick*. Moreover, after the transformation, many other moments become significant too, since one's unconditional commitment must be expressed in one's day-to-day activity.

But the eternal is also absolutely important in one's life. Not the disinterested, abstract eternity of Plato, but the passionately involved eternity that Kierkegaard calls "eternity in time." Normally, the significance of events in one's life is subject to constant retroactive reinterpretation,[10] but in the case of an unconditional commitment that defines the self, one's identity is as eternal as a definition. Kierkegaard says the knight is free to "forget the whole thing," but in so doing the knight would "contradict himself," since it is "a contradiction to forget the whole of one's life's content and still be the same" (*FT*, p. 72).

Further events will be interpreted in the light of the content given the self in the *Augenblick*, not vice versa. The way a commitment can produce a privileged moment is not something that disinterested thought can understand. Kierkegaard says: "A concrete eternity in one who exists is the maximum of passion ... The proposition inaccessible to thought is that one can become eternal although one was not such" (*P*, p. 261).

In sum, if you define eternity in an involved way as that which remains constant throughout your life, then your identity is eternal. That is, if you are unconditionally committed to a particular person or cause, that will be your identity forever, that is, for the rest of your life. This is a kind of involved eternity that must, in order to exist, be temporal. The paradoxical fact is that "I become for the first time eternal only in existence" (*P*, p. 481). But this does not make me any less temporal. "The existing individual *in time* ... comes to relate to the eternal *in time*" (*P*, p. 478).

The finite and the infinite. Kierkegaard calls an unconditional commitment an infinite passion for something finite. But just what makes an infinite passion count as infinite? It can't be just a very strong feeling; rather, it must in some sense transcend the finite. For Kierkegaard, an infinite passion can legitimately be called infinite because it opens up a world. Not only what actually exists gets its meaning from its connection with my defining passion; anything that could possibly come into existence would get its meaning for me from my defining commitment. In that sense the commitment is infinite.

Of course, the object of my infinite passion is something *finite*. We are interested in the smallest particularities of our beloved. Any such finite being is vulnerable, and yet the meaning of my life depends on it. This makes a defining commitment very risky. It would certainly be safer to define one's life in terms of some sort of theoretical quest or in terms of some abstract idea – say the eventual triumph of the proletariat – but that is not concrete enough to satisfy the need to make the finite absolutely significant. So it follows, as Kierkegaard says, that "without risk, no faith" (*P*, p. 176).

In sum, when you have a defining commitment, the *finite* object of your commitment is *infinitely* important, that is, the object of your passion is both something particular and also world defining. In short, it is the concrete condition for anything showing up as meaningful.

The necessary and the possible. We have seen that when you have a defining commitment you get an identity that is who you are, and it is *necessary* to being you. But although your identity is fixed, it does not dictate an inflexible way of acting, as if it were a compulsion. One has to be able to adapt to even the most radical changes in the defining object. All such adaptive changes will, of course, be changes *in* the world, not changes *of* the world. Kierkegaard calls this freedom to adapt *possibility* because, even though the central concern in one's life is fixed, one is free to adapt to all sorts of possible situations.

There is, however, an even more radical kind of freedom, the freedom to change one's world, that is, to change one's identity. To be born again *and again*. Although Kierkegaard does not say so in so many words, once we see that eternity can begin in time, we can see that not only can eternity *begin* at a moment of time (the

Augenblick), eternity can *change* in time. For example, Kierkegaard says Abraham had faith that if he sacrificed Isaac "God could give him a new Isaac" (*FT*, p. 65). This could happen because God is "that everything is possible" (*SD*, p. 71), and that means that even the inconceivable is possible. On Kierkegaard's view, one can only change worlds by being totally involved in one, deepening one's commitment, taking all the risks involved, until it breaks down and becomes impossible, and a new world appears by a discontinuous leap.

Thus, according to Kierkegaard, the radically impossible only makes sense if one is unconditionally committed to the current world. Otherwise, we have such flexibility that everything is possible, and although some events are highly improbable, they are not inconceivable. For the truly impossible to be possible, we must be open to radically new worlds which we can't even make sense of until we are in them. Only if one relates wholeheartedly to the world established by one's defining commitment, can one experience a gestalt switch in which one's sense of reality is totally transformed.

5.6 CONCLUSION

From his examination of all types of despairing ways to try to relate the factors, Kierkegaard concludes that the only sphere of existence that can give equal weight to both sets of factors is a religion based on an infinite passion for something finite. Kierkegaard is clear that "What is paradoxically edifying [in Christianity] therefore corresponds to the definition of God in time as an individual human being; for if that be the case, the individual relates to something outside himself" (*P*, p. 470).

But, given the logic of Kierkegaard's position, it follows that the object of defining commitment does not have to be the God-man. Indeed, in *Concluding Unscientific Postscript* Kierkegaard says, "subjectively [reflection is on] the individual relating to something *in such a way* that his relation is truly a God relation" (*P*, p. 168).

In *The Sickness unto Death*, Kierkegaard claims to have shown that unless the self relates itself to itself by relating to something else, it is in despair; that is, only if it has an unconditional commitment can the self get the two sets of factors together in such a way that they reinforce rather than oppose each other. At the end of his definition of the self, Kierkegaard concludes rather abstractly: "This is the formula which describes the state of the self when despair is completely eradicated: in relating to itself and in willing to be itself, the self is grounded transparently in the power that established it" (*SD*, p. 44). "Grounded transparently" means acting in such a way that what gives you your identity shows through in everything you do. But what is the power (lower case) that established the self? Presumably it is whatever finite and temporal object of infinite, eternal passion gives the self an identity and so establishes the self as a new being.

Then the claim that God established the factors must mean that by making it possible for people to have defining commitments – in the first instance to Him – and so be reborn, Jesus revealed that both sets of factors are equally essential and so can and must be brought into equilibrium. This is the truth about the essential nature of the self that went undiscovered until Jesus revealed it. In this way he established the Christian understanding of the self, in which we now live. This account leaves in despair all those who, like the Greeks, see the self as a combination, but it potentially saves all Christian selves by calling them to make an unconditional commitment to "God in time as an individual human being" (*P*, p. 470).

So, on this reading, for the self "to be grounded transparently in the power that established it" would mean that a person relates himself to himself by freely relating to someone or something finite with an infinite passion and so becomes eternal in time, thereby overcoming despair by manifesting in all aspects of his life that both sets of factors of the self are essential. Whatever outside the self constitutes it as the individual self it is – healing it of despair by giving it an identity and thereby making it a new being – that "something" would be its savior. All such Christian lives would thus be grounded in Jesus, the God-man, who, as the first object of unconditional commitment, first makes such salvation possible.

But on this account, Jesus would only be the power that establishes the self's identity, not the power that established the three sets of contradictory factors that the self must bring into equilibrium. What, then, is the power that established the whole relation?

The "power" doesn't seem to be God, since the term is in lower case and Kierkegaard doesn't say that the power *created* the relation. But Kierkegaard does say that one could not despair "unless the synthesis were originally in the right relationship from the hand of God" (*SD*, p. 46). To cash out this metaphor we need to remember that for Kierkegaard "God is that everything is possible" (*SD*, p. 70). Then we can see that it is thanks to God that the impossible synthesis of the contradictory factors that make up the self is nonetheless possible.

NOTES

1. Kierkegaard, *The Sickness unto Death*, p. 43; henceforth cited in the text as *SD*. Jane Rubin and I have made several changes in the text in order to clarify what we believe to be its meaning. First, we have substituted Walter Lowrie's "factors" for Hannay's "terms" in the definition of the self, because it provides a convenient shorthand for describing the constituents of the synthesis. Second, we have changed the term "freedom" to "possibility." In other passages in *The Sickness unto Death*, and in *The Concept of Anxiety*, Kierkegaard uses the term "freedom" to refer to one factor of the synthesis that is the self. Though Kierkegaard is inconsistent in his use of terminology, the distinction between freedom and possibility is clear. Consequently, we have changed the terminology in order to preserve the clear distinction between the two concepts. Finally, we have reversed the order of the possibility/necessity and eternal/temporal factors, since Kierkegaard discusses them in this order in the remainder of *The Sickness unto Death*, and we have changed the order of temporal/eternal to eternal/temporal in order to make it parallel with Kierkegaard's presentation of the other sets of factors.
2. *Pascal's Pensées*, no. 121.
3. *Pascal's Pensées*, no. 258 (Stewart trans., p. 151).
4. *Pascal's Pensées*, no. 353.
5. I have changed "wanting" to "willing" and have modified the translation slightly in other ways.
6. *Pascal's Pensées*, no. 139
7. Lowrie, "Translator's Introduction," p. 134.
8. Kierkegaard, *Concluding Unscientific Postscript*, p. 470. Henceforth cited in the text as *P*.
9. Kierkegaard, *Fear and Trembling*, p. 54. Henceforth cited in the text as *FT*.

10. Sartre suggests as an example a person who has an emotional crisis as an adolescent that he interprets as a religious calling and acts on by becoming a monk. Later he comes to interpret the experience as just an adolescent psychotic episode and leaves the monastery to become a businessman. But on his deathbed, he feels that his was a religious calling after all, and repents. Sartre's point is that our past is constantly up for reinterpretation, and the final interpretation is an accidental result of what we happen to think as we die.

RICHARD SCHACHT

6 Nietzsche: after the death of God

> God is dead; but given the way of men, there may still be caves for thousands of years in which his shadow will be shown. – And we – we still have to vanquish his shadow too ... When will we complete our de-deification of nature? When may we begin to *naturalize* our human selves [*uns Menschen ... zu vernatürlichen*] in terms of a pure, newly discovered, newly redeemed nature! (*The Gay Science* 108–9)

> The greatest recent event – that "God is dead," that the belief in the Christian god has become unbelievable – is already beginning to cast its first shadows over Europe ... But in the main one may say ... [not] many people know as yet *what* this event really means – and how much must collapse now because it was built upon this faith, propped up by it, grown into it; for example, the whole of our European morality. (*The Gay Science* 343)

6.1 EXISTENTIALISM, EXISTENTIAL PHILOSOPHY, AND EXISTENZ-PHILOSOPHY

There can be no doubt that Nietzsche figured importantly in the genealogy of existentialism. Along with Kierkegaard, he is commonly considered to have been one of its fathers – or perhaps grandfathers, if its paternity is to be attributed to Martin Heidegger and Karl Jaspers. An argument can certainly be made that Kierkegaard deserves the characterization "existentialist," his passionate Christianity notwithstanding; for he virtually defined the program of the movement with his famous criticism of "modern philosophy" (that is, Hegel) for "having forgotten, in a sort of world-historical absent-mindedness, what it means to be a human being ... each one for himself," his insistence that "If [one] is a human being then he is also an existing individual," and his contention that a human being does best to "concentrate his entire energy upon the fact that he *is* an existing individual."[1] But is the reinterpretation of human reality that Nietzsche calls for, and undertakes, to be understood at all similarly?

There certainly is a great gulf between them. Nietzsche considers this reinterpretation to be mandated by what he terms the "death" of Kierkegaard's God, while Kierkegaard links his conception of the kind of "subjectivity" he considers to be the "truth" of human "existing" to the idea of a "God-relationship" requiring a "leap of faith" – which Nietzsche explicitly disparages.[2] Moreover, Kierkegaard construes human "existing" in terms of a strong conception of "subjectivity" and makes much of an associated conception of selfhood, while Nietzsche scornfully exclaims: "is there anyone who has never been mortally sick of everything subjective and of its wretched ipsissimosity [i.e., self-fetishism]?" (*BGE* 207).[3]

If "existentialism" is defined as what Kierkegaard, Nietzsche, Heidegger, and Sartre have *in common*, it becomes a word with little if any positive meaning, because they would seem to have little more in common than a critical relationship to classical modern philosophy from Descartes to Hegel, and overlapping sets of philosophical admirers, adversaries, and detractors. If, on the other hand, it is defined as the *totality* of what and how they think, the upshot would be utterly incoherent. So Sartre himself complained (as early as 1947!) that the word "is being so loosely applied to so many things that it has come to mean nothing at all."[4]

In attempting to deal with this situation, I consider it useful to distinguish between "existentialism," "*Existenz*-philosophy," and "existential philosophy" – all of which are further to be distinguished from a competing development that also emerged in Europe at about the same time that goes by the name of "philosophical anthropology" (from which Heidegger explicitly distinguishes his enterprise in *Being and Time* in that very book,[5] and with which the post-existentialist Sartre of *Search for a Method* actually allies himself).[6]

"Existentialism," as an "-ism," is a term that has come to be strongly associated with a certain view of human existence and the human situation, to which it therefore might as well simply be considered to refer, as a terminological fait accompli. It is basically the picture one gets from Sartre, Camus, and their literary and philosophical kindred spirits. On this view, we are "home alone" in a godless and alien universe. There are no absolutes in the realms of value and morality. There is no "happily ever after," and no real possibility of one. Human life is ultimately meaningless, and the human condition is fundamentally hopeless. In the immortal words of Monty Python's "Bright Side" song, "Life is quite absurd, and death's the final word."[7] On the other hand, we are *free* in a most radical sense, the limitations and contingencies of our abilities and lives and circumstances notwithstanding – free in the decisions and choices we make from among the possibilities open to us. We are completely responsible for our decisions and choices, and all that really matters is the integrity or authenticity with which we are capable of making them as we exercise our freedom. The fundamental absurdity and futility of it all make our lot a difficult one to bear, and many avoid facing up to it by fleeing into various forms of self-deception and inauthenticity. But there is a kind of dignity, value, and even happiness attainable by rising above the temptation to do so and realizing our absurd freedom, thereby giving our existence the only kind of human meaning that is not an illusion.

This is without question a possible construal and assessment of human existence – and, as fleshed out in the associated literature (novels, short stories, plays, movies), a vivid and gripping one. It enjoyed considerable vogue in the decades following the Second World War, and still does in some quarters. It undeniably addresses the question of "what it means to be a human being," and more specifically, to be "an existing individual." It certainly is not Kierkegaard's view of the matter, however – even though he was well aware of it as a human possibility (as one of the most extreme forms of "despair," serving as the springboard for his "leap of faith" that alone can remedy it). It likewise was not shared by such major figures as Heidegger and Jaspers, for whose thinking provision certainly must be made in this general connection. That is one reason why they so emphatically rejected the label of "existentialist" and sought to disassociate themselves from "existentialism."

That poses a problem, since an apt rubric for what they are all doing would be useful. Fortunately, a solution is readily available, in the form of the notion of "*Existenz*-philosophy," or the "philosophy of *Existenz*," that is commonly used for this purpose in German-speaking Europe. The term "*Existenz*" here is used to refer specifically to "existing" in the manner that a human being exists – not merely in the sense of being alive, but of being (as Kierkegaard puts it) "an existing individual," "each one for himself," as one goes about living and leading one's life and confronting the inescapability of one's finitude and mortality. Both Heidegger and Jaspers make major use of the German term "*Existenz*" in this connection, and make its analysis or elucidation the central task of their major contributions to the literature under consideration. That is what *Existenz*-philosophy is: the analysis or elucidation of human *Existenz*, conceived as an actual or possible dimension of human reality. I shall appropriate the term and use it (without italics) accordingly. It has to do with what Kierkegaard called the irreducible "subjectivity" of human existing, with the experiential character and general circumstances of such "first-person singular" existing, and (at least in some instances) with its purported basic ("ontological") structures.

Existenz-philosophy so construed is thus to be conceived in terms of *what it deals with* (like "philosophy of mind" and "philosophy of action"), rather than in terms of any conclusions about its topic, or any particular construal of human existing (such as the one just sketched). Its only general assumptions are that its topic is a *real* one (something that is humanly real or possible), a *fundamental* one (something that is part of the very fabric of human reality), and a *key* one (something that is of special significance in the makeup of human reality). So understood, Heidegger, Jaspers, Kierkegaard, and Sartre can all be considered Existenz-philosophers (or philosophers of Existenz). Some (such as Heidegger and Sartre) think that human Existenz can be *analyzed* in appropriate special concepts, often introduced as technical terms specifically for this purpose; while others (like Kierkegaard and Jaspers) think that it can only be indirectly *elucidated*.

"*Existential* philosophy" is an expression used by many commentators as a synonym or alternative version of "Existenz-philosophy." It may also (and, I believe, more helpfully) be used to refer to the sort of *approach*, perspective, or way of proceeding that tends to be favored by Existenz-philosophers, but that can be used to analyze or elucidate realities in addition to human Existenz itself. One version of it is the adaptation of Husserl's phenomenological method that is often referred to as "existential phenomenology," which analyzes phenomena from the perspective of the way in which they are experienced by the "existing" human being. The other main version of it involves the use of more literary and informal forms of language evocative of kinds of such experience to elucidate the matters under consideration. Existential literature (novels, plays, short stories, cinema) offers many cases in point; but so do the Existenz-philosophical writings of Kierkegaard and Jaspers, and of Sartre at times as well.

It is characteristic of Existenz-philosophy to take such existential-philosophical (that is, existential-phenomenological or existential-literary) perspectives not only to be most *appropriate* to the consideration of human Existenz, but also to be *privileged* over all others in the interpretation of human reality – even though the possibility of other (e.g., biological, social, cultural, historical, psychological) perspectives upon human reality that are relevant to its comprehensive interpretation may be acknowledged. This is in marked contrast with a rival development in European philosophy in the middle two quarters of the twentieth century that came to be known as "philosophical anthropology." Philosophical anthropology – for which human reality is most properly conceived and approached as a form of *life* – takes other such perspectives upon human reality equally seriously, and indeed tends to regard first-person-singular perspectives and phenomena to be very much in need of supplementation and interpretation by way of what can be learned about it from them.[8] This difference has made philosophical anthropology's developing rivalry with Existenz-philosophy in the reinterpretation of human reality a deep one.

Finally (for present purposes), it is common for Existenz-philosophers to distinguish between different fundamental ways in which it is possible for human beings to "exist," one of which is taken to be distinctly superior to the other or others. So Kierkegaard distinguishes between different types of "subjectivity"; Heidegger, between "authentic" and "inauthentic" existing; Jaspers, between genuine "Existenz" and the failure to attain it; and Sartre, between existing in "bad faith" or "self-deception" and existing with what might be called "integrity" with respect to one's radical freedom and responsibility.

Nietzsche's introduction to philosophy was by way of Schopenhauer, for whom all "representation" in consciousness was in stark contrast with the fundamental reality of "the world as will," and all individuation was a kind of illusion. The twin origins of Existenz-philosophy in Kierkegaard's passionately Christian championing of the radically subjective "self" and in Husserl's intensely anti-naturalistic neo-Cartesian program of a "pure phenomenology" are radically different – and equally (but for very different reasons) repugnant to Nietzsche. Yet Nietzsche did come to loom large in the thinking of many philosophers in the twentieth-century existential tradition. Indeed, it is probably fair to say that he was at least something like the catalyst that was necessary for Existenz-philosophy to be born of the unlikely pairing of Kierkegaard and Husserl. In what follows, I will briefly discuss a number of aspects of Nietzsche's thought, some of which were relevant to the emergence and development of Existenz-philosophy, and others of which render his association with it problematic.[9]

6.2 "THE DEATH OF GOD"

Nietzsche's thought might very broadly be viewed as an attempt to work out what he took to be the profound consequences of what he famously called "the death of God" – that is, the demise of "God" as an idea deserving of being taken seriously – in a way that would grant the truth of Schopenhauer's basic assessment of the human condition but would find a way to be as profoundly affirmative of life as Schopenhauer was negative about it. Nietzsche first announced this development quite matter of factly in the first edition of *The Gay Science* (1882), at the beginning of its third "Book," but he made it clear (in figurative language) that he took it to have major implications for the agenda of philosophy:

> *New struggles* [*Kämpfe*]. – After Buddha was dead, his shadow was still shown for centuries in a cave – a tremendous, gruesome shadow. God is dead; but given the way of men, there may still be caves for thousands of years in which his shadow will be shown. – And we – we still have to vanquish his shadow too! (*GS* 108)

By God's "shadow" Nietzsche means the many ways in which the God-idea has influenced our interpretations and evaluations – some of which he proceeds immediately to indicate and address, beginning with ways in which we tend to think about the world and ourselves (*GS* 109). He takes up the theme again a few pages later, in a way that is anything but matter of fact, in the famous "Madman" section (*GS* 125), the point of which is to make clear what a traumatic development the death of God could turn out to be. It appears again at the beginning of his next book, *Thus Spoke Zarathustra* (1883–85), early in its Prologue, with less anguish but in a way that indicates that it is the entire work's point of departure (*Z* I: P:2).

When Nietzsche published a second (1887) edition of *The Gay Science* the year after he returned to philosophical prose publication with *Beyond Good and Evil* (1886), he began the new fifth "Book" he added to the original four by sounding the same theme once more, making clear in passing what he means more specifically: "The greatest recent event – that 'God is dead,' that the belief in the Christian god has become unbelievable [*unglaubwürdig*, literally "unworthy of belief"] – is already beginning to cast its first shadows over Europe." Here the "shadow" image is being used differently, and more ominously; and Nietzsche goes on to indicate that what makes this "event" chilling is the thought of "how much must collapse now that this faith has been undermined [*untergraben*] because it was built upon this faith, propped up by it, grown into it; for example, the whole of our European morality" (*GS* 343).

Nietzsche's basic point is that the idea of God is an idea whose time has come and gone – or at any rate, is on its way out. "Why atheism today?" he asks in *Beyond Good and Evil*, and answers: "'The father' in God has been thoroughly refuted [i.e., debunked]; ditto, 'the judge,' 'the rewarder'" (*BGE* 53). What remains of the God-idea is a mere abstraction that has nothing to be said for it and a combination of problematic origins and all-too-human motivations that render it undeserving of even being taken seriously. Nietzsche indicates how he proposes to dispose of it in a passage in *Daybreak* (1881):

In former times, one sought to prove that there is no God – today one indicates how the belief that there is a God could *arise* and how this idea acquired its weight and importance: a counter-proof that there is no God thereby becomes superfluous. – When in former times one had refuted [i.e., critically demolished] the "proofs of the existence of God" put forward, there always remained the doubt whether better proofs than those just refuted might not be found: in those days atheists did not know how to clear the table [*reinen Tisch zu machen*]. (*D* 95)

That is, atheists previously had not figured out how to get the whole issue *off the table* and lay it to rest: namely, by depriving it of all credibility, showing that its origins and motivations weigh against it rather than for it, and thus – in the absence of countervailing supportive evidence or arguments – *subverting* it. Nietzsche indicates some of the sorts of things he has in mind two sections earlier, when he writes: "what if God were *not* 'the truth' and it were precisely this that were demonstrated – if he were the vanity, the lust for power, the impatience, the terror, the enraptured and fearful delusion of men?" (*D* 93). This may not amount to a "disproof" or "refutation" in the logical sense of these terms; but for Nietzsche it disposes of the God-idea compellingly and decisively, and should be convincing for any "free spirit" of sufficient sophistication and intellectual integrity. The real task of "the philosophy of the future" that he heralds and seeks to inaugurate is not to dwell on the matter and belabor the point. It is rather to proceed to reckon with its interpretive and evaluative consequences.

6.3 THE ADVENT AND OVERCOMING OF NIHILISM

Nietzsche had a great deal to say about "nihilism." One of his great concerns was with what he called "the advent of nihilism" – the "rebound from 'God is truth' to the fanatical faith 'All is false'" (*WP* 1).[10] He believed that while a certain sort of nihilism – that is, the rejection of all metaphysical, religious, evaluative, and moral absolute principles transcending this life in this world in their status and reality – can be a healthy thing philosophically and humanly (for those capable of doing without them, at any rate), it also is a great danger; for it is profoundly negative in its basic thrust and must be superseded if it is not to become a life-negating fatality for humanity. "Nihilism represents a pathological transitional stage," he observed in another note from the same period (1887); "what is pathological is the tremendous generalization, the inference that there is no meaning at all" (*WP* 13). So he concludes the Second Essay of his *On the*

Genealogy of Morality (1887) with an impassioned evocation of the possibility of a post-nihilistic humanity of "creative spirit" and "compelling strength" sufficient to overcome it:

> This man of the future will redeem us not just from the ideal held up till now, but also from the things *which will have to arise from it*, from the great nausea, the will to nothingness, from nihilism ... this Antichrist and anti-nihilist, this conqueror of God and of nothingness – *he must come one day.* (*GM* II:24)

The "ideal held up till now" is that of a transcendent God considered to be the absolute basis of all value, meaning and truth; and "the thing which will have to arise from it" is nihilism – the conviction that, in the absence of any such basis, the ideas of value, meaning and truth collapse – here diagnosed as a kind of withdrawal symptom resulting from previous addiction to that ideal. "A nihilist," Nietzsche quips, "is a man who judges of the world as it is that it ought *not* to be, and of the world as it ought to be that it does not exist" (*WP*, 585A).

The key to overcoming nihilism, Nietzsche came to understand, is ironically somewhat similar to his strategy for disposing of the God-idea: that is, by a kind of *cure* – in this case by coming to understand and freeing ourselves from the (false but seductive) "God or bust ('nothing matters')" dichotomy, and from the absolutism addiction that disposes one to give up on and disparage anything that does not satisfy the craving for it. Liberation from that addiction by itself, however, is not enough. Truth and value must be given a new footing. And that, for Nietzsche, is possible – by shifting their locus to this life in this world. Life itself holds the key to the meaning of life; for the meaning of life, beyond its self-renewing vitality, is nothing more or less than its own enhancement and enrichment.

Nihilism for Nietzsche thus is not to be overcome by way of the discovery of some new transcendent absolute reality, truth, or value standard beyond this life and world to replace God, by reference to which they and our own existence can be assessed and are endowed with meaning and worth. It is to be overcome instead by learning to think of reality, truth, and value differently, in a manner attuned to the basic character and developmental possibilities of life as they reveal themselves in human life and history and in the life around us – and to come to *affirm* them for what they are and have it in them to become, rather than to condemn them for not being otherwise.

So, Nietzsche writes, a genuine philosopher "demands of himself a judgment, a Yes or No, not [merely] about the cognitive disciplines [*Wissenschaften*] but about life and the value of life" (*BGE* 205). That judgment can go either way; for it is neither a cognitive judgment nor a value judgment in terms of some standard of value external to life. Rather, it is an expression of one's basic disposition with respect to life as one takes it to be. Schopenhauer had said "No" to it, and that is what Nietzsche takes the nihilist fundamentally to be doing. The overcoming of nihilism for him is a matter of finding a way to a "Yes" to life that is genuine and deep. And that sort of affirmation is not merely intellectual; it is a matter of one's having come to learn to *love* it, for what it fundamentally is, as it fundamentally is.

At a basic level, Nietzsche takes it to be the case that a healthy living creature, "being alive, loves life" (*BGE* 24). It is, in some more or less primordial dispositional way, "affirming" of life and of the kind of life it is (even if that may involve doing things that risk or result in its own individual "going under," as he likes to put it). But for creatures like ourselves, Nietzsche observes near the end of the first edition of *The Gay Science*, there is nothing that is more important and needful where our dispositions are concerned than "learning to love" (*GS* 334). And several sections later, at its conclusion, he uses one of his most famous images – that of "the eternal recurrence" of everything in one's life and in the world more generally – to construct a kind of test to reinforce it in its application in the larger context of the affirmation of life: "how well disposed would you have to become to yourself and to life *to crave nothing more fervently* than this ultimate eternal confirmation and seal?" (*GS* 341).

A part of what the death of God entails is that life can have no meaning bestowed upon it from on high. It can, however, come to have another kind of meaning, beyond that of its own mere preservation and continuation. That meaning has to do with what Nietzsche calls its *enhancement* (*Erhöhung*, literally "heightening" or making "higher"). This idea is what he memorably conveys by means of another of his most familiar images – that of "the *Übermensch*" or "overman" – when in his literary-philosophical masterpiece,

Thus Spoke Zarathustra, he has his character Zarathustra begin his preaching and teaching by saying:

> *I teach you the Übermensch* ... The *Übermensch* is the meaning of the earth. Let your will say: the *Übermensch shall be* the meaning of the earth! I beseech you, my brothers, *remain faithful to the earth*, and do not believe those who speak to you of otherworldly hopes! (*Z* I: P:3)

Nietzsche employs the figure or image of the *Übermensch* here as a kind of symbol of the enhancement or creative transformation of human life, elevated above and beyond the plane of merely animal existence and yet again above and beyond that of life that is human but "all-too-human," to the level of forms of exceptional humanity that he considers to be "higher" than ordinary human life typically is in one qualitative way or another. In using it, Nietzsche refers to no particular specific type of human being but points in the same general direction as he does in the passage from the end of the Second Essay of *Genealogy of Morality* cited above. There he envisions the possibility of a form of humanity that would be characterized not only by greater health and vitality but also by higher and richer spirituality and creativity than has been attained even by the most notable of exceptions to the human rule previously (including the "sovereign individual" discussed in *GM* II:2), continually "overcoming" and surpassing itself, and further transforming and enriching human life on this earth. That conception of human possibility is the heart of Nietzsche's response to the danger posed by nihilism, in the aftermath of the death of God.

6.4 A "PHILOSOPHY OF THE FUTURE"

Nietzsche wrote *Zarathustra* to give expression to his discovery of this new post-religious, post-metaphysical, and also post-nihilist way of thinking, which he believed heralded a new dawn for humanity and for philosophy alike. He gave his next book, *Beyond Good and Evil*, the subtitle "Prelude to a Philosophy of the Future." In it he attempts to set the stage for the new kind of philosophy, to indicate what some of the main tasks on its agenda would be and how it would pursue them, and to get on with it. As its title is meant to suggest, his "philosophy of the future" is to be *post-moral* (as well as post-religious, post-metaphysical, and post-nihilist), in the sense of being purged of the "moralism" of thinking under the influence of "good-versus-evil" morality and of moral values that are assumed to trump all others. It is to be analytical and critical; but its twin basic tasks are constructive *interpretation* (and reinterpretation) and *evaluation* (and revaluation).

It is one of the themes of *Beyond Good and Evil* that Nietzsche's kind of interpretive and evaluative philosophy is to be carried on in an "experimental" rather than "dogmatic" manner, recognizing that no interpretation or evaluation of anything of significance will ever be beyond the possibility of challenge and improvement. It is another that such inquiry needs to be multiply "perspectival," in the case of anything as complex and diversely relational as art, music, morality, human reality, or life more generally, let alone such notions as "truth," "value," or "creativity." A related point, sounded as early as *Human, All Too Human* (1878), is that in dealing interpretively and evaluatively with most matters – and in particular with anything relating to human reality – one is dealing with things that have *become* what and as they are and thus must be approached not only analytically but also "genealogically" or "historically" – which is to say, *developmentally*:

> Lack of historical [i.e., developmental] sense is the family failing of all philosophers ... They do not want to learn that man has *become*, that the faculty of cognition has become ... But everything has become: there are *no eternal facts*, just as there are no absolute truths. Consequently, what is needed from now on is *historical philosophizing*, and with it the virtue of modesty. (*HATH* I:2)

To this Nietzsche importantly adds that "historical philosophy," very differently from the "metaphysical philosophy" from which he seeks to distinguish it, "can no longer be separated from natural science, the youngest of all philosophical methods" (*HATH* I:1).

This is a theme that recurs in his later writings. He insists that philosophers of the kind he calls for and attempts himself to be must be as sophisticated scientifically as possible, and that scientific inquiry is essential both to the reinterpretation of human reality and to the attempt to foster the enhancement of human life and the attainment of a "higher" humanity. So, in the same work, he celebrates "physics" (shorthand for natural science generally) precisely for this reason. Proclaiming that "*we want to become those we are* [i.e., have it in us to become] – human beings who are new, unique, incomparable, who give themselves laws, who create themselves," he then continues:

> To that end we must become the best learners and discoverers of everything that is lawful and necessary in the world: we must become *physicists* in order to be able to be *creators* in this sense – while hitherto all valuations and ideas have been based on *ignorance* of physics [i.e., natural science] or were constructed so as to *contradict* it. Therefore: up with physics [*hoch die Physik*]! And even more so [*höher noch*, higher still] that which *compels* us to turn to physics – our intellectual integrity [*Redlichkeit*]! (*GS* 335)

Nietzsche is by no means prepared, however, to grant the natural sciences the last word with respect to many matters, and in particular with respect to human reality and the human world. So, for example, he writes: "A 'scientific' interpretation of the world" in which it is supposed that "mechanics is the doctrine of the first and last laws on which all existence must be based as on a ground floor," would be "a crudity and naiveté, if not a lunacy, an idiocy," driving home his point by way of the example of "how absurd" a purely "'scientific' assessment of music would be" (*GS* 373). This point is of great importance in connection with the question of how his kind of "naturalism" is to be understood.

6.5 NIETZSCHE'S "NATURALISM"

The most direct and important instance of this insistence for Nietzsche, as this passage itself indicates, is the reinterpretation of human reality – that is, of "*der Mensch*" ("man" in the generic sense) or "the type *Mensch*," as the form of life it has come to be. So, earlier in the same book, after announcing "the death of God" (*GS* 108), he goes on immediately to call first for a "de-deification of nature" – a purging of our conceptions of the world and nature of all of the "shadows of God" and related anthropomorphisms that have long characterized our thinking about them – and then for a thoroughly "naturalistic" reinterpretation of ourselves as human beings who are a part of this newly understood nature: "When may we begin to '*naturalize*' our human selves [*uns Menschen ... zu vernatürlichen*] in terms of a pure, newly discovered, newly redeemed nature!" (*GS* 109). His implicit answer is: here and now, for this is the general project of the book. The sections that follow – "Origin of Knowledge" (*GS* 110), "Origin of the Logical" (*GS* 111), the origin of "scientific thinking" (*GS* 113), the origin of our "humanity" (*GS* 115), the origin of "morality" (*GS* 116) – provide immediate illustrations of what he has in mind.

Nietzsche holds that human reality is originally and fundamentally a form of animal life; and that everything it has "become" has come about through developmental processes of an entirely mundane (worldly) nature. So he has Zarathustra proclaim: "Body am I entirely, and nothing else; and soul is only a word for something about the body" (*Z* I:4). Putting the point more prosaically in *The Antichrist* (1888, a title better translated as "*The Antichristian*"), he writes:

> We no longer derive man from "the spirit" or "the deity"; we have placed him back among the animals ... The "pure spirit" is a pure stupidity: if we subtract the nervous system and the senses – the "mortal shroud" – *then we miscalculate* – that is all! (*A* 14)

Beyond Good and Evil, like *The Gay Science*, revolves around the project of reinterpreting human reality naturalistically – such human phenomena as morality and religion included. These phenomena may well have been among the "many chains [that] have been laid upon man," as Nietzsche figuratively puts it, "so that he should no longer behave like an animal" – and that have indeed resulted in the actual "separation of man from the animals" (*HATH* II: II:350). But they nonetheless have their own "natural histories" that are parts of our own – indeed, the part of *Beyond Good and Evil* dealing with morality bears the title "Natural History of Morals" – and so are to be treated accordingly, even though they have contributed significantly to what Nietzsche calls our "de-animalization [*Enttierung*]" (*D* 106).

> To translate man back into nature ... to see to it that man henceforth stands before man as even today, hardened in the discipline of science, he stands before the *rest* of nature ..., deaf to the siren songs of old metaphysical bird catchers who have been piping at him all too long, "you are more, you are higher, you are of a different origin!" – that may be a strange and crazy task, but it is a *task* – who would deny that? (*BGE* 230)

This is a "task" Nietzsche continued to pursue in *The Genealogy of Morality* – the topic of which is not only the "genealogy" or (very human) origin and development of a number of significant moral phenomena associated with modern-day morality, but also those of a number of salient features of human reality more generally. These developments include breeding "the beast of prey 'man'" into "a tame and civilized animal, a *household pet*" (*GM* I:11); "the labor performed by man upon himself" by means of the "ethics of custom and the social straitjacket" through which "man was actually *made* calculable" (*GM* II:2); the further process through which "nature" was able "to breed an animal *that may promise*" – that is, that is capable of making and keeping promises – which Nietzsche calls "the paradoxical task that nature has set itself in the case of man" (*GM* II:1); and "the *internalization* of man," through which "man first developed what was later called his 'soul'" and his "entire inner world," by way of the "inhibition" of the "outward discharge" of aggressive drives.

Nietzsche's naturalism is scientifically attentive (as *GS* 335 makes clear); but it is by no means "scientistically" reductionist, in the sense of supposing that the whole of human reality can in principle be comprehended and expressed in terms of the technical languages, conceptual schemes, and empirical-theoretical explanations of the natural sciences. His diatribe against "'Science' as prejudice" (that is, "'*Wissenschaft*' as dogma" *GS* 373), cited above, with "music" invoked as star witness, makes that evident as well. His naturalism is one that not only is open to the idea of emergent development (in which processes converge in a way that results in the emergence of something qualitatively different), but features it prominently. Indeed, it stands ready to meet the challenge of those who would point to various sorts of cultural, intellectual, and "spiritual" phenomena as evidence of something "more than" or "different from" anything of entirely "natural" origins by undertaking to make them naturalistically intelligible.

Nietzsche's naturalism extends to his thinking with respect to values and morals. So, in a note from 1887 to which he gave the heading "Toward a Plan," the first item he lists on his agenda is: "In place of *moral values*, purely *naturalistic* values. Naturalization of morality" (*WP* 462). So also, in *Twilight of the Idols* (1888) a year later, he writes: "Every naturalism in morality – that is, every healthy morality – is dominated by an instinct of life; some commandment of life is fulfilled by a determinate canon of 'shalt' and 'shalt not'" (*TI* IV:4). Nietzsche's thinking is meant to be "beyond" the tyranny of the concepts of "good and evil" associated with what he here goes on to call "*anti-natural* morality – that is, almost every morality that has so far been taught, revered, and preached." Indeed, in its rejection of all such anti-natural moralism and associated non-naturalistic "moral values" – "*there are altogether no moral facts* (*TI* VI:1) – it may even be characterized (as he himself characterizes it) as "immoralist." But while he does reject the idea of any absolute values somehow existing independently of this life and world, he is intent upon a naturalistic reorientation of value theory, and of moral theory as well in derivative association with it.

6.6 NIETZSCHE'S "AESTHETICISM"

This characterization is intended to underscore the crowning importance Nietzsche attaches to aesthetic and artistic concepts and values in his thinking with respect to life and the world in general, and to human reality and possibility in particular. It is related to his emphasis on the ideas of the "enhancement [*Erhöhung*]" of life and its quality, and of the kind of humanity he calls "higher [*höher*]" and "superior [*vornehm*, often translated as 'noble']" in relation to the all-too-human general rule in human life, of which his image of "the overman [*Übermensch*]" is the apotheosis and symbol. The term "aestheticism" here refers more specifically to the way in which he conceives of the difference-making characteristics at issue – difference-making not only in terms of what he calls "ranking" or "order of rank," but also with respect to their human-experiential significance. What renders the term appropriate in this context is Nietzsche's emphasis on the idea of *creation* and *creativity*, his heavy reliance upon artistic imagery and upon art and the artist as paradigms of what he has in mind (and seeks to generalize), and his identification of *culture* as the dimension of human reality that is the locus of all such differentiation and development.

The term "aestheticism" is thus both useful and apt as a further positive indication of the general direction of his post-moralism, and of the development of his kind of post-absolutist as well as post-nihilist value theory. It is not in conflict with his value-naturalism but rather is an outgrowth and extension of it. His fundamental aesthetic values are not independent of what he refers to above as "naturalistic values" but rather are grounded in and developed out of the latter, which animate them even as they are transfigured in them. They thus remain naturalistic values, while yet also representing their creative transfiguration and supersession.

Nietzsche's aestheticism is on full display in *The Birth of Tragedy* (1872), in which he writes that "it is only as an *aesthetic phenomenon* that existence and the world are eternally *justified*" (*BT* 4, repeated in *BT* 24); and that "art is not merely imitation of the reality of nature but rather a metaphysical supplement of the reality of nature, placed beside it for its overcoming" (*BT* 24). By "metaphysical" here he means something transcending and contrasting with the merely natural – and yet he also considers the two basic impulses he identifies in art, "the Apollinian and its opposite, the Dionysian, as artistic energies which burst forth from nature herself," thus making the "overcoming" of nature in or by means of art its own self-overcoming through its self-"transfiguration" (*BT* 2). Moreover, he writes, in the Dionysian arts of music and dance, one "is no longer an artist, he has *become* a work of art," and that "we have our highest dignity in our significance *as* works of art." (*BT* 1 and 24; emphasis added.)

Nietzsche subsequently abandoned the characterization of art as a kind of "metaphysical" activity, but not the idea of art as the creative transformation of the natural, through which the natural – and we as its transformers and the true loci of its transformation – attain a significance and worth which it and we would otherwise lack. This idea is at the heart of what he means by "value creation." He likewise retained the idea of the redeeming transfiguration of nature through man's artistic self-transformation, writing in a note from 1885 that "man becomes the *transfigurer of existence* when he learns to transfigure himself," calling this "the great conception of man" (*WP* 820). And he further retained the idea of "becoming a work of art," writing (in an aphorism in *The Gay Science* entitled "*One thing is needful*"): "To 'give style' to one's character: a great and rare art! It is practiced by those who survey all the strengths and weaknesses of their nature and then fit them into an artistic plan" (*GS* 290).

On the other hand, Nietzsche subsequently came to think less of art in the sense of "the fine arts" in this connection than of the artistic character or quality that can be extended and cultivated more broadly in human life and experience – for which, however, he stresses our indebtedness to art in this narrower sense. So he writes:

> *What one should learn from artists.* – How can we make things beautiful, attractive, and desirable for us when they are not? ... Here we could learn something ... from artists who are really continually trying to bring off such inventions and feats .... [But] with them this subtle power usually comes to an end where art ends and life begins; but we want to be the poets of our lives – first of all in the smallest, most everyday matters. (*GS* 299)

A little later in the same book Nietzsche expands upon the idea of a transformation of human reality in such a way that "all nature ceases and becomes art" in a passage in which he sounds one of his favorite themes: "We *want to become those we are* [*wollen Die werden, die wir sind*] – human beings [*Menschen*] who are new, unique, incomparable, who give themselves laws, who create themselves" (*GS* 336). Here he joins characteristics commonly associated with true works of art to two other characteristics, which he associates with true artists: autonomy and creativity.

Creativity is one of the central themes of *Zarathustra,* as Nietzsche through Zarathustra elaborates upon his meaning in having Zarathustra proclaim the "overman" to be "the meaning of the earth: "He who creates, creates man's goal and gives the earth its meaning and its future" (*Z* III: 12:2). That same thought is reflected more prosaically in a later (1887) note in which Nietzsche considers "to what extent one can endure to live in a meaningless world *because one organizes a small part of it oneself*" (*WP* 585A). It remains central to the reconsideration of values for which *Beyond Good and Evil* prepares the way, and to his elaboration of the "new language" with respect to value – centering it upon "value for life" (*BGE* 4) – with which Nietzsche proposes to replace moralistic thinking, even of a hedonistic or utilitarian kind: "All those ways of thinking that measure the value of things in accordance with *pleasure* and *pain* ... [are] naivetés on which everyone conscious of *creative* powers and an artistic conscience will look down, not without derision, nor without pity." He then goes on, in a memorable passage in this same section, to contrast "all-too-human" humanity and the higher humanity of which the "overman" is emblematic as follows:

In man *creature* and *creator* are united: in man there is material, fragment, excess, clay, dirt, nonsense, chaos; but in man there is also creator, form-giver, hammer-hardness, spectator-divinity, and seventh day: do you understand this contrast? (*BGE* 225)

This "contrast" illuminates Nietzsche's conceptions of what he calls the "all-too-human" and the "enhancement of life." The latter involves the overcoming of the former, and the developmental attainment of a higher humanity, the general character of which is summed up in his phrase "union of spiritual superiority with well-being and an excess of strength" (*WP* 899). And spiritual superiority for him is by no means something purely or even primarily inward. Rather, it is fundamentally a *cultural* matter. The enhancement of life, for Nietzsche, essentially involves the enhancement of human *cultural* life; "higher humanity" and "higher culture" are concepts that for him go hand in hand. So he writes, in the note from 1887 cited earlier that bears the heading "Toward a Plan" and lists items on his philosophical agenda: "In place of 'society,' the *culture-complex* as my chief interest (both as a whole and with regard to its parts)" (*WP* 462).

That interest is already evident in *The Birth of Tragedy*; it becomes very explicit in *Schopenhauer as Educator* (1874). This third of Nietzsche's four *Untimely Meditations* (as he called them) is of particular interest in the present connection, because it is in effect Nietzsche's aestheticist manifesto, setting the stage for *Zarathustra* and the "philosophy of culture" that is a crucial feature of his developing reinterpretation and reassessment of human reality. He begins in a way that would seem to make his association with existentialism appropriate:

The man who does not wish to belong to the mass needs only to cease taking himself easily: let him follow his conscience, which calls to him: "Be yourself! All you are now doing, thinking, desiring, is not you yourself." (*SE* 1, p. 127)[11]

However, Nietzsche immediately takes this thought in an unexpected direction. The "self" that one is encouraged to "be" (or become), setting oneself apart from "the mass" of all-too-human humanity, is no distinct identity one is to discover and be true to, or even to establish as one's own by way of an authentic choice or decision: "your true nature lies, not concealed deep within you, but immeasurably high above you, or at least above that which you usually take yourself to be" (*SE* 1, p. 129). Nietzsche does not immediately explain what he means by this, but his language here hints broadly that he has in mind the attainment of a significantly "higher" sort of humanity than "the mass" represents.

Nietzsche's underlying thought in this essay is that "man is necessary for the redemption of nature from the curse of the life of the animal," which in the spirit of Schopenhauer is said to be the fate of meaningless striving and suffering. Our challenge is to rise above an existence that is no better than this, to a humanity that transcends animality in a way that lifts this curse and thereby "redeems" nature through its transformation – in ourselves – into something that is more than merely natural, by endowing our own striving and suffering existence with a kind of meaning that merely natural existence (and its striving and suffering) lacks. But, Nietzsche asks, "where does the animal cease, where does man begin?" For, he contends, in our all-too-human ordinary existence, "usually we fail to emerge out of animality, we ourselves are the animals whose suffering seems senseless." Genuine humanity is "*higher*" humanity: "We are pressing toward man as toward something that stands high above us" (*SE* 5, pp. 157–58).

Nietzsche then goes on to contend that those who point the way, provide a glimpse and anticipation of that higher and truer humanity, and thereby "lift us up," are "those true men [*Menschen*, human beings], *those who are no longer animal, the philosophers, artists and saints*" (*SE* 5, p. 159). These three types are singled out because they represent three ways of transcending the plane of fundamentally animal existence: by way of insight, creativity, and self-mastery. And it is the cultivation and combination of these traits that are said to make possible "*the completion and fulfillment* [*Vollendung*] *of nature.*" This, Nietzsche says, enables us to "*discover* a new circle of duties" – duties involving our doing whatever we can to advance the cultivation of these traits, through the "production" and assistance of those exceptional human beings through whose efforts they are furthered. Moreover:

These new duties are not the duties of a solitary [individual]; on the contrary, they set one in the midst of a mighty community held together, not by external forms and regulations, but by a fundamental idea. It is the fundamental idea of *culture* [*Kultur*]. (*SE* 5, pp. 160–61)

It is in these terms that Nietzsche here answers the question: "how can your life, the individual life, receive the highest value, the deepest significance? How can it least be squandered?" His answer is: "by *consecration to culture.*" He elaborates: "Anyone who believes in culture is thereby saying: 'I see above me something higher and more human than I am; let everyone help me to attain it, as I will help everyone who knows and suffers as I do.'" And unless one happens to be among the "rarest and most valuable exemplars" of humanity and culture in and through whom they are further enriched and enhanced, "consecration to culture" means "living for the good" of those who *are* such "exemplars" in whatever way one can (*SE* 6, pp. 162–63).

Nietzsche undoubtedly had Richard Wagner – his paradigmatic creative genius – in mind when he wrote this. He subsequently outgrew this bit of "great man" Romanticism, and generalized the idea along the lines of Zarathustra's exhortation that one do whatever one has it in oneself to do to contribute to the advent of the "overman" (*Z* I: P:4) – that is, to the enhancement of human life. The emerging focus of his concern, as he puts it in his Preface to *Genealogy*, was with the attainment – or non-attainment – of "the *highest power and splendor* actually possible to the type man [*Mensch*]" (*GM* P:6). It remained the case, however, to the end of his productive life, that the kind of human greatness he has in mind is to be conceived in terms of both human-spiritual and human-cultural "power and splendor," as two sides of the same coin. They together are the twin loci of his conception of the "highest" humanity conceivable and attainable. "What matters most," he writes in *Twilight*, just before the abrupt end of his productive life, "always remains culture" (*TI* VII:4).

6.7 NIETZSCHE'S DIONYSIANISM

Finally, mention must be made of Nietzsche's distinctive this-worldly alternative to (or kind of) religiousness, which is perhaps best characterized (following his own characterization of it) as "Dionysian." It could not be more different from Kierkegaard's radical God-centered Christianity – or, on the other hand, from the flatly secularist, utterly de-divinized worldviews of Sartre and Camus. The philosophical theologian Paul Tillich, in whose courses I first encountered Nietzsche, characterized him as an *"ecstatic* naturalist," and that characterization is well warranted. In the spirit of Zarathustra's proclamation that "body am I entirely, and soul is only a word for something about the body," one might say that for Nietzsche "divine" is only a word for something about life and the world; but that "something" is an important "something" in each case.

So Nietzsche is moved to feel the need of such notions as "joy," "affirmation," "faithfulness to the earth," *"amor fati,"* and "eternal recurrence" to characterize the kind of fundamental attitude or relation to life and the world that he considers not only to be humanly possible but to be humanly optimal. They are expressive and indicative of what he calls a "Dionysian" kind of sensibility (and even religiousness) that is as far beyond nihilism as it is beyond all religious and metaphysical "otherworldliness" and life-denying "ascetic ideals." If human life is to flourish beyond the possibility of all disillusionment, not only must we become capable of *enduring a recognition* of the fundamental character of life and the world, and of the human condition in this life and world; we must come to be able truly to affirm, embrace and love them. Nietzsche's Dionysianism is that love and celebration. So, in a late (1888) note, he speaks of "a Dionysian value standard for existence," and writes:

> Such an experimental philosophy as I live anticipates experimentally even the possibilities of the most fundamental nihilism; but this does not mean that it must halt at a negation, a No, a will to negation. It wants rather to cross over to the opposite of this – to a Dionysian affirmation of the world as it is, without subtraction, exception, or selection – it wants the eternal circulation [i.e., recurrence]: the same things, the same logic and illogic of entanglements. The highest state a philosopher can attain: to stand in a Dionysian relationship to existence – my formula for this is *amor fati*. (*WP* 1041)

"Amor fati [love of fate]" is Nietzsche's counterstroke to the Judeo-Christian idea of *"amor Dei* [love of God]" as the formula for the

essence of religious faith. In place of making the unconditional love of a God imagined to exist beyond this life and world the cornerstone of the living of one's own life in this world, and also in place of a nihilistic negation of this life and world in the absence of such a God, Nietzsche envisions the alternative of an unconditional acceptance, affirmation, and love of what we are in any event stuck with: the world as it fundamentally is and will ever continue to be – notwithstanding the fact that our own individual and collective human existence cannot change the way it is and is itself but a fleeting ephemeral instance of the kind of affair it is. "Saying Yes to life even in its strangest and hardest problems," he writes at the conclusion of *Twilight* – "*that* is what I called Dionysian [in *BT*]," even referring to himself as "the last disciple of the philosopher Dionysus" (*TI* IX:4). Nietzsche's Dionysianism differs from what he calls by that name in *Birth of Tragedy*, however, in that it incorporates elements of what he had there called "Apollinian" as well, as does the "tragic" sensibility that he had conceived as the issue of their union; and in fact his Dionysianism might be seen as his version of that very sensibility.

As Nietzsche came to realize, one's *attained sensibility* makes all the difference. In *The Birth of Tragedy*, looking at life and the world through the lenses of the Schopenhauerian interpretation and sensibility that he had adopted, he had written: "Suppose a human being has thus put his ear, as it were, to the heart chamber of the world will and felt the roaring desire for existence pouring from there into all the veins of the world [...] – how could he fail at once to *break*?" (*BT* 21). By the time of *Human, All Too Human* (six years later), however, he had attained the new sensibility that was to animate his thinking from then onward – which he credits to *art*:

> Above all, [art] has taught us for thousands of years to look upon life in any of its forms with interest and pleasure, and to *develop our sensibility so far* [*unsere Empfindung so weit zu bringen*] that we at last cry: "life, however it may be, is good!" This teaching imparted by art to take pleasure in life and to regard the human life as a piece of nature ... has been absorbed into us, and now reemerges as an almighty requirement of knowledge. One could give up art, but would not thereby relinquish the capacity one has learned from it. (*HATH* 222)

As Nietzsche very importantly observes in *The Gay Science*, "One must learn to love" (*GS* 334) – or at any rate, one must learn to do so if one's love is to be strong enough to survive the recognition of the things about life and the world that Schopenhauer took to warrant their condemnation and rejection. And it is of the utmost importance for Nietzsche that they *can* come to be loved, beyond all revulsion and disillusionment, and without the mediation of the various forms of illusion that he had deemed indispensable to the achievement of this result in *The Birth of Tragedy* – precisely through the further cultivation of the kind of sensibility for which we have the arts to thank.

In a note from the mid 1880s Nietzsche suggests thinking of "the world as a work of art that gives birth to itself" (*WP* 796) – and, he might have added, that also destroys itself and then gives birth to itself yet again, in a never-ending alternation of creation and destruction. And again: "An anti-metaphysical view of the world – yes, but an artistic one" (*WP* 1048). Nietzsche's Dionysianism is thus conjoined with his aestheticism, as its generalization and celebration. It involves learning to think of oneself as – and to become – something analogous to a work of art giving birth to itself, in a culture and a form of life and world that each may likewise be so construed, with a sensibility that enables one further to learn to love it all for the aesthetic phenomenon it is seen to be – its ephemerality notwithstanding, redeemed by the consolation of its endless recurrence.

6.8 CONCLUSION

Is Nietzsche an existentialist? His thought is philosophically unconventional, post-religious (and anti-Christian), post- (and indeed anti-) metaphysical, sometimes polemical, and often passionate; but that does not answer the question in the affirmative, for the same things may be said of the thought of Bertrand Russell. His embrace by subsequent paradigmatic existential philosophers likewise does not answer the question; he has also been embraced by others hostile to existential philosophy, of a variety of orientations. In terms of the distinctions suggested at the outset, Nietzsche's Dionysian aestheticism is either his alternative to or his version of existentialism; his naturalistic "historical" philosophical anthropology is either his alternative to or his version of Existenz-philosophy; and his science-friendly but culturally informed interpretive genealogical-psychological *fröhliche Wissenschaft* is either his alternative to or his version of phenomenological existential philosophy. His kind of philosophy, so understood, is certainly quite different from Sartre's or Heidegger's, not to mention Kierkegaard's. If it too is to be considered a kind of existentialism, Existenz-philosophy, and existential philosophy, however, so much the better – for them.

NOTES

1. Kierkegaard, *Concluding Unscientific Postscript*, p. 100.
2. In *Thus Spoke Zarathustra*, I:3. (For referencing conventions, see n. 9 below.) This was without his ever having read Kierkegaard. Nietzsche never had the opportunity to read him because he could not read Danish, and Kierkegaard had not yet been translated into German.
3. *BGE* = *Beyond Good and Evil*. For referencing conventions, see n. 9 below.
4. Sartre, *Existentialism is a Humanism*, p. 20.
5. Heidegger, *Being and Time*, e.g. pp. 38, 71–75, 170.
6. Sartre, *Search for a Method*, Preface.
7. "Always Look on the Bright Side of Life," from Monty Python's movie *Life of Brian* (1979). Tune and lyrics by Eric Idle.
8. See Schacht, "Philosophical Anthropology."
9. I shall follow the usual practice of identifying and referring to Nietzsche's works by the abbreviations of their customary English-language titles (listed below) after my first mention of them, and of identifying passages by section or part-and-section numbers in most cases, rather than page numbers, to make it easy to find them in any edition or translation that might be used. I shall generally cite the Kaufmann or Hollingdale translations, but on occasion shall modify them where I consider different renderings to be desirable. Full publication information can be found in the Bibliography. "P" within a reference refers to a work's Prologue.

   A *The Antichrist*
   BGE *Beyond Good and Evil*
   BT *The Birth of Tragedy*
   CW *The Case of Wagner*
   D *Daybreak*
   EH *Ecce Homo*
   GM *On the Genealogy of Morality*
   GS *The Gay Science*

HATH	*Human, All Too Human*
NCW	*Nietzsche contra Wagner*
SE	*Schopenhauer as Educator*
TI	*Twilight of the Idols*
TL	"On Truth and Lie in a Nonmoral Sense"
UDH	*On the Uses and Disadvantages of History for Life*
UM	*Untimely Meditations*
WP	*The Will to Power*
Z	*Thus Spoke Zarathustra.*

10. Much of what Nietzsche had to say about nihilism is to be found in notes from his notebooks of 1883–88 that are gathered in the first part of a volume of selections from these notebooks published posthumously under the title *The Will to Power*. The status and significance of the material in this volume and in his notebooks is much debated. See Schacht, *Making Sense of Nietzsche*, ch. 6.
11. In identifying citations from this work, page numbers as well as section numbers are given, owing to the length of the sections. The page numbers are those in Hollingdale's translation of SE in *Untimely Meditations*.

LAWRENCE J. HATAB

7 Nietzsche: selfhood, creativity, and philosophy

One of the central themes in existential philosophy is the problem of meaning, a problem that follows upon the modern scientific objectification of nature. Modern science gave priority to mathematics in a mechanical model of motion and causality; accordingly, values and purposes were no longer seen to be intrinsic to nature (as they had been in ancient and medieval thought). If values and purposes were not "objective" and were nevertheless still to find a place in philosophy, they could only be thought in terms of the human "subject." Yet such a divide created a kind of chasm between the meaningfulness of life and life's natural environment, a chasm that has endured in philosophy ever since. Because human beings exist in nature – which lacks intrinsic meaning – what possible status can be given to meaning-claims about values and purposes? One of the marks of existential philosophy – at least in representative thinkers such as Kierkegaard and Sartre – has been to reverse the priority of scientific, rational objectivity and give precedence to human subjectivity in questions of meaning. In other words, Kierkegaard and Sartre accept the idea of objective being and rational "essences" (as universals that define existing particulars), but they refuse to privilege such notions when it comes to meaning formation, since these notions foster either a nihilistic denial of meaning or an attempt (as in Kant and Hegel) to reconfigure meaning in purely rational terms. In matters of human concern such as values, then, we have Kierkegaard's reversal (the claim that subjectivity is the truth) and Sartre's reversal (the claim that existence precedes essence). Both thinkers emphasize that the self is radically free with respect to the claims of objectivity and essence when *choosing* the incorporation of meaning into an individual human life.

In this chapter I want to explore the questions of meaning and selfhood in Nietzsche's thought, as well as the related questions of creativity and Nietzsche's methods of philosophical writing. What we find is that Nietzsche's approach to these basic themes – especially the issue of selfhood – differs significantly from this standard picture of existentialism.

7.1 FROM METAPHYSICS TO NATURALISM

We can gain entry to Nietzsche's philosophy by beginning with his critique of metaphysics. According to Nietzsche, "the fundamental faith of the metaphysicians is *the faith in opposite values*" (*BGE* 2).[1] The Western religious and philosophical tradition has operated by dividing reality into a set of binary opposites such as constancy and change, eternity and time, reason and passion, good and evil, truth and appearance – opposites that can be organized around the concepts of being and becoming. The motivation behind such divisional thinking is as follows: becoming names the negative and unstable conditions of existence that undermine our interest in grasping, controlling, and preserving life in the face of the pervasive force of uncertainty, variability, destruction, and death. Being, as *opposite* to becoming, permits the governance or exclusion of negative conditions and the attainment of various forms of stability untainted by their fluid contraries.

Nietzsche wants to challenge the priority of being in the tradition, so much so that he is often read as simply reversing this scheme by extolling sheer becoming and all its correlates. This is not the case, even though Nietzsche often celebrates negative terms rhetorically to unsettle convictions and open up space for new meanings. In fact, Nietzsche replaces oppositional exclusion with a sense of *crossing*, where the differing conditions in question are not exclusive of each other but are reciprocally related.[2] Nietzsche suggests that "what constitutes the value of these good and revered things is precisely that they are insidiously related, tied to, and involved with these wicked, seemingly opposite things" (*BGE* 2). Rather than fixed contraries, Nietzsche prefers "differences of degree" and "transitions" (*WS* 67). Even the idea of sheer becoming cannot be maintained, according to Nietzsche. Discernment of such becoming can only arise once an imaginary counter-world of being is placed against it (*KSA* IX, pp. 503–4).

In restoring legitimacy to conditions of becoming, Nietzsche advances what I call an *existential naturalism*. The finite, unstable dynamic of earthly existence – and its meaningfulness – itself becomes the measure of thought, one that runs counter to various attempts in philosophy and religion to "reform" the supposedly originally flawed condition of lived experience by way of a rational, spiritual, or moral "transcendence" (*GS* 109; *TI* 3, 16). In turning to "the basic text of *homo natura*" (*BGE* 230), Nietzsche is not identifying his philosophy with what we would call scientific naturalism, which in many ways locates itself on the "being" side of the ledger. For Nietzsche, nature is more unstable and disruptive than science allows; it includes forces, instincts, passions, and powers that are not reducible to objective categories. Stressing a darker sense of "nature red in tooth and claw," Nietzsche claims that "the terrible [*schreckliche*] basic text of nature must again be recognized" (*BGE* 230). Naturalism, for Nietzsche, amounts to a kind of philosophical methodology, in that natural forces of becoming will be deployed to redescribe and account for all aspects of life – including cultural formations – and for the emergence of even seemingly anti-natural constructions of "being."

For Nietzsche, "the death of God" stands for the demise of anti-natural thinking, yet the consequences reach far beyond religion. It is not simply atheism, since it acknowledges the fact that, historically, divinity has been "living" as a powerful productive force. From Plato through the Enlightenment, a divine mind had been the ultimate reference point for origins and truth, a standing warrant for all sorts of cultural constructs in moral, political, philosophical, even scientific domains. With the eclipse of God, all inferences from theological grounds must come undone as well (*TI* 9, 5). The death of God therefore announces the demise of truth; or, at the very least, it signals that "the will to truth becomes conscious of itself as a *problem*" (*GM* III, 27). Even though divinity is no longer an intellectual prerequisite in the modern world, we still have confidence in the "shadows" of God (*GS* 108), in supposedly secular truths that have nonetheless lost their pedigree and intellectual warrant. This matter is especially significant with respect to modern moral and political constructs.

The consequences of God's death are enormous because it threatens us with nihilism, the loss of meaning and intelligibility. The secular sophistication of the modern world has unwittingly "unchained this earth from its sun," so that we are "straying as through an infinite nothing" (*GS* 125). The course of Western thought has led it to turn away from its historical origins, but the unsuspected result has been that "the highest values devalue themselves" (*WP* 2). So we are faced with a stark choice: either we collapse into nihilism or we rethink the world in naturalistic terms freed from the reverence for being-constructs. "Either abolish your reverences or – *yourselves*! The latter would be nihilism; but would not the former also be – nihilism? – This is *our* question mark" (*GS* 346).

For Nietzsche, the threat of nihilism – the denial of any truth, meaning, or value in the world – is in fact parasitic on the Western tradition, which has judged conditions of becoming in life to be deficient and has "nullified" these conditions in favor of rational, spiritual, or moral corrections. If, in the wake of the death of God, the loss of these corrections is experienced as nihilistic, it is because the traditional models are still presumed to be the only measures of truth, meaning, and value – and thus the world seems empty without them (*WP* 12A). For Nietzsche, however, philosophers should embrace the death of God with gratitude and excitement, not despair, because it opens new horizons for thought (*GS* 343). Various motifs in Nietzsche's texts can be read as counter-nihilistic attempts to rethink truth, meaning, and value in naturalistic terms, in a manner consistent with conditions of becoming. One very important example of this is Nietzsche's idea of will to power.

"The world viewed from inside ... would be 'will to power' and nothing else" (*BGE* 36). A world of becoming, for Nietzsche, cannot simply be understood as a world of change. Movements are always *related* to other movements and the relational structure is not simply expressive of differences, but also of resistances and tensional conflicts (*WP* 568). Will to power names, in dynamic terms, the idea that any affirmation is also a negation, that any condition or assertion of meaning must overcome some "other," some obstacle or counterforce.[3] Moreover, Nietzsche claims that "will to power can manifest itself *only* against resistances; therefore it *seeks* that which resists it" (*WP* 656; my emphasis). A similar formation is declared in *Ecce Homo* in reference to a warlike nature: "It needs objects of resistance; hence it *looks for* what resists" (*EH* I, 7). We must notice the following implication: Since power can *only* be what it is in relation to resistance, one's power to overcome is essentially related to a counter-power; if resistance were eliminated, if one's counter-power were destroyed or even neutralized by sheer domination, one's power would evaporate, it would no longer *be* power. Power is *overcoming* something, not annihilating it: "there is no annihilation in the sphere of spirit" (*WP* 588). Power is more a "potency" than a full actuality because it retains its tensional relation with its Other. Accordingly Nietzsche's phrase *Wille zur Macht* could be translated as "will *toward* power," which would indicate something other than a full "possession."

Will to power, therefore, cannot be understood in terms of individual states alone, even successful states, because it names a tensional force-field *within which* individual states shape themselves by seeking to overcome other sites of power. Power cannot be construed as "instrumental" for any resultant state, whether it be knowledge, pleasure, purpose, or even survival, since such conditions are epiphenomena of power, of a drive to overcome something (*GM* II, 12, 18). For this reason, Nietzsche depicts life as "that which must always overcome itself" (*Z* II, 12). This also accounts for Nietzsche's objection to measuring life by "happiness," since the structure of will to power entails that *dissatisfaction* and *displeasure* are intrinsic to movements of overcoming (*WP* 696, 704). Thus conditions of sheer satisfaction and completion would dry up the energies of life.

From this it becomes evident that meaning is always reciprocally related to "otherness" and can thrive only in the midst of challenges to meaning. All scientific, religious, moral, and intellectual developments began as elements of dissatisfaction and impulses to overcome something, whether it be ignorance, worldliness, brutality, confusion, or competing cultural models. Even pacifism – understood as an impulse to overcome human violence and an exalted way of life taken as an advance over our brutish nature – can be understood as an instance of will to power, and any doctrine that would reject will to power in Nietzsche's sense would undermine the conditions of its own historical emergence as a contention with conflicting forces.

7.2 PSYCHOLOGY AND PERSPECTIVISM IN PHILOSOPHY

A central feature of Nietzsche's naturalism is that his diagnosis of the philosophical tradition goes beyond a conceptual critique of beliefs and theories: "the path to fundamental problems" is to be found in psychology (*BGE* 23), which, for Nietzsche, is more than a mere "science of the mind." Nietzsche maintains that the origins of problematic constructs of "being" are not primarily found in mistaken beliefs but in psychological weakness in the face of a finite world, an *aversion* to the negative conditions of life which he describes as "decadence, a symptom of the *decline of life*" (*TI* 3, 6). Thus a certain kind of psychological strength is needed to affirm life and rethink it in ways that are more appropriate to its natural conditions of becoming. This becomes a *normative* aspect of Nietzschean psychology, which does not operate with a universal human nature but offers a delineation of *types* along a continuum of weakness and strength. Nietzsche objects to the idea of human equality[4] and promotes a hierarchical arrangement of types: "My philosophy aims at an ordering of rank" (*WP* 287). His celebration of creative types over the herd mentality is grounded in the "strength" involved in risking new ventures, as opposed to the "weakness" of needing the shelter of conformity.

In general terms Nietzsche maintains that no form of thought is "value-free." Elements of desire and interest are always operating in human thinking – what we think about has to *matter* to us. Even principles of "disinterest" or "objectivity" serve certain values. When we are asked not to act out of personal interests, the principle itself is animated by values and interests: "The 'disinterested' action is an *exceedingly* interesting and interested action" (*BGE* 220).

With Nietzsche's insistence that philosophy cannot be separated from personal interests and meaning-formation, his turn to psychology means that knowledge cannot be based in an absolute, fixed, objective standard, but in a pluralized perspectivism: "There is *only* a perspective seeing, only a perspective 'knowing'" (*GM* III, 12). There are many possible takes on the world, and none could count as exclusively correct. A plurality of perspectives entails not only different, but also conflicting interpretations; thus even the coexistence of conflicting positions must be accepted as characteristic of "knowledge." Nietzsche expresses his outlook as follows: "Profound aversion to resting once and for all in any one total view of the world. Enchantment [*Zauber*] of the opposing point of view" (*WP* 470).

This perspectivism informs Nietzsche's approach to the question of the meaning of life. His aim is not to find a decisive answer to "Why are we here?" but to explore the *problem* of finding meaning in a world that ultimately blocks our psychological interest in happiness, preservation, knowledge, and purpose. To be precise, the question is not "What is the meaning of life?" but "Can there be meaning in life?" Is life as we have it meaningful, worthwhile, affirmable *on its own terms*? Nietzsche's diagnosis of the Western tradition is that, in one form or another, the answer to this question of meaning in natural life has been "No." No culture or form of thought has ever denied that our immediate existence is characterized by negative constraints – change, suffering, loss, and death – that limit our possibilities. Thus it would appear that, measured against our highest aspirations, life as we first have it is tragic. "Concerning life, the wisest men of all ages have judged alike: *it is no good*" (*TI* 2, 1). Whether in scientific, rationalistic, religious, or moralistic terms, initial conditions of existence have been judged to be deficient, confused, fallen, alien, or base – in need of correction or to be transcended altogether. For Nietzsche, however, all such judgments are nihilistic, and he sees as his task the affirmative revaluation of this tragic existence itself: "I want to learn more and more to see as beautiful what is necessary in things; then I shall be one of those who make things beautiful. *Amor fati*: let that be my love henceforth ... And all in all and on the whole: someday I wish only to be a Yes-sayer" (*GS* 276).

It is crucial to see that the existential task of life-affirmation in response to the *question* of meaning and the danger of nihilism is the core issue in Nietzsche's thought, that which underpins and animates all his supposed "doctrines" such as will to power, perspectivism, and eternal recurrence.[5] For this reason, Nietzsche's texts cannot be read solely as a collection of philosophical doctrines or propositions that call for assessment by conceptual, empirical, or logical criteria.[6] Nietzsche's philosophical work is intelligible only in light of an existential project – that of choosing between a looming nihilism or a revaluation of life. His own thinking accomplishes this by bringing together "in a *decisive* way" (*WP* 1058) two notions that had previously been held apart: *becoming* and *the value of existence*. In opposition to traditional metaphysical philosophy, his guiding concern is to find meaning and value *in* becoming.

7.3 SELFHOOD

Nietzsche's critique of objective being entails, on the positive side, the idea that all thought is creative, a product of human valuation rather than a process of pure, objective "discovery" (see *Z* I, 15). Yet this focus on creativity and Nietzsche's appeal to psychology often challenges our assumptions about human selfhood, especially if we come to them with the sort of existentialist conceptions of subjectivity and consciousness that we find in Kierkegaard or Sartre. Nietzsche's approach to selfhood is enormously complicated, and, as we will see, even his proto-existential celebration of "creative individuals" cannot be read as a radical individualism – whether as generalizable to all selves or as limited to a discrete "type."

Because human selfhood, for Nietzsche, is always emergent within a dynamic of life forces, his thinking undermines our usual notions of self-identity. He rejects the modern model of an individual, unified, substantive, autonomous self, an enduring substance or a unified subject that possesses attributes and stands "behind" activities as a causal source (*BGE* 19–21). Selfhood is *performance*: "There is no 'being' behind doing, effecting, becoming; 'the doer' is merely a fiction added to the deed – the deed is everything" (*GM* I, 13). Traditional, mistaken, models of selfhood are subsidized, above all, by language. Human experience and thinking are decentered processes, but the "grammatical habit" of using subjects and predicates, nouns and verbs, tricks us into assigning an "I" as the source of thinking (*BGE* 17). Human experience is much too fluid and complicated to be reducible to linguistic units (*BGE* 19). The vaunted philosophical categories of "subject," "ego," and "consciousness" are nothing more than linguistic fictions that cover up the dynamics of experience, created to mask from us the precariousness of an ungrounded process. Ultimately for Nietzsche, the self is not an organized unity but an arena for an irresolvable contest of differing drives, each seeking mastery (*BGE* 6, 36). There is no single subject, but rather a "multiplicity of subjects, whose interplay and struggle is the basis of our thought and our consciousness" (*WP* 490).

Nietzsche's tensional psychology does not, however, entail that the self is an utter chaos. A certain shaping of the self is possible, but only through a demanding procedure of counter-cropping the drives such that a kind of mastery is achieved. To achieve this is to attain "freedom," but such freedom is not anything like the "essence" of selfhood in the existentialist sense. Nietzsche thinks that the modern promotion of universal freedom is careless and even dangerous (*TI* 9, 41). According to Nietzsche (and this is missed in many interpretations) freedom and creative self-development are not for everyone: "Independence is for the very few; it is a privilege of the strong" (*BGE* 29). That most human beings are bound by rules and are not free to cut their own path is, from the perspective of life, necessary. The "exception" and the "rule" are *both* necessary for human culture. Exceptional types *further* the species, but the rule *preserves* it (*GS* 55). Thus the exception can never become the rule, can never be a model for all humanity (*GS* 76). Unless one keeps this point in mind, Nietzsche's promotion of creative individuals is easily misunderstood. Freedom from constraints is restricted to those who are strong enough for, and capable of, high cultural production. "My philosophy aims at an ordering of rank: not at an individualistic morality. The ideas of the herd should rule in the herd – but not reach out beyond it" (*WP* 287).

Though the meaning of freedom in Nietzsche's thought is not always clear, it *is* clear that he rejects both the modern idea of free will and that of mechanistic determinism: the former because of his dismissal of atomic individualism and the latter because of his voluntaristic alternative to mechanistic causality (*BGE* 21). Freedom, for Nietzsche, is nothing like a substantive faculty or power possessed by a "subject"; it is a relational term that accords with the tensional structure of will to power. The human sense of freedom arises from the delight in overcoming obstacles (*BGE* 19); indeed, the measure of freedom can only be gauged "according to the resistance that must be overcome" (*TI* 9, 38). Thus, rather than talk of free and unfree will, it is better to speak of strong and weak wills, according to their capacity or incapacity for struggle and experimentation (*BGE* 21).

Just as Nietzsche's views on the relation between selfhood and freedom do not always track existentialist expectations, his views on selfhood and *consciousness* could hardly be less Sartrean. He dismisses the centrality of consciousness – the idea that the conscious mind is our highest nature – and denies that it defines our identity through some capacity to control instinctive drives. According to Nietzsche, consciousness is a very late development of the human organism, neither particularly strong nor effective (*GS* 11).

> The problem of consciousness (more precisely, of becoming conscious of something) confronts us only when we begin to comprehend how we could dispense with it; and now physiology and the history of animals place us at the beginning of such comprehension ... we could think, feel, will, and remember, and we could also "act" in every sense of that word, and yet none of all this would have to "enter our consciousness" (as one says metaphorically). The whole of life would be possible without, as it were, seeing itself in a mirror. For even now, for that matter, by far the greatest portion of our life actually takes place without this mirror effect; and this is true even of our thinking, feeling, and willing life, however offensive this may sound to older philosophers. (*GS* 354)

Of course, by "consciousness" here Nietzsche does not mean simple "awareness" but rather self-consciousness, a reflective "mirror." Such consciousness is not the opposite of instinct, but rather an epiphenomenal *expression* of instincts; even the reflective thinking of a philosopher "is secretly guided and forced into certain channels by his instincts" (*BGE* 3).

Since consciousness seems to arise in *internal* self-reflection, the traditional emphasis on consciousness has gone hand in hand with doctrines of atomic individualism, which hold self-identity to be independent of social relations. For Nietzsche, in contrast, consciousness itself is a social construction, a function of language understood as *communicative* practice, a *common* apprehension of signs.

> Consciousness is really only a net of communication [*Verbindungsnetz*] between human beings; it is only as such that it had to develop; a solitary human being who lived like a beast of prey would not have needed it ...
>
> In brief, the development of language and the development of consciousness ... go hand in hand ... The emergence of our sense impressions into our consciousness, the ability to fix them and, as it were, exhibit them externally, increased proportionately with the need to communicate them to *others* by means of signs. The human being inventing signs is at the same time the

human being who becomes ever more keenly conscious of himself. It was only as a social animal that man acquired self-consciousness. (*GS* 354)[7]

If Nietzsche is right, then even *self*-consciousness, understood as a kind of internal representation or dialogue, is a function of social relations and the traffic in signs. Accordingly, self-knowledge is not the philosophical primitive it is often taken to be, but is only a function of the internalization of socio-linguistic signs that operate by fixing experience into stable and common forms.

Thus it is impossible to grasp one's "individual" self in self-reflection, because the *instruments* of reflection are constituted by the *omission* of what is unique in experience.

[G]iven the best will in the world to understand ourselves as individually as possible, "to know ourselves," each of us will always succeed in becoming conscious only of what is not individual but "average."... Fundamentally, all our actions are altogether incomparably personal, unique, and infinitely individual; there is no doubt of that. But as soon as we translate them into consciousness *they no longer seem to be*. (*GS* 354)

For Nietzsche, individualism is disrupted by the fact that most of what we recognize as human is a *social* phenomenon. Nevertheless, we cannot ultimately *reduce* human nature to conscious linguistic and conceptual categories, because there is an element of non-conscious experience – the "personal, unique, and infinitely individual" – that eludes these structures.

Nietzsche's thesis concerning language and consciousness raises a number of questions. How far does the conjunction of self-consciousness and socially based language extend? Is selfhood nothing more than a linguistic-communal phenomenon? Is language nothing more than a network of common signs that averages out experience? If that is so, how are the creative departures from the norm possible that seem to be presupposed by Nietzsche's endorsement of creative types, and thus creative language?

The puzzling relation between consciousness, language, and selfhood is a focused version of a central theme in Nietzsche's philosophy: the idea that knowledge is nothing but the way that becoming is "fixed" by language and grammar. For instance:

Our usual imprecise mode of observation takes a group of phenomena as one and calls it a fact: between this fact and another fact it imagines in addition an empty space, it *isolates* every fact. In reality, however, all our doing and knowing is not a succession of facts and empty spaces but a continuous flux ... The word and the concept are the most manifest ground for our belief in this isolation of groups of actions. (*WS* 11)

Knowledge appears to be an "error" – instigated by language – when measured against life-forces that precede such formation. In *The Gay Science* (355), right after the section on the communal function of language, Nietzsche claims that knowledge originates in reducing the unfamiliar to the familiar, a reduction based on *fear* of the strangeness of experience. Yet Nietzsche often insists that "errors" such as these are necessary for human functioning and survival. Indeed, to identify them as errors is not an objection to them (*BGE* 4). Nietzsche calls the communal character of words "the most powerful of all powers" because of its life-serving value (*BGE* 268); indeed, after outlining the prejudices of language, Nietzsche adds: "we think *only* in the form of language ... we cease to think when we refuse to do so under the constraint of language" (*WP* 522). The linguistic order of thinking is "a scheme that we cannot throw off." A comparable claim is given in a published work: "we have at any moment only the thought for which we have the words at hand" (*D* 257).

Selfhood, too, appears to be a function of such "fixing" (*GS* 354); individual self-awareness has no privileged status. It may be, then, that individuality in the existential sense is not completely graspable, but perhaps it is thinkable as a negative trace, as something *relative* to consciousness and language in terms of what is *not* discernible in words and self-awareness. We might gain traction in this matter by returning to the question broached earlier: How is creativity thinkable in the light of the communal function of language?

Consider this aside in the passage we have been considering: after a long duration of the communicative practices of language, "the ultimate result is an excess of this strength and art of communication – as it were, a capacity that has gradually been accumulated and now waits for an heir who might squander it" (*GS* 354). Artists and writers are said to belong among such heirs and squanderers. Perhaps creative language is such squandering; and indeed, the idea of squandering seems to fit claims Nietzsche sometimes makes about artistic creativity being a non-voluntary compulsion arising from an over-flowing surplus of energy (e.g., *BGE* 213; *Z* I, 22). Yet the question remains: How can language be truly creative if it is bound by common forms and effects? The answer turns on what Nietzsche means by creativity.

We have already seen that for Nietzsche the existence of the norm is essential for the maintenance of human culture, but it turns out that it is necessary for, and intrinsic to, creativity itself. The freedom of the creative type does not do away with structures and constraint; it requires them as the basis for shaping new ones (see *WS* 122). Creativity is a complicated relationship between openness and form. Certain "fetters" (*Fesseln*) are required both to establish the cultural overcoming of purely natural states (*HATH* I, 221) and to provide a comprehensible shape to new cultural forms (*WS* 140). Creative freedom, therefore, is not the opposite of normalization, discipline, or constraint; it is a disruption of structure that yet needs structure both to prepare and to consummate departures from the norm (see *GS* 295 and *BGE* 188). For Nietzsche, creativity is a kind of "dancing in chains" (*WS* 140). It is, as he says elsewhere, an individual *interpretation* of inherited schemes of language (*WP* 767). Expressing admiration for Greek poetry's deployment of conventions, Nietzsche questions "the modern rage for originality" (*WS* 122, 127), and in *Will to Power* (809) he talks of the aesthetic state as "the source of languages," as a "superabundance of means of communication," and as "the high point of communication and transmission between living creatures." Furthermore, "every mature art has a host of conventions as its basis – insofar as it is a language. Convention is the condition of great art, *not* an obstacle."

Creative language, therefore, is not the opposite of common meanings and communication, although it will disrupt and alter ordinary familiarity. Similarly, since the original fuel for creativity is not the conscious self but a dynamic of subliminal, sub-linguistic drives and instincts, the idea of a "creative individual" can be understood only in a performative sense, through the contrast between innovation and established patterns. This is why Nietzsche calls the free spirit a "relative concept," rather than some discrete identity (*HATH* 225). Although *The Gay Science* (354) seems to render individuality inaccessible to self-awareness and language, the choice is not really between an unspeakable uniqueness on the one hand and communal speech on the other. Creativity must manifest itself in communicative language, and what is individual is both drawn from subliminal drives and indicated in its effects relative to the norm. Moreover, the performative and relative character of the creative individual would be consonant with Nietzsche's insistence that there is no "doer" behind the deed, that the deed is all there is (*GM* I, 13).[8]

The idea that creativity is not a function of individual consciousness is often expressed in Nietzsche's work. For instance, we hear that creativity precedes individuality, since "the individual is itself just the most recent creation" (*Z* I, 15). And *Will to Power* (289) offers the stark claim that "all perfect acts are unconscious." In *Beyond Good and Evil* (17) we are told that "a thought comes when 'it' wishes, and not when 'I' wish." There are two senses of "unconscious" operating in Nietzsche's analysis – a *depth* sense and a *surface* sense. The depth sense refers to instinctive drives and life forces that are not available to awareness; the surface sense refers to spontaneous, non-reflective activity, behavior, and cultural functions. Since Nietzsche holds that thinking is among the activities that can operate without being "mirrored" in consciousness, and since thinking is grounded in language, we can talk of non-reflective language as well. This would help to explain various texts in which Nietzsche talks about an *immediacy* in artistic language or thought processes – in other words, a direct disclosure not only without reflection but without *any* intercession beyond its self-presentation.

In *The Birth of Tragedy*, Nietzsche describes the immediate disclosive effects of tragic poetry on the audience, which is so direct that it is not even "symbolic" or "fictional" (see *BT* 7, 8, 21), and in certain later discussions he reiterates this sense of poetic immediacy. In *Will to Power* (811), artists are described as intoxicated with an overwhelming force of extreme sensuous acuity, which produces a "contagious" compulsion to discharge images that are "immediately enacted" in bodily energies: "An image, rising up within, immediately turns into a movement of the limbs." *The Gay Science* (84) likewise discusses the origin of poetry in discharges of rhythmic force that compel both body and soul toward disclosive effects. And in *Ecce Homo*, Nietzsche tells of how *Zarathustra* and eternal recurrence "came to" him in August 1881, as a quasi-prophetic inspiration that "invaded" and "overtook" him, an involuntary necessity that made him feel like a mere "mouthpiece," and where image, parable, and reality seemed indistinguishable (*EH* III; *Z*, 1).

Immediacy of experience is something that Nietzsche frequently invokes to counter the primacy of self-consciousness in modern philosophy, the domain of "this entirely dismal thing called reflection" (*GM* II, 3). Reflection is dismal because it displaces what Nietzsche thinks are the healthy, instinctive, and spontaneous energies in life. Yet we cannot say that Nietzsche utterly dismisses reflection. Philosophy is impossible without some degree of reflection, and Nietzsche always considered himself a philosopher. The tension in Nietzsche's thinking here partially accounts for his non-traditional philosophical style and the elusive character of his thinking, for philosophy has typically not only reflected *on* experience but has sought to *govern* experience and thought through reflective criteria. Nietzsche, in contrast, pursues the essentially ambiguous task of reflecting upon that which precedes and always eludes reflection – in a word, *life* – while allowing it to speak in its own terms. It is this ambiguity that sounds in the perplexing opening line of the *Genealogy*: "We are unknown to ourselves, we knowers, even to ourselves, and with good reason" (*GM* P, 1). Nietzsche's thought is sometimes classified as a form of "philosophy of life" (*Lebensphilosophie*), and this is correct as far as it goes. Yet Nietzsche seems unique in recognizing and sustaining the fundamental enigma in thinking about life. A philosopher, as a living being, is something like a dog chasing its own tail. If selfhood is taken to be some "what" that lies behind our "becoming what we are," then Nietzsche's communicative practices aim to talk us out of selfhood. In this light another puzzling remark in *Ecce Homo* might make more sense: "To become what one is, presupposes that one not have the faintest notion *what* one is" (*EH* II, 9).

7.4 SELFHOOD AND MEANING

As we noted, some versions of existentialism gather the question of meaning on the other side of objectivity, in subjectivity or consciousness. For Nietzsche, however, meaning – as an antidote to nihilism – is to be found in overcoming all such self-centered constructions that look for meaning in human interests alone. Any meaning that can stand up to the realities of our situation must incorporate the *limits* that the human individual encounters in the larger economy of *life*. It is from this perspective that we should approach the significance of Nietzsche's notorious *Übermensch*, which figures prominently in *Thus Spoke Zarathustra*. The *Übermensch* should not be taken as the promise of a higher, progressive type of human being – an association that Nietzsche repudiates (*EH* III, 1) – but as a more anonymous, structural concept that prepares the possibility of life-affirmation. When the figure is first announced (*Z* P, 3), it is connected with the "overcoming" (*Überwinden*) of the human, and it is directly named *der Sinn der Erde*, "the meaning of the earth"; that is, it is not someone who affirms the meaning of the earth but the meaning itself. In fact, Zarathustra says that human existence so far is "*unheimlich* and still without meaning." The *Übermensch* will "teach humans the meaning of their existence" (*Z* P, 7); it calls us to remain "faithful to the earth" (*Z* P, 3). This clearly fits with Nietzsche's naturalistic alternative to otherworldly doctrines, his affirmation of finite, earthly conditions. Such affirmation requires that we "get over" humanity (*überwinden* can mean getting over something, like a cold), that we "recover" from the polar opposition of "human" and "world" that has traditionally fostered self-serving conceptual illusions and attempts to rescue us from finitude.

> *Man*! What is the vanity of the vainest man compared with the vanity possessed by the most modest who, in the midst of nature and the world, feels himself as "Man"! (*WS* 304)

Nietzsche directly calls into question the dyadic human–world distinction (*GS* 346), and the various "crossing" motifs in *Zarathustra* (*über* can mean "across") suggest that *Übermensch* names a break with the past that will integrate humanity with the limits of natural earthly life. *Übermensch*, therefore, is better understood as a structural model for a new way of *experiencing* the world than as a new type of person or entity. It suggests what I would call "world-experience," by which I mean a kind of experience of meaning that is no longer "fixed" either in the human subject or in objects independent of human meanings. World-experience is, rather, a fluid circulation of intersecting forces that undermines *any* locus of fixed identity, either in "us" or in "reality." Evidence for this idea of world-experience can be found in a notebook entry that also touches on Nietzsche's critique of the individual: "*Stop feeling like such a fantastic ego*! Learn to throw off, step by step, *your alleged individuality*! ... Go beyond 'me' and 'you'! *Experience cosmically*!" (*KSA* IX, p. 443).

How can we characterize world-experience? I think a helpful analogy can be found in creative, artistic experience, which Nietzsche, as we have seen, insists is not grounded in the conscious self but in a *process* that is wider and deeper than conscious intention and reflection. For Nietzsche, creative activity is *übermenschlich* in being a *release* into creative powers that reach beyond our normal conscious experience of evident "things." In a notebook passage Nietzsche associates the *Übermensch* with an activity that exceeds ordinary human experience. He speaks of a counter-movement to the average man, a "luxurious surplus [*Luxus-Überschusses*] of mankind," where a "stronger way [*Art*], a higher type [*Typus*] steps into the light, which possesses different conditions of origin and maintenance than the average man. My concept, my *parable* for this type is, as one knows, the word '*Übermensch*'" (*KSA* XII, p. 462).

7.5 SELFHOOD AND PHILOSOPHICAL STYLE

As we noted earlier, Nietzsche rejects the notion that philosophy is an impersonal pursuit of knowledge; even the most "objective" philosophical style conceals a "personal confession," an "unconscious memoir." A philosopher's thought bears "decisive witness to *who he is*" (*BGE* 6). In considering a philosophical claim, one should ask: "what does such a claim tell us about the man who makes it?" (*BGE* 187). Philosophy can never be separated from existential interests, and so "disinterested knowledge" is a fiction (*BGE* 207; *GM* III, 12, 26). Perspectives of value are more fundamental than objectivity or certainty. There is no being-in-itself, only "grades of appearance measured by the strength of *interest* we show in an appearance" (*WP* 588). If all this is so, then in assessing a philosophy the standard of demonstrable knowledge should be exchanged for the more open concept of "interpretation" (*GS* 374). Interpretation is the "introduction of meaning [*Sinn-hineinlegen*]" and not "explanation" (*KSA* XII, p. 100).[9] Moreover, as we saw in considering Nietzsche's perspectivism, philosophy in this sense includes the necessity of conflicting interpretations – a point that should be kept in mind when Nietzsche is accused of embracing contradictory positions across different texts, or even within the same text. Assuming that Nietzsche knew what he was doing, we can say that such passages enact his warning against oppositional thinking by deliberately disturbing a fixed position through the insertion of a counter-position. Moreover, his hyperbolic attacks can be seen as a rhetorical strategy to unsettle thinking and reveal possibilities otherwise concealed by commonplace assumptions.

In considering the history of thought, what initially stands out is the unresolved character of basic questions, the endurance of critique and counter-critique. This suggests that there may be limits to our ability to provide definitive answers to our deepest intellectual questions. Rather than give up on such questions or resort to mystical, transcendent, even relativistic solutions, Nietzsche focuses on philosophy as an embodied expression of psychological forces. Critical assessment of the philosophy that emerges from such a focus would no longer turn on cognitive tests ("How can you prove X?") but on psychological explorations and probes ("Why is X *important* to you?"). If, for Nietzsche, all philosophy is value-laden and cannot be encapsulated in descriptive, objective terms amenable to logical demonstration, that will hold of his own as well – a point of which he is quite aware: "What have I to do with refutations!" (*GM* P, 4). Nietzsche often indicates that philosophy – including his own textual work – is a circulation of writing and reading that stems from, and taps into, personal forces and dispositions toward life. Indeed, the question of philosophical style may be connected with the limits of conscious language previously discussed. Nietzsche calls (good) style "the actual communication of an inner state" (*EH* II, 4), which effectively enacts signs, tempo, rhythm, and gesture to render an inner state accessible to an audience, perhaps a selective one. Can "inner state" here refer to that which escapes the "common signs" of language in *The Gay Science* (354)?

None of this means that philosophy is nothing more than personal expression, even though the first-person singular appears so often in Nietzsche's texts. For one thing, Nietzsche deploys the "we" as much as the "I." Moreover, this prevalence of the "I" and the "we" also implies a pervasive second-person perspective, that of "you" the reader. Hence, to fully appreciate Nietzsche's texts we must engage them in their addressive function; our own response is inseparable from their meaning. Nietzsche's stylistic choices – hyperbole, provocation, allusions, metaphors, aphorisms, literary forms, and historical narratives not confined to demonstrable facts or theories – show that he presumed a reader's involvement in bringing sense to a text, even to the extent of exploring beyond or thinking against it. Nietzsche's books do not advance "doctrines" as a one-way transmission of finished thoughts. He assumes readers who are active, not simply reactive; they must think for themselves (*EH* II, 8). Aphorisms require an "art of interpretation" on the part of readers (*GM* P, 8); Nietzsche wants to be read "with doors left open" (*D* P, 5). However, such openness does not mean that Nietzsche's texts are nothing but occasions for interpretive free-association either. Nietzsche's *own* voice and positions are central to his writings, and he takes forceful stands on philosophical questions. Yet he did not write as – and did not want to be read as – a typical philosopher constructing arguments in pursuit of "objective truth." Whatever truth turns out to mean in Nietzsche's philosophy, it cannot be a strictly objective or logical enterprise, because truth must be *alive* in writers and readers.[10]

Nietzsche's styles of writing comport with similar techniques practiced by many other existentialist writers who aim to challenge purely objectivist or universalist assumptions about philosophical thought. At the same time, it is important to remember that Nietzsche's conception of philosophy and writing cannot be reduced to "self-creation." He describes the higher philosopher as "the man of the most comprehensive responsibility who has the conscience for the overall development of mankind" (*BGE* 61). He even calls genuine philosophers "commanders and legislators" (*BGE* 211). Even when creative individuals break away from the social conventions of their time, they carry the seeds of future "spiritual colonization" (*GS* 23). Throughout his writings, Nietzsche was always a philosopher of culture (see *TI* 8, 4). Even though self-creation is a necessary condition for innovative thinking, for Nietzsche the ultimate aim of creativity must be culture-creation and new outlooks that will enhance human existence as a whole.

NOTES

1. Cited numbers refer to text sections, except in the case of *KSA*. I have occasionally modified published translations.

A	*The Antichrist*
BGE	*Beyond Good and Evil*
BT	*The Birth of Tragedy*
D	*Daybreak*
EH	*Ecce Homo.* The four main chapters are indicated by roman numerals, with book titles in chapter III abbreviated accordingly.
GM	*On the Genealogy of Morality*
GS	*The Gay Science*
HATH	*Human, All Too Human*
KSA	*Sämtliche Werke: Kritische Studienausgabe*
TI	*Twilight of the Idols.* The chapters are numbered in sequence by arabic numerals.
UDH	*On the Uses and Disadvantages of History for Life*
UM	*Untimely Meditations*
WP	*The Will to Power*
WS	*The Wanderer and His Shadow,* Part II of *Human, All Too Human.*
Z	*Thus Spoke Zarathustra.* The four parts are indicated by roman numerals, the sections by arabic numerals according to Kaufmann's listing on pp. 112–14.

2. I borrow the term "crossing" from Sallis, *Crossings.*
3. See Richardson, "Nietzsche's Power Ontology," which nicely shows how will to power is a comprehensive concept, rather than limited in scope as some scholars maintain.
4. See Hatab, *A Nietzschean Defense of Democracy,* ch. 2.
5. See Reginster, *The Affirmation of Life.* On eternal recurrence, see Hatab, *Nietzsche's Life Sentence.*
6. See Soll, "Attitudes toward Life." Reading Nietzsche is more like being "propositioned" by a seducer. He even says that philosophy is more seduction than argument (*D* 330).
7. A similar point is made in a later work, *TI* 9, 26. Something like Nietzsche's account of consciousness and language can be supported by findings in developmental psychology. The notion of "inner speech" or "private speech" – self-directed verbalization – can account for *how* language is implicated in self-consciousness. Research shows that inner speech is the most important factor in the development of self-awareness, the capacity to become the object of one's own attention, one's own thoughts and behaviors. On this see Morin, "Possible Links between Self-Awareness and Inner Speech." A kind of "distance" between the observer and the observed is required for the self-awareness *of* observation. Inner speech provides this kind of distance. It is important to stress that such a development is derived from the original *social* milieu of language, so that self-awareness arises from the reproduction of social mechanisms by way of self-directed language. Private speech in young children (talking to oneself in task

performance) is essential for the cognitive and behavioral development of the child, because here the child takes over the regulative role of the social world. On this see Winsler *et al.*, "The Role of Private Speech." Language begins as collaborative tasking and conversation; private speech is a redirection of this milieu toward independent functioning. Cognitive and behavioral capacities begin in a social-linguistic network, and private speech begins a process that over time leads to the *internalization* of these capacities that now can operate "silently," as it were. In sum, mature development, individuation, and self-consciousness are the result of an internalization of the social-linguistic environment, mediated by inner or private speech. Such research lends credence to Nietzsche's analysis, although the language-consciousness conjunction in his account raises more radical philosophical questions about the very nature of human selfhood and the meaning of individuation.

8. While culture-creation disrupts established forms of life, it is meant to settle into *new* forms of culture. In this respect we should consider Nietzsche's recognition of "second nature," which he calls a "new habit, a new instinct" that coalesces after a "first nature" of cultural inheritance has been altered or replaced – keeping in mind that the first nature in question was once a second nature replacing a first nature, and that this new second nature will become a first nature that will face disruption in the future after its own settlement (*UM*: *UDH* 3).
9. For more on this question of interpretation see Schrift, *Nietzsche and the Question of Interpretation*; see also Cox, *Nietzsche: Naturalism and Interpretation.*
10. An excellent study in this respect is D. Allison, *Reading the New Nietzsche.* Other significant works that stress the importance of existential effects rather than mere propositional knowledge are Nehamas, *Nietzsche: Life as Literature*, and Janaway, *Beyond Selflessness.*

WILLIAM BLATTNER

8 Heidegger: the existential analytic of Dasein

8.1 HEIDEGGER'S ONTOLOGY IN *BEING AND TIME*

On page 67 of *Being and Time* Heidegger writes, "The 'essence' of Dasein lies in its existence."[1] This formula was the inspiration for Jean-Paul Sartre's better known thesis that "existence precedes essence."[2] What can it mean to say that our "essence" lies in our existence, and why does Heidegger put "essence" in quotation marks? We may assume that by the latter device Heidegger means to indicate that the sense in which Dasein has an essence is rather different from the sense in which non-human things have essences, or perhaps even that Dasein does not really have an essence at all. In the preceding paragraph he writes,

> The "essence" of this entity lies in its to-be [*Zu-sein*]. Its being-what-it-is (*essentia*) must, so far as we can speak of it at all, be conceived in terms of its being (*existentia*). (*BT*, p. 67; H, p. 42)

The phrase "to-be" is more gerundive than gerund; it expresses the idea that we have our being to be, as we may have tasks to do or miles to walk.[3] Our essence, our "what-we-are" (or better, "who-we-are"), is determined by how we live, and how we live is structured by how we are *called upon* to live. Called upon by whom or what? By ourselves. (We shall explore this thought later.) In the paragraph in which Heidegger makes this statement he infers from it that Dasein is not an entity "present-at-hand."

Concretely speaking, what can it mean to say that how we live determines who we are, our "essence"? It means at least that no essence, nature, or concept that logically precedes the concrete life we lead determines who we are. In his *Existentialism is a Humanism*, Sartre contrasts being human with being a paper-cutter.

The paper-cutter has an essence, or ideal model, which the manufacturer realizes in the process of production. If we think of God the creator as a master artisan, then we can think of him as realizing or actualizing ideal models of types of entity in his act of creation, so that cats realize the essence felinity and human beings the essence humanity. This way of interpreting the traditional conception of essence is derived from Heidegger's phenomenological reconstruction of ancient Greek metaphysics, in which he construes the *eidos* or nature of a thing as the ideal image of the thing that is "seen in advance" by the artisan and which guides her act of production.[4] We need not consider whether this is an accurate interpretation of ancient Greek metaphysics, for with the rise of modern natural science the understanding of nature shifted away from essences in the classical sense and towards the notion of law-governedness. Nature is a domain of entities governed by precise and exceptionless laws. José Ortega y Gasset quotes the seventeenth-century scientist and philosopher Robert Boyle, *via* Ernst Cassirer, thus: "*natura* is the rule or system of rules according to which phenomena behave – in short, their law."[5] This vision of nature reaches its apex in Kant's *Critique of Pure Reason* in 1781. With this shift the nature of a thing is reconceived as the set of laws that explain its features and behavior, which is very close to what John Locke meant by a "real" in contrast to a "nominal" essence.[6]

To say, then, that our essence lies in our existence implies that we have no essence independently of how we as a matter of fact live our lives. No set of scientific laws explains how we live. Concretely speaking, what does this mean? Ortega y Gasset writes, "Man is an infinitely plastic entity of which one may make what one will, precisely because of itself it is nothing save only the mere potentiality to be 'as you like.'"[7] That is, there are no limits to what we may be (we are "infinitely plastic"), and we have unfettered voluntary control over this infinite plasticity (we may be "whatever we like"). This cannot be correct, however. Let me first explain why and then show how Heidegger avoids this extreme conception of freedom.

I may dream of being a naturalist and explorer (like Meriwether Lewis), or of being a professional baseball player, or of being a Swabian, but I am not able to be any of those things. I cannot be a naturalist and explorer, because that role or niche no longer exists. I cannot be a professional baseball player, because I do not have the requisite physical attributes. I cannot be a Swabian, because I was born and reared in California. That is to say, then, that world-history, physical attributes, and personal history all limit what I can be.[8] So, it is clearly incorrect to say that we are "infinitely plastic."

Heidegger insists upon the two forms of historical limitation by way of his concept of thrownness: Dasein is "delivered over to" its "There"; its being is "factical." "Factical" is a term that Heidegger develops as a contrast to "factual." Factuality is the way in which things are determinate, have definite features. Facticity is the way in which Dasein is determinate and has definite features. Dasein is determinate insofar as it has been delivered over to a situation or thrown into it. We are thrown into our history, both world-history and personal biography, as well as thrown into our communities and language(s). These phenomena capture the sense in which, at any moment of our lives, we are already someone in particular. We cannot be "as we like" but are restricted in the range of possibilities that are available to us by our history.

How about physical attributes? Does Heidegger acknowledge their role in limiting our "plasticity"? The answer here is more complicated. When he distinguishes facticity and factuality in para. 12 he writes,

> for even entities which are not worldless – Dasein itself, for example – are present-at-hand "in" the world, or, more exactly *can* with some right and within certain limits be *taken* as merely present-at-hand. To do this, one must completely disregard or just not see the existential constitution of being-in. But the fact that "Dasein" can be taken as something which is present-at-hand and just present-at-hand, is not to be confused with a certain way of "presence-at-hand" which is Dasein's *own*. This latter kind of presence-at-hand becomes accessible not by disregarding Dasein's specific structures but only by understanding them in advance. (*BT*, p. 82; H, pp. 55–56)

Heidegger thus asserts that it is possible to "take" Dasein as merely present-at-hand by ignoring its "existential constitution," that is, its self-understanding and all that attends the latter. If we do not ignore Dasein's existential constitution, but rather attempt to describe its "own" form of "presence-at-hand," what are we describing? Heidegger may mean to assert that there is an entirely disjoint set of features that Dasein has, when considered properly, or he may intend to suggest that those features of Dasein that one may be *tempted* to treat as present-at-hand actually have a complex ontological status that involves taking them up into Dasein's existential constitution.

For an example of the latter sort of pattern we may look at Heidegger's treatment of demise and perishing in II.I. "Perishing" is the term he uses for the ending of the life of any living organism (*BT*, p. 284; H, pp. 240–41). It is clear that human beings, as living organisms, suffer perishing. Heidegger adds:

> Dasein too "has" its death, of the kind appropriate to anything that lives; and it has it, not in ontical isolation, but as codetermined by its originary kind of being ... We designate this intermediate phenomenon as its *demise*. (*BT*, p. 291; H, p. 247)

When we die, it is not simply that the life-functions of our body cease; rather, our projects are left unfulfilled, our goals have been achieved (or not), we leave grief in our wake, etc. Our *lives*, not just our organic functioning, end. We may transfer this model of ontological co-determination from perishing/demise onto other physical features of human life. We do not just have hair of some physical color, but are blondes or brunettes or redheads; we are not just of some objective height, but are tall or short; we have stature. We do not just have a biological sex,[9] but are masculine, feminine, transgender, gender-ambiguous, and so on. We do not normally encounter our biological features in brutely physical form, but rather as expressed in an existentially co-constituted way. Further, existentially co-constituted physical features are not reducible to brute physical characteristics. It is not even clear that the existential features always have *necessary* brute physical bases, as for example when a transgender individual is entirely accepted as a person of the target gender. From the preceding considerations we may conclude that Dasein's factical determinations (gender, stature, etc.) are not identical with its factual determinations (biological sex, objective height, etc.).

We can formulate this line of thought succinctly thus: who one is in each case is a person, not just a body. There are two ways to look at this idea, *metaphysically* and *ontologically*. Construing the thesis metaphysically, and recurring to the modern conception of nature, we might argue that our biological constitution does not scientifically explain our factical determinations. This is more than simply to say that the fact that Kiefer Sutherland is 5 ft. 8½ in. tall does not of itself entail that he is of short stature – after all, every year he saves the United States from a terrorist catastrophe! Physical height and personal stature can fail to be identical, even though the latter is scientifically explained by a larger ensemble of physical determinations, including presumably one's physical height. So, to take Heidegger's thesis metaphysically is to argue that Dasein's factical determinations are not explainable scientifically in terms of its biological and material constitution.

This thesis has overtones of the more traditional mind–body debate. Once philosophers abandoned the simplest form of identity theory (a one-to-one correspondence of mental state types with neural firing types), they began to experiment with more holistic mind–body identity theories. So, for example, perhaps my stature at a time is explained by the total state of my body at a time, including my nervous system. This suggestion does not seem very plausible, however, since my stature is surely not a fact (or as Heidegger would say, a "Fact"[10]) merely about me or dependent solely upon aspects of my life in isolation. Rather, my stature is surely a *socially constituted* Fact. I cannot have stature all on my own, but only in a social context in which height matters, for example.

Let me pause for a paragraph to note that this last observation draws in another important theme in Heidegger's existential analytic of Dasein: "The world of Dasein is a *with-world*. Being-in is *being-with* others. Their being-in-themselves within-the-world is *Dasein-with*" (*BT*, pp. 154–55; H, p. 118). Heidegger maintains that Dasein is an essentially social creature. It is true, of course, that one may find oneself at any given time entirely alone, in the sense of having no companionship, no neighbors, and no friends. However, "Being-with is an existential characteristic of Dasein even though no other is present-at-hand or perceived" (*BT*, p. 156; H, p. 120). That is, to lack companionship, for example, is a deficient manner of sharing a world with others. Such a condition is a lack, and is generally felt to be such by those who suffer it, because we are essentially social creatures. One might object that some people are, after all, anti-social, but being anti-social is a way of sharing a world, "sharing" not in the sense in which a preschool will teach children to share their toys, but rather in the sense in which one is in a world with others even if one rejects them. An entirely *asocial* life is rather hard to imagine. For one thing, an *entirely* asocial life would have to be one without language, for to speak a language is among other things to conform to a set of standards of word-usage that are monitored and regulated by one's language-community.

Returning now to metaphysics: given that stature is a socially constituted Fact, it cannot be explained solely by the total state of one's body. One might argue, however, that all this shows is that one's stature is explained scientifically by the complete state of bodies belonging to one's community (including their nervous systems). So, it seems that at every turn the attempt to flesh out the idea that we are persons rather than bodies *metaphysically* runs into a further layer of imaginable scientific explanation that might undercut the thesis. It is noteworthy that Heidegger makes no attempt to defend the idea in this form. His interest is *ontological*, rather than metaphysical. Let me spell out some details of the ontological position Heidegger adopts and then only afterwards make some comments on the distinction in play here between metaphysics and ontology.

Recall that back at the very beginning of this chapter we briefly encountered Heidegger's notion that "The 'essence' of this entity lies in its to-be [*Zu-sein*]" (*BT*, p. 67; H, p. 42). The "to-be" in this formula, I noted, is not the infinitive "to be" (*Sein*), but rather the gerundive "to be" (*Zu-sein*). In what sense is Dasein defined by a gerundive? Heidegger uses a number of different turns of phrase to convey his idea: we are *delivered over* (*überantwortet*) to our being; our being *is an issue* for us or concerns us (*darum geht es uns*).

In I.5, para. 29, "Being there as Disposedness,"[11] Heidegger explains:

> In attunedness,[12] Dasein is always disclosed attunedly as *that* entity to which it has been delivered over in its being; and in this way it has been delivered over to the being which, in existing, it has to-be. (*BT*, p. 173; H, p. 134)

Attunement discloses to us our "that we are and have to-be," and it does this by revealing things within-the-world, others, and our own lives as mattering in determinate respects. In the extended example of an attunement that Heidegger offers, fear, he indicates that among the essential functions of fear is to reveal some entity as fearsome, as threatening us or something important to us.[13] He analyzes fear as having three components – that "in the face of which one fears" (the object), that "about which one fears," and "the fearing itself" – and this tripartite structure is meant to be a constitutive structure of attunement in general. My interest here is the about-which, concerning which Heidegger writes:

> *That which* fear fears *about* is that very entity which is afraid – Dasein. Only an entity for which in its being this very being is an issue, can be afraid. Fearing discloses this entity as endangered and abandoned to itself. (*BT*, p. 180; H, p. 141)

This is to say that one cannot fear unless one's being matters to one, is an issue for one. If one were utterly indifferent to one's well-being, one might notice a threat, in the sense that one would note an entity or process which, if left to its own course, might compromise one's life or physical integrity. That sterile threat, however, would not *matter* to one, and thus one would not experience the *affect* of fear.[14]

Another way to put Heidegger's point would be to say that our own being always *has a claim on us, makes a demand of us*. To be a person is to respond to the normative pull of that for the sake of which one leads one's life. He introduces the conception of the for-the-sake-of-which in chapter 3 of Division I, para. 18 (*BT*, p. 116; H, p. 84).

> Why does the understanding – whatever may be the essential dimensions of that which can be disclosed in it – always press forward into possibilities? It is because the understanding has in itself the existential structure which we call *projection*. With equal primordiality the understanding projects Dasein's being both upon its for-the-sake-of-which and upon significance, as the worldhood of its current world. (*BT*, pp. 184–85; H, p. 145)

By "possibilities" Heidegger means ways that Dasein can be or live, and these "ways of living" embody self-understandings. I press forward into my career as a teacher, into my role as a father to my sons, etc. These possibilities are those for the sake of which I do what I do, my for-the-sakes-of-which. To describe these particular for-the-sakes-of-which as a "career" and a "role" is potentially misleading, since "the 'for-the-sake-of' always pertains to the being of *Dasein*, for which, in its being, that very being is at *issue*" (*BT*, pp. 116–17; H, p. 84). That is, I *am* a teacher and I *am* a father, and it is for the sake of *being* those things that I do what I do. Put more plainly, my daily activity is organized in terms of and makes sense as an attempt to *be* a father and a teacher, among other things. These possibilities or self-understandings constitute the *point* of my daily activity, serve as the aims of my living.

So, to describe Dasein as a person, rather than merely as a body, is to characterize it in this normative language of aims or purposes, of for-the-sakes-of-which. Heidegger identifies such normative description of Dasein as one of the ways we may "consider" Dasein, in contrast with considering Dasein as something factual, e.g., as a body. Now, if this is merely a way we may *consider* Dasein, does that mean that Dasein is not "really" an entity that is defined or constituted by its for-the-sakes-of-which? The premise of this question is a pre-Kantian assumption about the nature of ontology. Let me explain.

Traditional metaphysics took as its goal to discover the necessary structure or inherent nature of things. Two examples of such metaphysical ambition are the attempt to prove (or disprove) the existence of God, and the attempt to determine whether material objects are infinitely divisible or resolve into indivisible "atoms" of matter. To probe such questions and develop answers to them, traditional metaphysics sought to establish that reason itself – or perhaps our concepts themselves – requires or entails, e.g., that God exists or that matter is infinitely divisible. That is to say, then, that traditional metaphysics sought to infer results about the constitution of things from the limits of what we can conceive or from the rules of the power of rationality we must employ.

In his *Critique of Pure Reason* Immanuel Kant asked by what presumption we may assume that the world conforms itself to the constraints of our concepts or our faculty of reason. He argued that we are not in a position to make pronouncements on the constitution of things as they are "in themselves" or independently of our power of representing or understanding them, unless we can first establish that things *must* conform to our ability to understand them (our faculty of understanding). There is no way to do that, however. Thus, we must limit the philosophical claims we make to the way things must present themselves to our experience. Transcendental or "Critical" philosophy turns away from the inherent constitution of a transcendent world and towards the formal structure of our ability to represent objects or have a world. Heidegger calls this more modest philosophical aspiration "ontology," and it contrasts with pre-Kantian metaphysics.[15]

Thus, when Heidegger distinguishes the factical person from the factual body he is not advancing a metaphysical thesis about the identity or distinctness of two entities as they are in themselves. Rather, he is identifying two formally distinct sorts of *phenomena*. A phenomenon is *"that which shows itself in itself*, the manifest" (*BT*, p. 51; H, p. 28), and its form, as I am using the term here, is what Heidegger calls the "mode of being" of the phenomenon. We may think of the mode of being as a set of criteria that determine in each case *whether* a phenomenon of the relevant sort *is*.[16] In Descartes's ontology, to be physical (an extended thing) is to be located in space and to be mental (a thinking thing) is to be conscious. Whereas Descartes developed metaphysical arguments for the distinctness of mind (thinking things) and body (extended things), in the *Paralogisms* chapter of the *Critique of Pure Reason* Kant argued that the question of distinctness cannot be answered, hence should not be asked: the question oversteps the scope of philosophy as an analysis of the structure of objectivity. Put in Heideggerian terms, philosophy is limited to analyzing the criteria of being, whereas questions of identity and distinctness are factual questions about the inventory of entities. Thus, whether "in themselves" stature and gender are identical with, or supervene upon, some complex set of biological features is an empirical question we are not in a position to ask or answer philosophically.[17]

8.2 HEIDEGGER'S EXISTENTIALISM

The thesis that Dasein is constituted by a set of gerundive self-understandings does not merely underwrite the ontological distinction between persons and bodies. Heidegger argues that it also has implications for what he calls the "factical ideal" (*BT*, p. 358; H, p. 310) of human life to which we should be drawn. Because its "essence" lies in its existence, he argues, Dasein confronts a challenge it would not otherwise face. He calls this challenge "anxiety" and "death." It is important to note that by "death" Heidegger does *not* mean to refer to the ordinary phenomenon to which the word usually refers. He claims to be describing a more "primordial" or "originary" form of death in which the ordinary phenomenon is grounded. The same holds for his use of "guilt," as we shall see.[18]

Anxiety discloses Dasein as "uncanny" or "not at home."[19] Heidegger adds:

In anxiety what is environmentally ready-to-hand sinks away, and so, in general, do entities within-the-world. The "world" can offer nothing more, and neither can the Dasein-with of others. Anxiety thus takes away from Dasein the possibility of understanding itself, as it falls, in terms of the "world" and the way things have been publicly interpreted. (*BT*, p. 232; H, p. 187)

In anxiety Dasein is not at home in the world, because the world offers it no possibility for understanding itself. However, *only* the world can provide Dasein with the content of its self-understanding. Thus, much later in *Being and Time* Heidegger writes of resoluteness, which is the authentic disclosure of life,

In resoluteness the issue for Dasein is its ownmost ability-to-be, which, as something thrown, can project itself only upon definite factical possibilities. Resolution does not withdraw itself from "actuality," but discovers first what is factically possible; and it does so by seizing upon it in whatever way is possible for it as its ownmost ability-to-be in the Anyone. (*BT*, p. 346; H, p. 299)

So, *only* the world can provide content for Dasein's self-understanding, but in anxiety the world can offer nothing. Thus, in anxiety Dasein cannot understand itself. It is for this reason that Dasein feels uncanny or not at home in anxiety.

Understanding and disposedness are "equi-originary" (M&R: "equiprimordial"), that is, jointly necessary and mutually conditioning.

As *existentialia* disposedness and understanding characterize the originary disclosedness of being-in-the-world. By way of attunedness Dasein "sees" possibilities, in terms of which it is. In the projective disclosure of such possibilities, it is already in each case attuned. (*BT*, p. 188; H, p. 148)

To "see" a possibility – that is, to grasp it and to be able to project oneself upon it or press forward into it – Dasein must be attuned to or tuned into that possibility. Put in plainer language, to understand a possible way to be, Dasein must "care" about the possibility; the possibility must matter to Dasein. This is a general truth about

Dasein, Heidegger thinks. An attunement in which Dasein is indifferent to all of its possibilities satisfies the formal requirements of disposedness, but it neither provides any motivational force for pressing ahead into a possibility nor differentially attunes Dasein to its possibilities so that it is moved to press forward into this possibility rather than that. Indeed, Heidegger writes that in anxiety, "entities within-the-world are of so little importance in themselves that on the basis of this *insignificance* of what is within-the-world, the world in its worldhood is all that still obtrudes itself" (*BT*, p. 231; H, p. 187). So, "anxiety discloses Dasein *as being-possible*" (*BT*, p. 232; H, p. 188) because it strips Dasein of all of its ordinary entanglements in life, its ordinary commitments and self-understandings, which require being differentially attuned to the significance of what is possible. In anxiety Dasein is unable to be anyone determinate or concrete; it is only possible.

Death is precisely the condition of not being able to be: "Its death is the possibility of no-longer-being-able-to-be-there ... Death is the possibility of the simple impossibility of Dasein" (*BT*, p. 294; H, p. 250).[20] Heidegger's discussion of death in *Being and Time* is complex and somewhat meandering, as he works his way through a number of related concepts before focusing on his technical conception of death. As we saw above, Heidegger distinguishes perishing (the ending of organic life) from demise, the ending of the life of a person. Demise coincides with the perishing of Dasein as an organism, but is "co-determined" or modified by Dasein's originary kind of being, that is, by its existential constitution.[21]

Such demise is not death, however, in Heidegger's technical sense. Indeed, in a highly paradoxical passage Heidegger writes, "Death is a way to be, which Dasein takes over as soon as it is" (*BT*, p. 289; H, p. 245). Death is a *way to be*? But is it not "the possibility of the simple impossibility of Dasein"? The language implies that there is a way in which Dasein can be in which it is also impossible. How can that make sense? It makes sense if the sort of impossibility to which Heidegger refers is construed in a purely existential sense, namely, as the impossibility of self-understanding. Under what conditions would self-understanding be impossible? As we saw above, in anxiety Dasein cannot understand itself; it cannot press forward into being anyone in particular. Since it is indifferent to all possible ways of being Dasein, it is frozen by the "total insignificance of the world." Dasein experiences existential death when it suffers from anxiety. Thus, Heidegger writes, "Thrownness into death reveals itself to Dasein in a more originary and impressive manner in the disposedness of anxiety" (*BT*, p. 295; H, p. 251). This is a "purely existential" death, in contrast with demise, which is a phenomenon co-determined by Dasein's existential and biological constitutions.

Death in this technical sense has a number of identifiable features, Heidegger argues. It is ownmost, non-relational, unsurpassable, certain, and indefinite. He characterizes the *non-relationality* of death as follows: "When it stands before itself in this way, all its relations to other Dasein have been undone" (*BT*, p. 294; H, p. 250). That is, in death others cease to matter, since after all, in death everything ceases to matter. This has nothing to do with "facing one's end alone," but rather with the dissolution of one's interpersonal relations in the experience of existential death. Death's status as *ownmost* is closely related to its non-relationality, and Heidegger tends to discuss them together. Death is ownmost in a double sense. It is the only possibility of existence that one has no matter what else might be true of one, because it is a *formal* possibility of existence, not a concrete factical possibility. What is more, because in death Dasein is stripped of its factical self-understandings and its relations to others, it is "*fully* assigned to its ownmost ability-to-be" (*BT*, p. 294; H, p. 250). This means that in death one is peculiarly prepared to confront and perhaps embrace one's ability to be authentic. (We shall discuss this below.)

Death is also *unsurpassable*, or unable to be overtaken, because Dasein cannot immunize itself from death; it is always possible. That is, death is *certain* and *indefinite*. This does not mean that the probability that one's life will end is 100 percent, and it does not mean that one's life could end at any time. Those are observations appropriate to demise, not to existential death. Rather, existential death is indefinite in that it is not made possible or available by any concrete factical configuration of life. The possibility of being a parent requires biological maturation and a cultural niche for child-bearing and -rearing. Death, because it is a formal possibility of Dasein, is always possible and tied to nothing in particular. Because it is always possible, we can "hold death for true," as Heidegger reconstructs the concept of certainty on which he relies. It is possible to integrate[22] death into one's self-understanding in such a way that it suffuses everything, or as Heidegger sometimes puts it, "penetrates" deeply into one's existence. To do this is to achieve authenticity.

In what way do death and anxiety clear the way for authenticity? In death and anxiety Dasein encounters at first hand and practically (rather than merely as a philosophical insight) that it has no essence. In practice what this means is that Dasein comes to understand the vulnerability of its factical life. It is useful to note a distinction between contingency and vulnerability. By "contingency" is generally meant that our commitments, entanglements, and attunements are not grounded in some transcultural or at least defining nature of Dasein. Rather, they are simply the life one finds oneself with, the life into which one is thrown. "In anxiety, according to Heidegger, we are faced with the ultimate contingency of the [Anyone-possibilities] we pick up from the public world," writes Charles Guignon.[23] Anxiety reveals a "basic groundlessness and meaninglessness" of one's life, as Hubert Dreyfus and Jane Rubin describe it.[24] However, groundlessness or contingency is only *distressing*, as opposed to a sterile philosophical observation, if one longs for certainty or metaphysical grounding. Put a little differently, it is not at all clear why the appropriate response to groundlessness or contingency is not just a shrug of the shoulders à la Richard Rorty.[25] Heidegger seems to think that the absence of essence leads to a crisis, or at least a critical practical insight that requires facing up to anxiety and resolutely liberating oneself from the "illusions of the Anyone" (*BT*, p. 311; H, p. 266).

Vulnerability is a phenomenon that can demand of Dasein that it learn to live in a new way. Consider a commitment or passion that has taken on a dominant role in one's life: marriage, children, a career that really matters to one (what can be described in somewhat antique language as a "calling"). To experience these for-the-sakes-of-which as vulnerable or fragile[26] can be deeply unsettling. When my wife and I were married, her brother worked tirelessly that day to help set up the venue and then to clean up. When my wife thanked him, he said, "That's okay, Sis, you only get married once or twice." That isn't what one wants to hear on the day after one's wedding, but it is a commonplace of modern American life: marriages are vulnerable. It is one thing to acknowledge this intellectually or sociologically – "I recognize that my marriage might be one of the 45 percent or so of marriages in the USA that end in divorce" – and another to integrate it into the way in which I live my marriage. What could this mean?

One proposal might be that to integrate vulnerability into the way I live my marriage is to be prepared at every turn to give it up, in the sense of not taking it too seriously, not letting it penetrate into one's existence and suffuse everything one does. This is a truly odd suggestion, however. This sort of attitude makes sense for gambits and strategies: my strategy for losing weight might be a fad diet; but of course, if that doesn't work out I have to be prepared to give it up and try a different approach. It can also make sense for ambitions: one imagines that politicians who strive for high office must be aware all along that they might not succeed, and they must be prepared to give up their ambition.[27] To have such an attitude about marriage, children, and callings (as opposed to jobs) is harder to imagine and suggests, I think, an affective disorder rather than an existential achievement.[28]

A far better proposal is that to be aware of the vulnerability of one's deepest commitments and entanglements is to be prepared to *struggle* for them. To "take a friendship for granted," as we sometimes say, is to fail to attend to it and nurture it. One must attend to it and nurture it *because* it is vulnerable. Another way one might describe this, the way *Heidegger* describes it, is thus:

> *For the Anyone, however, the situation is essentially something that has been closed off.* The Anyone knows only the "*general situation*," loses itself in those "*opportunities*" which are closest to it, and pays Dasein's way by a reckoning up of "accidents" which it fails to recognize, deems its own achievement, and passes off as such. (*BT*, pp. 346–47; H, p. 300)

One might think of the general situation as an unimaginative and conformist approach to the factical situation of life, and that would be right as far as it goes. Note, however, that if one relates to one's life in such a conformist and leveled-off manner, one will specifically be out of touch with the threats to one's commitments and entanglements, threats that make them vulnerable. One will not then know when one must struggle for them.

The flip side is that living in the general situation, instead of the current factical situation, one can also fail to notice to when one is called upon to abandon existing commitments and change one's way of life. In what way would the current situation call upon one to modify or change one's commitments? According to Heidegger's analysis, we always press forward into a definite way of living on the ground of how the various options that confront us at a time matter to us. Thus, if our attunements shift, we can thereby be called upon to adjust the way we project ourselves forward into life. If instead of attending to these changes in one's attunement one heeds rather "what one says" about how one should live – the dominant interpretation of life in one's community – then one is in a sense not listening to oneself but listening rather to the Anyone or the general situation. This is the flip side of being prepared to struggle for one's commitments, because it too involves a practical acknowledgement that one's commitments and entanglements are vulnerable. To be vulnerable means, in part, that it can come to pass that they have collapsed and it is time to move on. It is important to note, however, that being prepared to move on does *not* mean not taking them seriously or regarding them as "ultimately meaningless," as Dreyfus and Rubin reconstruct Heidegger's thought. It means, rather, acknowledging their dissipation when it happens.

Thus, integrating the vulnerability of what matters into one's style of projection involves *both* being prepared to struggle for one's projects in the face of their fragility *and* being prepared to move on when they have "died." How does one know which sort of response is appropriate? There is no rule for telling. Rather:

> But on what basis does Dasein disclose itself in resoluteness? On what is it to resolve? *Only* the resolution can give the answer. One would completely misunderstand the phenomenon of resoluteness if one should want to suppose that this consists simply in taking up possibilities which have been proposed and recommended, and seizing hold of them. *The resolution is precisely the disclosive projection and determination of what is factically possible at the time.* (*BT*, p. 345; H, p. 298)

Resoluteness just is the openness to hearing what the situation is saying. To be able to see what the situation demands, rather than to be lost in the public idle talk that demands of Dasein that it live pretty much like everyone else, requires that Dasein *want* to understand what the situation requires. Heidegger calls this wanting to understand "wanting to have a conscience," which is another name for resoluteness (*BT*, p. 343; H, pp. 296–97).

Why "conscience"? Why does Heidegger use this term in this context, especially when he also insists that his interpretation of human existence is not a moralizing interpretation (*BT*, pp. 210–11; H, p. 167)? As we saw above, to understand oneself is not just to have a cognitive grasp or interpretation of one's life, but rather to be called upon to understand oneself in a definite way, to be responsive to a normative demand. This normativity is not necessarily a *moral* normativity (though there is no reason why moral norms cannot be included within its scope). It is normativity in the sense of standards: pressing forward into being a father sets standards for one's life, standards that are embodied in the ways in which possible courses of action matter to one. To be possessed of conscience in this more general – we may call it "transcendental" – sense is to be responsive to the normative demands inherent in one's for-the-sakes-of-which. Transcendental conscience discloses one as the target of norms, as the one who is called forth to understand and live up to who one is.[29]

Conscience calls us forth to our "own self," to being who we are, and resoluteness opens us to the demands of the current factical situation. Acting on the demands of conscience – that is, being resolute – thus requires a resolute (or persistent, steadfast) responsiveness to the concrete factical situation in which one lives. This situation is vulnerable, which has two implications: its normative demands require struggle, but they are also changing, which requires flexibility, the ability to change and adapt responsively to the world. For this reason, Heidegger argues, the factical ideal of "self-constancy" is not the continuity or stubbornness of either an "expressivist"[30] attachment to a true, deep, inner self, or an unbending essentialist subjugation to eternal moral laws. Rather:

> *The constancy of the self*, in the double sense of steadiness and steadfastness, is the *authentic* counter-possibility to the non-self-constancy which is characteristic of irresolute falling. Existentially, *self-constancy* signifies nothing other than anticipatory resoluteness. The ontological structure of such resoluteness reveals the existentiality of the self's selfhood. (*BT*, p. 369; H, p. 22)

"Anticipatory resoluteness" is resoluteness that has fully integrated the vulnerability of Dasein's world, commitments, entanglements, passions, and attunements into the manner in which it is resolutely open to the current factical situation.

To be open to the world in this way is to be open to one's self, for as Heidegger puts the point somewhat darkly, "Dasein *is* its world existingly" (*BT*, p. 416; H, p. 364).[31] Because Dasein is not a subject that stands apart from the world, that could exist without the world, but is rather thoroughly enmeshed and entangled in the world, to listen to one's self, to the call of conscience, and to listen to the situation, what is factically possible here and now, is the same thing. Indeed, the norms to which one is subject and to which one must respond, the norms that one "hears" in the call of conscience, inhere in the factical world. They do not derive from some transcendent self standing outside the world, as does the Kantian categorical imperative, nor are they based in some unchanging cosmic order, as is Natural Law. They are based in "one's own self," which is the current situation into which one is thrown and on the ground of which one must press forward into life.

NOTES

1. I generally rely on Macquarrie and Robinson's 1962 translation of Heidegger's *Sein und Zeit*, but make alterations as I feel are necessary. In citing the text, I abbreviate *Being and Time* as *BT* and give the page references to both the English and the German texts – thus, here: (*BT*, p. 67; H, p. 42), where the "H" reference is to the 15th German edition, published by Niemeyer. To indicate a systematic divergence in technical terminology from Macquarrie and Robinson's translation, I note their translation like this: "M&R: state of mind." I will also refer to chapters of *Being and Time* in the standard format: "1.3" to refer to Division 1, ch. 3.
2. The differences between the formulations is technical at best and not worth worrying about in this context, at least as long as one sees that by "precedes" Sartre does not mean priority in time, but rather conceptual priority. See Sartre, *Existentialism is a Humanism*.
3. The gerund (or verbal abstract noun built on the infinitive) in German is simply "*Sein*," as in Heidegger's many uses of the word "being" throughout *Being and Time*, which are all capitalized by Macquarrie and Robinson, but which I switch to lower case in my quotations. "*Zu-sein*" is a verbal abstract noun built on the gerundive: "*ich habe viel zu tun*," "I have much to do." Macquarrie and Robinson are inconsistent about the hyphen in the gerundive "to-be"; I insert it in every case.
4. Heidegger, *The Basic Problems of Phenomenology*, Part 1, ch. 2.

5. Ortega y Gasset, "History as a System", p. 191. He cites Cassirer, *Das Erkenntnisproblem in der Philosophie und Wissenschaft der neueren Zeit*, vol. II, p. 433.
6. A nominal essence is an essence in the classical sense discussed in the previous paragraph. Locke thought of the real essences as the micro-physical constitution of a thing. The formulation I give generalizes away from his corpuscularean assumptions. See Locke, *An Essay Concerning Human Understanding*. I owe my clarity on Locke, such as it is, to James Mattingly.
7. Ortega y Gasset, "History as a System," pp. 203–4.
8. Ortega y Gasset actually concedes all these points. He tends to assert his view in a provocatively strong form and then walk it back. Vis-à-vis history he writes, *"Man, in a word, has no nature; what he has is ... history"* ("History as a System," p. 217). Vis-à-vis physical attributes he writes "man's being is made of such strange stuff as to be partly akin to nature and partly not, at once natural and extranatural" ("Man the Technician," p. 111).
9. Which is actually not such a simple phenomenon, for we have to distinguish morphological secondary sexual characteristics from chromosomal constitution to account for conditions such as Swyer syndrome.
10. A fact (*Tatsache*) is a factual determination. A Fact (*Faktum*) is a factical determination.
11. I follow Taylor Carman in translating Heidegger's term "*Befindlichkeit*" as "disposedness." M&R's "state-of-mind," even hyphenated, suggests that disposedness is a characteristic *of mind*. "Disposedness" is meant to suggest the manner in which one is at any given time disposed, both "how one is, and how one is faring" (*BT*, p. 173; H, p. 134) and the manner in which one is situated or "thrown" into the world.
12. I translate Heidegger's term "*Stimmung*," which is the ordinary German word for mood or spirits, as "attunement." Heidegger appropriates the ordinary word and uses it both to refer to a wider range of phenomena than are normally designated by "mood" and to emphasize a particular aspect of these phenomena, namely, the way in which they "tune us in" to what matters.
13. Heidegger develops this example at length in para. 30. That he uses fear as his chief example of an attunement indicates quite clearly that he doesn't really have moods in mind, since fear is an emotion rather than a mood. For more detail on this point, see my *Heidegger's "Being and Time,"* pp. 80–84.
14. It is for this reason that Heidegger writes, "We do not first ascertain a future evil (*malum futurum*) and then fear it" (*BT*, p. 180; H, p. 141).

15. In contrast to Heidegger Kant calls traditional metaphysics "ontology." "The proud name of ontology must give way to the modest one of a mere analytic of pure understanding" (*Critique of Pure Reason*, A247/B303).
16. This is the way Heidegger appropriates what he calls the medieval thesis that "to the constitution of the being of an entity there belong existence and essence." See *The Basic Problems of Phenomenology*, Part I, ch. 2.
17. It may even be that such questions are not factual, but rather senseless. If the mode of being involves not just criteria of the *being* of an entity (*whether* it is), but also identity conditions (whether *x* and *y* are one entity or two), then it would seem that one cannot even ask whether two entities with different modes of being are really one and the same, since their identity conditions differ. This strikes me as the correct reply, but I cannot find texts in which Heidegger adopts it.
18. And perhaps for anxiety too, though if so my reading of anxiety is wrong. Katherine Withy developes this line of thought in her "Heidegger's Angst is Not (Only) a Mood."
19. I am summarizing my interpretation of anxiety and death from my "The Concept of Death in *Being and Time*" and from *Heidegger's "Being and Time."*
20. See Thomson, "Heidegger's Phenomenology of Death in *Being and Time*," for more on death.
21. It is not clear that they always coincide. Nietzsche spent the last eleven years of his life in a catatonic state. In most respects his biographical life ended in 1889, though legally he was still alive, and this legal status had numerous biographical implications, including that his sister did not gain full control of his literary estate until he perished.
22. There is a neat contrast in the German that is hard to capture in English: unsurpassable: *unüberholbar*; integrated: *eingeholt*. "When, in running forth, resoluteness has *integrated* [M&R: *caught up*] the possibility of death into its ability-to-be, Dasein's authentic existence can no longer be *surpassed* by anything" (*BT*, p. 355; H, p. 307).
23. Guignon, "Becoming a Self", p. 129.
24. Dreyfus and Rubin, "Kierkegaard, Division II, and Later Heidegger", pp. 307–8.
25. Rorty, *Contingency, Irony, and Solidarity*.
26. Thanks to Rebecca Kukla, who suggested this word to me.
27. Contrast Hilary Clinton's dignified and enthusiastic endorsement of Barack Obama in 2008 with Richard Nixon's infamous "you won't have Nixon to kick around anymore, because, gentlemen, this is my

last press conference" (as transcribed by *The New York Times*, Nov. 7, 1962 and quoted at http://en.wikiquote.org/wiki/Richard_Nixon).

28. It is also a rather shallow way to live, though it is hard to know how to argue for this characterization in a philosophically principled fashion. Think of Kierkegaard's searing comparison with investment strategies in the "Preamble from the Heart" in *Fear and Trembling* (p. 72).
29. This interpretation of conscience is influenced by Crowell, "*Sorge* or *Selbstbewußtsein*?" and "Subjectivity," as well as Kukla, "The Ontology and Temporality of Conscience." I discuss the details of their construal of conscience in my "Transcendental Conscience."
30. As per Taylor, *The Ethics of Authenticity*.
31. In "Transcendental Conscience" I argue that it is important to see that the self to whom the conscience addresses itself, which Heidegger calls "the authentic self" or "one's own self," is not a self *other than* the everyday "Anyone-self" who is enmeshed in socially constituted for-the-sakes-of-which. The "authentic self" is an essential, formal dimension of the Anyone-self.

KARSTEN HARRIES

9 The antinomy of being: Heidegger's critique of humanism

9.1 THREE QUESTIONS

Heidegger's "Letter on Humanism"[1] was written in November 1946, first as a response to a letter by the French philosopher Jean Beaufret, who ever since late 1940 had worked tirelessly to introduce the French to Heidegger's thought. Already in the fall of 1945 Beaufret had Jean-Michel Palmier deliver to Heidegger a series of four articles he had written, "À propos de l'existentialisme," accompanied by a letter.[2] Heidegger appreciated the understanding of *Being and Time* they demonstrated. On September 12, 1946, Beaufret met Heidegger for the first time in his hut in Todtnauberg. Later, in November, he sent Heidegger another letter, asking him to clarify the relationship of his thought to Sartre's existentialism. In it he posed these questions: (1) "How can we restore meaning to the word 'humanism'"? (GA9, p. 315/219); (2) How does ontology relate to ethics? (GA9, pp. 352–53/254–55); (3) "How can we preserve the element of adventure that all research contains without simply turning philosophy into an adventuress?" (GA9, p. 362/263). Heidegger's reply, dated November 23, was later reworked and published in 1947, together with "Plato's Doctrine of Truth," significantly not in Germany, but in Switzerland, as part of a series edited by a former disciple, Ernesto Grassi. The shadow of his association with National Socialism lay heavy over Heidegger. This long, but quickly written essay is his first publication after the end of the Second World War.

Beaufret's three questions led Heidegger to survey the way his thought had evolved since *Being and Time* – evolved, but not really progressed beyond what had there been accomplished. More than one world had collapsed for him: by the time he was working on *Being and Time*, he had lost the Catholic faith of his youth; by 1933 he had lost faith in philosophy's ability to provide the needed reorientation, a loss that let him turn briefly to Hitler as the only hope, he then thought, remaining to a Germany that had lost its bearings; by 1936 he had lost faith in Hitler, whom he had come to understand in the image of Aaron as another creator of a golden calf. This loss let him turn to the poet Friedrich Hölderlin. In his poetry he found a promise of homecoming for a homeless humanity.

The end of the Second World War must have reinforced Heidegger's sense of having lost his home. That in the spring of 1946 he should have suffered a mental breakdown is hardly surprising. This sense of homelessness was compounded by the fact that the French occupation authorities not only forced him to share his rather small Freiburg home with the family of a French sergeant and a Silesian refugee – leaving him and his wife only his study, thus making him a stranger in his own house (GA16, p. 426) – but even threatened to confiscate his precious library. In December of that year he got final word of what he had expected for some months, that his request to be allowed to resume his lecturing, now as a professor emeritus, at the University of Freiburg had been refused. Given his association with National Socialism, he was judged unfit to teach. And that association, short-lived though his rectorate and his active participation in the movement had been, did indeed presuppose that a humanism that looked back to the ancients and to the Italian Renaissance, and that had once stood for what had been best in German education, had lost its significance for Heidegger long before 1933. When he received Beaufret's letter Heidegger must have known about his distance from this humanism.

Still, given his dire situation at the time, he was pleased by the attention he received from French visitors and journals, and especially pleased to make the acquaintance of Beaufret. Heidegger was of course aware how much French interest in his work was linked to Jean-Paul Sartre, who was then at the height of his popularity and whose lecture, "Existentialism is a Humanism," given on October 29, 1945, had been a cultural event of the first order that echoed also in Germany. In that lecture Sartre had named Heidegger as a fellow representative of that atheist existentialism Sartre endorsed and now offered to a world in ruins as a new humanism. Heidegger himself had recently been loaned a copy of *Being and Nothingness* by a young French soldier and admirer, Frédéric de Towarnicki. The book, it appears, impressed him.[3] Towarnicki hoped to arrange a meeting with Sartre. The difficult times prevented it; they were to meet only in 1952.[4] Beaufret's follow-up letter, inviting Heidegger to clarify not just the relationship of his thought to humanism, but more especially to its Sartrean version, came thus at an opportune moment.

One might have expected that Heidegger, given his situation, would have welcomed the opportunity to wrap himself, too, in the humanist mantle. Instead he called every humanism, indeed every "ism," into question (GA9, p. 315/219), implicitly linking humanism to both communism and National Socialism and more generally to the darkness of the age. To be sure, Heidegger is quite aware that his critique of humanism, presupposing his understanding of the essence of the humanism, invites misunderstanding:

> Because we are speaking against "humanism" people fear a defense of the inhuman, and a glorification of barbaric brutality. For what is more "logical" than that for somebody who negates humanism nothing remains but the affirmation of inhumanity? (GA9, p. 346/249)

Answering his own rhetorical question, he points out that there is indeed a sense in which his thinking – which would call human beings to come back home to "the truth of Being" – can claim to be a more profound humanism, misleading though he thinks the label would be, bound as humanism, as Heidegger understands it, is to metaphysics, a history that Heidegger links to the plight of European culture.

As this qualification hints, Heidegger's understanding of humanism invites challenge. His sketch of humanism's metaphysical essence offers only a caricature. It was Ernesto Grassi, to whom Heidegger owed the publication of his "Letter," who insisted in many subsequent publications,[5] without ever convincing Heidegger, that Italian humanism, and especially the thought of Giambattista Vico, offers an alternative to metaphysical thinking that Heidegger should have welcomed. Hans-Georg Gadamer, another Heidegger student, was to insist similarly on the importance of the humanist tradition in the opening chapter of *Truth and Method*.[6] But if Heidegger's blindness to that tradition invites question, more important is his rejection of what he took humanism to be, and especially his insistence on the profound distance that separated his own thinking from that of Sartre, who now was claiming the humanist label for himself. And since Heidegger knew how much Sartre's existentialism owed to *Being and Time*,[7] he also had to ask himself whether what he had written there did not invite such a misreading. He thought it important to correct such a misunderstanding.

To many, that correction is better described as a revision of his own *Being and Time*, as a turn away from human being (Dasein) to Being (Sein). Does not Heidegger himself speak in the "Letter on Humanism," and this for the first time, of a *Kehre*, a reversal, in his thought?

But how is this *Kehre* to be understood? Heidegger insists in this essay that "there has been no change of standpoint." Indeed, as the many quotes from *Being and Time* in the "Letter" demonstrate, the former has in no sense been left behind. As Heidegger here describes this so-called *Kehre*, it is better understood not as a reversal in the direction of Heidegger's path of thinking but as an attempt to enter more deeply into the matter to be thought, the question of Being. To understand the necessity of this *Kehre* is to understand the center of Heidegger's thought. It thus will demand our special attention.

9.2 HEIDEGGER'S CRITIQUE OF HUMANISM

That it was Ernesto Grassi who published the "Letter on Humanism" together with "Plato's Doctrine of Truth" is significant. Grassi had published the latter essay, based on a lecture course given in the winter semester 1930/31 (GA34) and written down in 1940, already once before, in 1942, in the second volume of the annual *Geistige Überlieferung*.[8] He knew therefore that Heidegger's understanding of humanism in the "Letter" had been anticipated in the conclusion of the Plato essay and that the two essays belonged together. "Plato's Doctrine of Truth" develops an interpretation of the allegory of the cave to show that in Plato we find the transformation of truth understood as *aletheia*, or disclosedness, into truth understood as correctness that, according to Heidegger, is the beginning both of metaphysics and at the same time of "humanism." The measure of such correctness is the Platonic idea, understood as the timeless essence of what is. To grasp the idea is to get hold of the true being of things.

In the "Letter on Humanism" Heidegger proposes to use the word "humanism" in its essential and widest sense. Every humanism is said to presuppose a determination of the essence of man, the *animal rationale.* As such it is inextricably joined to metaphysics, accompanying its beginning, unfolding, and end. To the progress of metaphysics corresponds thus the progress of humanism, which in ever different ways places man at the center of all that is, without necessarily making him therefore into the highest being: there can be and has been a Christian humanism. Appealing to some supposedly timeless essence of man, every humanism seeks to bring human being closer to the presupposed idea. As Heidegger explains it in "Plato's Doctrine of Truth," in projecting an ideal image of man, and thus an ethics, humanism thus seeks to

> lead [human beings] to the liberation of their possibilities, to the certitude of their destiny, and to the securing of their "life." This takes place as the shaping of their "moral" behavior, as the salvation of their immortal souls, as the unfolding of their creative powers, as the development of their reason, as the nourishing of their personalities, as the awakening of their civic sense, as the cultivation of their bodies, or as an appropriate combination of some or all of these "humanisms." (GA9, p. 236/181)

The "Letter on Humanism" presupposes this meaning of the word. That neither Plato nor Italian humanism quite fits under this umbrella Grassi had known at least since he wrote his *Habilitationsschrift, Il problema della metafisica platonica* (1932) under Heidegger's direction.[9]

When he chose to republish "Plato's Doctrine of Truth" together with the "Letter on Humanism," Grassi no doubt remembered that when it was to be published the first time, the office of the Nazis' chief ideologue, Alfred Rosenberg, found the evident relativism of Heidegger's understanding of humanism incompatible with that "German political humanism" on which National Socialism had to insist. That the essay was published at all in those difficult times Heidegger owed to Grassi's good connection to Mussolini, who personally intervened.[10] The charge that was then raised against Heidegger by Nazi ideologues has to be made by anyone who believes that a viable humanism must rest on a firm foundation. That includes Sartre, who finds such a foundation in the Cartesian *cogito.* Heidegger not only denies any such foundation; he insists that every humanism that understands itself to rest on such a foundation has lost sight of the antinomial truth of Being, towards which the word *aletheia* gestures. And in this respect, he insists, Sartre's existentialism must indeed be considered a humanism.

By asking how the word "humanism" could once again be given a sense that might reorient a thoroughly disoriented world, Beaufret was implying, as Heidegger points out, that he wanted to hold on to a term that Heidegger thought had lost its meaning, that he wanted to pour new wine into a venerable vessel (GA9, pp. 344–45/247). But the end of metaphysics, as Heidegger understands it, means the breaking of that vessel. The "word has lost its meaning. It has lost it through the insight that the essence of humanism is metaphysical, which now means that metaphysics not only does not pose the question concerning the truth of Being, but also obstructs the question, insofar as metaphysics persists in the oblivion of Being" (GA9, p. 345/247).

9.3 HEIDEGGER'S HUMANISM?

But did Sartre's existentialism not promise to pour new wine into the venerable old vessel of humanism? To be sure, the Heidegger-admirer Beaufret must have had misgivings about the flavor of this particular wine. Beaufret was thus asking Heidegger to clarify his own position in relation to Sartre's *Existentialism is a Humanism*, which, like *Being and Nothingness* (1943), did not conceal Sartre's debt to *Being and Time* and especially to its understanding of authenticity. Was this then perhaps an acceptable humanism after all?

To be sure, Sartre himself observes, and with good reason, that, given what he had written in *Being and Nothingness*, "Many will be surprised by what I have to say here about humanism" (*EH*, p. 18). By insisting that concrete existence, here and now, is situated, but free and unbound by some essence, Sartre would seem not to fall under Heidegger's definition of humanism. Indeed in that book he had accused Heidegger of an unjustifiable humanism that prevented him from simply accepting the human condition:

> What am I? A being which is not its own foundation, which qua being, could be other than it is to the extent that it does not account for its being.

This is the first intuition of our own contingency which Heidegger gives as the first motivation for the passage from the un-authentic to the authentic. There is restlessness, an appeal to the conscience (*Ruf des Gewissens*), a feeling of guilt. In truth, Heidegger's description shows all too clearly his anxiety to establish an ontological foundation for an Ethics with which he claims not to be concerned, as also to reconcile his humanism with the religious sense of the transcendent. The intuition of our contingency is not identical with a feeling of guilt. Nevertheless it is true that in our own apprehension of ourselves we appear to ourselves as having the character of an unjustifiable fact. (*BN*, pp. 127–28)

Sartre is right to note the anguish that colors the rhetoric of *Being and Time*. He is right, too, when he speaks of Heidegger's "anxiety to establish an ontological foundation for an Ethics with which he claims not to be concerned." To be sure, as a work in fundamental ontology *Being and Time* has to remain formal and abstract; as a quasi-transcendental inquiry it can only describe possibilities of human existence, without prescribing where human beings are to stand. Terms like "authenticity" and "inauthenticity" are thus supposed to function in a purely descriptive manner. But despite such claims, Heidegger is indeed concerned to provide the foundation for an ethic that has appropriated the truth of Nietzsche's pronouncement that God is dead. And so, after many pages and Heidegger's repeated insistence that terms such as "inauthenticity" or "idle talk" are not being used in a derogatory sense (GA2, pp. 57, 222/68, 211), he finally acknowledges that we cannot in the end divorce ontological inquiry from the ontic stance of the inquirer, and that is to say, from an ideal image of man:

Is there not, however, a definite ontical way of taking authentic existence, a factical ideal of Dasein, underlying our ontological Interpretation of Dasein's existence? That is so indeed. But not only is this Fact one which must not be denied and which we are forced to grant; it must also be conceived in its *positive necessity*, in terms of the object which we have taken as the theme of our investigation. (GA2, p. 411/358)

As Sartre recognizes, Heidegger's choice of words communicates the ideal underlying and steering his ontological investigations. *Being and Time* does more than describe existential possibilities; it calls its readers to that acceptance of our own guilty being that Heidegger terms "resoluteness," where the word "guilt" retains much of its religious aura. Heidegger would have us understand his fundamental ontology also as a fundamental ethics. There is indeed a great deal that can be cited in support of Herman Philipse's claim that in *Being and Time* "the historical development of ethical foundationalism has reached its final stage. The attempt to ground ethics on secure first principles first shifted from heteronomy to autonomy, and then from Kantian universalizability to unrestricted freedom."[11]

To be sure, that characterization fits Sartre better than Heidegger, and, as Sartre recognized, it is a mistake to overlook what so profoundly separates their thinking on freedom. Sartre does not share Heidegger's anguish. He would seem to see no need for a transcendent guarantee or ground of values other than the subject itself.

> But instead of seeing that the transcendences there posited are maintained in their being by my own transcendence, people will assume them upon my surging up in the world; they come from God, from nature, from my "nature," from society ... These abortive attempts to stifle freedom under the weight of being (they collapse with the sudden upsurge of anguish before freedom) show sufficiently that freedom in its foundation coincides with the nothingness that is at the heart of man ... Human nature cannot receive its ends, as we have seen, either from the outside or from a so-called "inner" nature. It chooses them and by this very choice confers upon them a transcendent existence as the external limit of its projects. From this point of view ... human reality in and through its very upsurge decides to define its own being by its ends. It is therefore the positing of my ultimate ends which characterizes my being which is identical with the sudden thrust of freedom which is mine. (*BN*, pp. 568–72)

Heidegger's appeal to dwelling in "the truth of being" – the basis for what he means by "ethics" – does indeed invite Sartre's charge that Heidegger, too, would "stifle freedom under the weight of being."

9.4 SARTRE'S HUMANISM

Sartre's insistence that to be free means to be free to determine whatever ends one chooses to pursue suggests that his existentialism is opposed to any humanism. And yet Sartre's embrace of the humanist label in *Existentialism is a Humanism* is unequivocal and justified by the way he here gives his understanding of authenticity a Kantian twist, difficult to reconcile with what we find in either *Being and Nothingness* or in Heidegger's *Being and Time*:

Existentialists like to say that man is in anguish. This is what they mean: a man who commits himself, and who realizes that he is not only the individual that he chooses to be, but also a legislator choosing at the same time what humanity as a whole should be, cannot help but be aware of his own full and profound responsibility. True, many people do not appear especially anguished, but we maintain that they are merely hiding their anguish or trying not to face it. Certainly, many believe that their actions involve no one but themselves, and were we to ask them, "But what if everyone acted that way?" they could shrug their shoulders and reply, "But everyone does *not* act that way." In truth, however, one should always ask oneself "What if everyone did what I am doing?" The only way to evade that disturbing thought is through some kind of bad faith. (*EH*, p. 25)

So understood, existentialism can indeed be seen as a humanism. It is difficult not to think here of Kant's categorical imperative, which would have us act only in such a way that we could will the maxim of our action to become a universal law, despite, and difficult to reconcile with, Sartre's explicit rejection of any view that would understand each individual as "a particular example of a universal concept – man" (*EH*, p. 22), which confronts the individual with an ought. Existentialist authenticity here appears incompatible with Kantian autonomy. "In Kant's works, this universality extends so far as to encompass forest dwellers – man in a state of nature – and the bourgeois, meaning that they all possess the same basic qualities. Here again, the essence of man precedes his historically primitive existence in nature" (*EH*, p. 22).

But how are we to reconcile Sartre's rejection of such an appeal to essence with his claim that one ought always to ask oneself what would happen if everyone did as one is doing. Does this not bend authenticity, as analyzed by Heidegger in *Being and Time* and appropriated by Sartre in *Being and Nothingness*, back in the direction of Kantian autonomy? To be sure, Sartre insists that "freedom, under any concrete circumstance, can have no other aim than itself, and once a man realizes, in his state of abandonment, that it is he who imposes values, he can will but one thing: freedom as the foundation of all values" (*EH*, p. 48). That would seem to suggest that, developing Heidegger's analysis of authenticity in *Being and Time*, for Sartre, as for Kierkegaard, purity of heart is to will one thing: freedom.

But like Kant, Sartre appears unable to finally make sense of freedom without binding it to a commitment to human solidarity. And indeed, a few pages later Sartre explicitly agrees with Kant "that freedom wills itself and the freedom of others" (*EH*, p. 49). "As soon as there is commitment, I am obliged to will the freedom of others at the same time as I will my own. I cannot set my own freedom as a goal without also setting the freedom of others as a goal" (*EH*, pp. 48–49). Authenticity, according to Sartre in this essay, entails a commitment to the freedom of others. "Consequently, when, operating on the level of complete authenticity, I have acknowledged that existence precedes essence, and that man is a free being who, under any circumstances, can only ever will his freedom, I have at the same time acknowledged that I must will the freedom of others" (*EH*, p. 49). Anthony Manser is right to observe that not only here Sartrean authenticity is "very similar" to Kant's categorical imperative.[12]

But is Sartre's understanding of freedom compatible with the way he here embraces what looks rather like Kant's practical reason? Not everything would seem to be allowed to the authentic actor. This, however, is difficult to reconcile with this remark: "Dostoevsky once wrote: 'If God does not exist, everything is permissible.' This is the starting point for existentialism. Indeed, everything is permissible if God does not exist, and man is consequently abandoned, for he cannot find anything to rely on – neither within nor without" (*EH*, pp. 28–29). Heidegger could perhaps accept this conditional. And, as Sartre recognized, Heidegger refuses to settle for such a forlorn existence. That explains the late Heidegger's nostalgic turn towards Being, which is also a turn towards, if not an embrace of, religion. But can Sartre accept his conditional? He, too, refuses to accept a purely negative freedom. He, too, looks back, although not to religion but to the Enlightenment, to Kant's practical reason.

To be sure, Sartre is critical of Kant in *Existentialism is a Humanism*. Like many before him, he accuses Kant of providing us with a rule so formal that it does not help the individual to decide what to do in a particular situation. His example is a student who has to decide whether to stay with his mother or join the Resistance. In such situations, Sartre, suggests, the categorical imperative offers no help. The student is left with the anguish of the decision that faces him. But to admit this is not to say that Sartre's student is left free to do whatever he wants. Kant's categorical imperative appears here as a necessary, if not sufficient, condition of authentic action. In that sense, Sartre's understanding of authenticity remains tethered to Kantian autonomy. Sartre, one might say, here calls attention to a lacuna in Kant's moral philosophy.

It is a lacuna similar to one that we also meet with in Kant's philosophy of nature, a lacuna to which Kant himself called attention: Any judgment of fact presupposes the subjection of the manifold of sensibility to the understanding. Such subjection, however, requires that the gulf that separates understanding and sensibility be bridged. In the *Critique of Pure Reason* Kant assigns that bridging function to the imagination. How does the imagination accomplish this task? Kant has no good answer and speaks of "an art concealed in the depth of the human soul."[13]

And must something analogous not also hold in the moral realm?[14] Here too there is need for an imaginative bridging of the gulf that separates what pure practical reason demands and the countless concrete possibilities human actors face. In *Existentialism is a Humanism* Sartre assigns that bridging function to a free commitment, issuing from the individual's situation, passion and desire (*EH*, p. 24). But if it is thus grounded in individual taste, authentic action must nevertheless also remain responsive to the universal. There is thus a sense in which Sartre remains faithful to Enlightenment humanism. The atheist Sartre would seem not to have understood Nietzsche's proclamation of the death of God as radically as Heidegger, who long before 1933 had lost faith in the ability of reason to bind freedom.

It must have touched Heidegger strangely to find himself referred to, by someone then widely thought of as the leading philosopher of the post-war world, as a fellow atheist existentialist. To be sure, Heidegger had long since lost his faith in God. But, like Nietzsche, "that last passionate seeker of God and German philosopher" (GA16, p. 111), Heidegger experienced that death as a loss of all that once gave dignity and measure to human beings, a loss he had to struggle with throughout his life. How was such dignity now to be understood? Does such talk still make sense in a world ruled by an objectifying reason that threatens to reduce human beings to free subjects facing a mute world of objects or, alternatively, as material to be used and abused as those in power see fit? Sartre's essay, communicating what we can call an evangelical atheism that presented itself as a humanism for the modern age, must have seemed to Heidegger an attempt to seek shelter in the ruin of an Enlightenment world that, with the death of God, had lost its foundation.

9.5 THE DEATH OF GOD

It is hard to exaggerate the importance of Nietzsche's thought for those thinkers who, like Heidegger, matured in a Germany left in shambles by the First World War. Not just a political order had perished; perished had the conviction that *Bildung*, committed to ideals bequeathed to us by the Greeks and Romans, could offer the answer to that nihilism diagnosed by Nietzsche. When Nietzsche speaks of the death of God – a phrase explicitly, anxiously, and ominously endorsed by Heidegger in his "Rectorial Address" (GA16, p. 111) – he is thinking first of all of the biblical God; and unlike Sartre, who experienced the death of God as empowering, Heidegger suffered that death. Had he not once hoped to become a theologian?

What has killed this God, what has devalued what once were the highest values, Nietzsche insists, is we ourselves; more precisely, our Promethean will to power, which would have us assert ourselves as the masters of all that is, refusing to accept that this project of mastery has led to the progressive erosion of what once gave meaning to life. Heidegger speaks instead of the progress of metaphysics, which seeks to lay hold of the being of beings, to grasp it and thus render human beings the masters and possessors of nature, including their own nature. Is this not the hope of every humanism?

And why should we heirs of the Enlightenment not put humanity in the place left vacant by the death of God? The Enlightenment was confident that reason could take the place of all the authorities that different revolutions had swept aside. Such optimism has supported modernism, as it has supported science, liberal democracy, and international communism. Is the pursuit of truth not a pursuit of what alone should bind freedom?

But what truth? And does freedom remain freedom when thus bound? Some philosophers have seen no great difficulty here: Descartes, for example, following Thomas Aquinas, insists that the will binds itself willingly and freely to whatever it clearly knows and thereby perfects itself and comes to rest. And similarly, according to Kant, freedom perfects itself when it binds itself to the rule of reason. But such perfected freedom is at some distance from that being I am, bound to the body and possessed of a freedom that reveals itself in the question "why be moral?" This freedom does not belong to human beings insofar as they are members of Kant's kingdom of ends, but to Kierkegaard's solitary individual, who experiences what Kant calls our membership in the kingdom of ends as problematic, as something he or she can refuse. Heidegger was such a solitary individual who was no longer able to accept the authority of the categorical imperative as a no longer transcendent but transcendental – and that is to say human – absolute. He could not make sense of such a human absolute. Is Kantian autonomy supported by more than a misplaced faith that would put reason in the place left vacant by the death of God? The end of metaphysics denies that very place to us. This would seem to leave the subject's own radical freedom as the only source of value.

And was this not one lesson Jean-Paul Sartre had learned from Heidegger's *Being and Time*, ever since he first encountered it when still a student at the Sorbonne, in conversations with the early Heidegger admirer Kuki Shuzo, who had engaged Sartre to teach him French and join him in philosophical discussion?[15] In such freedom Sartre sought the key to a humanism truly of today, even if in *Existentialism is a Humanism* he found it necessary to temper such emphasis on freedom with Kantian intuitions.

9.6 HEIDEGGER'S *KEHRE* RECONSIDERED

But was Sartre not right to suspect Heidegger of wanting to stifle freedom under the weight of Being? What positive message does the "Letter on Humanism" have to offer except some hermetic gestures towards the saving power of the truth of Being? Heidegger does not make things easy for the reader. Instead of showing us the way home he seems to call us first of all to silence, as indeed in *Being and Time* already he had offered as the only example of authentic *Rede* or discourse the wordless call of conscience, in which the human being calls himself to come home to himself. This call now has become the call, not of the self to itself, but of Being:

> But if man is to find his way once again into the nearness of Being he must first learn to exist in the nameless. In the same way he must recognize the seductions of the public realm as well as the impotence of the private. Before he speaks man must first let himself be claimed again by Being, taking the risk that under this claim he will seldom have much to say. Only thus will the preciousness of its essence be once more bestowed upon the word, and upon man a home for dwelling in the truth of Being. (GA9, p. 319/223)

The quoted passage raises all sorts of questions – first of all the central question of *Being and Time*: what is the meaning of Being? And how are we to understand that nearness of Being to which we are to find our way? What is the relationship between Being and language? What does it mean to "dwell in the truth of Being"?

Being and Time remained a fragment. The philosophical project on which Heidegger had embarked – to use Husserl's phenomenological method to elucidate the meaning of Being – could not be carried to completion. And what prevented it was the matter to be thought: the essence of Being. In its approach, *Being and Time* still belongs with a transcendental metaphysics, even if the sought meaning of Being has to elude such an approach. The incompleteness of *Being and Time* is due to the impossible goal Heidegger had there set himself. "It is everywhere supposed that the attempt in *Being and Time* ended in a blind alley [*Sackgasse*]" (GA9, p. 343/246). In the "Letter on Humanism" Heidegger does not really disagree; he leaves the supposition standing, hinting that not only his philosophy but philosophy as such had reached with this book something like a dead end. "The thinking that hazards a few steps in *Being and Time* has even today not advanced beyond that publication. But perhaps in the meantime it has in one respect come further into its own matter" (GA9, p. 343/246).

This further movement led Heidegger to redescribe the path of his thinking, not as a *Sackgasse*, but as a *Holzweg* (GA13, p. 91). And so he gave the most important collection of essays he published the title *Holzwege*. But what is the difference? Do not both *Sackgasse* and *Holzweg* suggest a way that misses the intended goal? But the German "*Holzweg*" has a quite specific meaning: it suggests a path cut by foresters to allow some trees that have been cut down to be brought out of the forest. A *Holzweg* therefore ends in a clearing or *Lichtung*. In a sense such a path does lead nowhere. For a hiker to be on a *Holzweg* means that he has lost his way. But is such a loss of way – what the Greeks called *aporia* – not the beginning of authentic thinking? Such thinking, Heidegger now insists, must question philosophy as it has come to be established – i.e., metaphysics – and leave it behind.

The *aporia* into which Heidegger's path of thinking leads us is tied to an antinomy buried in Heidegger's understanding of the relationship of human being, language, and Being.

> But man is not only a living creature who possesses language along with other capacities. Rather, language is the house of Being in which man ek-sists by dwelling, in that he belongs to the truth of Being, guarding it. (GA9, p. 333/237)

The expression "house of Being" is ambiguous. On the one hand it suggests something like: the limits of language are the limits of the world. To "be" for us, things must take their place in the always already structured spaces provided by our language. In that sense Being, the presencing of beings, can be said to depend on language and thus on human beings. Much in Heidegger suggests such a reading that makes language constitutive of whatever we can think or experience.

On the other hand, is every language not a phenomenon in the world and can be investigated as such? Does the whole of reality not encompass language, and are we not thus forced to speak of beings, and thus of Being, as transcending language? One can support the claim that reality transcends language by pointing out that responsible speech must respond to things that have being independent of human beings. Something like this would seem to be demanded by all claims to truth. But there is always the counter-question: how is this response to be thought? Do things have being for us without language?

Heidegger confronted this antinomy already in *Being and Time* in his attempt to think the ontological difference, the difference between beings and Being, the latter referring to the way things disclose themselves to Dasein, i.e., to human being. When we approach that difference from the perspective of transcendental philosophy, we will want to say: Being is constitutive of and therefore transcends beings. Beings can present themselves only to a being that is such as we are, a being that, embodied and dwelling in language, is open to a world in which beings have to take their place and present themselves if they are "to be" at all. The way beings present themselves is always mediated by the body and by language and founded in the being of Dasein as care. In the "Letter on Humanism" Heidegger will repeat the sentence: "Only as long as Dasein is, is there [*gibt es*] Being" (GA9, p. 336/240).

But Heidegger qualifies this when he speaks, in par. 43 of *Being and Time*, of the dependence of Being (*but not of beings*) and reality (*but not of the real*) on care, i.e., on the always understanding and caring being of human beings (GA2, p. 281/255). In the "Letter on Humanism" this qualification becomes: "But the fact that the *Da*, the lighting as the truth of Being itself, comes to pass is the dispensation of Being itself ... the sentence does not mean that the Dasein of man in the traditional sense of *existentia*, and thought in modern thought as the actuality of the *ego cogito*, is that being through which Being is first fashioned" (GA9, p. 336/240). There is therefore a sense in which beings and the real can be said to transcend that Being (*Sein*) which is said to be relative to Dasein. To be sure, these beings could not "be" in Heidegger's sense without human beings. Only human consciousness provides the open space that allows things to be perceived, understood, and cared for. That space is a presupposition of the accessibility of things, of their being. But this is not to say that we in any sense create these beings. Our experience of the reality of the real is thus an experience of beings as transcending Being. This demands a distinction between two senses of Being – the first transcendental sense relative to Dasein, and in this sense inescapably historical; the second transcendent sense the ground of Dasein's historical being, and thus also of Being understood transcendentally. But any attempt to lay hold of that ground must inevitably fail. Here our thinking bumps against the limits of language. And yet this ground, Heidegger insists, calls us, if in silence, opening a window in our modern world, a world shaped by the progress of metaphysics. The evolution of Heidegger's thought since *Being and Time* can thus be described as supplementing the silent call of conscience with the silent call of Being, where there is a suggestion that only as a response to the latter can there be the authentic speech that would seem to be inseparable from authentic dwelling. To speak here of a *Kehre*, as Heidegger himself does for the first time in print in the "Letter on Humanism" (GA9, p. 328/231), is misleading in that it suggests a reversal. But, as Heidegger points out, "there has been no change of standpoint." The question of Being remains central. The so-called *Kehre* is thus better understood, as Heidegger himself here describes it, not as a philosophical advance but as a more thoughtful attempt to attend to the matter to be thought (GA9, p. 343/246–47). What makes it necessary is the antinomial essence of Being, which denies the thinker a foundation.

9.7 THE END OF PHILOSOPHY

Those who want to read *Being and Time* as Sartre read it may be tempted to understand the *Kehre* in the light of a remark Nietzsche made about Wagner's progress.

Half his life Wagner believed in the revolution as ever a Frenchman did ... What happened? A misfortune. The ship struck a reef; Wagner was stuck. The reef was Schopenhauer's philosophy. Wagner was stranded on an opposite worldview. What had he transposed into music? Optimism. Wagner was ashamed? Even an optimism for which Schopenhauer had coined an evil epithet – *infamous* optimism. He was ashamed a second time. He reflected a long while, his situation seemed desperate. – Finally, a way out dawned on him: the reef on which he was shipwrecked – what if he interpreted it as the *goal*, as the secret intent, as the true significance of his voyage? To be shipwrecked here – that was a goal, too. *Bene navigavi, cum naufragium feci.*[16]

Heidegger had a similar disappointment. He too once believed in revolution. His ship, too, had struck a reef. Had he too not been, once, as Sartre calls himself in *Existentialism is a Humanism*, an optimist, looking to authentic resolve to bring about that revolution that was to replace with something new the ruin that European culture had become? But his too had been a false optimism. He too had placed hopes where there was nothing left to hope. So what was he to do? Reinterpret his philosophical journey so that the dead end, the reef on which he was shipwrecked, was the real goal of the journey: the clearing in which we are touched by the nearness of Being.

In such nearness, if at all, a decision may be made as to whether and how God and the gods withhold their presence and the night remains, whether and how the day of the holy dawns, whether and how in the upsurgence of the holy an epiphany of God and gods can begin anew. But the holy, which alone is the essential sphere of divinity, which in turn can alone afford a dimension for the gods and or God, comes to radiate only when Being itself beforehand and after extensive preparation has been illuminated and is experienced in its truth. Only thus does the overcoming of homelessness begin from Being, a homelessness in which not only man but the essence of man stumbles aimlessly about. (GA9, p. 338–39/242)

In the *Spiegel* interview Heidegger was thus to proclaim despairingly, "Only a god can still save us" (GA16, p. 671).

It is tempting to understand the "Letter on Humanism" in this way. But it was not his disastrous alliance with National Socialism and his subsequent disappointment that led to Heidegger's *Kehre*. The *Kehre* is demanded by Heidegger's understanding of Being, as we find it already in *Being and Time*. The Sartrean appropriation of Heidegger was always a misreading, as Sartre recognized. Of special importance here is Sartre's refusal to accept Heidegger's analysis of being-unto-death as providing the only key to the being of the self, to its finitude, its temporality and historicity, and thus to the meaning of authenticity. According to Sartre, all that is needed is the Cartesian *cogito*. It alone provides philosophy with a foundation: "As our point of departure there can be no other truth than this: *I think therefore I am*. This is the absolute truth of consciousness confronting itself" (*EH*, p. 40). That the *cogito* as such does not yield a robust self, Sartre recognizes. For Sartre, as for Heidegger, human being is always a being with others in a particular situation. But Sartre, Heidegger suggests, fails to question what has cast us into this situation. Already in chapter 5 of *Being and Time*, and more forcefully in the "Letter on Humanism," Heidegger insists that however we are to understand what has thrown us into the world – Heidegger speaks of "Being itself [*das Sein selbst*]" – it must be understood historically. A key charge he raises against Sartre, against metaphysics, and especially against every humanism that would appeal to some trans-historical essence of human being, is that it does not take history seriously enough and thus ignores the shape of that modern world to which we are inextricably bound. This lets him make some uncharacteristic, at the time no doubt timely, remarks about Marx.

Homelessness is coming to be the destiny of the world. Hence it is necessary to think that destiny in terms of the history of Being. What Marx

> recognized in an essential and significant sense, though derived from Hegel, as the estrangement of man has its roots in the homelessness of modern man. This homelessness is specifically evoked from the destiny of Being in the form of metaphysics and through metaphysics is simultaneously entrenched and covered up as such. Because Marx by experiencing estrangement attains an essential dimension of history, the Marxist view of history is superior to that of other historical accounts. But since neither Husserl, nor – so far as I have seen till now – Sartre recognizes the essential importance of the historical in Being, neither phenomenology nor existentialism enters that dimension with which a positive dialogue with Marxism first becomes possible. (GA9, pp. 339–40/243)

But the essential homelessness of modern man – which as Marx recognized is his historical fate – is not adequately understood in terms of certain historical developments such as the rise of capitalism. Instead, Heidegger insists, we need to consider the way our modern age, this "age of the world picture," as Heidegger had called it (GA5, pp. 75–113), represents the culmination of the progress of metaphysics in science and technology and with it the forgetfulness of Being. That age has to transform the human being into a free subject who just happens to find him- or herself in this world, possessed of this body, born in this place, speaking this language – just as it has to transform all things into mute objects. It is this understanding of world and self that provides Sartre, too, with his point of departure.

9.8 HUMANISM AFTER ALL?

Sartre had good reason to claim that Heidegger sought "to reconcile his humanism with the religious sense of the transcendent." Such a sense is implicit in Heidegger's suggestion that thinking is indeed an adventure – and not just as "an inquiry into the unthought" but by being "bound to the advent of Being, to Being as advent" (GA9, p. 363/264), where such an advent holds out the promise of the return of the holy and perhaps of God. Thinking cannot force such an advent. All it can do is prepare for it by exhibiting the way every metaphysics, and thus every humanism, presupposes a historically conditioned way in which beings have presented themselves to the thinker. The reef on which the project of metaphysics suffers shipwreck is history. But in thus thinking the essential limit of metaphysics, such thought opens a window to what transcends the reach of metaphysics and thus philosophy. Just as Kant's antinomies were meant to prove that the reality known to science may not be identified with reality, lest we lose sight of the humanity of human beings that is a presupposition of every ethics, so what I called the antinomy of Being, an antinomy inscribed into what Heidegger calls the truth of Being, is to show that reality may not be identified with what philosophy can know, lest we lose sight of the humanity that in the end is the concern of every genuine humanism. And in that sense Heidegger can claim that his critique of humanism is born of care for our humanity.

> Where else does "care" tend but in the direction of bringing man back to his essence? What else does that in turn betoken but that man (*homo*) become human (*humanus*)? Thus *humanitas* really does remain the concern of such thinking. For this is humanism: meditating and caring, that man be human and not inhumane, "inhuman," that is, outside his essence. (GA9, p. 319/223–24)

NOTES

1. References in the text are to the following volumes of the Martin Heidegger *Gesamtausgabe* (Collected Works). When I use a translation, the page reference follows the German original, separated by a /. Full details can be found in the Bibliography.

   GA2 *Sein und Zeit* / *Being and Time*
   GA5 *Holzwege*
   GA9 *Wegmarken* / "Letter on Humanism," "Plato's Doctrine of Truth"
   GA13 *Aus der Erfahrung des Denkens*
   GA16 *Reden und andere Zeugnisse eines Lebensweges*
   GA34 *Vom Wesen der Wahrheit. Zu Platons Höhlengleichnis und Theätet.* Two works by Sartre will also be cited in the text abbreviated as follows:
   BN *Being and Nothingness*
   EH *Existentialism is a Humanism.*

2. Beaufret, "À propos de l'existentialisme." See Kritzman *et al.*, *The Columbia History of Twentieth-Century French Thought*, p. 252.
3. de Towarnicki, *À la rencontre de Heidegger.*
4. Mehring and Thomä, "Eine Chronik," p. 534.
5. See especially Grassi, *Heidegger and the Question of Renaissance Humanism.*
6. Gadamer, *Truth and Method.*

7. For a succinct account of Sartre's indebtedness to Heidegger, see Janicaud, "Heidegger und Jean-Paul Sartre."
8. Grassi *et al.*, *Geistige Überlieferung*. Cf. Ott, *Martin Heidegger*, p. 271.
9. Grassi, *Il Problema della metafisica platonica*. See Rubini, "Philology as Philosophy."
10. Ott, *Martin Heidegger*, p. 272.
11. Philipse, "Heidegger and Ethics," p. 458.
12. Manser, *Sartre*, p. 163.
13. Kant, *Critique of Pure Reason*, A141.
14. See Schrader, "Basic Problems of Philosophical Ethics."
15. Kuki Shuzo was the first to dedicate a book to Heidegger's thought. The report on Sartre's encounter with Kuki is found in a letter to Charles Morris by one Zygmunt (I assume the Zygmunt in question was the sociologist Zygmunt Bauman). See "Question on Letter to Charles Morris on Heidegger & Sartre." See also Light, *Shuzo Kuki and Jean-Paul Sartre*.
16. Nietzsche, *The Birth of Tragedy*, p. 164.

STEVEN CROWELL

10 Sartre's existentialism and the nature of consciousness

10.1 SARTRE AND MODERN IDEALISM

When Jean-Paul Sartre died in 1980 his body lay in state and was viewed by more than fifty thousand people.[1] It is safe to say that few of these were there because the deceased had authored a volume with the forbidding subtitle, "An Essay in Phenomenological Ontology," or because he had helped to free modern thought from the spell of transcendental idealism. Sartre died a notorious public intellectual – "the hated conscience of his century"[2] – and it was his pugnacious advocacy of unpopular causes, his commitment to resistance in all its forms, his well-known novels and plays, and, of course, his association with the legends of "existentialism," that fascinated the crowd. Sartre dominated French intellectual life as no one had before and no one has since, but by 1980 the idea that his *philosophy* was worth critical consideration seemed quaint. *Being and Nothingness*? Old hat. Naïve. Pre-linguistic-turn. Metaphysical. *Phenomenological.* Sartre's idiom seemed irrevocably tied to the subjectivism and psychologism that structuralism and analytic philosophy had finally laid to rest. No matter that Sartre himself had deconstructed the metaphysical subject; the emphasis on consciousness in *Being and Nothingness* marked it as *passé*. Hadn't Sartre himself abandoned *Being and Nothingness* in favor of Marxism, which "remains ... the philosophy of our time"?[3]

Nevertheless, Sartre *was* a philosopher; he *did* grapple brilliantly with philosophical problems bequeathed by the modern tradition; and his existentialism *can* be evaluated in terms of the purely philosophical motives of its birth. Before Sartre was an existentialist he was a phenomenologist, and, as this chapter will argue, he understood key elements of his existentialist theory of the self to be direct consequences of adopting the phenomenological approach to consciousness. Today consciousness has again become a respectable topic in philosophy. Thus it may be possible to rescue Sartre's existentialism from the bars and cafés of popular fantasy and bring it once more into the debate.

The present chapter's approach to Sartre's vast and often unruly thought is quite limited. Its guiding question may be formulated as follows: what must "I" be – what is it to be a self – if we "abandon the hypothesis of the contents of consciousness"?[4] This move entails rejecting a whole set of philosophical assumptions deriving from Descartes and three centuries of his followers. Descartes conceives the mind as a kind of theater populated by "ideas" of extra-mental entities. Such contents of consciousness – "representations" – are actual entities, ontologically distinct from the entities they represent. In ordinary life we do not believe that the things we see, feel, and touch are modifications of the mind, that they belong "in us" rather than in the world; we think they are tables, chairs, and other people. Descartes found reasons to question this sort of realism, however, and such reasons have been hard to shake – at least for philosophers. The result has been a continuing struggle with idealism: broadly, any position which holds that the world is only present to us mediated by mental entities – a position that often brings skepticism in its wake. This philosophical idealism is the target of Sartre's existentialism, which sees itself as putting an end to the Cartesian legacy by fulfilling the promise of Edmund Husserl's phenomenological approach to consciousness. Hence, if we are to understand Sartre's contribution to freeing us from the Cartesian "way of ideas," we must first understand something of Husserl's.[5]

10.2 HUSSERL'S LEGACY: THE INTENTIONALITY OF CONSCIOUSNESS

Phenomenology, as Husserl understands it, is a particular way of approaching philosophical problems; specifically, it is reflective description and analysis of experience as it is lived from the first-person perspective. Its interest in consciousness arises from this, since "consciousness" designates the field of first-person experience. In principle there are any number of ways to approach consciousness in this sense – for instance, by explaining it as the result of causal processes in the brain or as a late stage of evolutionary development – but any such approach presupposes a prior familiarity with what it is trying to explain. If this prior understanding of consciousness is faulty, the explanation is likely to go astray. According to Husserl this has been the fate of modern psychology, since its prior understanding of the nature of consciousness derives from Descartes's faulty representationalist model. Hence the need for phenomenology: a reflective description of consciousness that avoids third-person theories.

Husserl's great discovery was that if one "brackets out" such theories, one uncovers the semantic character of consciousness – the fact that conscious states and attitudes refer to things in the world. This semantic character – in phenomenological terms, "intentionality" – is intrinsic to consciousness: all consciousness is consciousness *of* something *as* something. Two things are to be especially noted here. First, intentionality is a descriptive feature of consciousness, not one that is *attributed* to it through the hypothesis of contents – mental entities or representations – that function referentially. Perceiving a tree and being conscious of a representation of a tree (say, in a photograph) are two different things, and the former does not need the latter for its meaning. The second point concerns this meaning itself. Phenomenological reflection does not reveal a world of meaningless sensations, atomistically separated from one another, which would need to be integrated by cognitive algorithms. Rather, it accepts that our experience is of daunting challenges, threatening storms, loveable oafs, inviting pools, and impossible dreams, and it seeks to investigate how such meanings arise and reinforce or conflict with one another in experience itself. In phenomenological jargon, reflection traces the "constitution" of the meaningful objects of experience.

For instance – to use an example from *Being and Nothingness* – the constitution of a Ming vase as "fragile" is something quite other than its being composed of a certain sort of material. Clay is clay, whatever shape it may take, and the fact that there is now one piece of it and then (after dropping it) there are several does not mean that the clay is fragile. It has just been "rearranged" (*BN*, p. 40). The *vase* is fragile, and though it is composed of clay, it is *constituted* as a vase by certain norms that determine what it is supposed to be, what it is *meant* to be. These norms must be present *in* experience:

it is not enough that they somehow pertain to the vase; I must act in light of them, understand them. Only so can I see the vase as fragile; that is, as exposed to a certain sort of failure – namely, failure to hold, through the redistribution of what it is made of, the shape necessary to its proper functioning. There are other ways it can fail, of course – by being leaky or awkward, for instance – and these too are constituted in certain ways. Thus fragility is established through experienced relations of meaning, relations which phenomenology sets out to explore.

It is important to recognize that phenomenology is not psychological reflection in the sense of introspecting my particular mental states. The vase and its fragility belong to the world. In Sartre's language, which he borrows from Husserl, the vase is "transcendent" – that is, it is not "immanent" to my mind, a content of consciousness; it is *other* than my consciousness of it. Thus, to be constituted in consciousness does not mean to be rendered subjective. The field of meaning-relations is the "transcendental field," and it includes all transcendent entities whatsoever.[6] Tables and chairs are transcendent in this sense, but so are numbers, logical laws, and social institutions – as are quarks, comets, brains and, of course, other people and *their* mental states.

In *The Transcendence of the Ego*, an early essay that in many ways lays the groundwork for *Being and Nothingness*, Sartre insisted on this point against those who saw phenomenology as a return to Cartesian idealism:

> [N]othing is more unjust than to call phenomenologists "idealists." On the contrary, for centuries we have not felt in philosophy such a realistic current. The phenomenologists have plunged man back into the world; they have given full measure to man's agonies and sufferings, and also his rebellions. (*TE*, p. 104)

It is telling that in speaking of the "world" into which phenomenology has plunged us once more, Sartre does not invoke the world of quarks, molecules, and brains, nor even the world of tables, chairs and cats on mats, but the world of agonies, sufferings, and rebellions – a world, in short, where that which is agonizing, or tormenting, or oppressive is as real as anything else. The phenomenological realism that Sartre champions is not any kind of materialism but what we may call a *realism of meaning*.

Given this understanding of the constitution of transcendence and the resulting realism of meaning, the *ego* presents a problem. For it is certainly not a particular mental process like perceiving, willing, imagining, or judging – something immanent – but nor does it seem to be something in the world, a transcendent object. In confronting this issue Husserl came to speak, paradoxically, of a "transcendence in immanence." For Sartre, however, this paradox is evidence of a deep confusion about the nature of consciousness – namely, the idea that all conscious states exhibit an ego whose states they are, the source or agent or patient of those states. In Husserl's technical terms, the "transcendental field of consciousness" is "egological"; there is a "transcendental ego." In speaking of the *transcendence* of the ego, Sartre pointedly rejects this view: "We should like to show here that the ego is neither formally nor materially *in* consciousness; it is outside, *in the world*. It is a being of the world, like the ego of another" (*TE*, p. 31). The emptying out of consciousness – abandoning "the hypothesis of the contents of consciousness" – expunges not only representations but the ego as well. Thus, in answer to our leading question – what must I be if consciousness has no content? – *The Transcendence of the Ego* offers a *non*-egological account of consciousness. Central to this account is the concept of "non-positional self-awareness," which will play a key role in *Being and Nothingness*.

10.3 THE EGO AND NON-POSITIONAL SELF-AWARENESS

Can one conceive of a "purely impersonal consciousness" (*TE*, p. 37)? Ever since Descartes, the connection between the "I" and the "think" has been a puzzle. Sartre rejects Kant's purely formal solution – the "I think must be *able* to accompany all my representations" – for the question concerns "the existence *in fact* of the I in consciousness" (*TE*, p. 35). Is it a fact that all conscious experience is also always experience of an I who experiences? Sartre answers this question by distinguishing between the way things appear when we reflect on some (past or ongoing) experience and the way things appear "pre-reflectively," within that experience itself.

When I reflect on my experience of running to catch up with a bus, I appear to myself as an agent (I choose to run), as being in a certain state (I desire to catch the bus), and as possessing a certain quality (I am late "again"). But Sartre denies that such reflection captures experience as it is lived, where, in contrast, there is only "consciousness of the streetcar-as-having-to-be-overtaken." I am "plunged into the world of objects; it is they which constitute the unity of my consciousness ... but *me*, I have disappeared ... There is no place for *me* on this level" (*TE*, p. 49). For Sartre, such pre-reflective experience has no need of an ego to unify its elements into a single experience because the *object* provides the necessary unity; all my gestures, perceptions, and states "intend" or "mean" the identical object: the bus-to-be-caught. "By intentionality consciousness transcends itself. It unifies itself by escaping from itself" (*TE*, p. 38). Furthermore, *were* there to be an ego in consciousness it would "tear consciousness from itself," it would "slide into consciousness like an opaque blade" (*TE*, p. 40). At the pre-reflective level, the presence of an ego would compete with the object of which I am conscious: all experience would be of two objects, one "outer" and one "inner." But not only is this not how we experience the world; things *could not* be experienced in this way, since to be (pre-reflectively) conscious of any object is to constitute it as other than the act of consciousness itself, as transcendent. There is no "inner" space in which I might locate such an object: both inner and outer can only be constituted in relation to what Sartre (following Husserl) calls an "absolute" consciousness (*TE*, p. 96), which would be consciousness of the norms that constitute the distinction between inner and outer. Interiority (psychological subjectivity) is just as transcendent as exteriority.[7] The ego, an objective identity, belongs to the world.

But if in this sense "all is ... clear and lucid in consciousness," if no ego inhabits it, it is nevertheless the case that all consciousness is "self-consciousness" in a different sense. The very lucidity of consciousness, its openness to the world, is possible only because "it has no need at all of a reflecting consciousness to be conscious of itself" (*TE*, p. 45). In being aware of the streetcar-to-be-overtaken, my experience does not involve awareness of a second object, *me*; but it does involve awareness of *itself* – a pre-reflective, non-objectifying, "non-positional" (*TE*, p. 41) consciousness of being what it is. To be conscious of something is to be conscious of being so. To the extent that perception is a conscious state or act, my perception of this landscape or that streetcar is aware of itself *as* perceiving. It is sometimes thought that cases of so-called "blindsight" – where subjects seem to be able to make discriminations in the environment corresponding to those they would make were they self-consciously perceptive, even though they claim to see nothing – show that consciousness need not be aware of itself. But such cases show, at most, only that perceiving involves an information-processing aspect that can function independently from its character as conscious experience. But neither can the self-awareness of conscious states be understood as a "higher-order" state (such as reflection) that targets them as objects, since in order to provide the target state with its conscious character a higher-order state would itself have to be conscious, yielding an infinite regress. For such reasons, Sartre holds that non-positional self-awareness is the very being of consciousness, "the law of its existence." Indeed, "the existence of consciousness is an absolute because consciousness is consciousness of itself" (*TE*, p. 40).

The concept of non-positional self-awareness is central to *Being and Nothingness* – "Behind the cogito of Descartes we must find the pre-reflective cogito" (*BN*, p. 13) – and for Sartre, this peculiar mode of awareness demands that we completely rethink what it is to be a self. It shall thus serve as our guiding thread as we enter his labyrinthine "bible of existentialism."

10.4 BEING-IN-ITSELF AND BEING-FOR-ITSELF

Readers of *Being and Nothingness* immediately confront the fact that Sartre is writing with three primary interlocutors in mind: Husserl, Hegel, and Heidegger.[8] This is not always a blessing, for it introduces layers of motivation into the text that can obscure its overall argument. From Husserl Sartre takes his starting point, the intentionality of experience. This is what, in the book's dense Introduction, he calls "the phenomenon," distinguishing it from Kant's notion of mere (subjective) *appearance*. The phenomenon is the thing itself as it appears. From Heidegger Sartre takes the form of the question he proposes to explore: because the phenomenon seems to escape both traditional realism and idealism, it is necessary to ask about the *being* of the phenomenon. Heidegger held that phenomenology is essentially ontology – an approach to the question of the "meaning of being" – and, like Sartre, he held that

Dasein (human being) was first in the order of ontological inquiry. Sartre differs from Heidegger, however, in insisting that one must begin with "the *cogito*," that is, with *consciousness* – a term that Heidegger avoids.[9] For this reason, Sartre's ontological analysis of the phenomenon starts with the framework of the "revealing" and the "revealed," for the articulation of which he turns to his third interlocutor, Hegel: to understand the being of the phenomenon one must recognize two distinct "regions" of being, "being-in-itself" (*être-en-soi*) and "being-for-itself" (*être-pour-soi*). Since this has given rise to the impression that Sartre's existentialism is essentially a neo-Cartesianism, we must get clear about how these terms function before we can appreciate his very non-Cartesian account of the self.

Sartre's argument in the Introduction turns on the claim that the phenomenon involves two forms of what he calls "transphenomenality." On the one hand, the tree that I perceive over there is not *reducible* to the series of appearances in which it is given to me. This transphenomenality of the object is being-in-itself. On the other hand, the tree is not something *other* than this series of appearances either; appearing belongs to its very nature. This means that the phenomenon makes reference to a *different sort* of transphenomenality, one that constitutes it as appearing, as "revealed." Sartre calls this the "dimension of transphenomenality in the subject," being-for-itself. It thus looks as though the phenomenon is a product of "two absolutely separated regions" (*BN*, p. 26).

On the one hand, being-in-itself is what consciousness reveals, and if one tries to characterize this transphenomenal dimension without any appeal to consciousness, one can only say that it "is," it "is in-itself," and it "is what it is" (*BN*, p. 29). A famous scene from *Nausea* invokes this "absurd" aspect of the in-itself:

> So I was in the park just now. The roots of the chestnut tree were sunk in the ground just under my bench. I couldn't remember it was a root anymore. The words had vanished and with them the significance of things ... And then, all of a sudden, there it was, clear as day: existence had suddenly unveiled itself.[10]

Struggling to characterize this revelation, Roquentin seizes upon the gap between the generality of explanation and the "in the way" (*de trop*) character of what is: "The world of explanations and reasons is not the world of existence." You cannot pass "from its function as a root, as a breathing pump, to *that*, to this oily, callous, headstrong look."[11] As the characteristics, properties, and functions of things melt away and the absurdity of the contingent "invades" him, Roquentin finds the "naked world" revealing itself as "all thick, a jelly," a "sticky filth ... tons and tons of existence, endless."[12] On the other hand, being-in-itself is *revealed*, and this can only be thanks to something altogether other than it, consciousness. Consciousness must therefore be a type of being that is *not* what the in-itself is: it *is not*; it is *not-itself*; it is *what it is not*. From a logical point of view such characterizations are absurd; nor does Sartre base any arguments on them. Instead, he uses them in a purely heuristic way to trace the implications of that non-positional self-awareness he uncovered in *The Transcendence of the Ego*.

As the negative definition of being-for-itself makes plain, these two transphenomenal regions are not symmetrical. Appearing is necessary to the *root* (the phenomenon), but this is not true of being-in-itself; it need not be revealed. Consciousness, however, is nothing but being-revealing and so depends on something other than it, which it reveals. From the fact that all consciousness is consciousness of *something*, then, Sartre derives what he calls an "ontological proof": "consciousness is born *supported* by a being which is not itself" (*BN*, p. 23). This dependence is expressed in a formula that Sartre employs in many variations throughout *Being and Nothingness*: consciousness is "what it is not and is not what it is." It is "what it is not" because it depends on what it is not (being-in-itself) in order to be at all; and it is "not what it is" because, in this very dependence, its identity is undermined. Because in being positionally aware of something consciousness is non-positionally aware of itself, it can never *coincide* with the world it reveals, not least with that which it takes *itself* to be. At this level of abstraction such claims can seem frivolous, and there is no doubt that Sartre sometimes allows his language to play. But this non-identification is the phenomenological basis for the familiar existential idea that human reality is fundamentally alienated.

With the mention of "human reality" we reach Sartre's goal. For he introduces his ontological terms only in order to *cancel* the appearance of metaphysical dualism they suggest.

It appears that we have barred all doors and that we are now condemned to regard transcendent being and consciousness as two closed totalities without possible communication. It will be necessary to show that the problem allows a solution other than that of realism or idealism. (*BN*, p. 26)

That solution consists in overcoming the fallacy of misplaced concreteness to recognize that transcendent being and consciousness "constitute only moments" of what is *genuinely* concrete or real: "man within the world in that specific union which Heidegger ... calls 'being-in-the-world'" (*BN*, p. 34). It cannot be that the in-itself and for-itself are themselves things or substances out of which the phenomenon is *composed*. Such a metaphysical dualism would indeed reintroduce all the problems of Cartesianism. But Sartre's is a *phenomenological* ontology, and so these terms must be understood as principles of the *constitution* of the phenomenon, as norms that establish meaning.[13] The subsequent 765 pages of text are devoted to showing how human reality is "that being which includes within itself these two radically separated regions of being" (*BN*, p. 30), and it is the phenomenological description and analysis of this "inclusion" that gives birth to existentialism as a distinctive picture of the self in the world.[14]

10.5 NEGATION AND POSSIBILITY

The first chapter of *Being and Nothingness* is entitled "The Origin of Negation," and it is not initially clear why Sartre's investigation into human reality should begin in this way. The upshot of Sartre's quest for origins is that "man is the being through whom nothingness comes into the world" (*BN*, p. 59), that human reality is something like a "worm" that "lies coiled in the heart of being" (*BN*, p. 57). But why is the question of negation or nothingness important in the first place? Part of the answer lies in Sartre's aim of accounting for the being of the phenomenon – that is, for the being of meaning. Meaning cannot be understood apart from *possibility*, and possibility, in turn, cannot be understood as a function of being, the in-itself, actuality. Hence an ontological account of meaning requires an account of non-being and so of negation. Let us unpack these points a bit more fully.

First, the kind of possibility that Sartre has in mind is not logical possibility, which is indifferent to actuality. The actual dollar in my pocket is no less a logical "possibility" than are the ten that are not there. Sartre's ontological concept of possibility, on the other hand, *contrasts* with what is actual: what is possible *is not*, since it is *merely* possible. But if this is so, then, second, our consciousness of possibility – our consciousness not only that there is a dollar in my pocket but that there might not be, that there could be ten – demands some explanation. How does negation come to infect the plenum of being-in-itself? The consequences are far-reaching, since consciousness of possibility is involved in all intentionality, all experience of a meaningful world.

To see this, recall our Ming vase. To perceive the fragility of the vase is to be conscious of the possibility of its non-being in the form of its destructibility. This "being conscious of non-being" cannot simply be a matter of our judging that the vase is fragile, since the judgment presupposes a prior awareness of its fragility. It is not as though I first see the vase and then judge that it is possible for it to break; rather, I *step lightly* around it, I *handle it gently*. In Sartre's terms, I have a "pre-judicative comprehension of nothingness as such and a conduct *in the face of nothingness*" (*BN*, p. 40). I perceive fragility ("an objective fact") and accommodate my behavior to it. Such behavior evinces a "concrete intuition" of non-being. This is not merely to grasp the logical possibility that the vase could break; if it were, it would be incomprehensible why I would not simultaneously act in light of the logical possibility that it might fly away. Rather it is to *perceive* this *specific* possibility of non-being: fragility.

Sartre calls these beings whose encounter presupposes a "pre-judicative comprehension of nothingness," *negatités*. Among them he lists distance, change, repulsion, regret, and distraction (*BN*, p. 55), but the point is quite general: to encounter anything *as* something (to encounter something as a person, a person as desirable, a table as wobbly, a tree as tall, a knob as a handle) is to act toward it in light of some possibility. What something means is a function not just of what it *is* in the sense of the in-itself, but of what it *can be* – that is, of certain norms that govern its ability to maintain identity through change. A "desirable" person is not just a jumble of attributes but those attributes in light of possibilities of satisfying or failing to satisfy certain attitudes on the part of another. A table is not in-itself wobbly, but only in light of a norm according to which it "ought to" but "does *not*" maintain itself in a certain position. This does not mean that the table is not "really" wobbly; it just means that its *being* so cannot be understood solely with the principle of being-in-itself.

If the possibility in light of which things show up as this or that cannot derive from the in-itself, where does it come from? Sartre is certainly not the first philosopher to point out the connections between determination (meaning) and negation (possibility), but he argues that previous philosophers have not appreciated the implications of this connection for our understanding of *ourselves*. It is true that "non-being always appears within the limits of a human expectation" (*BN*, p. 38). For instance, "it is man who renders cities destructible, precisely because he posits them as fragile and as precious and because he adopts a system of protective measures with regard to them" (*BN*, p. 40). But to say that such determinations are tied to our expectations explains nothing, since the problem reappears. What, after all, *is* an expectation? It is a *negatité*, a conscious state that includes negation in its definition ("awareness of what *is not* but likely will be"). What, then, must *consciousness* be if something like an expectation is possible? It is in answer to this question that Sartre introduces the existential concept of an inescapable, and therefore "monstrous" (*TE*, p. 100), *freedom*.

10.6 POSSIBILITY AND FREEDOM

An expectation cannot be conceived as some actual state or "content" of consciousness, for in that case the reference to possibility (negation) it contains would be unintelligible. Nor can such negation be conceived as a logical operator, since such an operation would be subject to the same objection: as a kind of *being*, it could never break through the actual to open up the conditional space of meaning. If, in Sartre's famous example, I expect to find Pierre in the café and gradually become conscious of his absence, "I am of necessity forced to produce an act of thought which no prior state can determine or motivate ... Inasmuch as my present state would be a prolongation of my prior state, every opening by which negation could slip through would be completely blocked" (*BN*, p. 63). Thus, to understand something like expectation it is necessary to reject the psychological model according to which consciousness is a "stream of *Erlebnisse* [experiences]," a continuum of states that are causally or "motivationally" ordered. On a model where one state motivates the next, conditionality is at best a third-person construct. If that were the whole truth about consciousness, our first-person experience of expectation – and all other consciousness of possibility – would be a complete mystery. But it is not the whole truth; it is, as *The Transcendence of the Ego* argued, only the image that consciousness presents when taken as the object of psychological *reflection*.

The (ontological) truth about consciousness, in contrast, is that it cannot contain anything at all, cannot be a "series of *Erlebnisse*," cannot have any content. Consciousness exhausts itself in being consciousness of the world. At the same time, it cannot simply *be* the world; hence it must be non-positional self-awareness of *not being* the world. To be perceptually aware of a tree, for instance, is to be non-positionally aware of perceiving, and this is necessarily to be aware of *not being* the tree. Perhaps I feel myself to be "at one" with the tree, to *be* the tree; I totally identify with it. Nevertheless, to the extent that the tree is *experienced* in this way there is a non-positional consciousness of *not* being it. This entails that consciousness can neither contain, nor be actually connected to, anything. Non-positional self-awareness is thus the origin of negation: by its very essence consciousness must "disassociate itself from the causal series," must "effect a nihilating withdrawal" from being, must necessarily and always be "putting itself out of circuit in relation to [the] existent" (*BN*, pp. 58, 60f.).

Thus Sartre transforms Husserl's distinction between a psychological and a phenomenological view of consciousness into a doctrine of freedom with radical implications for our conception of ourselves. Selfhood occupies an uneasy place between being-in-itself and being-for-itself precisely because the freedom of consciousness means that I can never coincide with any *determinate* thing (what I or others take myself to be), with any "nature." To exist as conscious is to be free, and this is to lack a nature or "essence" that would account for what I am or ought to be: "Human freedom precedes essence in man and makes it possible; the essence of human being is suspended in his freedom" (*BN*, p. 60). The existential slogan that "existence precedes essence" derives from the nature of consciousness as freedom. Selfhood is thus nothing substantial but is, as Sartre noted in *The Transcendence of the Ego*, "performance" (*TE*, p. 94).

10.7 FREEDOM AND ANGUISH

For Sartre, the "proof" of ontological freedom lies in its being a necessary condition for meaning, the phenomenon (*BN*, p. 70). Freedom is not, therefore, established by considering the will, or the nature of action. To say that I am radically free is not to say that my ego is a peculiar worldly entity that, unlike other entities, possesses the property of being the cause of its own actions. This familiar picture of "free will" is merely the obverse of the deterministic picture of the self, and both are what Sartre calls "patterns of flight" that I adopt in reflection so as to conceal the inescapable ontological freedom of consciousness. "Determinism, before being a theoretical conception, is first an attitude of excuse" (*BN*, p. 78). When I am ashamed of some pattern of behavior, I chalk it up to irresistible impulses or to my poor upbringing. On the other hand, when I am proud of something I do, I treat it as emanating from my free choice, from my "true" self: a "little God which inhabits me and possesses my freedom as a metaphysical virtue" (*BN*, p. 81). In both cases I treat myself as a substance and my freedom as a capacity that I sometimes exercise and sometimes do not. But ontological freedom precedes such selfhood; it is the very "being of consciousness." If that is so, and if consciousness is always non-positionally aware of itself, then "consciousness ought to exist as consciousness of freedom" (*BN*, p. 65). And if "what we are accustomed to call a revelation of the inner sense or an original intuition of our freedom" (*BN*, p. 82) does not count as consciousness of freedom, what *does* count? For Sartre, it is "in *anguish* that man gets the consciousness of his freedom ... anguish is the mode of being of freedom as consciousness of being" (*BN*, p. 65).

To say that I experience my ontological freedom in anguish is to say that it is in anguish that I come face to face with the "disengagement from the causal series" that is the essence of consciousness.

Why should my experience of the nothingness that separates consciousness from its past and future be experienced precisely as anguish? It is because such experience reveals my *alienation* from myself, the fact that my desire to be something necessarily fails, that my existence is not supported by any essence. Anguish is the affective recognition that, as Sartre puts it, "there is never a motive *in* consciousness; motives are only *for* consciousness" (*BN*, p. 71), and he provides two famous examples to show what this means: vertigo is "anguish in the face of the future," and addiction is "anguish in the face of the past."

Walking along a narrow ledge, I begin to fear that I might stumble on a stone and plummet into the abyss. To get a grip on my fear, I "take measures" – that is, I reflectively posit myself as the proximal cause of my behavior: I propose to walk very carefully, to stand close to the sheltered side, etc. In so doing, I treat the outcome as "my *possibility*" and thereby simultaneously acknowledge that the decisive conduct will emanate from my *future* self. Sartre notes that this would not produce anguish "if I could apprehend myself in my relations with these possibles as a cause producing effects" (*BN*, p. 67), but though I can *think* this way, I cannot *apprehend* myself as such a cause. The anguish that is vertigo is precisely the apprehension of myself as "other than" a cause. If the self that I will be might avoid falling, it is equally possible that it will throw itself into the abyss, and nothing "I" do can determine the outcome. My future self is indeed *me* (otherwise I would not care about what it will do), but "I *am* not the self I will be." What I am *now* is "not the foundation for what I will be" in the way a cause is the foundation of its effect. As Sartre puts it, "*I am the self which I will be, in the mode of not being it*" (*BN*, p. 68). My freedom is experienced as the anguish of vertigo because "the self which I am depends on the self which I am not yet to the exact extent that the self which I am not yet does not depend on the self which I am" (*BN*, p. 69).

In a similar way, the addict experiences anguish when he is confronted with the nothingness that separates his present from his past. Having lost everything, a compulsive gambler vows never to gamble again. The indignities, the miseries inflicted on his family, etc., are vivid to him and motivate his commitment to quit. He goes forth confident that these motives have the force of causes and will shield him from his compulsions. Of an evening, however, he finds himself before the gaming table and in anguish experiences his freedom: the motives are still "there" – that is, he remembers them, can imagine his poor family, etc. – but they have no force. He discovers that such motives are not *in* consciousness but only *for* consciousness, and that if they are to have any force at all they must be reconstituted *as* motives by his present self. The anguish of addiction is thus an experience of freedom in the sense of the inefficacy of resolve. In it, the gambler learns that he is not the self he was, in the mode of being it. He *is* that man – the gambler, the failure, the one who resolved to quit – but this "essence" is useless to him. To make this point, Sartre quotes Hegel: *Wesen ist was gewesen ist*. Essence is what has been (*BN*, p. 72).

To say that existence precedes essence, then, means that I can neither rest in nor disavow my identity. What I have done belongs to what Sartre calls my "facticity." I have been this or that person, and from a third-person point of view my facticity explains me: I am ruined "because" I gambled away my fortune, gave in to my impulses, etc. However, facticity is only ever the other side of my "transcendence," my freedom. What I have done is "a demand without being a recourse" (*BN*, p. 73); I have to own up to it, but it does not excuse (because it does not cause) what I subsequently do.

10.8 ENGAGEMENT, VALUES, AND BAD FAITH

If freedom is the essence of consciousness, and if anguish is the consciousness of freedom, why are we not always in anguish? Sartre answers that in some sense we are, but because we "are what we are not and are not what we are," we can engage in strategies of self-deception and Pascalian "distraction" in order to mask this freedom from ourselves.

The most common form of distraction is simply to act, to lose oneself in the world. A pre-reflective consciousness of possibilities is not sufficient to give rise to anguish; rather, those possibilities have to be made explicit in reflection. Ordinarily, however, "we act before positing our possibilities"; possibilities are disclosed precisely in the process of being realized. To act is to render the gap between my present and future self infinitely small. "The alarm which rings in the morning refers to the possibility of my going to work ... but to apprehend the summons of the alarm *as a summons* is to *get up*" (*BN*, p. 75). By getting up I forestall the emergence of a consciousness of possibility as "my" possibility, and so of anguish: I could not get up, refuse to work, die. To act is to be carried along as though compelled by a series of demands posed by the world, and this is possible because *engaged* consciousness is not the naked subjectivity of the pre-reflective *cogito* but rather that subjectivity as "clothed," so to speak, in the many roles it has always already adopted, its "practical identities":[15] lover, writer, breadwinner, resistance fighter. I jump out of bed at the sound of the alarm clock because the alarm addresses me – "the breadwinner" – as a demand, and so long as I act as the breadwinner I will get up. Being engaged in a practical identity thus "precludes the anguished intuition that it is I who confer on the alarm clock its exigency – I and I alone" (*BN*, p. 76).

This notion of "exigency" is the heart of Sartre's existential account of values, including moral values. For Sartre, values are "ideal." This does not mean that values are timelessly true as opposed to merely conventional or historically relative. Rather, values are ideal because they are "demands which lay a claim to a foundation," while "this foundation can in no way be *being*" (*BN*, p. 76). The foundation of value cannot lie in being-in-itself because a value is a kind of *ought*. A pattern of behavior (say, truth-telling or courage) becomes a value only by being contrasted with another pattern and preferred to it. But the one pattern "is" no less than the other. Hence, according to Sartre, it is beside the point to argue that one system of values is objectively valid or rationally justified, for this does nothing to change its ideality. What makes it *valuable* that some pattern is rationally justifiable or objectively valid? Why ought one to prefer a pattern of behavior that is rationally justifiable over one that is not? On Sartre's analysis, there is the potential for anguish in the gap that separates the *demand* character of a value (its normativity) from its *exigency* (its normative force).

> Value derives its being from its exigency and not its exigency from its being. It does not deliver itself to a contemplative intuition which would apprehend it as *being* value ... On the contrary, it can be revealed only to an active freedom which makes it exist as value by the sole fact of recognizing it as such. (*BN*, p. 76)

Values are exigent (i.e., they exhibit themselves as genuinely *valuable*) only in being acted upon. The minute they emerge to an objectifying reflection as "values," however, they have no *conceivable* exigency. They cannot be reflected upon in their character as values – cannot be made explicit as *possible* modes of behavior, in contrast to operating tacitly as norms of my engaged actions – "without being at the same time 'put into question'," and that means, without standing on the other side of the divide that separates them from their normative force. "It follows," according to Sartre, "that my freedom is the unique foundation of values and that *nothing*, absolutely nothing, justifies me in adopting this or that value, this or that scale of values. As the being by whom values exist, I am unjustifiable" (*BN*, p. 76).[16]

"Ordinary morality," in contrast, is a kind of discourse that attempts to divert us from the anguished recognition of freedom. Values, in the form of norms or oughts, are built into the social roles in light of which I pre-reflectively act. Because I act as a breadwinner, I value getting up and perceive the alarm clock as an exigent demand: I get up. So too, because I am a bourgeois I do not spit on the sidewalk, I tell the truth, and I do not steal. If I see someone who spits on the sidewalk, lies constantly, and robs people blind I am indignant at the "baseness" of such a person. But my respectability and the baseness of the other are "moral values" only because I am engaged in the world as a bourgeois; the "moral" quality of such behavior does not pre-exist my commitment to it. "My indignation has given to me that negative value 'baseness'" – i.e., it is *because* I am indignant that a pattern of behavior appears base (as including within its character an ought-not-to-be). To another who does not share my bourgeois commitments, such a pattern may have nothing base about it. Which of us is correct? We both are. That is the ideality of values. Ordinary morality rests on my freedom and commitment, a fact that I discover in anguish. On this analysis, it is little wonder that individuals and groups cling to their "family values" with the tenacity of pit bulls.[17]

Pre-reflective engagement in the world is not our only response to the "monstrous" consciousness of our freedom. We noted that the usual talk of freedom and determinism is a pattern of flight meant to conceal the anguish of ontological freedom, but this sort of reflective "rationalization" is easily disrupted by pre-reflective reality. A more subtle pattern of flight is what Sartre calls "bad faith" (*mauvaise foi*). Bad faith is not a matter of explicit reflection but a way of pre-reflectively playing hide-and-seek with oneself, a kind of self-deception made possible by the fact that selfhood is constituted by consciousness of being what it is not and not being what it is.

Bad faith is the attempt to avoid admitting to oneself the meaning of one's behavior, even as one is engaged in it. Because one must acknowledge such meaning in order to conceal it, the possibility of bad faith is paradoxical. Nevertheless, because I do not possess my identity in the way "an inkwell *is* an inkwell" (*BN*, p. 102) – that is, in the manner of the in-itself – I can both formulate the project of self-deception and deflect the demand for sincerity in such a way as to avoid shame or other painful self-avowals.[18] For instance, despite a pattern of behavior that can only be described as "cowardly," I can fail to notice this fact about myself. Each element of the pattern is reduced merely to what it is – not part of a pattern but a particular choice, with extenuating circumstances in each case. Simultaneously, I can view myself as being courageous, since it is always possible that I will be "when it counts." In this way I emphasize my transcendence – namely, the fact that I "am" these supposedly cowardly acts, but only in the mode of *not being* what I am. If you want me to admit "sincerely" that I am indeed cowardly, I can deflect you since, as Sartre notes, "the project of sincerity is itself in bad faith" insofar as it demands that I see myself as having the fixed identity of a thing. I can insist that "I am not a coward" – which would be the simple truth were I to mean by it that I am not a coward "in the mode of being it" (i.e., I am what I am not). But I am in bad faith because I deflect your demand for sincerity in the very terms you use: I deny being a coward in the same ontological sense in which a table is not a chair. But in that sense, I *am* a coward; cowardice is the meaning of my behavior. At a certain level I "know" this; bad faith is a "meta-stable" project (*BN*, p. 113). But the very ontology that makes bad faith possible entails the possibility of an epistemology in bad faith: I can always trade on the fact that "to believe is to know that one believes, and to know that one believes is no longer to believe," since "it is *only* to believe" (*BN*, p. 114) – that is, to admit that there is always room for doubt. The self in bad faith is a perpetual sophist.

10.9 SELF AS PERFORMANCE: PROJECT AND SITUATION

By the end of Part One of *Being and Nothingness*, Sartre has outlined the picture of human reality that emerges when we abandon the hypothesis of the contents of consciousness and see non-positional self-consciousness as negation (freedom). One's life, on this view, is performance: "a constantly renewed obligation to remake the *Self* which designates the free being" (*BN*, p. 72). Note that the Self *designates* the free being; that is, it is the image or sign of such a being, that which freedom *constitutes* itself as being. In Sartre's language, selfhood is a "project" – a choice or "original projection of myself" (*BN*, p. 77), a commitment to specific patterns of behavior (roles or ways of being) that one finds in one's world. By making such roles my own, the world takes on whatever meaning and value it has for me; it becomes my *situation*. "Our being is immediately 'in situation,' that is, it arises in enterprises and knows itself first insofar as it is reflected in those enterprises" (*BN*, p. 77). From within a situation the meaningful world appears to be a brute "given." Nevertheless, it is only through my commitment to a project that it has any meaning at all.

> I emerge alone and in anguish confronting the unique and original project which constitutes my being ... Nothing can ensure me against myself, cut off from the world and from my essence by the nothingness which I *am*. I have to realize the meaning of the world and of my essence; I make my decision concerning them – without justification and without excuse. (*BN*, pp. 77–78)

Sartre's picture of the self thus radicalizes the traditional concept of autonomy: to "be" *just is* to be responsible for giving oneself the law of one's being, to act in accord with the norms of some project or role. Sartre illustrates the idea of bad faith by describing a waiter who is "playing at *being* a waiter" (*BN*, p. 102). The waiter is in bad faith because, by means of his affectations and exaggerated movements, he wishes us to grasp him as a thing, entirely coinciding with his role. But such bad faith is only an extreme case of what we all do all the time, and must do if we are to *be* anything at all. At a deeper level, Sartre's picture of the self as a player of roles points toward what he calls one's "fundamental project" (*BN*, p. 721) – a basic choice of being that expresses itself in all I do as a certain style of self-presentation, a certain pattern of decision-making and responsiveness to the world's solicitations. Although the fundamental project is conscious, it is a deeply sedimented sense of self that is not easily brought to reflective awareness. To uncover and interpret it requires what Sartre calls "existential psychoanalysis," of which he attempts to provide examples in works such as *Baudelaire* and *L'Idiot de la famille*. At bottom, though, the ontological structure of selfhood is contradictory and "man is a useless passion" (*BN*, p. 784). For human reality is structurally the attempt to be "a consciousness which would be the foundation of its own being-in-itself by the pure consciousness it would have of itself" – an ideal, essentially contradictory, "which can be called God" (*BN*, p. 724)

But while Sartre's picture of selfhood is rooted in the nature of consciousness, it should be obvious that the human reality he describes cannot be *reduced* to consciousness, to what he calls "the ontological structure of the for-itself" (*BN*, p. 394). For though an isolated individual consciousness is conceivable (*BN*, p. 376) – solipsism is a logical possibility – *human* reality is not solipsistic but social. To act is to act in accord with *already given* norms and roles, even if my project is precisely to challenge them. The phenomena – the meanings involved in my projects – are inconceivable if there are no others in the world; phenomenologically speaking, no solitary consciousness could constitute them. Hence there are, as a matter of fact, other people. The world of human reality *cannot* be the world of Descartes's evil demon, nor the world of a brain in a vat.

This fact is not without consequences for an understanding of selfhood, for it means that I – *I myself* – have an aspect of my being that escapes me insofar as it is my being-for-others. My being-for-others is no mere image in the mind of the other person; it is an ontological feature of what *I* am. Even if consciousness contains no contents – even, that is, if there is no self or ego behind the scenes – a certain sort of substantial self comes to "haunt" consciousness, because there are others in the world who bestow upon me an "outside" that I must acknowledge as "me" without being its source. I am thus alienated from myself not only through the negativity of consciousness; I am also alienated from myself through my being-for-others.

10.10 BEING-FOR-OTHERS AS THE DEATH OF POSSIBILITIES

If the meaning of what I encounter derives from my projects, how are we to make sense of that experience in which I encounter not an object but another for-itself, another subject, another freedom? In traditional terms, this is the "problem of other minds," and Sartre's existential approach to it is one of his most important contributions to philosophy.

Sartre's account of social reality in *Being and Nothingness* – which is hyperbolically dramatic and rather underdeveloped – is less important than his reformulation of the problem, which had traditionally been posed in terms of knowledge. How do we know that that thing over there is "minded," that it is a subject? Behavior establishes the fact with a certain probability, but Sartre argues that such probability depends for its sense on an original experience in which the Other is "given to me directly as subject" (*BN*, p. 341). I may never be absolutely certain that this thing before me is minded, but this very uncertainty presupposes that the concept of "another" consciousness is intelligible to me, and this cannot be derived from *self*-consciousness alone. What, then, is our original experience of the other subject as subject? Sartre approaches the problem by way of a two-staged phenomenology. First, he describes how encountering the other as an object differs from encountering the many other objects in the world. Then, in his famous analysis of the Look (*le regard*), he uncovers the experience of the other as subject which the former presupposes. We shall examine each in turn.

In his *Cartesian Meditations*, Husserl described how perceiving another person involves awareness of a peculiar sort of absence.[19] *All* perception involves absence: when I see a house, the front side is visible while the back side is "absent," not directly visible. However, I am aware that were I to walk around the house, the back side, always already there, would come into view. To perceive another person, however, is to be aware of the absence of something that can *never* come into view as itself: the subjectivity of that person, his or her consciousness. This experience does not entail that consciousness is "inside," in some inaccessible realm. If that were so, I could conceivably gain access to it by developing a sixth sense, devising some apparatus to detect it, or in some other way. But the other person "escapes" me far more radically than any such inaccessible interiority. As Sartre puts it, I experience the Other's absence as a kind of "drain hole" through which the things in *my* world "run off" and disappear (*BN*, p. 343). To see a man sitting on a park bench is to experience the way the park's features, shaped by my project of taking a stroll, begin to organize themselves around another object in my landscape, turn their faces in a direction that is both objective and unfathomable.

But having described the experience of the other as object, Sartre argues that this sort of absence cannot be foundational. It presupposes that I have already experienced the Other as subject. But how is that possible? Sartre's innovation lies in recognizing that such an experience can only be one in which I experience *myself* as an *object for* the Other.

> If the Other-as-object is defined in connection with the world as the object which sees what I see, then my fundamental connection with the Other-as-subject must be able to be referred back to my permanent possibility of *being seen by* the Other. It is in and through the revelation of my being-as-object for the Other that I must be able to apprehend the presence of his being-as-subject. (*BN*, pp. 344–45)

What is it to experience oneself as an object? It cannot be a matter of *thinking* of oneself objectively – reflecting on one's mental states or other qualities – for the question concerns *pre*-reflective experience, subjectivity engaged in the world. Sartre thus describes how being an object is experienced *affectively*; specifically, it is in the experience of *shame* that I cannot but acknowledge that I am an object and so also that the Other is the subject for whom I am and before whom I am judged. "Shame is by nature *recognition*. I recognize that I *am* as the Other sees me" (*BN*, p. 302). To be "seen" by the Other is to discover oneself as an entity in the world – not for oneself but for *the Other*.

Sartre makes this vivid in his first-person description of a man peeking through a keyhole at a scene of seduction. The voyeur is completely absorbed in his experience; the world is spread out before him according to the meanings constituted in his act of looking and, though there is a non-positional self-awareness of that act, no "self" inhabits the experience, any more than a self inhabits my experience of running after the bus. All is pure for-itself, so to speak.

Suddenly, there are footsteps; the flood of shame signifies, as Sartre says, an "essential modification" in the experience. Specifically, "I now exist as *myself* for my unreflective consciousness" (*BN*, p. 349). The fact that it is for my *unreflective* consciousness that I now exist as myself is crucial here. We are not yet on the level of reflection or self-objectification, but I am nevertheless no longer a mere for-itself but a *self* – a modification of my being that *I* could not have produced:

> So long as we considered the for-itself in its isolation, we were able to maintain that the unreflective consciousness can not be inhabited by a self; the self was given in the form of an object and only for the reflective consciousness. But here the self comes to haunt the unreflective consciousness ... This means that all of a sudden I am conscious of myself as escaping myself, not in that I am the foundation of my own nothingness but in that I have my foundation outside myself. (*BN*, p. 349)

In short, though consciousness can have no contents and so cannot be "inhabited" by the self, it can be *haunted* by the self I am – as I am for the Other. The nature of the experience is such that it is pointless to deny that this is a genuine aspect of *my* being – to claim, for instance, that it is only a mental picture the Other has of me, a mere representation. As Sartre puts it, "my shame is my confession" (*BN*, p. 350). Being-for-others is every bit as much *my* being, my self, as is the for-itself. I am ashamed because "I have an outside."

The Other, then, does not merely inhabit the world but transforms my *situation*, the way the world takes on meaning and value as a space of possibilities. Specifically, to experience the other as another subject is to experience the *death* of my possibilities in the existential sense.[20] Initially, Sartre's voyeur "lives" his possibilities as pure instrumentalities: the shadows to the left are his "cover"; the keyhole is his "window on the scene"; the stairwell is the pure possibility of "escape." Hearing footsteps, however, changes such instrumentalities into objective *probabilities*: the shadows no longer signify pure "concealment" but *also* the possibility of being discovered in them; the keyhole is no longer merely his access to the world but *also* the evidence of his crime; the stairwell no longer presents itself as the immediate instrument of escape but *also* as the region whence approaches his captor (*BN*, p. 354). To experience the death of my possibilities is thus to experience the birth of a social world. The situation is now not only something in which objects are there for me, but something in which I too am "situated" as an object, an object for the Other.

10.11 THE SOCIAL WORLD AS A SPACE OF CONFLICT

With the analysis of the Look Sartre begins to explore dimensions of selfhood that do not derive directly from the nature of consciousness – for instance, its embodiment and its sociality. Though these aspects of his thinking are also crucial to the existential picture of the self, we cannot develop them further here.[21] Nevertheless, we may conclude by considering one final aspect of our theme, one that arises from the fact that I am not merely a "being in situation" but also a being who *is situated* by the Other's consciousness. For Sartre's analysis of the Look makes possible a richer account of the "me" which, in *The Transcendence of the Ego,* still appeared as a function of my own objectifying self-reflection. *Being and Nothingness,* in contrast, recognizes that the Me is originally produced by the Other, that an isolated for-itself could never objectify itself in that way. Instead, the Me is the stakes of a permanent *contest* between my freedom and that of the Other. Social reality thus emerges as a space of enduring conflict between subjectivities, each of whom struggles to retain the position of "I," the subject, and to refuse what the Other makes of me: "Hell is – other people!"[22] In this way the fundamental meaning of autonomy and self-determination is recast in existential terms – not as a given of consciousness but as something to be wrested from the Other: rebellion.

Because "two freedoms can exist for one another" only as the death of each other's possibilities, social relations are necessarily conflictual. Each freedom attempts to "negate" (i.e., define) the other, maintain the subject position and, with that, its possibilities *as* possibilities. To lose one's possibilities is to be constituted as Me by the Other, but since the Other defines me always in light of some specific project, the Me that emerges is *concrete,* a definite aspect of my being that I am without being its origin. Indeed, all the "qualities" that I objectively apprehend myself as being stem originally from the Other: "I am situated as a European in relation to Asiatics or Negroes, as an old man in relation to the young, as a judge in relation to delinquents, as a bourgeois in relation to workers, etc." (*BN*, p. 373).

If it is said that I am *already* American, male, white, and so on apart from any relation to the Other, this is true only from a third-person point of view.[23] From the first-person perspective of the for-itself, the meaning of these things cannot be realized as objective qualities since I am separated from them by negation, by the pre-reflective self-awareness of *not being* them. Thus what it *means* to be a Jew or a woman is discovered first of all through the eyes of the anti-Semite or man.[24] For this reason, I discover this Me as an alienated yet real dimension of my being and, in seeking to overcome this alienation (i.e., to restore my subjectivity) I must *refuse* the Me, constitute it as merely an "image," a "mental representation" entertained by a bigot or male chauvinist. But to do so I must first of all assume it. Thus "this Me which has been alienated and refused is simultaneously my bond with the Other and the symbol of our absolute separation" (*BN*, p. 380).

But it is clear that the contest does not take place on a level playing field. Although in principle the struggle between freedoms is symmetrical and under the control of neither – the Look can emerge at any time, as when an actor, lost in his role, suddenly becomes aware of the individuals in the audience looking at him and promptly forgets his lines (*BN*, p. 394) – the social world is a world of concrete asymmetry and inequality. The institutions of such a world are configured in such a way as to privilege "power," one form of subjectivity over another. Patriarchy, capitalism, racism, heterosexism: these are names for social institutions that insure that women, workers, non-whites, and homosexuals start off and largely remain in the object-position. Though gender, for instance, is a quality that arises only "between" subjects in the conflict over freedom, certain institutions are designed to make it appear that gender qualifies only one of the subjects: women are "female" subjects whereas men are simply subjects, the norm of subjectivity as such, pure for-itself and freedom. Sartre's existential theory of the self thus contains elements for a critical analysis of social and political institutions that would recognize such distorting "ideologies" and work toward the concrete liberation they impede. Whether his existentialism is *sufficient* for such a project of political action and liberation is something that Sartre himself came to doubt. But he never doubted that the existential analysis of the self was a *necessary* condition for any adequate ethics or politics.

NOTES

1. See Bernasconi, *How to Read Sartre*, p. 1.
2. As the title of John Gerassi's book proclaims.
3. Sartre, *Search for a Method*, p. 30.
4. Sartre, *Being and Nothingness*, p. 71. Henceforth cited in the text as *BN*.
5. A pioneering treatment of Sartre's relation to phenomenology is Natanson, *A Critique of Jean-Paul Sartre's Ontology*. Recent discussions relevant to the approach taken in this chapter can be found in Morris, *Sartre*; Mouille, *Sartre et la phénoménologie*; and Reisman, *Sartre's Phenomenology*.
6. See Sartre, *Transcendence of the Ego*, p. 93. Henceforth cited in the text as *TE*.
7. *The Transcendence of the Ego* is largely devoted to showing how "immanence" or the "inner" is constituted – not as the essence of the self but as a distinct worldly "region" of psychological reality. For an analysis of this text, see Priest, *The Subject in Question*.
8. For a commentary on *Being and Nothingness* that is attuned to Sartre's dialogue with phenomenology and the tradition of post-Kantian transcendental philosophy, see Gardner, *Sartre's Being and Nothingness*.
9. For more on these matters, see Fell, *Heidegger and Sartre*.
10. Sartre, *Nausea*, p. 126–27.
11. Sartre, *Nausea*, p. 129.
12. Sartre, *Nausea*, p. 134.
13. One might call them "categories," though this introduces complications that we cannot take up here. On the relation between the Hegelian "categorial" elements and the phenomenological elements in Sartre's philosophy see Hartmann, *Sartre's Ontology*.
14. See Cabestan, *L'Être et la conscience*.
15. See Korsgaard, *The Sources of Normativity*.
16. For a critical look at Sartre's arguments for this thesis, see Detmer, *Freedom as a Value*, pp. 133–76.
17. For an overview of Sartre's approach to ethics, see Anderson, *Sartre's Two Ethics*.
18. R. Moran, *Authority and Estrangement*, develops Sartre's ideas here in more analytic terms.
19. Husserl, *Cartesian Meditations*, p. 109.

20. This idea has applications in psychiatry, as the chapter by Ratcliffe and Broome in this *Companion* shows.
21. On embodiment, see Wider, *The Bodily Nature of Consciousness*. Important aspects of Sartre's social and political thinking are discussed in the chapters by Flynn and Bernasconi in this *Companion*.
22. Sartre, *No Exit*, p. 45.
23. Blattner discusses this point in terms of Heidegger's concept of "facticity," in Chapter 8 of this *Companion*.
24. See Sartre, *Anti-Semite and Jew*; Beauvoir, *The Second Sex*.

THOMAS R. FLYNN

11 Political existentialism: the career of Sartre's political thought

As a student in the *lycée*, the young Sartre did not show a serious interest in political theory or in practical politics generally. His natural tendencies were anarchic. But his close friend and classmate at the École Normale Supérieure, Paul Nizan, joined the Communist Party (PCF) at age twenty-three (a decision Sartre considered shocking [*monstre*]). Sartre's interests were more literary and philosophical than political at that time. He resisted the siren call of socialism, for example, that had turned the heads of many of his classmates at the École, including Raymond Aron.[1] Eschewing party adherence, as he would the rest of his life, Sartre nonetheless was strongly opposed to colonialism, which he regarded as a sordid form of state takeover. Sartre harbored a basic egalitarian spirit from his early teens and, as he recalls, thought of the French control of Algeria whenever the injustice of colonialism came to mind (*Cér.*, p. 478). As his life-long companion Simone de Beauvoir remarks, they showed little concern for politics after graduation and did not even vote in the critical general election of 1936 that ushered in the socialist program of the *Front populaire*. But even in those years, as Sartre assures us, his "heart was on the Left, of course, like everyone else's."[2]

11.1 STUDENT, SCHOLAR, TEACHER (1915–1939)

Although he came under the influence of the charismatic pacifist professor known as Alain at the Lycée Henri IV, Sartre's own pacifism seems to have been rather short-lived and superficial. By the time he entered military service during the "Phony War" of 1939–40, Sartre had all but shed those inclinations in the face of the Nazi attack. Still, in his *War Diaries* he records on several occasions the tension at play in his personal life between the Stoicism that had attracted him in college, which Sartre associated with Alain's pacifist arguments, and his personal quest for authenticity.[3] But it was anti-militarism and not opposition to violence per se that fed Sartre's "pacifism." This will surface in his *War Diaries* and thereafter.

Sartre interrupted his teaching appointment at a *lycée* to spend the academic year 1933/34 at the French Institute in Berlin under a fellowship to study contemporary German philosophy, especially Husserlian phenomenology. In view of his extreme involvement in matters political after the war, it is astonishing that he seemed to ignore the National Socialist "revolution" that was taking place virtually outside his window. Sartre seems to have remained the detached scholar during his residence at the Institute.

Yet he was not insensitive to the political implications of his early work in phenomenology. Expressing a view of Communist philosophy that he will repeat ten years later, Sartre concludes his critique of Husserlian phenomenology, *The Transcendence of the Ego* (1936), by approving of historical materialism and rejecting "the absurdity of metaphysical materialism." He suggests that the theory of an egoless consciousness, proposed in that text, should suffice as "a philosophical foundation for an ethics and a politics which are absolutely positive."[4] Note this conjunction of the ethical and the political. It will become a recurrent theme throughout Sartre's subsequent work.

A measure of Sartre's political commitment during the 1930s was his attitude toward the Spanish Civil War (1936–39). Though he certainly sided with the Republicans, as did many of his close friends, and in 1937 published a powerful short story, "The Wall," which dramatized that war experience, he remarked later that it was not "his" war.[5] "When I wrote *The Wall*," he admitted, "I had no real knowledge of Marxist thought, I was simply in complete opposition to the existence of Spanish fascism."[6]

His close, long-lasting friendship with Paul Nizan certainly added to Sartre's distrust of the Communist Party, a distrust that never fully left him, even during the period of his "fellow-traveling" in the early 1950s. Nizan, who died at the battle of Dunkirk in May of 1940, had renounced his allegiance to the Party the year before because of its support of the nonaggression pact between

Hitler and Stalin. The Party responded by vilifying Nizan as traitor and government informer. In 1947, Sartre joined François Mauriac, Raymond Aron, and many others in a public letter to the leaders of the PCF challenging them either to furnish evidence behind their smear campaign against Nizan's name or to retract these accusations publicly.[7]

11.2 VINTAGE EXISTENTIALISM (1938–1946)

Sartre returned to Paris after several months of incarceration in a Nazi Stalag following the fall of France, quite intent on playing a part in the Resistance. With Maurice Merleau-Ponty and others, he gathered a group of intellectuals under the banner of "Socialism and Freedom [*Liberté*]" in March of 1941. It attracted about fifty members but lasted scarcely nine months. It could not compete with other resistance organizations, especially the PCF, which had abandoned its pacifist stance once the Germans invaded the Soviet Union in June of that year. But the values of "socialism" and "freedom" continued to inspire and guide Sartre's public life. Indeed, in his valedictory interview with Simone de Beauvoir (1974), Sartre reflected on his experience of true community as a prisoner and wished that it could have been conjoined with freedom:

> We founded the movement Socialism and Freedom (*Liberté*). The title was my choice because I had in mind a socialism in which [freedom] existed. I had become a socialist by then, owing in part to our life in the sad socialism of prisoners that nonetheless was a collective life, a community. (*Cér.*, p. 494)

> The Marxists in France gave no place to the notion of freedom, [to the notion that people] could form themselves according to their own options and not as conditioned by society ... The idea that a free man could exist beyond socialism – when I say "beyond" I don't mean at some later stage but surpassing the rules of socialism at every moment – that's an idea that the Russians have never had. That's what I had in mind by calling our little group in 1940, 1941 "Socialism and Freedom." Though it is very difficult to realize beginning with socialism it's the connection, socialism–freedom, that represents my political inclination. It was my political bent and I've never changed it. Today I'm still defending socialism and freedom in my discussions with [the Maoists], Gavi and Victor. (*Cér.*, p. 502)

In the early years following the liberation of Paris by the allies in 1945, Sartre accepted an invitation to join David Rousset and Gérard Rosenthal in the inauguration of a non-communist non-party of the Left called the "Revolutionary People's Assembly" (RDR).[8] Its aim was to reconcile Communists and Socialists into a common front against capitalism at home and colonialism and superpower politics abroad. It was in search of a "third" option between either side of Cold War politics, though clearly from a Left-leaning perspective. Noteworthy is Sartre's rationale for joining this group: his appeal to "situation" as "an idea capable of uniting the Marxists and non-Marxists among us."[9] In his masterwork *Being and Nothingness* (1943), Sartre had characterized "human reality" as "being-in-situation." In his seminal essay "Materialism and Revolution," published the year before joining the RDR, he had concluded: "It is the elucidation of the new ideas of 'situation' and of 'being-in-the-world' that revolutionary behavior specifically calls for."[10] It is commonly acknowledged that this futile foray into organized politics soured him on the genre. Still, he would continue to recommend that members of the working class join the Communist Party, which Sartre came to see as its sole voice in what for years he had referred to as "class conflict." He would not join the Party himself, but he did support four years of fellow-traveling with the PCF from 1952 to the Soviet crushing of the Hungarian revolution in 1956.

In his last interview with Beauvoir, Sartre admits: "I was never in favor of a socialist society before 1939." He described his position up to that point as "an individualism of the Left" (*Cér.*, pp. 479–80). If his experience in the army and in the prisoner-of-war camp taught him the importance of social solidarity, he was still in thrall to the individualist ontology he was formulating in *Being and Nothingness*. It based interpersonal relations on the objectifying gaze of competing individuals, resulting ontologically in a kind of stare-down and politically in a Hobbesian war of all against all. In a famous phrase from that book, Sartre claims that "the essence of the relations between consciousnesses is not the [Heideggerian] *Mitsein* (being-with); it is conflict."[11] Five years later Sartre described this stage of his thought as "a rationalist philosophy of consciousness."

11.3 ETHICS AND POLITICS (MEANS AND ENDS)

In a major address delivered at the opening session of UNESCO at the Sorbonne, November 1, 1946, Sartre set forth the responsibility of the writer in the post-war world: He must "give his thoughts unceasingly ... to the problem of the end and the means; or alternatively, the problem of the relation between ethics and politics."[12] He concludes with reference to the possibility of yet another world war and warns of the writers' descent from responsibility into culpability if they failed to address the threat of this greatest of world catastrophes.

This issue of end/means forms another enduring theme in Sartre's thought. What saves him from an ethical consequentialism is the fact that his ethical and political theories include *non-negotiables*. One such is the free organic individual (the responsible subject who can never be used as a means only); another is the value-concept of freedom (the idea, which Sartre believes to be implicit in any choice, that freedom is itself taken to be a value).[13] They will set the parameters at each turn of his thought. In fact, one can chart a roughly parallel development of his ethics and his politics dating from his "discovery" of the philosophical significance of society during the war and the Resistance and continuing to the hypotheses entertained in his discussions with Benny Lévy in the aftermath of the "events of May, 1968" in the 1970s. Sartre's experience of "solidarity" among his fellow prisoners led to his realization that "concrete" freedom (as distinct from the abstract freedom that simply defines the individual as such) requires that the field of options for others be expanded as well. As he states in *Existentialism is a Humanism*, "In thus willing freedom, we discover that it depends entirely on the freedom of others, and that the freedom of others depends on our own" (*EH*, p. 48).

11.4 HUMANISMS AND THE POLITICAL

Sartre displayed a strong animus against several types of humanism in the novel that made him famous, *Nausea* (1938). Yet a year later, Private Sartre is applying that negative view to political principles in his *War Diaries*, minus the total rejection displayed in the novel:

If we are looking for political principles today, we have really only four conceptions of man to choose between. The narrow conservative synthetic conception ([the parochial one of] *Action française*, for example); the updated narrow synthetic conception (racism, Marxism); the broad conservative synthetic conception (humanitarianism); the analytical conception (anarchic individualism). But nowhere do we find any reference to the human condition, determined on the basis of individual "human reality." (Entry for November 21, 1939 [*WD*, p. 28])

The problem, in his opinion, is that, of the many meanings of "humanity," "the modern meaning – the human condition of every individual – has not yet been unveiled" (*WD*, p. 25). Though Sartre continued to oppose the "humanism" of the Radical Socialists like his step-father, Joseph Mancy, one could now say of him what Beauvoir said of herself: "The spring of 1939 marked a watershed in my life. I renounced my individualistic, antihumanist way of life. I learned the value of solidarity."[14]

What is that "modern" meaning that will engender the political principles of the future? With the wisdom of hindsight, we can say that it is a *humanism of "situation."* Parsing that term as Sartre uses it, we find that every situation is at once objective, practical, or "lived," and historical. How these three features will enter into Sartre's political and social thought remains to be seen, but it is already clear that the elements of its conception are germinating in the young conscript's mind. Let us consider each of them in turn.

Objective possibility. Contrary to the impression given by *Being and Nothingness*, one cannot change a situation by merely willing it. The metaphor of the time being "ripe" for a certain historical event to occur captures the sense of objective possibility. Sartre is applying this concept to his notion of "situation" when he remarks that "it is history which shows some the exits and makes others cool their heels before closed doors."[15] By the time he makes that claim, in *The Communists and Peace* (1952), Sartre is in league with the PFC, though, as ever, in his own way. But he was already appealing to this aspect of "situation" in 1946 when dealing with anti-Semitism:

Since [the anti-Semite], like all men, exists as a free agent within a situation, it is his situation that must be modified from top to bottom. In short, if we can change the perspective of choice, then the choice itself will change. Thus we do not attack freedom, but bring it about that freedom decides on other bases and in terms of other structures.[16]

Sartre's growing sense of objective possibility thickens his understanding of "freedom" from a quasi-Stoic "freedom to think otherwise" (what elsewhere he called "freedom as the definition of man") to a full-fledged notion of "positive" or "concrete" freedom that requires the change of socio-economic conditions; that is, "the bases and the structures" of our choices. As he writes in the Introduction (*Présentation*) to the new journal that he and his friends are launching, *Les Temps Modernes* (1945), the task the editors set for themselves in view of the abstract freedom of the individual is to expand his possibilities of choice; that is, to increase his concrete freedom.[17] This is a call for some form of "socialism."

Praxis and lived experience (le vécu). In *Being and Nothingness* Sartre described "situation" as an ambiguous mixture of facticity and transcendence – or, less technically, the "given" and the "taken" – in our concrete lives. What the introduction of "praxis" and "lived experience" adds to the concept of situation is a dialectical and broadly experiential character. Although praxis (purposive human activity in its socio-historical context) had already entered Sartre's vocabulary in *What is Literature?* (1947)[18] – as well as in his posthumously published *Notebooks for an Ethics*, composed in 1947/48 – it plays a far greater role in *Search for a Method* (1957)[19] and the *Critique of Dialectical Reason* (1960).[20] There it supplants consciousness (being-for-itself), the fundamental category of *Being and Nothingness*, as the vehicle of transcendence and freedom.

The appearance of the concept of lived experience (*Erlebnis, le vécu*) was as significant as that of praxis. Lived experience was introduced, Sartre tells us, to do justice to the situational and the subconscious aspects of "consciousness." As he explains: "*le vécu* – lived experience – is precisely that ensemble of the dialectical process of psychic life, in so far as this process is obscure to itself because it is a constant totalization, thus necessarily a totalization which cannot be conscious of what it is."[21] And elsewhere he concedes: "I suppose it represents for me the equivalent of conscious-unconscious."[22]

This major modification of Sartre's psychology enables him to appeal to "Freudian" concepts without resorting to the concept of the unconscious, which he had vigorously criticized in *Being and Nothingness*. The unblinking eye of Sartrean consciousness is retained and our unqualified responsibility preserved. Henceforth, an "existential" approach to Marxism will embrace psychological phenomena as more than the superficial, "ideological" matters they were held to be by orthodox Marxism. This path of "lived experience" reveals its promise in the several "biographies" of famous literary artists that Sartre pens in the second half of his life. Once asked by Maoist friends why he continued to labor over his gigantic study of Gustave Flaubert, Sartre defended his undertaking as the attempt to produce a model "Socialist" biography.[23]

The historical. Sartre elaborates this dimension of our situation by appeal to a Hegelian saying that our "essence is our past" (*das Wesen ist was gewesen ist*). If "situation" is an ambiguous mix of facticity and transcendence, of the in-itself and the for-itself, of the given and the taken, then the temporal dimension of our facticity is precisely our biography. But as Sartre's individualist ontology expands, this description grows apace: our facticity is read as our history, not merely our biography; it is "our" story, not simply mine.

Now this fits nicely into the Marxian theory of history and class consciousness, where the "subject" of history is the working class. Sartre will subscribe to such a view in the *Critique of Dialectical Reason*, but during his vintage existentialist stage he lacks the social ontology to warrant talking of a collective or "class" subject in more than a purely psychological sense. The problem is his individualist theory of interpersonal relations, based on the phenomenon of the Look. He has not overcome the limits of what he would later call "analytic reason," even as he is insisting that human reality is a totality, not a collection – the first principle of existential psychoanalysis (*BN*, p. 568).

11.5 POLITICAL EXISTENTIALISM (1947–1952)

Aside from the stark contrast between pre- and post-war Sartre, the other stages of his life bleed into one another. So the present period begins with the elaboration of the concept of "committed literature" developed in *What is Literature?* but previewed in Sartre's UNESCO address a few months earlier.

Various existential concepts are at work in the view of committed literature articulated in this essay. Chief among them is that of "situation," which Sartre here begins to elaborate in terms of the concepts of objective possibility, praxis, and the historical just discussed. Of the many questions which the committed writer must address to his contemporaries, none is more pressing than that of the relation between morality and politics (see *WL*, p. 154). This, in turn, raises the dilemma of a Communist Party which adopts the rhetoric of moral responsibility in its frequent appeal to social (in) justice, while sustaining a materialist dialectic which renders such ascriptions unwarranted. In other words, freedom and economic determinism are mutually incompatible. Such is Sartre's view of the matter.

The problem of means–ends, of morality and politics, continues to insinuate itself in *What is Literature?* Sartre addresses it explicitly toward the conclusion of the book:

> Such is the present paradox of ethics; if I am absorbed in treating a few chosen persons as absolute ends ... if I am bent on fulfilling all my duties towards them, I shall spend my life doing so; I shall be led *to pass over in silence* the injustices of the age, the class struggle, colonialism, Anti-Semitism, etc., finally, to *take advantage of oppression in order to do good.* (*WL*, p. 221; emphasis in original)

But the other side of the paradox is that by throwing myself completely into the revolutionary enterprise "I risk having no more leisure for personal relations – worse still, of being led by the logic of the action into treating most men, and even my friends, as means."

At this point, Sartre introduces an aesthetic value that, while it is appropriate for his audience (he is discussing the situation of the writer in 1947), harkens back to the conclusion of *Nausea*, where the protagonist seeks "salvation" through literary art. Though Sartre has by now concluded that "evil cannot be redeemed" (*WL*, p. 180), he does allow himself the Kantian thought that "the contemplation of beauty might well arouse in us the purely formal intention of treating men as ends." Still, his growing sense of objective (im)possibility counters that "this intention would reveal itself to be utterly futile in practice since the fundamental structures of our society are still oppressive" (*WL*, p. 221). Sartre counsels that "if we can start with the moral exigence which the aesthetic feeling envelops without meaning to do so, we are starting on the right foot." But our task is to "*historicize* the reader's goodwill." By this he means that we must turn the purely formal intention – to treat men in every case as an absolute end – into a specific intention by the *subject* of our writing that directs his intention upon his neighbors, upon the oppressed of the world. But we shall have accomplished nothing, he warns, "if we do not show him – and in the very warp and weft of the work – that it is quite impossible to treat concrete men as ends in contemporary society" (*WL*, p. 222).

This entails considering the "city of ends" – which Sartre also adopts from Kant – as a practical "ideal" toward which we should aim and approach "only at the end of a long historical evolution." Sartre acknowledges that this is the *strain* peculiar to the project he is proposing. Repeating what we identified as the leitmotif of his political and ethical philosophy, he insists that "we must militate in our writings in favor of the freedom of the person *and* the socialist revolution. It has often been claimed that they are not reconcilable. It is our job to show tirelessly that they imply each other" (*WL*, p. 223; emphasis in original).

A few years later, as Sartre was moving into the stage of full cooperation with the PCF, he published a large volume introducing the works of Jean Genet, *Saint Genet* (1952). On the final page, he concludes that Genet is us and that he faces us with the choice of our day: either to follow Bukharin – who in the infamous Moscow show trials of the 1930s confessed falsely to treason to preserve the unity of the Party – or to imitate the creatively free Genet. What it comes down to is a Kierkegaardian either/or: "Bukharin or the will *to be together* carried to the point of martyrdom; Genet or our solitude carried to the point of Passion."[24] As if to replay the freedom/socialist revolution alternative, which itself instantiates the end/means alternative, Sartre challenges us with the thought that we might succeed in reconciling this dichotomy – "be it only once and *in the realm of the imaginary*" – if only we have the courage "to go to the limits of ourselves in both directions at once" (*SG*, p. 644; emphasis added). Here as elsewhere, Sartre is urging us to increase the tension rather than reduce it – or perhaps better, to resolve it in the "as if" of a Kantian ideal. However, if one opts to "go to the limits of ourselves in both directions at once" (to emphasize the individual *and* the social), one may see this suggestion as Sartre's last salute toward what we might call a "Kierkegaardian dialectic," namely, one that simply intensifies the dichotomy rather than resolving it via a synthesizing "mediation." This would underline Raymond Aron's critique of Sartre's project of Marxist existentialism voiced in 1946: "A follower of Kierkegaard cannot at the same time be a follower of Marx."[25]

11.6 THE MISDIRECTED IMAGINARY: SARTRE'S FELLOW-TRAVELING WITH THE PCF (1952–1956)

Sartre was already having problems resolving the tension between end and means, politics and ethics. In 1948 he had abandoned writing the Ethics he promised at the end of *BN*, after producing several hundred pages of notes that were published posthumously as *Notebooks for an Ethics*. He later explained that the text was too idealist in nature and no longer expressed his current thoughts (see *Cér.*, p. 234). If one is looking for a more "realist" and even more "materialist" version of his ethical insights, one could do no better than to read his "profoundly autobiographical" play, *The Devil and the Good Lord*, which premiered June 7, 1951. It is commonly understood as mirroring Sartre's entire ideological evolution (*C/R*, 1:249). For someone who for most of his life sought to balance imagination and conceptualization, the literary and the philosophical, it is not surprising to note how creative literary works either anticipated or retrospectively exemplified the ideas articulated in Sartre's philosophical work. His play, *No Exit*, for example, communicates imaginatively much of the phenomenological ontology of *BN*. A major issue in *The Devil and the Good Lord* is the relation between ethics and politics – the Absolute and the (Peasant) Revolution. In its concluding scene Goetz, the new commander of the peasants and a convert from the other side, having just coldly killed a subordinate who questioned his authority, exclaims:

> The kingdom of man is beginning. A fine start! ... Never fear, I shall not flinch. I shall make them hate me, because I know no other way of loving them ... I shall remain alone with this empty sky over my head, since I have no other way of being among men. There is this war to fight, and I shall fight it.[26]

In an interview published the day this play opened, Sartre defends his sympathy with the Communists: "To the extent that I am inspired by a rather broad Marxism, I am an enemy for Stalinist Communists [viz. the PCF]" ... "Until the new order [the Revolution arrives], the Party will represent the proletariat for me, and I do not see how this situation could possibly change for some time ... It is impossible to take an anti-Communist position without being against the proletariat" (cited *C/R*, II:254).

These remarks were predictive. Soon Sartre added several new members to the team of *Les Temps Modernes*, which subsequently displayed a closer orientation with the Party. He cooperated with the PCF in defending Henri Martin, a sailor jailed for distributing tracts opposing the war in Indo-China. But his chief move in that direction was a set of essays published in *Les Temps Modernes* under the title *The Communists and Peace*, starting in July of 1952. Occasioned by the arrest of the acting head of the PCF on trumped-up charges in the aftermath of a massive demonstration against the arrival in Paris of the American general, Matthew Ridgway, this text, which illustrates Sartre at his most hyperbolic, ushers in the next years that in the eyes of many will fix Sartre permanently as a Communist. Yet Sartre had made it clear that he was agreeing with the Communists on specific, limited subjects, "arguing on the basis of *my* principles and not *theirs*" (*CP*, p. 68). This served to distinguish him from the Stalinist-oriented PCF during this period of relative cordiality.

Some of those principles would appear in Sartre's *Critique of Dialectical Reason*, especially ones that reveal an anti-Communist turn in the social ontology he is starting to form. But the conceptual framework had changed from *BN*. The means–end issue is being "historicized" and the "situation" is becoming concrete. Nowhere is this better expressed than in a footnote in a book that has been described as the best commentary on *The Devil and the Good Lord* (*C/R*, II:250), Sartre's *Saint Genet*:

> The abstract separation of these two concepts [Good and Evil] expresses simply the alienation of man. The fact remains that, in the historical situation, this synthesis [of these two] cannot be achieved. Thus, any ethic which does not explicitly profess that it is *impossible today* contributes to the bamboozling and alienation of men. The ethical "problem" arises from the fact that Ethics is *for us* inevitable and at the same time impossible.

Action must give itself ethical norms in this climate of nontranscendable impossibility. It is from this outlook that, for example, we must view the problem of violence or that of the relationship between ends and means. To a mind that experiences this agony and that was at the same time forced to will and to decide, all high-minded rebellion, all outcries of refusal, all virtuous indignation would seem a kind of outworn rhetoric. (*SG*, p. 186 n.; emphasis in original)

It seems that the high-minded non-negotiables of Sartre's ethical belief up to this point are being placed on the shelf of abstraction, or projected onto the sky of an idealist "as if." In effect, he is echoing the revolutionary's maxim that one must crack a few eggs to make an omelette.

Sartre confirmed his sympathy with the PCF with voyages that would come to embarrass him after his return. The first was to attend the Congress of the World Peace Movement in Vienna, December 12–19, 1952, where he was enthusiastically received and during which he prohibited the performance of his play *Dirty Hands*, because of the anti-Communist use to which it was being put by its Viennese producers. In May–June 1954, Sartre made his first of several visits to the Soviet Union. He returned singing its praises; for example, he made the astonishing claim that there was complete freedom of criticism in the USSR. Recalling these words twenty years later, he insisted that the series of remarks published after his return was the work of his secretary, Jean Cau, and that he was not taken in by what he saw there: "They showed me what they wanted me to see, obviously, and I had a lot of reservations" (*Cér.*, p. 462).

11.7 BETWEEN REVOLUTIONS (1956–1969)

With the discovery of the labor camps in the USSR and its violent quelling of the Hungarian workers' uprising in 1956, Sartre began to distance himself from the PCF once more. He wrote a lengthy essay, "The Phantom of Stalin," to explain his move. It called for the de-Stalinization of the PCF, while arguing that the Party nonetheless remained the best hope for the proletariat. Besides exorcizing the ghost of Stalin, his essay aimed at establishing common cause with other parties of the Left, including the Socialists (SFIO) which, in a not-conciliatory interview in *L'Express*, he described as the party of "those who torture in Algeria."[27] There were three other revolutions that drew Sartre's considerable attention during these twelve years: the war in Vietnam – especially the United States' involvement, leading him to participate in the Russell War Crimes Trial – the Algerian war of independence, and the Cuban revolution. Each could be considered the fruit of colonialism or neo-colonialism and, as such, they elicited the disgust that we noted the young Sartre harbored toward colonialism. More recently, he had written that colonialism is a system of impersonal, structural rules and associated practices and could apply to it what he remarked about another system, capitalism: "the meanness is in the system" (*CP*, p. 183). We have seen that the hallmark of Sartrean existentialism, even if it is attenuated during his years of fellow-traveling with the PCF, is a certain *irreducibility* that he reserves for the responsible individual. Only in the *Critique of Dialectical Reason* will he fashion the social ontology to support the position, but we can safely modify his claim about these social structures and institutions: the meanness is (not entirely) in the system. Whether it is the "two hundred families"[28] that, in popular opinion, moved their money to Swiss accounts when the Socialists came to power in 1936, thereby weakening the government, or the racist attitudes and practices that sustained the workings of neo-colonialism in 1950s Algeria, the appeal to system or "structural" necessity, in Sartre's view, does not excuse the populace. As he says or implies in his many essays and interviews on social issues: the responsibility settles on us all. Whether it be in our lack of concern for the structural injustices of a corrupt regime in Cuba, our sympathy with the actions of our national armies in Algeria or Vietnam, our unwillingness to protest against or willingness to benefit from the exploitation of the Arab population in Algeria or the locals in Southeast Asia, Sartre voices the rhetorical judgment: "We are all guilty." Doubtless this presumes a degree of solidarity, as well as an idea of collective responsibility, that Sartre has yet to justify beyond appealing to the "spirit of synthesis."[29] But his practice is calling for a theory that the *Critique of Dialectical Reason* will attempt to supply.

If the Spanish Civil War was "not his war," as Roland Dumas remarked years later, "The Algerian war was *his* war."[30] In January 1955, *Les Temps Modernes* had started a campaign in support of the Algerian rebels; in 1957 its issues were confiscated on four occasions by the government in Algeria. The November issue was seized by the Metropolitan government for the first time. Sartre's essay on a case of torture by French forces in Algeria appeared in the weekly *Express* March 6, 1958. That issue was confiscated. In the same month, Sartre published an essay in *Les Temps Modernes* entitled "We Are All Assassins." As the war progressed and the tide turned in favor of the rebels, Sartre's life was threatened on two occasions (July 19, 1961 and January 7, 1962) when bombs were exploded at the entrance to his apartment by members of the Organization of the Secret Army (OAS). The war ended July 3, 1962, when France granted Algeria independence after a referendum.

After a visit to Cuba, Sartre and Beauvoir returned singing Castro's praises. It was Castro's seeming commitment to "direct democracy" that attracted Sartre at the start and his subsequent intolerance of internal criticism that turned Sartre against the dictator. In effect, it was Sartre's unflinching commitment to socialism *and* freedom that moved him into Castro's orbit during this period and would just as unequivocally draw him out of it.

Sartre had long opposed French colonialism in Indo-China. He saw the intervention of the United States and its allies in Vietnam as repeating that injustice, but now the charge was "genocide" delivered by an International War Crimes Tribunal under the sponsorship of the famous philosopher and pacifist Bertrand Russell. As its executive president, Sartre announced in his opening address, May 2, 1967, that "the Tribunal would judge the crimes committed in Vietnam by the definitions and standards of existing international law and particularly the judgments of the Nuremberg Tribunal which judged German war crimes in 1945."[31] Since their only authority was "moral," the self-appointed group hoped to appeal to public opinion by publicizing the "crimes against humanity" that were now being ascribed to the victors of an earlier war. Sartre published an essay, "On Genocide," that was accompanied by a summary of the evidence and the judgment of the Tribunal written by his adopted daughter, Arlette El Kaïm-Sartre. The unanimous judgment of this body was that the United States was guilty of genocide in Vietnam during the period specified. Again the appeal was to human solidarity of rights and interests. As a variation on a Sartrean theme, the document concludes: "This crime [of genocide], carried out every day before the eyes of the world, renders all who do not denounce it accomplices of those who commit it, so that we are being degraded today for our future enslavement."[32]

11.8 BEYOND COMMUNISM, BEYOND MARXISM (1968–1980)

If photos of Soviet tanks crushing the Hungarian revolution destroyed whatever belief Sartre had maintained in the Stalinist orthodoxy of Soviet and French Communism, the Soviet-ordered invasion of Czechoslovakia by Warsaw Pact troops in 1968 to suppress its liberalizing "Prague Spring" ended his sympathy for Communism generally – with the possible exception of the Italian version, which he always considered *sui generis*. As he remarked to his Maoist discussants in the early 1970s, "The Communists ... don't give a fig about justice, what they want primarily is power" (*ORR*, p. 76).

The "events of May, 1968" marked a turning point in French politics and culture that continues to the present day.[33] If it would be excessive to label it, as some have done, the "Sartrean" revolution,[34] there is little doubt that these events resonated with his model of political existentialism, a model that includes elements of (1) moral indignation, (2) spontaneity, (3) camaraderie, (4) a heightened sense of disalienation, (5) distrust of party politics, (6) confidence in "direct action," and (7) visceral dislike of authority. We have seen these features emerge in various stages of Sartre's career in politics. Of course, if "politics" is limited to the exercise of voting and active relations with, if not membership in, political parties, the extent of Sartre's career is considerably reduced. But as he insisted to his Maoist friends: "Everything is political; that is, everything questions society as a whole and ends up disputing it" (*ORR*, p. 27).

When we add to this list of features (8) "violence," we see why Sartre found the youthful exuberance and impatience with mere verbiage characteristic of these events so attractive, especially in his last decade. In a set of conversations (really, interviews) from November 1972 to March 1974 with two "Maoists" – one of whom will become his last secretary[35] – Sartre took stock of his political biography in particularly explicit and challenging remarks. Among the many decisive statements uttered in this context was his admission that he had moved from an "irrealist idealism" at age eighteen (which is why he abandoned his ethics of authenticity sketched in the *Notebooks for an Ethics*), through an amoralist realism at forty-five (with the Communists), to rediscovery of a moralist realism that was now materialist, anti-hierarchical, and libertarian (with his post-Communist colleagues) (*ORR*, p. 79).

What Sartre calls "materialist" involves neither a reductionist mind–brain identity thesis, nor the Marxist determinism that he rejects as "economism." Rather, it denotes the elaboration of his basic concept of situation in terms of "objective possibility." There is determinism in nature, as Kant insisted, and in history too, as Hegel claimed, but "we can always make something out of what we've been made into" – which is the Sartrean existentialist mantra, extended via dialectical reasoning to encompass the material conditions of our existential life (*le vécu*). This irreducible wedge of subjectivity – which Sartre once described as "the limit of reflexive recoil" (*EN*, p. 32; *BN*, p. 65) – is the ontological ground of our freedom, whether abstract or concrete, and of our moral responsibility. This is why he can assert, against orthodox dialectical materialism, that morality is not merely a function of the superstructure but "exists at the very level of production" (*ORR*, p. 45). He agrees with the Maoists that "a worker is moral by virtue of the fact that he is an alienated man who reclaims freedom for himself and for all" (*ORR*, p. 45). In fact, this was a basic Sartrean conviction long before he encountered *les Maos*.

If the features of existentialist politics can be gathered from Sartre's ad hoc statements and essays, the theoretical foundation for this approach was laid in Sartre's *Critique of Dialectical Reason* and its introductory essay, *Search for a Method*. These works have been subjected to careful commentaries, but a brief reference to aspects of the argument of each will elucidate the epistemic and ontological grounding for the features of existentialist politics enumerated above.

Let us note at the outset that *Search for a Method* was not written as an introduction to *CDR*. It was a translation, with some additions, of an essay, "The Situation of Existentialism in 1957," published in a Polish journal at the request of its editor. So when it is attached to *CDR* one should not be surprised that the fit is not perfect. Addressing the question "Do we have today the means to constitute a structural, historical anthropology?" (*SM*, p. xxxiv), Sartre offers the hypothesis that we do. Such an anthropology should be a product of the union of existentialist psychology (and moral concerns) with Marxist dialectic (and social causality). The second of its three chapters is dedicated to "The Problem of Mediations." In Hegelian terms, whoever says "dialectic" says "mediation." The "existentialist" Kierkegaard allegedly rejected all mediation, but Sartre – both here and in the *Critique*, but especially in his massive study of Flaubert's life and times, *The Family Idiot*[36] – is at pains to analyze those factors that "mediate" between the abstract or general (structural) features of the historical situation and the concrete praxis of the free organic individual. It is this emphasis on mediating factors that enables Sartre to bring the Marxist "forces and relations of production" to bear on the lives of individuals. Chief among these mediators is the family, as we learn from Sartre's study of Flaubert. So one can say that the mediations preserved what Louis Althusser called "structural causality," but (*pace* Althusser) by means of the praxis of concrete individuals understood in existential terms.[37] With a bit of help from the Marxian dialectic, it looks as if Marx and Kierkegaard had been conjoined after all.

The "progressive-regressive method," which Sartre adopted from the Marxist sociologist Henri Lefebvre and introduced to bring this synthesis about, was the topic of the final chapter of *Search for a Method*. This method begins by describing the phenomenon in question – say, Flaubert's writing of *Madame Bovary*. The regressive movement proceeds analytically from the facts so described to the conditions of their possibility, working its way through layers of increasingly abstract conditions and "structures." One could designate this as the "sociological" or the Marxian phase of the process. In a subsequent "progressive" movement, an attempt is made to examine the "totalizing praxis" of individuals and groups by means of which they make historically concrete the "structures," institutions, and practices that the regressive movement had uncovered.

The goal is to achieve a certain understanding of the concrete by locating the particular individual or event in the context of class consciousness, for example, or the forces and relations of production operative at that time, thereby overcoming simplistic economic determinist analyses. Apropos such analyses Sartre remarks:

"Valéry is a petit bourgeois intellectual ... But not every petit bourgeois intellectual is Valéry. The heuristic inadequacy of contemporary Marxism," he continues, "is contained in those two sentences. Marxism lacks any hierarchy of mediations" (*SM*, p. 56). This is what existentialism proposes to supply.

In many ways, the progressive-regressive method is better exemplified by the Flaubert study than by the *Critique*. And in light of the above, one can understand why Sartre could defend his continued labor on that project when the Maoists were urging him to abandon it in favor of more politically useful work: "I consider this opus to be a socialist work in the sense that, if I succeed, this will allow us to advance in the understanding of men from a socialist viewpoint" (*ORR*, pp. 73–74). Still, it was the *Critique* (1960), not *The Family Idiot* (1971–72), that produced the theoretical underpinning for the qualities that link existential politics with the events of May 68.

What gives the *Critique* its particular relevance to the student revolt is what we might call the *"threefold primacy of praxis"* – namely ontological, epistemic, and moral – that grounds Sartre's social theory. Briefly, social wholes such as groups and institutions, and social facts such as the French Revolution, depend for their existential actuality on the praxes and relations of concrete individuals. As Sartre insists: "There are only men and real relations between men" (*SM*, p. 76). Whatever else one might appeal to in the social realm – "structures" or "systems" for instance – depend for their continued existence and efficacy on "free organic praxis" of individuals in relation. Such things also depend upon being comprehended, at some level, by those individuals. True, structures enjoy the "intelligibility" of the static concept. But the here-and-now realization of these phenomena rides on the praxis of individuals alone and in relation to one another. The self-awareness of praxis (comprehension) brings the abstraction of concepts into the realm of lived experience. What generates the moral indignation characteristic of uprisings like the events of May '68 is the realization that there are identifiable individuals at the base of the impersonal structures and systems to which people commonly appeal to escape moral responsibility. One is better justified in holding people morally accountable than in throwing blame on structures. Not that the "bases and structures of choice" should not be changed, as we saw in the case of the anti-Semite. But to do so requires the passionate commitment of individuals. That has been Sartre's claim throughout. As one revolutionary graffito proclaimed: "Structures don't take to the streets!"

In view of the foregoing, and in summary fashion, let me relate each of the above mentioned features of the events of May '68 to ideas developed in the *Critique*.

(1) *Moral indignation*. We have mentioned the primacy of the praxis of the free organic individual. This is illustrated throughout the two volumes of the *Critique*. At the base of the "practico-inert" conditioning (material heir to Sartre's earlier category of being-in-itself) is the sedimentation of prior praxes (of the colonists, for example, whose attitude and practices continue the effects of the system they have inherited).

(2) *Spontaneity*. In what Sartre, following Malraux, calls an "apocalyptic moment, the alienated individuals spontaneously fuse into a group; group membership entails new qualities" (*CDR*, p. 357).

(3) *Camaraderie*. Each member views every other as "the same" in practical identity and concern. In this way, the power of members surpasses that of a mere collection of isolated individuals.

(4) *A heightened sense of disalienation*. The alienating status of "serial alterity" is overcome through spontaneous group formation. Each becomes "the same" as the other in practical concerns, though not "identical" in totalitarian dissolution. The emerging group resembles the members of a team, whereas the alienated individuals are "other" to one another, like the television-viewing audience. Their "unity" is only apparent; a unity-in-otherness.

(5) *Distrust of party politics*. The party, even if it gives rise to small groups (cells), does so hierarchically and for its own preservation; the party wants power, not freedom.

(6) *Confidence in direct action*. Since the unity of the group is practical, not theoretical, its goals are generated from the group itself; the group as it is forming simply *is* its goal.

(7) *Visceral dislike of authority*. Authority, as Sartre implies in several places, is the "Other" in us.[38] In groups not tied

to direct action, a self-imposed authority structure arises that, Sartre believes, inevitably hardens into an institution such as the party or state – which is a phenomenon of the practico-inert and, as such, absorbs the free organic praxis into alienating, "serial" relations of pseudo-unity (conformity) and impotence (e.g., the faceless crowd).

(8) *Violence.* The basis of violence is interiorized scarcity; it will pervade society so long as material scarcity infects it. The "sworn group" (e.g., those who took the Tennis Court Oath in the French Revolution, Sartre's paradigm case of all of these features) introduces a relation of "fraternity-terror" that sustains a Rousseauian *sameness* via the threat of death for betrayal. Though Sartre had often described the violence characteristic of societies of oppression and exploitation, as well as the "counter-violence" of the oppressed and the exploited, only in the *Critique* does he connect this to the scarcity of material goods. This warrants his implicit reference to a "socialism of abundance" where violence would presumably be rare, if not excluded entirely.

In the interview he gave to Michel Contat as he turned seventy, Sartre remarked how it was Marxism as a philosophy of power that he rejected, while he continued to find several of its tenets valid – for instance, class struggle and surplus value. But he added: "We must develop a way of thinking which takes Marxism into account *in order to go beyond it*, to reject it and take it up again, to absorb it. This is the condition for arriving at a *true socialism*" (*L/S*, p. 61; emphasis added)

In a way that echoes the title as well as the thesis of "Socialism or Barbarism" – a French leftist group with which Sartre had ambivalent relations over the years – Sartre sums up his vision of the future: "Either man is finished ... or else he will adapt by bringing about some form of libertarian socialism." He explains what he sees as the coming revolution: "Revolution is not a single moment in which one power overthrows another; it is a long movement in which power is dismantled. Nothing can guarantee success for us, nor can anything rationally convince us that failure is inevitable. But the alternatives really are socialism or barbarism" (*L/S*, pp. 83–84).

11.9 "ALL POWER TO THE IMAGINATION"

A graffito on the walls during the events of May 1968 read: "*L'Imagination au pouvoir.*" This cry to leap from the political rut in which all the parties were stuck articulated the spirit of the rebels in the streets. It also echoed a persistent theme of Sartrean thought since he penned his thesis on the imagination for his diploma of higher studies (*DES*) in 1926/27. Though this topic has not been taken up explicitly here, since the present chapter's aims lie elsewhere, the path toward existential politics we have charted thus far confirms that Sartre was at heart a philosopher of the imaginary.[39] Given the major role played by the concept of the imagination throughout Sartre's thought – not to mention the ease with which he moved into imaginative literature and his skill at producing striking phenomenological descriptions – it should come as no surprise that his guiding values of "socialism *and* freedom" should assume synthesis "if only in the imagination" (*SG*). Such is his "vision" of the "new man," the "socialist man," whom we cannot yet experience but who will emerge with the advent of a "true" socialism (*ORR*, pp. 336–37). A remark repeated in his last discussions with Benny Lévy, which were published shortly before his death (1980), anticipates Sartre's hope for a society of fraternal equality and cognitive transparency. There he describes the ideal, the guiding star, of his political life in terms of the imaginary that has been his weapon as well as his trap throughout his public life:

> Socialism indeed makes no sense except as a dream (*comme l'état rêvé*), and a poorly conceived one at that, where man will be free; and it is that condition of freedom which people who desire socialism [are in fact seeking], whether they say so or not. (*ORR*, p. 347)

NOTES

1. Beauvoir, *La Cérémonie des adieux*, pp. 476–77; hereafter cited *Cér.* with page number.
2. Sartre, Foreword to Nizan, *Aden Arabie*, p. 51.
3. See Sartre, *Carnets de la drôle de guerre*, pp. 84–90; hereafter *CDG*. *The War Diaries*; hereafter *WD*.
4. Sartre, *The Transcendence of the Ego*, p. 106.

5. Perrin, *Avec Sartre au Stalag XII D*, p. 463. Cited by Cohen-Solal, *Jean-Paul Sartre*, p. 154; hereafter *JPS*.
6. Contat and Rybalka, *The Writings of Jean-Paul Sartre*, vol. I, *A Bibliographical Life*, p. 50; hereafter *C/R* with volume and page.
7. In 1948, Sartre would write *Dirty Hands*, a play that treats of the dilemma of a Party loyalist caught in the midst of the Party's change of policies that required him to redefine the motives of his previous actions initially undertaken at the Party's behest. Understandably, the Party was displeased by the opportunistic "thesis" of the play. Voicing dismay that his play was being presented as anti-Communist propaganda at a time when his relations with the PCF were warming, Sartre personally forbade its performance in Vienna while a congress of the World Peace Movement was taking place (December, 1952).
8. June 18, 1948 (*C/R*, p. 213).
9. Sartre *et al.*, *Entretiens sur la politique*, p. 38.
10. Sartre, "Materialism and Revolution," p. 253.
11. Sartre, *L'Être et le néant*, p. 502; *Being and Nothingness*, p. 429; hereafter *EN* and *BN* respectively.
12. Sartre, *La Résponsibilité de l'écrivain*, p. 59.
13. See Sartre, *Existentialism is a Humanism*, pp. 48–49; hereafter *EH*.
14. Beauvoir, *The Prime of Life*, p. 433.
15. Sartre, *The Communists and Peace*, p. 80; hereafter *CP*.
16. Sartre, *Anti-Semite and Jew*, p. 148.
17. Sartre, *Situations*, vol. II, p. 28; hereafter *Sit.* with volume and page number.
18. Where it is defined as "action in history and on history; that is, a synthesis of historical relativity and moral and metaphysical absolute, with this hostile and friendly, terrible and derisive world which it reveals to us" (*Sit.*, II:265; Sartre, *What is Literature?*, p. 194); hereafter *WL*.
19. Sartre, *Search for a Method*; hereafter *SM*.
20. Sartre, *Critique of Dialectical Reason*, 2 vols.; hereafter *CDR* with volume and page.
21. Sartre, "The Itinerary of Thought," p. 41.
22. Sartre, *Life/Situations*, p. 127; hereafter *L/S*.
23. See Gavi *et al.*, *On a raison de se révolter*, pp. 73–74; hereafter *ORR*.
24. Sartre, *Saint Genet*, p. 599; hereafter *SG*.
25. Aron, *Marxism and the Existentialists*, p. 30.
26. Sartre, *The Devil and the Good Lord*, p. 149.
27. Birchall, *Sartre against Stalinism*, p. 169.
28. Sartre, *Notebooks for an Ethics*, p. 415.

29. He distinguishes the spirit of synthesis, which he identifies with the holistic thinking of the proletariat, from the analytic spirit, associated with the bourgeoisie, which is individualist. The former anticipates the "dialectical reason" that he will study in the *Critique*, whereas the latter is fundamentally atemporal and anti-dialectical. The former gives us the "human condition" while the latter focuses on "human nature" (see *Sit.*, II:24).
30. Quoted from an interview October 15, 1984, with Cohen-Solal (*JPS*, pp. 440–44).
31. Sartre, *On Genocide*, p. 6.
32. Sartre, *On Genocide*, pp. 84–85.
33. The "events of May, 1968" denotes that explosive period in French political and cultural life when Parisian students took to the streets protesting the closing of the University at Nanterre, giving vent to a multiplicity of grievances from various quarters of society. This ignited a series of riots and clashes with the police that gained the support of tens of thousands who joined in the "movement." Labor unions became involved, though the PCF seemed to favor the status quo. The largest general strike in history was called, involving millions of workers throughout the country. The Gaullist government, at least momentarily, felt threatened. Though the physical danger was successfully met by the "Forces of Order," the moral and broadly cultural fabric of French society was rent and arguably liberalized in the aftermath.
34. A pseudonymous professor at the University of Paris (Nanterre) had characterized the May events in these terms. See Epistémon [Didier Anzieu], *Ces idées qui ont ébranlé la France*, pp. 78–87.
35. Benny Lévy (a.k.a. Pierre Victor). The so-called "Maoists" were a loose group of "Gauchistes" who stood to the far left of the Communists and valued each of the eight features of Sartrean thought just mentioned – especially spontaneity, violence, and deep ethical convictions. In his preface to a book, *Les Maos en France*, Sartre made clear his opening line: "I am not a Maoist" (*Sit.*, X:38). But then, their identity was as fluid as their convictions were anarchical.
36. Sartre, *L'Idiot de la famille*, 3 vols.; English translation, *The Family Idiot*.
37. "Jean-Paul Sartre is the philosopher of mediations *par excellence*," Althusser *et al.*, *Lire le Capital*, vol. II, p. 98. Sartre links Michel Foucault with Althusser as "philosophers of the concept" (referring to the static forms of the structuralists), whereas he defends the fluid and time-bound character of the "notion" (Jean Hyppolite's translation of Hegel's *Begriff*). Sartre's earlier distinction between "analytic" and "synthetic" reason or spirit becomes, in the *Critique*, the distinction

between analytical and dialectical reason. Analytical reason employs the "concepts" (the structures) of the practico-inert; dialectical reason utilizes the "notions" of praxis and its comprehension, which Sartre terms the "translucidity of praxis to itself" (*CDR*, 1:74). His argument with Foucault and his teacher, Althusser, is that structures are functions of the *practico*-inert. As the sedimentation of prior praxes, in Sartre's view, structures (e.g., "systems" such as colonialism, capitalism, or racism), notwithstanding their proper "intelligibility," are ontologically dependent on praxes for their efficacy. Because of this, Sartre argues that the meanness is (not entirely) in the system. (See *CDR*, 1:74–76, as well as Sartre, "Jean-Paul Sartre Répond.")

38. See, for example, *CDR*, 1:615–17, 627–28; *Family Idiot*, v:39.
39. I have developed this thesis elsewhere with additional evidence. See, for example, Flynn, "L'Imagination au Pouvoir" and "Sartre as Philosopher of the Imagination."

KRISTANA ARP

12 Simone de Beauvoir's existentialism: freedom and ambiguity in the human world

In July 1940, Simone de Beauvoir began a routine of going to the Bibliothèque Nationale most days from 2.00 to 5.00 p.m. to read G. W. F. Hegel's *Phenomenology of Spirit*. Hitler's armies had invaded and occupied Paris earlier, on June 14, 1940. She was teaching philosophy classes at a girls' *lycée* and living in her grandmother's empty apartment. Her close companion, Jean-Paul Sartre, who had been a soldier in a meteorological unit of the French Army, had been captured and was now being held in a German prisoner-of-war camp. Beauvoir was relieved to receive a note from him sent on July 2 saying he was being well treated, but life in Paris was dismal. Food was scarce, and the German troops were grim reminders of Parisians' lack of political freedom. Her reading routine helped soothe the dread, isolation, and alienation she felt. Beauvoir had always been a very earnest student. She had passed the demanding aggregation exam in philosophy at the young age of twenty-one. To supplement her knowledge of classical philosophical texts, she learned German and read texts in phenomenology. In 1935 she had read Edmund Husserl's *The Phenomenology of Internal Time-Consciousness* "without too much difficulty."[1] She also read Heidegger and translated long passages into French for Sartre.[2] Back when she was in college, her prodigious work habits had earned her a special nickname among her friends: *Castor*, or the beaver. Poring over a difficult philosophical text in a foreign language for three hours a day might seem a strange way to get through such times, but with her it made sense.

It was during these dark days that Beauvoir and Sartre both wrote major parts of the works that established them in the public eye: her novel *L'Invitée* (*She Came to Stay*), published in August 1943, and

Sartre's *Being and Nothingness*, published in June 1943. It was in a letter from the prisoner-of-war camp that Sartre first announced the title to her.[3] Both his stint as a soldier and his captivity in the camp provided him with large swathes of time he could devote to writing. Beauvoir shared in the birth of this work through their intensive correspondence, long conversations during his army leave, and her close reading of his notebooks. She found these ideas to be tremendously exciting, and some of them found their way into the novel she was writing. Sartre was influenced in turn by the insights in the long-polished draft of the novel he had read closely when he returned to Paris on army leave.[4] This interchange of ideas was nothing new to them. They had already established a close intellectual collaboration at this point, one that they maintained for the rest of their lives.

It is Beauvoir's close personal and intellectual relationship with Sartre, in fact, that has stood in the way of accurately assessing her contributions to existentialism. Sartre's *Being and Nothingness* was taken to be the decisive formulation of post-war French existentialism. Because of her close ties to Sartre, Beauvoir has until recently been seen primarily as his philosophical disciple, someone who applied his ideas in her fiction and non-fiction. Some even saw *The Second Sex*, Beauvoir's major work, groundbreaking in so many ways, as mainly an application of Sartre's ideas. Later in life Beauvoir tended to reinforce this impression. She was not a philosopher, she declared, Sartre was, so she adopted his philosophical ideas.[5] For her, a philosopher was someone who created a grand system like Hegel or Kant or Leibniz.[6]

But my opening vignette shows that Sartre was not the only philosophical influence on Beauvoir, despite her testimonials. While she did not write a systematic work of philosophy, she wrote two well-received philosophical essays, as well as theoretical articles for *Les Temps Modernes*. She also wove existentialist themes into her novels. In what follows I will show how, in these works, she developed important existentialist ideas that were distinctly her own. She began *She Came to Stay* in 1938; *The Second Sex* was published in two volumes in France in 1949. To my mind, these dates mark out her existentialist period. The central thesis of *The Second* Sex – that one is not born but becomes a woman – is undeniably an existentialist one. However, in that text she begins to move away from the existentialist focus of her earlier work, returning instead to a central theme of Hegel's – the dialectic of Lordship and Bondage – which had made a big impression on her in her reading sessions in 1940 at the Bibliothèque Nationale.

12.1 *SHE CAME TO STAY*: THE DEATH OF THE OTHER

Beauvoir chose a quotation from Hegel's chapter on Lordship and Bondage for the epigraph of *She Came to Stay*: "Each consciousness seeks the death of the other." In a letter to Sartre written in July 1940, she documents when she first encountered this idea, saying that it filled her with "intellectual ardor."[7] The novel narrates a complex romantic entanglement between four people who are more or less fictional counterparts of Beauvoir, Sartre, and two of their former students. Told from the point of view of Beauvoir's fictional counterpart, Françoise, the text is studded with passages about the impenetrability of another consciousness. Françoise reflects that the consciousness of her female rival is "like death, a total negation, an eternal absence, and yet, by a staggering contradiction, this abyss of nothingness could make itself present to itself and make itself fully exist for itself."[8] This metaphysical threat – the other woman's power to define her from the outside – leads Françoise to murder her in the end. The above quotation is just one place where connections to Sartre's theory of the for-itself and his account of the Look, presented in *Being and Nothingness*, are evident.[9] It is a matter of scholarly debate whether the parallels between the two works are due to Beauvoir's appropriation of Sartre's ideas, or vice versa.[10] However, the very existence of such a debate makes it clear that *She Came to Stay* is an existentialist novel.

Yet another passage in *She Came to Stay* introduces a different philosophical theme, one that became very important for Beauvoir in her later work and one that is uniquely her own. This passage occurs at the beginning of the novel as Françoise walks through the empty theater where she is working late at night.

> When she was not there, the smell of dust, the half-light, the forlorn solitude, all this did not exist for anyone; it did not exist at all. Now that she was there the red of the carpet gleamed through the darkness like a timid night light. She exercised this power: her presence revived things from

their inanimateness; she gave them their color, their smell. She went down one floor and pushed open the door into the auditorium. It was as if she had been entrusted with a mission: she had to bring to life this forsaken theater filled with darkness ... She alone released the meaning of these abandoned places, of these slumbering things. She was there and they belonged to her. The world belonged to her. (*SCTS*, p. 12)

In a subsequent essay, "Literature and Metaphysics," Beauvoir contends that there is a particular type of novel, the metaphysical novel, which presents a "metaphysical vision of the world."[11] The passage above is such a metaphysical vision. The ability to bring the sleeping theater back to life, which Françoise experiences in this passage, is what Beauvoir later named disclosure. "Disclosure" is the English word chosen by the translator of *The Ethics of Ambiguity* to render the French word *"devoilement."* Sartre used the terms *"devoilement"* and *"se devoiler"* in *Being and Nothingness* (there translated by Hazel Barnes as "revelation" and "to reveal"), but in a casual way.[12] Beauvoir brings the concept of disclosure into the foreground in her philosophical essays.

When Beauvoir has Françoise reflect that maybe without her the theater does not exist at all, she touches on a classical philosophical question: is there a world external to my consciousness? (In a later discussion with another character, Françoise concludes that the world does not vanish when no one is present, it just recedes into the misty distance.) However, neither in this novel nor in her subsequent work does Beauvoir really try to answer classical philosophical questions such as these. Rather, she is exploring what the phenomenologists call "intentionality," the relation between consciousness and the world of which it is conscious. Her concept of disclosure, prefigured in this passage from *She Came to Stay* and subsequently developed in her later works, owes much to two central figures in phenomenology, Edmund Husserl and Martin Heidegger.

When Heidegger uses the terms *"erschliessen"* and *"Erschlossenheit"* in *Being and Time*, they are translated into English as "to disclose" and "disclosure."[13] Heidegger uses the German term Dasein to refer to a human being – and to human *being* in general – which he characterizes as "being-in-the-world." By this he means that each of us exists within the world as it is disclosed. Beauvoir shows the influence of Heidegger on her thinking when she makes disclosure of the world a defining feature of human existence in her philosophical essays. But Heidegger is actually pointing to a more basic and holistic level of experience of the world. For him, the world is always already disclosed; it does not stand in need of disclosing. For Beauvoir, on the other hand, disclosure is a more active and voluntary operation. The reason is that Beauvoir retains a quasi-dualistic ontology, in which the disclosing consciousness stands over against the world disclosed. In his "Letter on Humanism," published in 1947, Heidegger strongly criticized what he saw as the underlying metaphysical assumptions of Beauvoir's and Sartre's existentialism. Existentialist humanism, he says, enthrones the "subject" as a "tyrant of being" who deigns "to release the beingness of being into an all too loudly bruited 'objectivity'" – a remark that uncannily fits the attitude that Françoise takes toward the objects she surveys in the empty theater.[14]

Heidegger drew from, but ultimately rejected, the phenomenology of Edmund Husserl. Beauvoir also drew from Husserl, especially in formulating her concept of disclosure. In Husserl's phenomenology, the contribution that consciousness makes to shaping the world of our experience is revealed by what he calls the transcendental *epoché*. To perform the *epoché* one must abstract from the question of whether the objects of consciousness actually exist. Whether or not these objects exist, they exist for us. They have meaning and significance, which ultimately derive from ourselves. In this respect, Beauvoir's concept of disclosure is closer to Husserl's notion of meaning constitution than to Heidegger's notion of disclosure. Beauvoir often speaks of how human beings give meaning and significance to the world. For her, the world that surrounds us is "the human world in which each object is penetrated with human meanings."[15]

12.2 "PYRRHUS AND CINEAS": FREEDOM AND THE MEANING OF LIFE

Beauvoir's first philosophical essay of her existentialist period, "Pyrrhus and Cineas," was written during the war and published right after the Liberation of France in 1944. It addresses an issue central to existentialism: what gives meaning to human life? The title comes from a story told by Plutarch. Asked by his advisor, Cineas, what he will do after he has conquered the whole world, Pyrrhus says he will rest. Cineas replies: "Why not rest right away?"[16] The French essayist Michel de Montaigne held Cineas' words to represent wisdom.[17] Beauvoir, in contrast, takes the side of Pyrrhus, though she does not endorse his imperialistic ambitions. There is nothing external to us that justifies our actions, but that does not make them pointless either. Neither God nor the good of humankind, neither death nor the pleasure of the moment, neither destiny nor the clockwork of the universe suffices to give meaning to human life. The only thing that does is a freely chosen goal. Life is meaningful because human beings make it so. Thus Beauvoir gives an existentialist answer to what is perhaps *the* existential question.

In this essay Beauvoir takes a distinctly different approach to depicting the relation between two consciousnesses, or freedoms, from the approach she took in *She Came to Stay.* Whereas in the novel (and in *Being and Nothingness*) another consciousness represents a limitation or a threat, Beauvoir proclaims here that because each of us is radically free we need others to provide a foundation and context for that freedom: "I need them because once I have surpassed my own goals, my actions will fall back on themselves, inert and useless, if they have not been carried off toward a new future by new projects" (PC, p. 135). According to Beauvoir's earlier understanding, the resistance to my projects represented by the other's freedom was a threat. Here it serves a positive purpose. I require another's freedom because "freedom is the only reality I cannot transcend" (PC, p. 31). Beauvoir here alludes to a metaphor from Kant's *Critique of Pure Reason*: the dove requires the resistance of the air to lift its wings.[18] However, in "Pyrrhus and Cineas" she still envisages one individual's freedom to be radically separate from another's. She clings to the Stoic conception of freedom as consisting in an interior sphere that cannot be breached: "As freedom, the other is radically separated from me; no connection can be created from me to this pure interiority upon which even God would have no hold" (PC, pp. 125–26). For this reason she claims that violence has no effect on the other's freedom, since it remains "infinite in all cases." Beauvoir will reject this position in her analysis of political and economic oppression in the last work from this period, *The Ethics of Ambiguity.*

As soon as *Being and Nothingness* was published, critics began to charge that existentialism excluded the very possibility of ethics.

In its closing pages Sartre had promised to devote a subsequent work to this subject. It never appeared, although many pages of notes and drafts were published after his death as *Notebooks for an Ethics*. If ethics is understood broadly to include the question that concerned, for instance, Socrates – how should we live our lives? – then Beauvoir is concerned with ethics in "Pyrrhus and Cineas." For instance, when Beauvoir asks what gives meaning to life there, one answer she considers is devotion to another. Such devotion is often misguided, she argues, and even if honest and sincere, necessarily misses the mark, since the other is radically free. Just as violence cannot touch the other's freedom, sacrifice and devotion cannot do anything for the other either. "I never create anything for the other except points of departure" (PC, p. 121). Some forms of devotion amount to an abdication of freedom, an attempt to escape its risk and anguish. The faulty reasoning goes: "Let's suppose the other needed me and that his existence had an absolute value. Then my being is justified, since I am for a being whose existence is justified" (PC, p. 117).

In *Being and Nothingness* Sartre holds any such attempt to flee one's freedom to be "bad faith." Even as early as her first philosophical essay, Beauvoir sees women in particular as liable to bad faith – attempting to escape the risk and anguish of freedom by assigning absolute value to the existence of another. In her novels from this period Beauvoir vividly depicts a range of female characters who fall into this trap. Elizabeth, a secondary female character in *She Came to Stay*, is one. Another is Hélène – the central character of Beauvoir's novel about the French Resistance, *The Blood of Others* – who feels that loving Blomart, the other central character, fills up the emptiness, the nothingness, inside her. Hélène previously looked to religion to fulfill the same function, to make her feel that she "must exist."[19] However, by the end of the book she realizes that everyone must justify their own existence for themselves. Beauvoir's final novel from this period, *All Men Are Mortal*, is framed by a story of the relationship of two people – a man who has mysteriously acquired immortality and a vain, anxiety-ridden actress. The actress, Regina, believes at first that she too can achieve immortality by existing in this man's eyes, but she finally realizes the cruel joke: his immortality renders everything in human life insignificant for him.

12.3 ARTICLES IN *LES TEMPS MODERNES*: EXISTENTIALISM AND POLITICS

Toward the end of 1945 Beauvoir published an essay, "Existentialism and Popular Wisdom," in the third issue of *Les Temps Modernes*, the new journal she helped found with Sartre, Maurice Merleau-Ponty, and others. She wanted to defend the new philosophical perspective she and Sartre were adopting from certain charges that had been lodged against it. Though neither she nor Sartre had coined the name "existentialism" – Gabriel Marcel had – both of them eventually adopted it. In her essay Beauvoir argues that existentialism is more honest and realistic than the sentimental idealism that many cling to, and more life-affirming than the "psychology of self-interest" that cynics and pessimists take refuge in.[20] Existentialism privileges human relationships: "Existentialists are so far from denying love, friendship, and fraternity that in their eyes the only way for each individual to find the foundation and accomplishment of his being is in these human relationships."[21] Of course, this description fits neither Sartre's account of the Look in *Being and Nothingness* nor Beauvoir's portrayal of dueling consciousnesses in *She Came to Stay*. However, in "Pyrrhus and Cineas" Beauvoir did come to regard individual freedoms as in some sense interdependent – a position that Sartre, too, seemed to adopt in *Existentialism is a Humanism*. In her subsequent essay, *The Ethics of Ambiguity*, Beauvoir argues at length for this position.

In her memoirs Beauvoir describes how living through the events culminating in the Second World War taught her the importance of the political realm. After the war she and Sartre became ever more involved in political activities. Starting with her novel *The Blood of Others*, she began to address the political situation in her writing as well. In a second essay in *Les Temps Modernes*, "Moral Idealism and Political Realism," Beauvoir examines different political stances through an existentialist lens. There she describes the balancing act that engaging in "lucid political action" involves.[22] An authentic ethics is political and an authentic politics is ethical. However, existentialism rules out appealing to any already existing set of moral standards and ideals. This is the "false objectivity" that Beauvoir has already rejected in "Pyrrhus and Cineas." Political realists on both the Left and the Right who argue that the end justifies the means also forget that the ends they pursue are not objectively given. Human ends are given value through the free acts of the people struggling to achieve them.

In his introductory essay to the first issue of *Les Temps Modernes* Sartre had called for a *littérature engagée*, or committed literature. As a faithful contributor to the journal, Beauvoir saw herself as a politically committed intellectual in this sense. For her, existentialism is a philosophy that has something important to say about political and social issues. Sartre stressed how the writer is always situated in a particular time, place, social stratum, etc. In these early years, neither Sartre nor Beauvoir recognized the important role gender plays in defining one's situation, and it was not until she began writing *The Second Sex* and looked deeply into what it was like to be a gendered subject that Beauvoir's political commitments took on mature form.

Another essay Beauvoir wrote for *Les Temps Modernes*, "An Eye for an Eye," takes up a specific issue of political morality: in it she argues that the execution of war criminals was morally justified. The crimes of the Nazis and their French collaborators are different from ordinary crimes because, in attempting through torture, humiliation, and other methods to reduce others to the status of mere things, they ignore their very humanity. Of course she recognizes that human existence has a material aspect, but that is not all there is to it. The "tragic ambiguity" of human existence is to be both a material thing and a consciousness.[23] Real evil – she even calls it absolute evil – comes about when one acknowledges only one's own subjectivity and treats the other solely as a material thing. Violent reprisal is justified because it turns the tables on the perpetrator of such evil. The victim reasserts his or her freedom and subjectivity, and the perpetrator viscerally grasps the material side of his or her existence. Each is equally human. However, because (as the phenomenological tradition emphasizes) one can only experience one's own subjectivity, the moral ideal is not strict equality for Beauvoir, but rather reciprocity. It is to recognize that "an object for others, each man is a subject for himself."[24] The affirmation of this reciprocity is, accordingly, "the metaphysical basis of the idea of justice."[25]

12.4 *THE ETHICS OF AMBIGUITY*: EXISTENTIALIST ONTOLOGY AND AUTHENTIC FREEDOM

In "An Eye for an Eye" Beauvoir says that the human being "is at the same time a freedom and a thing, both unified and scattered, isolated by his subjectivity and nevertheless co-existing at the heart of the world with other men."[26] She returns to the ambiguity of human existence in the opening passages of her last philosophical essay, *The Ethics of Ambiguity*, published serially first in *Les Temps Modernes* in 1946, and then on its own in 1947. There she stresses the inextricable connection between these two aspects of human life. A human being "is still part of the world of which he is a consciousness."[27] Consciousness emerges out of material reality and relates itself to it. Death and birth are two moments when the human being's material side is ascendant: "there is an original helplessness from which man surges up" (*EA*, p. 12). Human beings start life dependent on others, and they continue to be. Furthermore, the human body can always be "crushed by the dark weight of things" (*EA*, p. 7). In this essay Beauvoir traces the origins of existentialism back to Kierkegaard and claims that "from its very beginnings existentialism defined itself as a philosophy of ambiguity" (*EA*, p. 9). She then turns to the opposition between consciousness and material reality explored in Sartre's *Being and Nothingness*, the opposition between being-for-itself and being-in-itself. It is this duality, she says, that makes an ethics possible: "for a being who, from the very start, would be an exact coincidence with himself, in a perfect plenitude, the notion of having-to-be would have no meaning. One does not offer an ethics to a God" (*EA*, p. 10). Since human existence is ambiguous in this way, existentialism, as a philosophy of ambiguity, is not only able to found an ethics; it is "the only philosophy in which ethics has a place" (*EA*, p. 34).

There is an initial challenge, however, that existentialism – or at least an existentialism like Beauvoir's and Sartre's that stresses the magnitude of human freedom – must face before sketching out an ethics. In *Being and Nothingness* Sartre proclaims (and Beauvoir echoes this in *The Ethics of Ambiguity*) that all values, including ethical values, are created and freely adopted by human beings. Since values have their foundation in freedom, an existentialist ethics must rest upon freedom. But Sartre and Beauvoir also hold that human beings can never escape their freedom. If everyone is always free, why is it that not everyone acts morally? Beauvoir faces up to this problem in *The Ethics of Ambiguity* and finds a solution. She posits that there are two different levels to human freedom. The first level, the freedom that all human beings possess, she calls natural freedom; perhaps a better term is ontological freedom. The second level she calls moral freedom. It is an authentic freedom that people achieve only when they accept their original ontological freedom and no longer seek to escape it through devotion to others, to religion, or to a false objectivity in the ways Beauvoir depicted in earlier writing. According to *The Ethics of Ambiguity*, then, authentic freedom consists in willing oneself free.

On the existentialist view, we cannot, by an effort of will, escape our freedom; however, as Beauvoir explains, we can fail to will ourselves free. In *The Ethics of Ambiguity* Beauvoir presents five different personality types that represent five different ways that people live out this failure. The first she calls the sub-man, who retreats into apathy and inaction. Such people can be manipulated easily by fanatics and zealots, since unquestioning obedience to some external certainty can seem to give meaning to their lives. Fanatics and zealots do not question their values and ideals, but, as Beauvoir points out, in this they are no different than the vast majority of the conventional bourgeois. The latter are examples of Beauvoir's second personality type, the serious man – a type (as she notes) that Hegel, Kierkegaard, Nietzsche, and Sartre all singled out for scorn. A third type results from the psychic turmoil that attends the collapse of traditional values: the nihilist. Nihilists exercise their freedom by rejecting all the positive values that freedom creates, sometimes going so far as to destroy their fellow human beings who represent these values or actively choose to affirm them. Despite his penchant for destruction, the nihilist is a step higher than the serious man in Beauvoir's hierarchy. The nihilist is aware that values are the creation of human freedom, though this awareness fuels rage or coruscating pessimism. By contrast, Beauvoir's fourth personality type, the adventurer, experiences joy in living a life unrestricted by conventional expectations or values. Nevertheless, the adventurer's lack of commitment to shared goals or ideals cuts him off from meaningful connections with other people. The passionate man, in contrast – the final type Beauvoir describes – lives *through* his connection to someone else, or to some cause or land or treasure. Unlike the serious man, the passionate man realizes that he is the one who invests what he loves with such great value. Yet he fails to achieve authentic freedom for this very reason. It is a private, personal passion that can lead him to neglect others, or even to use them as a means to pursuing that very passion.

In *The Ethics of Ambiguity* Beauvoir relates her idea that there are different levels of freedom to the concept of disclosure, the power human beings have to bring the world to life, which she had described in *She Came to Stay*. Consciousness always discloses a world. But having now elucidated the ambiguity of the human condition – our dual existence as consciousness and material reality – Beauvoir explores a different aspect of disclosure. Disclosure is now seen to involve "uprooting" oneself from nature, from the realm of inert matter into which one can at any moment – and indeed sometimes wishes to – sink back. In an interesting passage she writes, "I should like to be the landscape which I am contemplating, I should like this sky, this quiet water to think themselves within me, that it might be I whom they express in flesh and bone" (*EA*, p. 12). Even under the worst circumstances human beings disclose the world. As Beauvoir's sub-man and nihilist discover to their regret, consciousness always ascribes some meaning to its surroundings. Furthermore, no world that is disclosed is mine alone; rather, it is "penetrated with human meanings." Even in the remotest corners of the earth, one is never wholly cut off from others: "One can reveal the world only on a basis revealed by other men" (*EA*, p. 71).

However, in order to achieve genuine freedom, Beauvoir says, one must will oneself to be free. Thus the two different levels of freedom she postulates involve two different attitudes toward disclosing the world. One can be a passive onlooker, or one can actively participate in forming and shaping the human world that one's consciousness discloses. To adopt the second attitude is to seek genuine freedom: "To wish for the disclosure of the world and to assert oneself as a freedom are one and the same movement" (*EA*, p. 24). But because in disclosing a world we remain in connection with other human beings, authentic freedom also has ethical implications. While some people may not want to acknowledge their dependence on others, the person aiming at genuine freedom brings this connection to the foreground and affirms it. To will oneself free is not just to will the disclosure of the world; it is also to will "that there be men by whom and for whom the world is endowed with human signification" (*EA*, p. 71). For Beauvoir, this means that "to will oneself free is also to will others free" (*EA*, p. 73). The only way that others can actively, and not just passively, disclose the world is if they too strive for genuine freedom.

In *The Ethics of Ambiguity* Beauvoir draws upon phenomenological analyses of temporality in order to show how the actions of each individual depend on others to give them meaning. Past, present, and future are not separate points but different dimensions of a single experience. Beauvoir stresses how the present is always linked to the future in the unity of a single temporal form: "Only the future can take the present for its own and keep it alive by surpassing it" (*EA*, p. 116). Systems as varied as Hegel's philosophy, political Marxism, and Christianity may attempt to bestow on the future "the immobility of being," but the future has no real existence apart from its connection to presently living human beings. Furthermore, no human being can alone determine what the future will be. As Beauvoir says, "it is other men who open the future to me" (*EA*, p. 82). They open it by disclosing a world in cooperation (or in conflict) with me. In *The Ethics of Ambiguity* Beauvoir holds the defining feature of oppression to be the way that it closes off the future and reduces life for its victims to "pure repetition." The oppressed suffer because they need others to provide the opportunities for them to realize their freedom. Yet the oppressor suffers as well. Beauvoir points out that the oppressor, too, needs others to be free in order to develop *authentic* freedom – again showing the influence of Hegel on her thought. To achieve genuine freedom I need for others to be free – genuinely free – so that they can open the future for me.

12.5 *THE SECOND SEX*: EXISTENTIALIST ROOTS, HEGELIAN INFLUENCES

Immediately after Beauvoir readied *The Ethics of Ambiguity* for publication she turned to writing *The Second Sex*, which was published in 1949. In this text, which extends to 577 pages in the French original, Beauvoir left the essay form behind to produce a work so comprehensive in scope as almost to defy classification. Eventually translated into many languages, it has had a worldwide impact.

Most feminists consider it to have been the impetus behind what is called the "second wave" of feminism.[28] *The Second Sex* remains the book for which Beauvoir is best known today.

Beauvoir initially intended this project to be a continuation of *The Ethics of Ambiguity*. It was to have had a personal focus, but one that would remain philosophical: she wanted to explain what it was to be both a woman and an existentialist.[29] Once she began to think about it, Beauvoir was surprised to discover how much being a woman had affected her life. Because her father's financial failures had made him unable to provide a dowry, her family expected her to pursue a career – a path that was unusual for a middle-class Frenchwoman of her day. Beginning in her college years, the male Parisian intellectuals with whom she came into daily contact treated her pretty much as an equal. Since her personal situation was atypical in these ways, to find out what it really meant to be a woman required a lot of research. Not only did she spend much time consulting texts at the library (very few of which she cites, unfortunately), she spent countless hours talking to women in France and the USA, where she traveled during this time.

Her conclusion is concisely summed up in the now well-known passage at the beginning of the introduction to the second volume of the French text: "One is not born, but rather becomes, woman. No biological, psychical or economic destiny defines the figure that the human female takes on in society."[30] This passage suggests the extent to which *The Second Sex* is an existentialist text. In accord with the central existentialist idea that existence precedes essence, *The Second Sex* argues that there is no special essence, or distinct biological nature or way of thinking, that only a certain portion of the human species possesses. In three successive chapters in the first volume Beauvoir shows how those who ascribe women's subordinate position in society to biology, psychological developments, or economic history are wrong. Of course, her criticisms were aimed at the intellectual opinions and social situation of her own time. Conditions have changed since she wrote *The Second Sex*. But addressing such changes lies beyond the scope of this chapter.

Beauvoir's chapter on biology has been the subject of much controversy. Feminists have charged that she describes women's experience of their bodies in unnecessarily negative terms. To pick one passage out of many, she compares human females to other female mammals by saying "in no other is the subordination of the organism to the reproductive function more imperious, nor accepted with greater difficulty" (*TSS*, p. 44; DS I, p. 69). Nonetheless, at the end of this chapter she explicitly adopts a perspective that seems to neutralize the philosophical importance of these observations. Female biology is different from male biology, and the female plays a different role in human reproduction, but that does not mean that the female has a fixed biological destiny. The proper perspective to take on the body is that of the phenomenological tradition – Beauvoir mentions Heidegger, Merleau-Ponty, and Sartre in this regard – in which "the body is not a *thing*, it is a situation" (*TSS*, p. 46; *DS* I, p. 72).[31] Given Beauvoir's previous emphasis on the ambiguity of human existence as both consciousness and material reality, it is not surprising that she ascribes importance to female biological functions. But from her existentialist perspective this is not the end of the story: "Woman is not a fixed reality, but a becoming," since, existentially speaking, no human being, male or female, is ever a fixed reality (*TSS*, p. 45; *DS* I, p. 72).

The approach that psychoanalytic schools of thought take to explaining women's behavior has the advantage that it concentrates on "the body lived by the subject" (*TSS*, p. 49; *DS* I, p. 77). Phenomenologically speaking, it seems unlikely that a human female's experience of her body could ever be the same as a male's. Unfortunately, Freudian psychology cannot succeed at explaining what it is like to live as a woman, because it takes the male body as its starting point. The female body is conceived as a deviation from the norm. The young girl's realization that her body lacks what the young boy's body has – the penis – is supposed to be decisive for her psychological development. But Beauvoir argues that having a penis only seems important to the young girl because the importance of being male is everywhere evident to her. Beauvoir seems to have more sympathy with a psychoanalytic approach than does Sartre, however, who presents a detailed critique of Freud's thought at various points in his work. She even advances her own account of the difference between the ways the young girl and the young boy experience their genitalia, and the consequences of this for their development. Yet in the end Beauvoir finds psychoanalytic explanations wanting because there is something more fundamental than anatomy and sexuality that determines one's experience of the world: "All psychoanalysts systematically refuse the idea of *choice* and its corollary, the notion of value: and herein lies the intrinsic weakness of the system" (*TSS*, p. 56; *DS* I, p. 85). To trace the roots of women's social inferiority back to forgotten or hazily remembered childhood incidents is to interiorize the process. Beauvoir's existentialism sees the individual subject always in relation to the world, and to the other people who populate it. Without the mediation of history and society, a human being with female anatomy could not "become" a woman.

Yet Beauvoir also rejects the explanation for male dominance given by Marxist theories of historical materialism. Although such explanations have a wider scope than psychoanalytic ones, they also neglect fundamental questions of why human beings come to adopt the value systems they do. Why did private property become the focal point of male-dominated economic systems? Beauvoir offers her own account of what drove certain key transitions in human history, though the chapters containing Beauvoir's speculations on what separated women from men in the early stages of human history have also been harshly criticized by feminists. In these sections of *The Second Sex*, as elsewhere, she returns to key elements of Hegel's thought – in particular his dialectic of Lordship and Bondage. According to Hegel, in order to advance to self-consciousness a consciousness must be willing to risk its life in a struggle to the death. Beauvoir speculates that this route was closed to females in prehistory because of the biological roles they played in human reproduction: "to give birth and to breastfeed are not activities, they are natural functions; they do not involve a project, which is why woman finds no motive there to claim a higher meaning for her existence; she passively submits to her biological destiny" (*TSS*, p. 73; *DS* I, p. 110). Thus, because they did not participate in war or hunting, females did not even rise to the level of the bondsman in Hegel's dialectic. Quoting Hegel, Beauvoir holds that they remained consigned to an animal type of life.

Inspired by Hegel, Beauvoir develops a new philosophical concept in *The Second Sex* – the concept of the social Other – in order to explain the unique position that women have occupied throughout history. In *She Came to Stay* Beauvoir had focused on how the dialectic of self-consciousness plays itself out between individual subjects. She returns to this idea in *The Second Sex*: "the subject posits itself only in opposition; it asserts itself as the essential and sets up the other as inessential, as the object (*TSS*, p. 7; *DS* I, p. 17). But reflecting the influence of Claude Lévi-Strauss, with whom Beauvoir studied at the Sorbonne, *The Second Sex* goes further by analyzing how this dynamic operates between different social groups: "The duality between Self and Other can be found in the most primitive societies, in the most ancient mythologies" (*TSS*, p. 6; *DS* I, p. 16). Ultimately, this Hegelian concept of the social Other becomes the dominant theoretical construct of the work, even to the point of eclipsing Beauvoir's original existentialist perspective.

Women, Beauvoir says, are the absolute Other, and their situation has been such that they have been unable to escape this status. Unlike other social groups, women have never turned the tables on men, making them into the Other in turn. Beauvoir suggests that this is because for woman "the tie that binds her to her oppressor is unlike any other" (*TSS*, p. 9; *DS* I, p. 19): males and females are necessary to each other. By thinking of woman in this way, as the absolute Other, Beauvoir is able to make sense of the wildly different – even contradictory – ways that women have been represented in the myths and literatures of various cultures. The female has been associated in turn with nature, artifice, life, death, animality, nurturing, sexuality, danger, and purity. In all these cases, woman is defined as what man is not. Men, being dominant in the culture, themselves define what it is to be a man.

In *The Second Sex*, Beauvoir's emphasis on the ambiguity of human existence retreats into the background. Instead she turns to a pair of opposed concepts from her earlier existentialist writing: immanence and transcendence. Immanence is associated with sinking back into the material side of existence, passivity, confinement to the present. Transcendence is conscious activity, a reaching beyond the situation one finds oneself in at any moment. In *The Second Sex* transcendence is similar to what, in *The Ethics of Ambiguity*, she called authentic or moral freedom. It involves an active disclosure of the world and involvement with others: "It is the existence of other men that wrests each man from his immanence and enables him to accomplish the truth of his being, to accomplish himself as transcendence, as flight towards the object, as a project" (*TSS*, p. 159; *DS* I, pp. 231–32).

However, the account of transcendence in *The Second Sex* differs from *The Ethics of Ambiguity*'s account of how individuals need each other in order to realize authentic freedom, for it emphasizes the role of *conflict* in this process. The ideal outcome of the conflict is "the free recognition of each individual in the other, each one positing both itself and the other as object and as subject in a reciprocal movement" (*TSS*, p. 159; *DS* I, p. 232), she says, hearkening back to her earlier definition of justice as reciprocity in "An Eye for an Eye." But, she contends, most males are not up to this challenge. Luckily for them, the existence of women as they have been shaped historically, culturally, and socially allows men to avoid this difficult step. Woman is constituted as a creature who does not exist as transcendence but as immanence – not wholly a material entity but "nature raised to the transparency of consciousness" (*TSS*, p. 161; *DS* I, p. 233). Thus Beauvoir draws from the Hegelian dialectic to explain how the male opposes himself to the female, but she postulates another possible outcome to it besides death or enslavement. By relegating women to immanence, men do not have to face up to the threat that another transcendence poses. That is why "no man would consent to being a woman, but all want there to be women" (*TSS*, p. 161; *DS* I, p. 234).

In the long chapters on the different stages of a woman's life in *The Second Sex*, Beauvoir explores how young women come to internalize this notion of themselves as the Other: "It is a strange experience for an individual recognizing himself as subject, autonomy and transcendence, as an absolute, to discover inferiority – as a given essence – in his self" (*TSS*, p. 311; *DS* II, pp. 46–47). In her earlier existentialist novels and essays Beauvoir had shown how at some level all human beings long to escape their freedom. *The Second Sex* goes into much detail about why women are presented with many more opportunities to give in to this temptation than are men. Women live among men in a male-dominated society. Thus "refusing to be the Other, refusing complicity with man, would mean renouncing all the advantages an alliance with the superior caste confers on them" (*TSS*, p. 10; *DS* I, p. 21). Beauvoir's readiness here to see women as complicit in their own oppression has drawn objections from some feminist readers.

Beauvoir describes how at puberty the young woman's body, the emanation of her subjectivity, becomes something other than her, an object that arouses new and sometimes startling responses from others: "She becomes an object; and she grasps herself as object; she is surprised to discover this new aspect of her being: it seems to her that she has been doubled; instead of coinciding exactly with her self, here she is existing *outside* of her self" (*TSS*, p. 349; *DS* II, p. 90). At this point the woman internalizes the alienation from her own body that is encouraged by the culture.[32] A new temptation arises: narcissism. Some women become intoxicated and take pride in this body they see in the mirror, which is theirs but somehow separate from them. Beauvoir places her analysis of female narcissism in a section at the end she labeled "Justifications," which also contains chapters on "The Woman in Love" and "The Mystic." Narcissism, romantic love and extreme religiosity are ways for women "to achieve transcendence through immanence" (*TSS*, p. 664; *DS* II, p. 455). Women, she says, seek to find in romantic love something essentially different from what men look for. Beauvoir's novels contain a number of unflattering portraits of women desperate to continue unsatisfying love affairs. *The Second Sex* provides the full context that allows their behavior to be understood.

For the most part the analysis of women's current situation in *The Second Sex* is descriptive, not prescriptive. Beauvoir mobilizes her philosophical knowledge and understanding to explain how women come to be alienated in their bodies and relegated to an inferior social position, but she does not say much about why this is wrong, nor about what should be done about it. Her reliance on Hegel's dialectic of Lordship and Bondage – which posits a drive to defeat or subjugate other consciousnesses – may make men's treatment of women comprehensible but it also makes it hard to hold them culpable. It is notable that Beauvoir has to revert to the standpoint of the existentialist ethics propounded in *The Ethics of Ambiguity* to explain why the subordination of one half of the human race to the other is wrong:

> The perspective we have adopted is one of existentialist morality. Every subject posits itself as a transcendence concretely, through projects; it accomplishes its freedom only by a perpetual surpassing towards other freedoms; there is no other justification for present existence than its expansion towards an indefinitely open future. Every time transcendence lapses into immanence, there is degradation of existence into 'in-itself', of freedom into facticity; this is a moral fault if the subject consents to it;

if this fall is inflicted on the subject, it takes the form of frustration and oppression; in both cases it is an absolute evil. (*TSS*, pp. 17; *DS* I, p. 31)

The freedom that entails a reaching out to other freedoms and an expansion into an open future is the authentic freedom that she described in *The Ethics of Ambiguity.* To deny women the capacity to develop authentic freedom is to commit a moral wrong.

In "An Eye for an Eye" Beauvoir called the fascists' attempt to reduce their victims to purely material existence an "absolute evil." Though the treatment accorded women throughout history has not been so harsh, it is wrong for the same reasons. It is a diminishment of women's true humanity. Therefore, women's situation needs to be changed. How? In one of the few places where she addresses this question Beauvoir again returns to the perspective of existentialist ethics:

[I]n woman ... freedom remains abstract and empty, it cannot authentically assume itself except in revolt: this is the only way open to those who have no chance to build anything; they must refuse the limits of their situation and seek to open paths to the future. (*TSS*, p. 664, *DS* II, p. 455)

In the decades that followed the publication of *The Second Sex* Beauvoir did engage in political action on behalf of women around the world. This was one way that she continued to fulfill the existentialist ideal of the committed intellectual.

12.6 CONCLUSION

Simone de Beauvoir was one of the most influential intellectuals of the twentieth century. Her rich, deep, and wide-ranging scholarly work *The Second Sex* has had a direct or an indirect effect on the lives of many. Although the situation of women (at least in some parts of the world) has changed since the time she wrote it, *The Second Sex* remains relevant. And though there were other intellectual influences on it as well, it is clearly one of the most significant works to have emerged from the existential tradition. The philosophical ideas that Beauvoir developed in her existentialist writings prior to *The Second Sex* also deserve attention. Her concept of ambiguity, with its stress on the material origins of human existence, seems especially promising. It provides an alternative to the excessively dualistic opposition between being-for-itself and being-in-itself found in Sartre's *Being and Nothingness*. Here, perhaps, connections can be made to the naturalism that seems to be all the rage in philosophy today. But Beauvoir's naturalism, if you can call it that, is an existential naturalism that insists that the natural world is at the same time a human world of consciousness and freedom. Our relation to nature must always retain an element of ambiguity, but given the dangers facing the natural world at the beginning of the twenty-first century, Beauvoir does well to remind us that a human being "is still part of this world of which he is a consciousness" (*EA*, p. 7).

NOTES

1. Beauvoir, *The Prime of Life*, p. 162.
2. Beauvoir, *Adieux*, p. 172.
3. Sartre, *Lettres au Castor*, vol. II, p. 285.
4. Sartre, *War Diaries*, p. 197; Beauvoir, *Letters to Sartre*, p. 258.
5. Schwarzer, *After the Second Sex*, pp. 57, 190.
6. Simons, *Beauvoir and* The Second Sex, pp. 10–11.
7. Beauvoir, *Letters to Sartre*, p. 328.
8. Beauvoir, *She Came to Stay*, p. 291. Henceforth cited in the text as *SCTS*.
9. Hazel Barnes traces what she sees to be the correspondence between Sartre's treatment of being-for-others in *Being and Nothingness* and the stages that the characters go through in *She Came to Stay*. See Barnes, *The Literature of Possibility*, pp. 121–37.
10. See Fullbrook and Fullbrook, *Simone de Beauvoir and Jean-Paul Sartre*, and Barnes, "Response to Margaret Simons," for the arguments on either side. Daigle and Golomb, *Beauvoir and Sartre*, provide a greater range of opinions.
11. Beauvoir, "Literature and Metaphysics," p. 275.
12. Barnes does not include either "disclosure" or "revelation" in her "Key to Special Terminology" at the back of the English translation of *Being and Nothingness*.
13. Heidegger, *Being and Time*, pp. 105–6.
14. Heidegger, "Letter on Humanism," p. 234. Heidegger's essay is directed at Sartre's essay *Existentialism is a Humanism*. There is no evidence that Heidegger ever read Beauvoir.
15. Beauvoir, *The Ethics of Ambiguity*, p. 74.
16. Beauvoir, "Pyrrhus and Cineas," p. 90. Henceforth cited in the text as PC.

17. Montaigne, "Of the Inequality That Is among Us," p. 196.
18. Kant, *Critique of Pure Reason,* p. 47.
19. Beauvoir, *The Blood of Others,* p. 83.
20. Beauvoir, "Existentialism and Popular Wisdom," p. 209.
21. Beauvoir, "Existentialism and Popular Wisdom," p. 213.
22. Beauvoir, "Moral Idealism and Political Realism," p. 189.
23. Beauvoir, "An Eye for an Eye," p. 248.
24. Beauvoir, "An Eye for an Eye," p. 249.
25. Beauvoir, "An Eye for an Eye," p. 247.
26. Beauvoir, "An Eye for an Eye," p. 258.
27. Beauvoir, *The Ethics of Ambiguity,* p. 7. Henceforth cited in the text as *EA*.
28. The "first wave" was the political activity that led to women getting the vote in the United States and Great Britain.
29. Bair, *Simone de Beauvoir,* p. 380.
30. Beauvoir, *The Second Sex,* p. 283; *Le Deuxième Sexe,* vol. II, p. 13; henceforth cited in the text as *TSS* and *DS* respectively. In my citations I have indicated the page numbers of the English translation first, and then the page numbers from the original French text: (*TSS*, p. 267; *DS* II, p. 13). The English page numbers refer to the recently published translation, which has important advantages over the first translation made in 1953.
31. Maurice Merleau-Ponty was a close friend of Beauvoir's in her youth. She had a very favorable opinion of his ideas on the body, as her glowing review of *Phenomenology of Perception* in the first issue of *Les Temps Modernes* in 1945 shows. See Beauvoir, "A Review of *The Phenomenology of Perception*."
32. I analyze this process in my "Beauvoir's Concept of Bodily Alienation."

TAYLOR CARMAN

13 Merleau-Ponty on body, flesh, and visibility

The central inspiring theme of Merleau-Ponty's philosophical thought is, in a word, the *body*. It is difficult to state his core insight, however, without making it sound trivial. Everyone knows that we *have* bodies and that the body is essentially involved (somehow or other) in perception and action. But what does it mean to "have" a body, and *how* (exactly) is the body implicated in our experience and our behavior? What is its relation to *us*?

To begin with, notice how misleading it is to say that I "have" a body, as if my body stands in a merely external relation to *me*. Wittgenstein once wrote, "If someone says, 'I have a body,' he can be asked, 'Who is speaking here with this mouth?'"[1] Yet we also speak loosely (and harmlessly) of "having" minds, though it seems absurd to say that a mind is something distinct from the person whose mind it is. Especially under the influence of Descartes, or at least the popular appropriation of Cartesianism, we are probably more inclined to say that we *are* our minds.[2] This is perhaps what we ought to say about the body, too, or at least what we ought to mean by saying that we have bodies: I don't *merely* have a body, I *am* my body. Even better, perhaps we ought to say that a body, like a mind, is an aspect of a person.

Merleau-Ponty's *Phenomenology of Perception* (1945), his magnum opus, amounts to a radical critique and repudiation of Cartesian dualism. Taken by itself, of course, that hardly distinguishes him from the vast majority of contemporary thinkers. For by the middle of the twentieth century almost no serious philosopher was a substance dualist, and nearly every educated person nowadays believes that we are somehow identical with, or constituted by, our bodies.

But Merleau-Ponty is not just one among the many opponents of metaphysical dualism. In fact, his contribution to philosophy bypasses traditional metaphysics almost entirely. That is to say, his phenomenology is not a theory of the mind from an objective theoretical point of view. His insistence on our bodily nature, and the bodily nature of perception, is not just an assertion of materialism. Instead, his point is that my *experience* of myself is wholly and exclusively an *experience* of a bodily self. I do not perceive my body, as Husserl inelegantly put it, as "a thing 'inserted' between the rest of the material world and the 'subjective' sphere."[3] In fact, usually I don't strictly speaking perceive my body as an object at all, which is why it is also misleading to say that I perceive myself and my body as identical or as coinciding, as if I had two representations, two concepts or descriptions – *myself* and *this body* – which happen to converge on one and the same thing, like the names "Morning Star" and "Evening Star." I never merely observe my body, Merleau-Ponty says, for "to do so, I would have to use a second body, which would itself be unobservable."[4]

It is better to say that I *live* or *enact* my body as the locus or manifestation of my attitudes, my perceptions, my actions in the world. As Merleau-Ponty puts it, "my body ... is my point of view on the world" (*PP*, p. 85/81), it is "my general ability [*pouvoir*] to inhabit" a world (*PP*, p. 359/363). The body is what constitutes the *structure* of my experience and my behavior. It is not, for me, an object of belief or observation, but a framework or horizon that constitutes what Merleau-Ponty, following Heidegger, calls my "being in the world" (*être au monde*).

The body is animated, so to speak, by what Merleau-Ponty calls the "body schema" (*schéma corporel*). The body schema is not a representation *of* the body, but the organization of our bodily awareness of the world, our practical ability to anticipate and (literally) incorporate the world in our actions and dispositions.[5] Such skills – or exercises of bodily "habit" – are not cognitive representations, nor are they in any sense internal to the mind, for as Merleau-Ponty says, "it is the body that 'understands' in the acquisition of habit" (*PP*, p. 168/167). The body comprises "stable organs and pre-established circuits" (*PP*, p. 103/100) that operate according to their own logic, as it were, below the threshold of self-conscious intention. My body preserves and maintains a "best grip" (*meilleure prise*) on the world (*PP*, p. 309/311); it is not "the object of an 'I think,'" but "an ensemble of lived meanings that finds its equilibrium" (*PP*, p. 179/177).

This descriptive account of the essential dovetailing of perception and bodily movement constitutes a profound challenge to the conceptual dualism still widely taken for granted, even by proponents of materialist theories of the mind. For Merleau-Ponty's argument is not that one and the same object in the world happens to answer to two distinct ideas we have in our store of concepts, namely mind and body, but that we have no clear ideas of mind and body except as impoverished abstractions from our precognitive understanding of ourselves as bodily perceivers and doers.

More than any of the other major figures in phenomenology, Merleau-Ponty sought to integrate the findings of the empirical sciences, especially psychology, into his own descriptions of perception and embodiment. In *Phenomenology of Perception*, for example, he devotes many pages to an analysis and discussion of a case of visual form agnosia, or what used to be called "mind blindness" (*Seelenblindheit*). A patient of the neurologist Kurt Goldstein, known in the literature only as "Schneider," suffered a brain injury in the First World War that left him "unable to perform 'abstract' movements with his eyes closed, that is, movements that are not relevant to any actual situation" (*PP*, pp. 119/118). He could still execute "concrete" movements, that is, "movements necessary for life, provided they have become habitual for him: he takes his handkerchief from his pocket and blows his nose, takes a match out of a box and lights a lamp" (*PP*, p. 120/118). So, for example, although Schneider could not deliberately point to his eyebrow, he could, with some effort, imagine himself into a situation in which he had to salute an officer, and thereby find his brow through the familiar bodily routine that he knew, as an objective matter of fact, would bring his finger into contact with it. Schneider, that is, had both concrete movement and abstract knowledge, but no abiding intuition of a stable environment, which ordinarily acts as a kind of bridge between our abstract thoughts and our motor skills.

Goldstein argued that Schneider's incapacity revealed a distinction between two neurological functions discreetly woven together in normal perception and behavior, namely our capacity for "pointing" to objects (*Zeigen*) and our capacity for "grasping" things for use (*Greifen*). Schneider can grasp, but he cannot point. This difference has been confirmed by subsequent research, most recently by Melvyn Goodale and David Milner, who have shown that two neural pathways in the brain, the ventral and the dorsal streams, are responsible for, in their words, "vision for perception" and "vision for action."[6]

But whereas Goldstein believed that Schneider's condition simply exposed the distinction between the two functions more clearly than normal experience does, Merleau-Ponty maintains, on the contrary, that the pathological state must be seen as a distortion and a privation of the normal case:

> Illness, like childhood and the state of the "primitive," is a complete form of existence, and the procedures it employs to replace normal functions that have been destroyed are themselves pathological phenomena. One cannot deduce the normal from the pathological, deficiencies from the surrogate functions, by a mere change of sign. We must take surrogates as surrogates, as allusions to some fundamental function they are trying to replace. (*PP*, p. 125/123)

We cannot simply assume that Schneider's "grasping" motor skills are the same as ours, open to view now in their pristine condition, disentangled from the "pointing" capacity he has lost. When we point to our brow, we do something altogether different from what Schneider does. We do not go through *any* tacit re-enactment or rehearsal of tactile memory or behavior, even very quickly and inconspicuously. We do not call upon an ensemble of exploratory movements, hoping to stumble on forms that then merely *seem* to be given to us in visual intuition. Instead, our bodies and worlds *really are* given visually in a way that Schneider's are not. Schneider's perceptual relation to things is profoundly unlike ours, not just different in a piecemeal way.

What is lacking in Schneider's sensorimotor experience? Not just objective spatial intuition, but a kind of bodily awareness that allows us to encounter the environment *as* a stable and abiding environment:

> What he lacks is neither motility nor thought, and we are led to recognize between movement as a third-person process and thought as the representation of movement an anticipation or arrival at a result, ensured by the

body itself as a motor power, a "motor projection" (*Bewegungsentwurf*) or "motor intentionality." (*PP*, p. 128/126–27)

Schneider's movements do not open up their own background, but are embedded in a kind of plenum: he cannot "grasp simultaneous wholes" or "take a bird's-eye view of" (*survoler*) his own movements (*PP*, p. 147/146); he cannot recognize his handwriting as his own, indeed "the world no longer has any *physiognomy* for him" (*PP*, p. 153/152). When he hears and retells a story, "he doesn't emphasize anything," but simply feeds it back "bit by bit" (*PP*, p. 154/153).

Merleau-Ponty never abandoned phenomenology, but by the mid 1950s his thought had taken a decidedly new direction. Some have argued that the change was profound, constituting a paradigm shift of the sort one finds in Heidegger and Wittgenstein, whose later thinking took a sharp turn from the early works that made them famous. When he died in 1961 Merleau-Ponty left behind an unfinished work, *The Visible and the Invisible*, which was published in 1964, along with working notes from his manuscripts. The fourth chapter of the published text, "The Intertwining – The Chiasm" (*"L'entrelacs – le chiasme"*), sketches out a new line of thought, with further, often cryptic elaboration in the notes. In the notes there are also occasional critical comments on his own earlier work, in particular *Phenomenology of Perception*, from which some have inferred a radical transformation in his entire approach.

Was the change radical? On the whole, I think not. Nevertheless, there are interesting and original ideas in *The Visible and the Invisible*, ideas that at times extend and elaborate themes in his earlier work, and even occasionally cast doubt on some of its basic assumptions.

What notion in particular did Merleau-Ponty abandon in his later work? In a word, the primacy of *consciousness*. Gestalt phenomena now suggest to him that, as he bluntly says, "perception is unconscious. What is the unconscious? That which functions as a pivot, an existential, and in that sense is and is not perceived." The unconscious "pivot" is still, in short, the body: "the *hinge* of the for itself and the for others – To have a body is to be looked at ... it is to be *visible*."[7]

This might sound like a minor terminological variation on the account of perception and the body that he had already developed in *Phenomenology of Perception*, but Merleau-Ponty evidently considered it a major departure with profound implications. What is at issue, it seems, is the *ontological* ground of phenomenology, which necessarily limits itself to conscious experience. In 1959 Merleau-Ponty writes, "Results of *Ph.P.* – Necessity of bringing them to ontological explicitation ... The problems that remain ... are due to the fact that in part I retained the philosophy of 'consciousness'" (*VI*, p. 237/183). And in July of that year, more critically:

> The problems posed in *Ph.P.* are insoluble because I start there from the "consciousness"–"object" distinction –
>
> One will never understand, starting from that distinction, how a particular fact of the "objective" order (a particular cerebral lesion) could entail a particular disturbance of the relation with the world – a massive disturbance that seems to demonstrate that "consciousness" as a whole is a function of the objective body – It is these problems themselves that must be dismissed by asking: *what is* the supposed *objective* conditioning? Answer: it is a way of expressing and noting an event of the order of brute or savage being that is ontologically primary. (*VI*, p. 253/200)

"Brute or savage being" is now prior to consciousness, and the task of philosophy is no longer simply to describe *conscious* experience, but to say how experience is possible as a mode of our *unconscious* bodily immersion in the world.

Why does Merleau-Ponty renounce the primacy of consciousness? The answer, I think, appears in the reference in the foregoing passage to "a particular cerebral lesion." Some fifteen years after his discussion of Schneider in the *Phenomenology*, that is, Merleau-Ponty is pondering again the potentially catastrophic effects of brain damage. As always, he rejects any sharp distinction between the mental and the physical, in terms of which purely mechanical events in the brain could be correlated with discrete psychological effects described in abstraction from the subject's entire bodily being in the world. Goldstein was wrong to think that Schneider's condition simply confined his motor actions to a purely tactile perception of his environment. On the contrary, Merleau-Ponty insists, Schneider has lost his visuomotor *awareness* of a stable, abiding world. Schneider's world is no longer *given* in conscious intuition.

What *does* Schneider have? A peculiar form of blind vision, so to speak, which remained deeply obscure on Merleau-Ponty's earlier account, the point of which was to emphasize Schneider's *loss* of motor intentionality, that is, the fully integrated visuomotor *experience* enjoyed by normal perceivers. Now that Merleau-Ponty no longer regards consciousness as basic to our being in the world, Schneider's peculiar "groping" immersion in the world appears at once stranger and more significant than ever. What is new in *The Visible and the Invisible*, then, is Merleau-Ponty's way of describing that unconscious ground of conscious experience, the ontological bedrock on which sense experience and bodily behavior both rest.

The ontological foundation of sensory receptivity and motor spontaneity is what Merleau-Ponty now calls "flesh" (*chair*). Flesh is the stuff common to ourselves and the world, what we and it are both made of, as it were. And yet the term is not just another name for physical matter: "flesh is not matter, it is not spirit, it is not substance" (*VI*, p. 184/139; cf. *VI*, p. 191/146). What then? The *sensibility* of things, the perceptibility both of the perceptual environment and of ourselves as perceivers – the *visibility* of vision, the *tangibility* of touch, the *exposure* of anything to which the world itself can be exposed in experience, including the bodily sense or experience of motor intentionality.

Merleau-Ponty had always insisted that to stand *before* the world, one must be *in* the world; he now goes further by insisting that to be *in* the world, one must be *of* the world. One must, so to speak, be of the same flesh as the world one inhabits and perceives. What is new in this is that it gives pride of place to what he had previously tended to brush off as merely "objective," namely the blind, unconscious bedrock of being that underlies perceptual experience. That blind, unconscious world now turns out to have profound significance precisely because *we are it*. In sensing, we ourselves must be thoroughly and inescapably sensible: "the body as sensible and the body as sentient," he explains, is "what we previously called objective body and phenomenal body" (*VI*, p. 180/136). But whereas previously he posited the objective body as secondary and relative to the phenomenal body of sensorimotor awareness – "the genesis of the objective body is only a moment in the constitution of the object" (*PP*, p. 86/83) – he now construes conscious experience as a whole, even its proprioceptive and motor elements, as grounded in a new kind of *pre*phenomenal being, namely the flesh of visibility.

It is our "brute or savage being," then, that makes possible everything explicitly realizable in phenomenological reflection. To see the world, we must already be in a kind of bodily communion with it. Merleau-Ponty puts this same idea to work in his celebrated essays on painting, the late "Eye and Mind" (1961), but also already "Cézanne's Doubt" (1945), which he wrote around the same time as *Phenomenology of Perception*. Like perception itself, Merleau-Ponty argues, painting is not just directed *toward*, but is also embedded *in* the world, and his philosophical aim, contrary to the tendency of some critics and art historians, is to "put the painter back in touch with his world."[8] Merleau-Ponty wants to capture, he says, the *depth* or *thickness* of the perceptual world, its intimation of *reality*, as opposed to its mere outward surface. We do not just see colors and shapes, but *things*, indeed things we see to *be* hard, soft, wet, dry, warm, cold, heavy, dense, light, and so on. How does that peculiar sense of solidity and reality manifest itself? In virtue of our bodily homogeneity with things, our unconscious continuity with the world as *flesh*. Flesh, the essential reversibility of perception, the fact that only something perceptible can perceive, is more basic than the conscious experience we have of ourselves as subjects inhabiting a world of objects distinct from us, a world we are *in* but not *of*.

Cézanne's artistic effort ran counter to that of Impressionists like Monet and Renoir, who sought to capture our immediate optical sensitivity to light and color: "Impressionism was trying to capture in the painting the very way in which objects strike our eyes and attack our senses. Objects were depicted as they appear to instantaneous perception."[9] The results were often lovely, but the project was misconceived, for we do not in fact *see* the light and the detached colors the Impressionists were trying to paint; we see *things* – trees, houses, pathways, open spaces, other people, not to mention contextual or situational things like threats, obstacles, and opportunities. Like empiricist philosophers and psychologists, the Impressionists were motivated more by abstract theoretical considerations than by concrete visual experience. Perception, they reasoned, is a product of sensory stimulation, an effect of our receptivity to discrete units of light and color. To paint the stimuli, one therefore ought to use the colors of the rainbow rather than, say, the browns and blacks of solid objects.

Like the theory of vision underwriting it, the aesthetic effect of Impressionist painting also turned out to be wrong, in unexpected ways. For shifting the viewer's attention away from the world and toward the proximal lighting conditions actually made things look *less* real, not more so: "depicting the atmosphere and breaking up the tones submerged the object and caused it to lose its proper weight," whereas "Cézanne wants to represent the object, to find it again behind the atmosphere" (CD, p. 16/12/62). Here Cézanne was not simply retreating to the methods of earlier masters; like the Impressionists, he wanted to paint our *perception* of things, but precisely in and by painting the things themselves. His work might therefore seem paradoxical, for "he was pursuing reality without giving up the sensuous surface" (CD, p. 17/12/63).

He did this, in part, by posing a radical challenge to traditional conceptions of visual perspective. According to Merleau-Ponty, Cézanne discovered intuitively and aesthetically what the Gestalt psychologists would later elaborate in theory, namely, that "lived perspective ... is not geometric or photographic perspective" (CD, p. 19/14/64). For one thing, photographic representation abolishes the size constancy built into real perception: the train on the movie screen gets suddenly bigger as it gets closer, until the picture frame can no longer contain it, whereas in real life the train gradually approaches until it is simply *here*. There is no "here" in the visual experience of cinema, for as viewers we stand outside the picture we see in a way we cannot stand outside the world we perceive. So too, "To say that a circle seen obliquely is seen as an ellipse is to substitute for our actual perception what we would see if we were cameras" (CD, p. 19/14/64). Cézanne therefore does not paint the glasses and plates on a table setting as geometrically perfect ellipses, but instead lets them bulge outward to evoke their real presence as things one could walk right up to and touch.

What Cézanne manages to paint, then, is not the light at our eyes, which, after all, we never (or hardly ever) see in its own right, but a world perceptually organized by our bodily involvement in it. The perspectival distortions in his paintings thus "contribute, as they do in natural vision, to the impression of an emerging order, an object in the act of appearing, organizing itself before our eyes" (CD, pp. 19–20/14/64–65). In this way, Cézanne's paintings attain a sense of reality beyond what the Impressionists could achieve in their attempt to paint light and the veil of appearance as such. In Cézanne, in short, we find that "insurpassable plenitude, which is for us the definition of the real" (CD, p. 21/15/65).

Merleau-Ponty returns to that sense of plenitude and reality in his last published work, the essay "Eye and Mind." The painter "'takes his body with him,'" says Valéry.[10] The body in question here is, of course, "not the body as a chunk of space or a bundle of functions, but the body that is an intertwining of vision and movement" (*Œ*, p. 16/162/124). It is misleading to draw a sharp distinction between the sensing subject and the sensible world, for "the world is made of the same stuff as the body" (*Œ*, p. 19/163/125). The body is on neither side of that putative divide between subject and world, for only something perceptible can perceive. The perceiver is neither an invisible zero point of consciousness nor an exposed surface. Instead, the body straddles the boundary between subject and object, visible and invisible, conscious and unconscious. Flesh is itself tangible in touching, visible in seeing, sensible in sensing; it is, in a word, "the reflexivity of the sensible" (*Œ*, p. 33/168/129). The bodily self is "a self caught up in things" (*Œ*, p. 19/163/124).

Vision and movement are also essentially intertwined, according to Merleau-Ponty, so that visible phenomena are always permeated with motor significance. What I see is defined for me in relation to what I can and cannot *do*. This constitutive connection with bodily movement means that no purely cognitive account of visual perception can capture its concrete intuitive motor significance: "This extraordinary overlapping" of perception and movement "precludes conceiving of vision as a function of thought" (*Œ*, p. 17/162/124). The mind does not move the body, as Descartes supposed; instead, what we call the mind is just an aspect of our bodily intelligence, which is constantly at grips with its environment: "My movement is not a decision made by the mind," rather "my body moves itself, my movement deploys itself" (*Œ*, p. 18/162/124).

The visual world is saturated with motor sense in virtue of our bodily continuity with the world we perceive. The enigma of painting, Merleau-Ponty maintains, is of a piece with the mystery of bodily existence: "since things and my body are made of the same stuff, vision must somehow take place in them; their manifest visibility must be repeated in the body by a secret visibility" (*Œ*, pp. 21–22/164/125). The visible world does not stand over against us as an object or an appearance, for there is a bond between us and it in virtue of which we are in a position to perceive it. To get a visual *grip* on things is not to apprehend their surface appearance, but to sense their bodily affinity with us, to commune with them, to inhabit them. As Cézanne put it, "The landscape thinks itself in me, and I am its consciousness" (CD, p. 23/17/67). What we see does not just occur, appear, or strike us from without, but invades us, speaks and makes sense to us: "All flesh, even that of the world, radiates beyond itself" (*Œ*, p. 81/186/145).

Like perception, painting concerns itself with the *visibility* of the visible: "painting celebrates no other enigma but that of visibility" (*Œ*, p. 26/166/127). Painting does not just duplicate appearances, but neither does it refer discursively or abstractly to non-visual sensory input, for instance tactile sensations. What painting accomplishes instead is the realization of the visible itself and as such: "It gives visible existence to what profane vision thinks is invisible" (*Œ*, p. 27/166/127). What we see in both painting and perception is "a texture of Being," which we do not merely observe or register, but occupy and inhabit. "The eye lives in this texture as a man lives in his house" (*Œ*, p. 27/166/127). The painter must therefore think magically, as if objects literally pass into him, or as if, as Malebranche facetiously put it, "the mind goes out through the eyes to wander among objects" (*Œ*, p. 28/166/128).

Of course, we do not typically see the way painters see: ordinarily we see *things*, whereas painters see and make visible the *visibility* of things. Seeing the visibility of the visible requires stepping back from our ordinary naïve immersion in things, just as, conversely, seeing things in the ordinary way requires *not* doing so: "To see the object, it was necessary *not* to see the play of shadows and light around it. The visible in the profane sense forgets its premises; it rests on a total visibility that is to be recreated and that liberates the phantoms captive in it" (*Œ*, p. 30/167/128). This deep bodily identification with the world, which is inherent in ordinary perception and visibly manifest in Cézanne's paintings, is evident in our intuitive identification with the bodies of others, and even more so in our identification with our own reflection in a mirror. According to Merleau-Ponty, our experience of others is not an experience of invisible minds concealed behind impersonal physical organisms. Instead, we experience others as sharing our world by sharing our embodiment:

"Other minds are given to us only as incarnate, as belonging to faces and gestures" (CD, p. 21/16/66). Similarly, my own mirror image is not a mere external presence. To see myself in a mirror is to *identify* unthinkingly with the body I see, which makes immediate reference to myself. This is how I am able to locate my own bodily feelings *in* the image itself. It is also why when I look at my reflection I never have the feeling of being *looked at*, for the eyes staring back at me are my own. I therefore draw no more analogy or inference from my mirror image to myself than I do from other bodies to other persons. What I see in the mirror is a kind of ghost: it is *me* – not *here* but *there*: "the ghost in the mirror draws my flesh outward, just as the invisibility of my body is able to animate [*investir*] other bodies I see ... man is a mirror for man" (*Œ*, pp. 33–34/168/129–30).[11]

Visibility, in Merleau-Ponty's sense of the word, is neither surface appearance nor sensory stimulation. It is the intuitively felt reality of things disclosed to us as part of a dense, opaque world, the milieu *in* which things show up, *amid* other things. Visibility and invisibility are not the mere presence and absence of visual input; they are our "absolute proximity" to and "irremediable distance" from things (*VI*, p. 23/8).

For Merleau-Ponty, then, "any theory of painting is a metaphysics" (*Œ*, p. 42/171/132); indeed, "the entire modern history of painting ... has a metaphysical significance" (*Œ*, p. 61/178/139). More specifically, "painting is an art of space" (*Œ*, p. 77/184/144). What kind of space? What aspect of space? Merleau-Ponty focuses on the phenomenon of *depth*. Not only is there depth in the world as we perceive it, but the very surfaces of paintings cannot help but evoke it, even when, as in the abstract geometric paintings of Piet Mondrian, they strive to be perfectly flat. Depth is not just one of the three dimensions of objective space, arbitrarily marked by one's line of sight: "something in space escapes our attempts to survey it from above" (*Œ*, p. 50/175/135). Depth is not some "unmysterious interval, as seen from an airplane, between these trees nearby and those farther away" (*Œ*, p. 64/180/140). For space itself is not external to me: "I live it from the inside, it encompasses me. After all, the world is all around me, not in front of me" (*Œ*, p. 59/178/138).

What then *is* depth? It is, of course, relative to perspective, hence dependent on us. Yet it is not simply the radial extension of objective space from the zero point of the observer; first because the observer's position is *not* just a zero point, but an organized, spatially extended body, and second because mere radial extension, geometrically defined, fails to capture what is essential to depth, namely its capacity to reveal and conceal, to occlude and disclose.

What Merleau-Ponty is describing in his account of depth is neither an objective property of space nor a subjective experience, but the very fact of our perceptual situatedness in a *world*. If nothing ever occluded or revealed anything else, if nothing stood behind or in front of anything – in short, if there were no *depth*, there would be no *world* we could see ourselves as occupying and inhabiting: "the enigma consists in the fact that I see things, each one in its place, precisely because they eclipse one another, and that they are rivals before my sight precisely because each one is in its own place" (*Œ*, p. 64/180/140).

It is this perspective-relative orientation of embodied perception that allows us to see the world as something separate from us, as independent of our point of view on it, as fully and genuinely *real*:

> Depth, so understood, is ... the experience of the reversibility of dimensions, of a global "locality" where everything is at once, from which height, breadth, and distance are abstracted, of a voluminousness we express in a word when we say that a thing is *there*. (*Œ*, p. 65/180/140)

Line, depth, and color evoke the *visibility* of the visible, the disclosedness of the world, which is always bound to horizons of invisibility, horizons that make up "the immemorial ground [*fond*] of the visible" (*Œ*, p. 86/188/147). Everything seen, in order to be seen, must be surrounded by a kind of halo of the unseen: "the hallmark [*propre*] of the visible is to have a lining of invisibility in the strict sense, which it makes present as a certain absence" (*Œ*, p. 85/187/147).

The visibility of the visible, the manifestation of sensory appearance, the disclosedness of the world cannot be adequately understood if we persist in the traditional dualistic interpretation of human beings as contingently embodied minds. A mind as such, even if it could entertain a thought or register a sense datum, could never encounter a world, which is why, as Merleau-Ponty says, "we cannot imagine how a *mind* could paint" (*Œ*, p. 16/162/123). Painting needs the body just as perception itself does: not as its external instrument or vehicle, but as its very manifestation in the world. The painter "takes his body with him," Valéry says: not in the way he takes his easel and his brushes, but as we take our bodies everywhere we go. We really ought to say instead, as Merleau-Ponty does, following the ancient, pre-Cartesian tradition, that the body "betakes" itself in what it does: "my body moves itself, my movement deploys itself" (Œ, p. 18/162/124).

Merleau-Ponty's persistent emphasis on the bodily nature of intelligence and perceptual awareness can sound obvious or trivial, but only if we temporarily forget the utter unnaturalness and untenability of received – still deeply entrenched – conceptions of ourselves as souls, minds, or as the currently fashionable metaphor has it, complex formal computational systems, which is to say, computers and programs.

NOTES

1. Wittgenstein, *On Certainty,* section 244.
2. In the Sixth Meditation, notwithstanding his official dualism, Descartes writes, "I and the body form a unit." *The Philosophical Writings of Descartes,* vol. II, p. 56 (AT VII, p. 81).
3. Husserl, *Ideen, Zweites Buch,* p. 161; *Ideas, Second Book,* p. 168. From Merleau-Ponty's point of view, this image, even if intended as a quaint or naïve approximation of the truth, is disastrously wrong.
4. Merleau-Ponty, *Phénoménologie de la perception,* p. 107; *Phenomenology of Perception,* p. 104; hereafter *PP* with page references to both editions. Of course, we can approximate something like this "body doubling" by means of mirrors or cameras. The point is that my first-person experience of my body *as mine* systematically deprives me of an observational relation to it.
5. Merleau-Ponty inherited the term "body schema" from the psychologist Henry Head, who explicitly distinguished between body *schema* and body *image.* See Gallagher, "Body Schema and Intentionality," pp. 226–29.
6. Goodale and Milner, *Sight Unseen,* pp. 45–48.
7. Merleau-Ponty, *Le Visible et l'invisible,* p. 243; *The Visible and the Invisible,* p. 189; hereafter *VI* with page references to both editions.
8. Merleau-Ponty, "Indirect Language and the Voices of Silence," *Signes,* p. 72; *Signs,* p. 57; *The Merleau-Ponty Aesthetics Reader,* p. 94. Merleau-Ponty is specifically contrasting his view with André Malraux's interpretation of modern abstract art as a retreat into abstraction and subjectivity. See Malraux, *The Voices of Silence.*

9. Merleau-Ponty, "Cézanne's Doubt," *Sens et non-sens*, p. 16; *Sense and Non-Sense*, p. 11; *The Merleau-Ponty Aesthetics Reader*, p. 61. Hereafter CD with page references to all three editions.
10. Merleau-Ponty, "Eye and Mind." *L'Œil et l'esprit*, p. 16; *The Primacy of Perceptive*, p.162 *The Merleau-Ponty Aesthetics Reader*, p. 123. Hereafter Œ with page references to all three editions.
11. Merleau-Ponty's observations here can be seen to anticipate recent studies concerning the neurological foundations of identification and empathy in the activation of mirror neurons. See Rizzolatti *et al.*, "Mirrors of the Mind."

IV The Reach of Existential Philosophy

JEFF MALPAS

14 Existentialism as literature

To what extent does existentialism constitute itself as a literary rather than a primarily philosophical phenomenon? Or, to put a slightly different but related question: what form does existentialism take when it is viewed *as literature* rather than as *philosophy*? Such questions arise as a fairly direct consequence of the fact that a number of key existentialist works (or works that have generally been regarded as such) have indeed been works of literature – Jean-Paul Sartre's *Nausea* (*La Nausée*, 1938[1]) and Albert Camus's *The Outsider* (*L'Étranger*, 1939) being two excellent examples – while some of the key figures within or close to the existentialist tradition have been literary rather than philosophical – arguably this is true of Camus, and certainly of Beckett. Rather than simply provide an exploration of existentialism in literature, or a survey of those literary works that figure within existentialism, this essay will also examine the idea of existentialism *as* literature, sketching a picture of existentialism as it emerges in literary rather than solely philosophical terms.

Although it is sometimes argued that existentialism stands in a special relationship to literature – that it is an especially "literary" mode of philosophizing – David E. Cooper argues that over-reliance on existentialist fiction has actually been a source of misconceptions about existentialism. Refusing to include Camus among the existentialists, or to allow that he might be a philosopher, Cooper claims that "existentialism ... is not a mood or a vocabulary, but a relatively systematic philosophy."[2] I am less persuaded than Cooper by the idea of existentialism as a "systematic philosophy" (if there is anything that is systematic in existentialism, then it is, it seems to me, just phenomenology[3]), and much more inclined to view existentialist literature as providing an important means of access to existentialist thinking or, at least, to what has to be viewed as a form of such thinking. While one approach to existentialism is through the philosophical works that make it up, another approach is surely through the literary works that represent a parallel, and sometimes alternative, mode of articulation and expression.

14.1 LITERATURE AND EXISTENTIALISM

"The novelist," says Milan Kundera, "is neither historian nor prophet: he is an explorer of existence."[4] Certainly the novel would seem to be centrally focused on the nature of human existence, albeit as portrayed through its concrete and singular instances. Is the novelist also, therefore, an existentialist?[5] The problem with such a conclusion is that it threatens to make existentialist literature almost co-extensive with literature as such, or at least with much modern literature. Yet existentialism is surely much narrower than this, on one account naming a historically specific phenomenon that is primarily focused around the literary and philosophical work of a loosely associated group of French thinkers and writers, centered on Jean-Paul Sartre and Simone de Beauvoir, in particular, from the late 1930s, and extending into the 1940s and 1950s. Moreover, even if one expands the scope of existentialism to encompass, first, its nineteenth-century precursors such as Kierkegaard and Dostoevsky, and, second, the German philosophers – especially Heidegger, who provided much of its conceptual underpinning – then existentialism nevertheless names what is still a fairly circumscribed body of thought and work.

Of course, much of the discussion of existentialism, past and present, has taken a far wider and more liberal view – nowhere more so than in the treatment of existentialism in literature.[6] Where literary works are concerned, existentialism is sometimes so broadly construed as to allow even Shakespeare to be included, along with a host of other dramatists, novelists, and poets. Writers as diverse as W. H. Auden, Philip K. Dick, Emily Dickinson, T. S. Eliot, William Faulkner, John Fowles, André Gide, Graham Greene, Henrik Ibsen, Hermann Melville, Iris Murdoch, Vladimir Nabokov, Harold Pinter, Tom Stoppard, and Miguel de Unamuno – to name but a few – have all been characterized, at one time or another, and with more or less justification, as belonging to the existentialist tradition. Indeed, one might wonder whether there is *any* modern literary figure of note who has not at some point been characterized in this way.

The broadening of existentialism that can be observed here, and which is especially problematic in regard to literature, is surely enabled and encouraged by a tendency to conflate the *existentialist* with the *existential*,[7] as well as by the way in which explicit existential themes have also come to be central to much modern literature as well as to certain streams within twentieth-century philosophy. Yet if "existentialism" is to be in any way a meaningful category, and if we are to maintain a sense of existentialism as a distinctive development within modern literature as well as philosophy, then it seems we do need to distinguish the existentialist from the existential. In fact, the distinction is not only necessary, but well founded. Apart from the mere verbal difference between the terms, "existential" not only has a longer history (the *Oxford English Dictionary* lists an occurrence from 1693[8]), but also a broader usage, an employment in a wider range of contexts (including logic), and a different meaning. "Existential" refers to that which pertains to existence (the *OED*'s 1693 citation talks of an "existential good," meaning the good that is associated with existing), whereas "existentialist" (and "existentialism") refers to a particular philosophical attitude or mode of philosophical inquiry – an attitude or mood that, in general terms, thematizes the problematic character of human existence in a world in which there is no pre-given source of meaning or significance.

On the basis of this distinction between the existential and the existentialist, we can identify important existential themes in the text of Shakespeare's *King Lear*, for instance, without thereby incorporating Shakespeare into the existentialist canon, and we can also acknowledge the way in which existential concerns have always been addressed in literature, as well as art, without turning all literature into *existentialist* literature.

Yet even if existentialism in literature is less ubiquitous than might sometimes be proposed, we may still ask whether there is not, as Kundera's comment might be taken to suggest, some special connection between existentialism and literature. If literature cannot itself be said to be given over to an existentialist perspective, might it not be the case that existentialism can be viewed as nevertheless given over, in some important way, to literary expression? The character of existentialism as centrally concerned with human existence – and as always *engaged* with human existence, both politically and personally – is surely itself such as to tend existentialism *as philosophy* towards the expression of existentialism *as literature*. Indeed, when one looks to that group of French writers whose works surely constitute the core of the existentialist canon – Sartre, Beauvoir, Camus, Marcel,[9] and Merleau-Ponty – it is striking that, with the exception of Merleau-Ponty (who may be viewed as more a phenomenologist than an existentialist), all gained reputations as literary figures, irrespective of their status as philosophers. Moreover, this literary emphasis might be taken to be evident from the very first in the "indirect" character of Kierkegaard's work, in Nietzsche's use of the figure of Zarathustra, and in the importance that can be assigned to the novels of Dostoevsky in prefiguring themes in later existentialist thought.

It has to be said, however, that the expression of philosophical ideas in literary form is not peculiar to existentialism (Plato presents us with an especially notable case in point), and, within the French tradition, in particular, literature and philosophy have often been intertwined – Rousseau being perhaps the best and most obvious example, but Voltaire being another.[10] Inasmuch as these two are both Enlightenment figures, one might view the entanglement of literature and philosophy in French existentialism as a continuation of a tendency already established within the culture of the French Enlightenment itself. Moreover, in what is perhaps (alongside Joyce's *Ulysses*) the greatest literary work of modernity, and certainly of modern French literature, Proust's massive *À la recherche du temps perdu*, one finds an example of a literary work that is also clearly philosophical in its orientation (it is not irrelevant that Proust was the nephew of Bergson) and that exerted an enormous influence, at least in France, on both the literature and philosophy that succeeded it. Not only in terms of works and individuals, however, but also institutionally, philosophy in France has always tended to spill over what might be thought to be its disciplinary boundaries, never remaining within the confines of the academy alone. Philosophy has thus located itself in the café and the *lycée*, the magazine and the newspaper, and not merely in the scholarly essay or the lecture room, while philosophers have often found themselves as much at home in the theater, the editorial office, and the school as in the university.

It is, however, significant that the apparent connection between existentialist philosophy and existentialist literature that one finds in France is not so clearly replicated when one looks to that other possible home for existentialism, Germany. One finds there, especially in the twentieth century, a much clearer demarcation between the philosophical and the literary – and this is so even in respect of supposed existentialist writing. Nietzsche is perhaps the exception, although a nineteenth-century exception. When one looks to those works of Jaspers and Heidegger that are usually assimilated to the existentialist tradition one find works, not of literature, but of philosophy (both Jaspers and Heidegger also occupied positions as professors in the discipline), while in the case of twentieth-century writers such as Hermann Hesse, some of whose writing is also treated as existentialist in character, one finds works that belong primarily to literature (with Hesse working outside academia). Perhaps most telling in the German case is the fact that while Heidegger's later writing is invariably treated as falling outside the existentialist canon – even though his early work, specifically *Being and Time*, is viewed as lying at its core – it is precisely in the later writing that Heidegger is often seen to present his work in less traditionally philosophical and more literary or "poetic" form, with much of the impetus of the later writing also deriving from the German romantic poet Friedrich Hölderlin.[11] In this respect, when it comes to Heidegger, the existentialist and the "literary" appear to stand, not together, but quite apart from one another.

One cannot, then, assume a conception of existentialism as *inevitably* tending towards expression in literary form. Yet even though existentialism cannot be simply viewed as a mode of philosophy always given over to literary expression, it is nevertheless also true there is a significant body of literature that is itself given over to existentialist ideas and approaches. Existentialism can thus be viewed as naming not only a *philosophical* attitude or approach, but also a certain *literary* genre or style that is most closely associated with French literature from the middle of the twentieth century, but that also relates to a wider group of nineteenth- and twentieth-century writers from Europe as well as the United States.

14.2 LITERARY PRECURSORS: DOSTOEVSKY, KAFKA, AND OTHERS

Existentialist thought is usually taken to be foreshadowed in the work of Søren Kierkegaard (1813–55) and Friedrich Nietzsche (1844–1900). Indeed, it is in Kierkegaard that we first find the development of a mode of thinking that takes the individual in its concrete existence as the primary philosophical focus. Moreover, both Kierkegaard and Nietzsche also present their ideas in ways that eschew the usual stylistic conventions of philosophical writing, adopting fictional and other devices to advance their thought. Much of Nietzsche's work appears in aphoristic form, sometimes relying – most notably in the case of *Thus Spoke Zarathustra* (*Also Sprach Zarathustra,* 1891), on narrative and even song – while Kierkegaard's method of "indirect communication" – which also makes use of stories and jokes, and was developed in explicit opposition to the academic prose of Hegelian thought – involves writing from multiple perspectives under a variety of pseudonyms, forcing the reader to a personal engagement with the material at hand.

Yet in spite of their unorthodox styles and techniques, the work of Kierkegaard as well as Nietzsche still remains much more firmly placed within the realm of philosophy than of literature. From a purely literary perspective, the key figure in the development of existentialism is not so much Kierkegaard or Nietzsche as Feodor Dostoevsky (1821–81). It would, of course, be a mistake to treat Dostoevsky as an "existentialist" writer, and not merely for reasons of anachronism. Dostoevsky's work is clearly much broader in scope and impact than such a label would suggest – he is, indeed, one of the great figures within nineteenth-century literature in a way that goes beyond any particular intellectual, literary, or philosophical style or movement. Nevertheless, Dostoevsky's writing takes up many themes and exhibits many of the characteristics that are also central to later existentialist literature, while Dostoevsky is himself taken up by, and is a significant influence on, philosophers and writers from Nietzsche to Sartre. Dostoevsky is especially important for Camus, who adapted Dostoevsky's *The Devils* (*Besy,* 1872) for the stage under the title *The Possessed* (*Les Possédés,* 1959).

Dostoevsky can be seen to set out, in the most vivid and powerful fashion, the problematic situation that underpins much existentialist thought – the situation of the solitary individual, the "outsider," who can no longer find any sure refuge in God or religion, for whom the usual standards of morality and conduct, even the standards of reason itself, no longer seem to hold, and whose very existence is rendered uncertain and ambiguous. It is this individual, often presented as torn within himself, as his own "double," who appears, in various guises, as the central figure in many of Dostoevsky's works from *Notes from Underground* (*Zapiski iz podpolya*, 1864) – a work famously described by Walter Kaufmann as "one of the most revolutionary and original works of world literature" and "the best overture to existentialism ever written"[12] – to *The Brothers Karamazov* (*Brat'ya Karamazovy*, 1880). Often he appears as a multiple figure – Golyadkin and his double in *The Double* (*Dvojnik*, 1864); Dmitri, Ivan, Alexei (Alyosha), and the illegitimate Smerdyakov, who are the four Karamazov brothers themselves (the double doubled). In *Crime and Punishment* (*Prestuplenie i nakazanie*, 1866), he is the student Raskolnikov, for whom murder becomes a form of philosophical experiment, while in other works – notably *The Idiot* (*Idiot*, 1869) and *The Devils* – this uncertain and ambiguous situation, and the antagonistic forces that obtain within it, is given form through the tragic and often violent interactions within a group of characters and the larger social and political forces that they represent.

Dostoevsky's explicit concern with ethical and psychological themes, his preoccupation with the disunity and fragmentation of the self, the often introverted and complex nature of his characters, and the ambiguous and uncertain outcomes to his stories, all anticipate elements of later existentialist writing. Yet it is notable that Dostoevsky's own response to the existential situation that he so acutely describes is much more akin to a Christian humanist ethic of love than to anything to be found in the work of existentialists such as Sartre. Thus, while the parable that forms a central element in *The Brothers Karamazov* – the tale of "The Grand Inquisitor" (perhaps the passage from Dostoevsky most often read by students of existentialist literature)[13] – provides no clear resolution within the confines of the section in which it appears, emphasizing instead the difficulty and ambiguity of the questions of freedom and responsibility it poses (the entire section is titled "Pro and Contra"), other sections of the work advance a rather more positive message, even if not made fully determinate, centered on the essentially ethical path adopted by Alyosha. Indeed, one of the most powerful images in *The Brothers Karamazov* is the scene in which Ivan asks of Alyosha whether he would consent to the torture of a single innocent child in return for the unalloyed happiness of the entire world.[14] Alyosha's answer is that he would not. It is an answer that will later be echoed, in real and urgent circumstances, by Camus.[15]

If in Dostoevsky one finds an account of the uncertainty and pain of the human condition that nevertheless demands of us a human and ethical response, no matter how difficult that may be, that same condition reappears in the work of Franz Kafka in a way that emphasizes its absurdity and apparent meaninglessness, but without any sense of the same ethical response. It is as if, in Kafka's universe, no such response is even conceivable. Written during the first two decades of the twentieth century, but mostly appearing for the first time in published form in the 1920s and 1930s (largely posthumously), Kafka's work paints a world all the more nightmarish for its juxtaposition of the abnormal and the irrational with the banal and apparently everyday.[16] In Kafka a man can be transformed into a gigantic beetle overnight (*The Metamorphosis*; *Die Verwandlung*, 1915) and yet attempt to continue a "normal" life as if he were merely afflicted by some temporary social embarrassment; a trial can be conducted without any indication of the crime at issue, the possible punishment, or the length and nature of the process (*The Trial*; *Der Process*, 1925). If it is the work of Dostoevsky that provides the literary precursor to the psychological and ethical preoccupations of existentialism, it is Kafka who prefigured something of the nausea of Sartre and the absurdity of Camus. In some respects, the situation that Kafka describes is the same situation of loss of meaning that also concerns Dostoevsky, but whereas Dostoevsky presents that loss in terms of an antagonism that exists within and between persons, and as instantiated in the form of real human suffering, Kafka presents it in the bizarre irrationality of ordinary, everyday life. Like the surrealists, with whom he has some obvious affinities, Kafka makes even the familiar appear suddenly strange and threatening.

Dostoevsky and Kafka are the two literary figures most frequently cited as forerunners of the existentialist writers of the 1940s and 1950s. Yet they are not the only writers of the nineteenth and early twentieth century who have been adopted by or assimilated to the existentialist tradition. Three other writers who are often read in this way – although in their case it is specific writings that are usually deemed of significance rather than their work taken as a whole – are Leo Tolstoy (1828–1910), the Norwegian Nobel-prize-winner Knud Hamsun (1859–1952), and the German poet Rainer Maria Rilke (1875–1926).

Tolstoy's *The Death of Ivan Ilyich* (*Smert' Ivana Il'icha*, 1886) tells the story of a successful man, a judge, conscious of his social status and success, who discovers he is dying and in the process also discovers the hollowness and artificiality of the life he has lived. Ivan Ilyich is only redeemed, and his suffering brought to an end in the last moments before death, through recognition of the importance of those around him and a sense of love and compassion. While Tolstoy's novel contains strongly Christian elements, it is also a powerful examination of the fragmentation of a life, as well as of the retrieval of its significance, in the face of the imminence of death – a death that is also unalterably and finally one's own.

Hamsun's *Hunger* (*Sult*, 1890), often seen as one of the founding works of modernist literature, recounts the psychological disintegration of a young writer as he struggles for basic survival outside the usual framework of society in the Norwegian city of Kristiania. Hamsun's work is strongly influenced by Dostoevsky and combines Dostoevsky's own psychological narration with a bleak portrayal of the corrosive and debilitating effects of modern city life. In this latter respect, Hamsun also represents a romantic reaction to modernity, one that is evident in other German writers but can be associated with Hamsun's own conservative political tendencies, given clearest expression in his Nazi sympathies during the Second World War.

Recognized as one of the greatest German poets of the last two centuries, Rilke wrote one novel, *The Notebooks of Malte Laurids Brigge* (*Die Aufzeichnungen des Malte Laurids Brigge*, 1910), which was cited by Sartre as a direct influence on his own writing. As its title suggests, the novel takes the form of a journal or set of notes – a loosely connected series of reminiscences, reflections, descriptions, and stories – as set down by a young writer living away from his native Denmark in Paris. Malte Laurids Brigge is both a writer and a foreigner in the city in which he lives. Yet preoccupied with the inevitability of death, and the character of time as moving us ever closer to it, Brigge also finds himself alienated in a more profound way than his circumstances might suggest, experiencing the world as empty and without meaning. An outsider existentially as well as socially, Brigge thus exemplifies the same figure we have already encountered in Dostoevsky, as well as in Kafka, Hamsun, and even Tolstoy (Ivan Ilyich is rendered an outsider by his approaching death) – a figure who will reappear in much later existentialist literature, including that of Sartre and Camus, as well as in other writers such as Hemingway and Hesse.[17]

14.3 SARTRE AND BEAUVOIR: METAPHYSICS, ENGAGEMENT, AND WRITING

It is doubtful if existentialism would have appeared as a distinctive mode of philosophical or literary expression at all were it not for Jean-Paul Sartre (1905–80) and Simone de Beauvoir (1908–96). Moreover, for both Sartre and Beauvoir, writing and philosophy were inextricably bound together – writing was, for them, essentially about *ideas* rather than mere artistic expression or aesthetic creation.

Awarded the Nobel prize for literature in 1964 (an award which he refused), Sartre's first and probably most widely read literary work is the novel *Nausea* – a work completed in the early 1930s, when Sartre was still a teacher in Le Havre. Presented as merely the edited version of materials found among the papers of a certain Antoine Roquentin and published "without alteration," the novel takes the form of a "metaphysical journal" recounting the thoughts and experiences of its supposed author in the town of Bouville (often taken to be a fictionalized version of Le Havre itself). Appearing almost as a kind of personal phenomenological report,[18] the novel recounts the increasing sense of revulsion and disgust Roquentin feels towards the world and towards existence. "Nausea" describes this feeling of revulsion – a feeling that is perhaps most vividly presented in Roquentin's description of his encounter with the "black, knotty mass, entirely beastly" that is the root of a chestnut tree under which he happens to sit.[19] In response to this experience of existential *Angst*, Roquentin is led to recognize the fundamental absurdity of existence – to recognize, that is, the fact of the absolute contingency of existence and its lack of any inherent meaning or purpose.

The idea of absurdity reappears in Sartre's other works (it can be seen as one of the underlying themes in the short stories that make up *The Wall* [*Le Mur*, 1939]), but increasingly it is the *response* to absurdity that takes precedence over the mere experience. Indeed, this partly reflects a shift in Sartre's own thinking that occurs during the 1940s and was made explicit in *What is Literature?* ("Qu'est-ce que la littérature?" 1947), in which Sartre argues for the importance of politically "committed" or "engaged" writing. The real question, then, is an ethical one: if human being is characterized by its freedom, as Sartre argues it is, then what is to be done with that freedom? It is this issue, always understood within a political as well as ethical frame, that is the main theme of the series of novels (originally planned as a quartet, although the fourth was never completed) that make up Sartre's *Roads to Freedom*.[20] The main character in the novels is a teacher, Mathieu Delarue, and much of the narrative deals with the emptiness that attaches to his life in the face of a freedom upon which he does not act, and the way in which that freedom is realized through action and commitment. The novel begins in July 1938, with the narrative extending into the period of the war and occupation, and draws heavily on Sartre's own war-time experiences (Delarue is thus taken to be a semi-autobiographical figure).

Notwithstanding the significance of his novels, it is Sartre's plays that have generally received greater critical acclaim. *The Flies* (*Les Mouches*, 1943) takes up a theme from the Greek tragedian Aeschylus. Orestes returns as a stranger to his home city, Argos, to take revenge on his mother, Clytemnestra, and his uncle, Aegisthus, for the killing of his father, Agamemnon. Here the theme is precisely human freedom, in particular Orestes' freedom from the gods, and his taking of responsibility for his own actions, horrific though they may be. *No Exit* (*Huis-clos*, 1944), one of the best-known of Sartre's plays, portrays the situation of three people who find themselves in hell (which takes the form of a French Second Empire drawing room). They find no torturer waiting for them, however, discovering instead that they are condemned to face one another for eternity without recourse to the usual subterfuges and deceits that make our life with others bearable – thus "There's no need for red-hot pokers.

Hell is – other people!"[21] In *The Devil and the Good Lord* (*Le Diable et le Bon Dieu*, 1951), Sartre's own favorite among his plays, we are presented with a portrayal, in the figure of the medieval warlord Goetz, of the way in which the apparent espousal of good can itself be a disguise for evil.[22]

Unlike Sartre, Beauvoir wrote almost nothing for the stage, completing only one play, *Who Shall Die?* (*Les Bouches inutiles*, 1945), and her literary work is instead focused on short stories,[23] a major series of autobiographical writings,[24] and, most importantly, her novels. Beauvoir's work exemplifies, however, a similar sense of political and intellectual engagement to that found in Sartre – as one might expect from one of the founding figures of modern feminism. Moreover, Beauvoir (who regarded herself as a "writer" rather than a philosopher) also talked explicitly of the "metaphysical novel," and defended the "genre" against other forms.[25] Yet there is a significant difference in the way ideas figure in their work. As André Maurois notes, in Sartre's writing philosophy "is the dough itself," while in Beauvoir's it "serves only as leavening, as yeast."[26] Beauvoir's own writing is strongly focused on her characters, their concrete situation, and the events and experiences that form the fabric of their lives. Indeed, it is partly because Beauvoir is such an accomplished novelist, and her characters and situations carry such a mark of reality upon them, that her work is able to do justice to the sense of *ambiguity* that also lies at the heart of her philosophical work: the nature of human life defies our attempts to give it clear and unequivocal meaning, it is always too multiple, too complex, too uncertain.[27] This also means, however, that the philosophical content of her novels is given in the rich complexity of the events and situations they depict, and not in any simply summarized structure of plot or character.

Human lives are essentially lives lived in relation to others, and almost all of Beauvoir's literary work focuses on the exploration of the relationality of human life as it is played out in particular, concrete circumstances. It pays special attention to the demands such relationality places upon us, and, although not always thematized as such, to the gendered character of the experience of and response to such relationality. It also explores the limitations that are placed on our freedom by the relations and situations in which we find ourselves.

These themes are particularly clear in *She Came to Stay* (*L'Invitée*, 1943) – the focus of Merleau-Ponty's essay "Metaphysics and the Novel."[28] *She Came to Stay* deals with the relationship between two people, Pierre and Françoise, as it is disrupted through the introduction of a younger woman, Xavière. The three-way relationship mirrors aspects of the situation involving Beauvoir, Sartre, and the young Olga Kosakievicz. A key idea in the book is the limited perspective we have on the lives of others – we can only grasp things from the perspective of our own situation – as well as the danger that our relation to others can itself bring. Thus Françoise's relation with Pierre, and also her own sense of self, is threatened by the intrusion of Xavière, finally leading Françoise, in the book's denouement, to the murder of Xavière. *The Blood of Others* (*Le Sang des autres*, 1945) also centers on the relationship between two people, Jean Blomart and Hélène Bertrand. Set in large part during the early 1940s (around the time at which it was written),[29] the novel provides a detailed portrait of the situated character of human freedom, and the ambiguous and uncertain choices that it sets before us. Jean and Hélène appear as contrasting figures – Jean is politically committed, joining the Communist Party and then the French Resistance, while Hélène is politically indifferent and self-centered. She is awakened to a sense of political activism, however, and sacrifices her life on a mission for the resistance organization led by Jean. The novel presents us with the inevitability of responsibility, even for those events over which we can exercise no choice. We are free, but not so free that we can escape our circumstances or the anguish and suffering that they bring.

In *All Men are Mortal* (*Tous les Hommes sont mortels*, 1946), Beauvoir explores our relations to death and to time – but the emphasis is on the way this connects to life. Fosca, the main character, is immortal, and his immortality is dedicated to the betterment of the world, yet Fosca discovers that his immortality becomes a source of detachment and indifference.[30] If there is meaning to be found in human life, it is only to be found, so Beauvoir suggests, in our involvement *in* life, and not in some abstract perspective on it.

The emptiness of any purely detached perspective, and so also of any intellectual involvement that is not concerned with concrete social and political issues, is also a theme in *The Mandarins* (*Les

Mandarins, 1954), the novel that won Beauvoir the prestigious Prix Goncourt. *The Mandarins* is a study of a group of Parisian left-wing intellectuals. In all of Beauvoir's work it is the concrete circumstances and relationships, and the way those relationships play out, which lies at the center. In the case of *The Mandarins*, the narrative that is presented is all the more dense and multi-layered, since it concerns what was essentially the contemporary situation – personal and existential, political and intellectual – in which Beauvoir and Sartre were themselves enmeshed in the post-war years. (The novel is often viewed, therefore, as a *roman à clef* – a novel that fictionalizes a group of real people). It thus continues Beauvoir's preoccupation with the concrete situatedness of literary and philosophical inquiry, as well as the ambiguity and complexity that it brings forth, while it also exemplifies the "metaphysical" novel as itself a novel of *engagement*.

14.5 "A PHILOSOPHY IN IMAGES": CAMUS AND THE SEARCH FOR LUCIDITY

It would be impossible to discuss existentialism from the perspective of literature without giving attention to the work of Albert Camus. Camus's 1942 novel, *The Outsider* (*L'Étranger* – there is no exact translation into English, with the American edition of the work titled "The Stranger" and the English "The Outsider"), is perhaps the best-known and most widely read work of "existentialist" fiction, and, together with the essay *The Myth of Sisyphus* (*Le Mythe de Sisyphe*, 1942), it is perhaps the most widely read existentialist work of all, whether literary or philosophical. That Camus is arguably, with the possible exception of Beckett, the most important, as well as the best known, literary figure within the existentialist canon provides good reason for attending more closely to him here.[31] Yet it also has to be said that within existentialism – if he was indeed ever "within" it in the first place – Camus also represents something of an anomalous figure, being himself an "outsider" in virtue both of personal background and philosophical commitment.[32]

Not only is Camus more familiar as a writer than as a philosopher (and although he preferred to style himself as such, he nevertheless also wrote that "a novel is never anything but a philosophy put into images"[33]), but his philosophical position stands somewhat apart from that of other existentialists, notably from that of Sartre. Moreover, as we saw above, his work is sometimes viewed as having little or no philosophical relevance. Yet just as one cannot omit Camus from any discussion of literary existentialism, neither should he be omitted from the philosophical discussion of existentialism. Indeed, increasing critical attention is now being paid to Camus as a philosopher and a writer. To some extent, this is due to the revival of interest in Camus's political views and his stance against the politics of violence – issues that have taken on a new resonance in light of the contemporary rise of terrorism and the supposed "war on terror" – but it also seems likely to be a measure of the strength of Camus as a writer, of the direct and personal style of his writing, and of the way in which his work as a whole – the critical and lyrical no less than the fictional – has remained relevant and accessible to a contemporary readership.

In contrast to the middle-class backgrounds of Sartre and Beauvoir, Camus came from a poor working-class family, growing up in the city of Algiers in what was then the French colony of Algeria. His father was killed in the First World War, and Camus was brought up by his mother and grandmother. Helped by the teacher to whom he later dedicated his Nobel prize, Louis Germain, Camus found his way to the University of Algiers, where he studied philosophy from 1932 to 1936 with Jean Grenier as his teacher. Grenier was a philosopher who focused on the concrete particularities of experience, as well as being something of a mystic, a lover of the Greeks, and a writer whose work was mainly in essay form.[34] In 1935 Camus began his *Notebooks* (*Carnets*, published under that title in 1951), and by 1938 he had decided on a career as a journalist, writing initially for the paper *Alger-Républicain* and then moving to France in 1939. By 1942 he had become involved with the French Resistance and was editing the underground news-sheet *Combat*. The publication of *The Outsider* in the early 1940s established his literary reputation, as did performances of his plays from 1944 onwards. The publication of Camus's *The Rebel* (*L'Homme revolté*, 1951) led to a public quarrel between Camus and Sartre and a breach between them that was never healed. In 1957 Camus became the youngest French writer ever to receive the Nobel prize for literature. At the time of his death, in 1960, he was working on what was to be a major novel with the title *The First Man* (*Le Premier Homme*, 1994) – a strongly autobiographical novel that was published posthumously in an edition edited by Camus's daughter Cathérine.[35]

Camus left behind a much smaller legacy of works than did Sartre – partly as a consequence of his early death, but also a result of his own difficulties in writing, particularly in the period leading up to his fatal car accident. One of the ironies, in fact, is that the accident occurred at a time when Camus had once again begun working on a new project – the draft of the posthumously published *The First Man* being with him in his briefcase when he died. Camus's work ranges across novels, short stories, plays, essays, and one major philosophical treatise, *The Rebel*. A great deal of his writing is also in the form of journalistic contributions, including those written for *Combat*.

Camus's most famous work is undoubtedly *The Outsider* – that "clear, dry work," as Sartre described it[36] – whose popularity has extended well beyond the 1940s, when it was first published.[37] *The Outsider* tells the story of Meursault, a clerk living in French colonial Algiers, who meets each day with a leaden indifference and inability to feel – an indifference that he seems incapable of hiding or covering up. What seems to matter most to Meursault – almost all he seems to care about, in fact – are issues of physical comfort or preference (coffee at his mother's funeral, the pleasure of swimming). The novel narrates the events leading up to Meursault's murder of an unnamed Arab on a beach,[38] the subsequent trial, and Meursault's conviction, and what occurs in the time during which Meursault awaits his execution. Meursault appears as an outsider not in virtue of his status or position – he is neither a writer nor a foreigner – but because of his inability to participate in the dissemblance that keeps absurdity at bay. In thc cnd Meursault finds redemption through the lucid recognition of the absurdity of his situation and the discovery that it does not matter. He finds a certain happiness, and even exultation, in the mere fact of existence and the experience of the world – a happiness that he realizes had been his all along.

The Outsider forms part of a trilogy of early works that were written in 1938–41 and that includes the essay *The Myth of Sisyphus* as well as the play *Caligula* (1944; written in 1938).[39] These three works all explore the idea of the absurd and the human response to it – a response that Camus characterizes most often (in the later works as well as the earlier) in terms of *rebellion* or *revolt*. In *Caligula*, Camus begins the story just after the death of Drusilla, Caligula's sister and lover. Brought by her death to recognize the absurdity of things, Caligula decides to exhibit that absurdity in his own actions, embarking on a reign characterized by caprice as well as brutality. Caligula thus finds a certain "happiness" in the face of absurdity, but it is, as he says, of a murderous kind, and the play ends with his own assassination.

While the works that Camus completed during the late 1930s and early 1940s focus largely on the situation of the individual and their response to absurdity – so that Camus seems to ignore, for instance, the moral issues relating to the murder that occurs in *The Outsider* – the works that come after are much more concerned with the individual as he or she stands in relation to others. Thus while the focus in the earlier works is on one's own death or the loss to oneself in the death of a lover (in *The Myth of Sisyphus* it is the question of one's own suicide), in the later works one's complicity in and response to the death and suffering of others is primary.[40]

The latter theme is explored in two of Camus's immediate post-war plays, *State of Seige* (*L'État de siège*, 1948) and *The Just Assassins* (*Les Justes*, 1950). *State of Seige* is set in the Spanish town of Cadiz and centers on the establishment and eventual overthrow of a dictatorial regime in the town – a regime that also brings plague along with it. *The Just Assassins* is a dramatization based on events surrounding the attempt to assassinate the Grand Duke Sergei Romanov in 1905, and it explores questions of revolt and idealism, violence and humanity. The group of revolutionaries on whom the play centers (almost all based on real historical figures) are divided over their willingness to enact murder to advance their cause, and, in particular, to countenance even the deaths of children as a possible consequence of their attempts to advance that cause.

Camus's second novel, *The Plague* (*La Peste*, 1947), is, in terms of its themes, similar to *The Just Assassins* and especially to *State of Seige* – although the development of those themes in the novel as opposed to either of the plays, including *State of Seige*, is also quite different. Narrated by one of the town's doctors, Bernard Rieux, who leads the fight against the disease (although the fact that he is the narrator remains hidden until near the book's end), *The Plague* tells of an outbreak of bubonic plague in the Algerian port town of Oran. Here Camus's concern is not so much with absurdity as with suffering, and the necessity of the revolt against it. Indeed, the evident parallels that the novel implicitly suggests between the plague and the German Occupation of France (which, in 1947, had only recently been ended) clearly indicate the way in which what is at issue is the resistance to tyranny and the refusal of evil. That evil, and the refusal of evil, is indeed central to the novel is made especially clear by Rieux's echoing of Alyosha's reply to Ivan in Dostoevsky's *The Brothers Karamazov* (something also evident in *The Just Assassins*).[41] Responding to the Jesuit Father Paneloux's advice, following the death of a child, that "we must love what we cannot understand," Rieux replies: "No Father. I've a very different idea of love. And until my dying day I shall refuse to love a scheme of things in which children are put to torture."[42] This rejection of suffering, and of the violence that often underlies it, is a central element in Camus's later thought, constituting the core of the humane and democratic politics of which he was a staunch advocate.[43] It is also indicative, of course, of one of the issues on which Camus and Sartre stand in sharp contrast to one another.

If *The Plague* appears uncompromising and unambiguous in the response to evil that it urges upon us, Camus's next novel, *The Fall* (*La Chute*, 1956), seems to present a more uncertain picture. The central character of *The Fall* is the ex-lawyer Jean-Baptiste Clamence. We first meet Clamence in an Amsterdam bar, and the novel is told as if we, the reader, were his interlocutor (or witness to just one side of an ongoing dialogue) in a developing series of encounters during which he narrates the story of his life. The key event in that life – the event that set Clamence on the path to his self-proclaimed role as a "judge-penitent" (a title the meaning of which only becomes clear as the novel draws to a close) – was his failure, many years before, to intervene in the night-time suicide of a young woman from a Parisian bridge. The event eventually leads Clamence to turn his back on his old life and take up residence in Amsterdam, where he ostensibly devotes himself to the welfare of those he meets.

While it seems as if Clamence is being remarkably frank about his own situation, about his duplicity and moral cowardice – as if he were a model of lucidity – it finally becomes evident that he tells his story with the aim of holding up a mirror to his interlocutors, thereby demonstrating their own moral inadequacy. Clamence relieves his own moral burden by drawing attention to the burden that is carried by others. Clamence thus appears as the opposite to Meursault in *The Outsider*: while Meursault seems incapable of hiding his indifference, remaining, in this respect, truthful, in Clamence we find a man who, in spite of the appearance of truthfulness, seems to be entirely dishonest.[44] A complex work, and not only in the form of its construction, *The Fall* has been variously interpreted – although no single interpretation seems adequate to the work as a whole. There is no doubt that elements of Camus's own life and character are incorporated into the figure of Clamence, and the novel also seems to depict the general loss of clarity and the moral ambiguity frequently taken to be characteristic of modernity.[45] Yet the novel is often read as an ironic commentary on the existentialist position itself, and especially on the existentialism of Sartre – an existentialism that appears to be preoccupied with individual authenticity but is incapable of recognizing its own insincerity; one in which guilt is universal but also, therefore, meaningless.[46]

In addition to the novels and plays, Camus published a volume of short stories, *Exile and the Kingdom* (*Exil et la royaume*, 1957), and three volumes of lyrical essays, *The Wrong Side and the Right Side* (*L'Envers et l'Endroit*, 1937), *Nuptials* (*Noces*, 1939), and *Summer* (*L'Été*, 1954). Although often overlooked, these essays, with their often highly evocative descriptions of particular places (frequently of places in Camus's native Algeria), are an essential part of his work. Indeed, the very sense of light and sun that pervades so many of these essays seems to exemplify the search for lucidity and clarity that itself drives so much of Camus's thinking and writing, even though, in his return to these places, the demand for lucidity is overtaken by a sense of concrete situatedness that itself resists complete elucidation.

What moves Camus more than anything else, underpinning his own insistence on the need for the renunciation of violence and recognition of life as the only real value,[47] is the sense of our being bound to the earth, to sea, and to sun, to a finite and fragile existence that always stands under the shadow of death and yet nevertheless allows of a certain happiness. As Camus writes in the essay, "Nuptials at Tipasa": "it is my life that I am staking here, a life that tastes of warm stone and the sound of the crickets."[48] It is this that brings Camus closer to late Heidegger than to Sartre and that is expressed in his insistence on his status as a writer rather than a philosopher. It also expresses his rejection of metaphysical pretensions or otherworldly hopes: "The only proofs must be ones that we can touch."[49] The theme is partly developed in the incomplete and posthumously published *The First Man* (*Le Premier Homme*, 1994). Containing similarly evocative descriptions that draw on Camus's own life and experience, the novel explores the character of a life as worked out in relation to the places in which it is lived. While Camus's refusal of violence and his emphasis on the necessity for a politics of dialogue was a part of what motivated his stance on the Algerian question, his position was also underpinned by his own sense of belonging and of place, his own sense of being *Algerian*.[50]

14.6 "THE SUFFERING OF BEING": BECKETT AND ABSURDISM

Existentialism and absurdism are often viewed as closely connected developments. Camus is one figure who stands at their intersection, although his place there is by no means an unequivocal one, while Sartre too can be seen as having an important and influential role in the development of absurdist drama, particularly in relation to Samuel Beckett (1906–89), who is perhaps its central figure. While absurdism is primarily located in the theater – with its key works being plays such as Beckett's *Waiting for Godot* and Eugène Ionesco's *Rhinoceros*[51] – Beckett was himself extremely productive as a novelist, short-story writer, and poet and was awarded the Nobel prize for literature in 1969.

The idea of the "theater of the absurd" is itself a creation of the literary critic Martin Esslin, as set forth in his influential book *The Theatre of the Absurd* (1961). Esslin includes under this heading not only Beckett but also Ionesco, Arthur Adamov, Jean Genet, and a list of other "avant-garde" figures – including Max Frisch, Günter Grass, Harold Pinter, and Edward Albee, all of whom objected to their categorization in this way. The concept of the absurd already appears in the work of André Malraux, who wrote in 1925 of a "basic absurdity" that lies at the core of European man,[52] and the idea clearly has its origins in the surrealist movement in the early part of the century.

The absurd appears, as we have seen, in the work of both Camus and Sartre (although Sartre argues that Camus's use of the term is different from his[53]). Yet according to Esslin, while Camus and Sartre "present their sense of the irrationality of the human condition in the form of highly lucid and logically constructed reasoning," the theater of the absurd "strives to express the senselessness of the human condition and the inadequacy of the rational approach by the open abandonment of rational devices and discursive thought."[54] In this respect, one of the most important devices in absurdist drama – and indeed in absurdist writing generally – is its use of humor. Thus Beckett's plays, while presenting a bleak picture of the human condition, are also full of jokes, verbal plays, and even pratfalls. In this respect, one might argue that absurdism is true to its name, not only in being "without sense," but in often being extremely funny. The only problem is that the joke is always, as it were, on us.

Not only is Beckett the best-known figure within absurdism (even though he contests his inclusion within it), but his work is also closest in its concerns to that of writers such as Sartre and Camus. Although, as already noted, Beckett was a prolific writer across a range of genres (his literary career began in 1929 and continued until his death in 1989), it is undoubtedly his plays that are the best known of his works. In particular, *Waiting for Godot* (*En attendant Godot* – the play was written and first published in French – 1952) has entered into popular culture as have few other works outside of Shakespeare.

Waiting for Godot was famously described by one newspaper critic as "a play in which nothing happens, twice," and yet which nevertheless keeps audiences glued to their seats.[55] Organized into two acts that share an almost identical structure, the play centers on two tramps, Estragon and Vladimir, joined for part of each act by two other characters, Pozzo and his servant Lucky, as they wait over two consecutive days for the arrival of another character who never appears, whose identity remains obscure, and whom neither Estragon nor Vladimir actually seems to know. The action, inasmuch as there is any, is without conclusion or resolution, and even the conversation constantly breaks down or is interrupted. The play is filled, not only with jokes, but also with strange words, biblical allusions, philosophical ruminations, and comments on the bleakness and futility of human life. The absurdity of existence is thus presented with no mitigation of that absurdity, and language itself starts to seem meaningless, incapable of carrying any significance. The only possible response, it would seem, is to laugh.

In *Endgame* (*Fin de partie*, 1957), we encounter another pair of odd characters – Hamm, who is old, blind, and unable to stand, and his young servant Clov, who cannot sit down. Also present are Hamm's legless parents, Ned and Nell, who live in nearby rubbish bins. The play seems to be set in a time when there is little left to the world, and its title suggests an allusion to the final stage in a game of chess. The play is, it seems, about endings, and the vain struggle against such endings, although the ending at issue seems to be one that could easily slip by almost unnoticed (as does the death of Nell). In *Krapp's Last Tape* (1958), a one-act monologue, we watch Krapp in his study on the evening of his sixty-ninth birthday as he does what he does every year: record himself as he reflects on the year gone by and listen to his past recordings. This time he listens to the one he recorded when he was thirty-nine, and we see the contrast, as does Krapp himself, between the man he was then and who he is now, between his hopes and expectations and the reality that has been realized, and we seem to see death standing behind him in the shadows.

What draws Beckett's work close to that of existentialists such as Sartre is not only his preoccupation with the idea of the absurd but also his bleak portrayal of the human situation – a portrayal that characterizes his novels and other works no less than his plays. Yet, unlike Sartre, Beckett seems to see little room for either freedom or political engagement. Instead, Beckett's work carries a strong sense of inevitable failure and of the complete inability of language or thought to make sense of the world in which we find ourselves, or even adequately to speak about the reality that confronts us. In this respect, Beckett is perhaps closer to Camus than to either Sartre or Beauvoir, although for Beckett there is no possibility of the sort of rebellious affirmation in the face of absurdity on which Camus places such emphasis. If Camus's work is ultimately about the value of human life and the possibility of happiness in spite of the inevitability of death, in Beckett, it is failure and death – "the suffering of being"[56] – and the ridiculous absurdity of existence that seem to be paramount.

14.7 PARALLELS AND SUCCESSORS: HESSE TO KUNDERA

The term "existentialist" is, as we saw earlier, often used in an expanded sense that encompasses much of modern literature as well as literature from past centuries. Such an expanded usage is obviously problematic. Yet while there are only a relatively small number of writers whose work can reasonably be characterized as "existentialist", there are many more writers who have produced individual works that may be thought to have some claim to be part of the existentialist canon, or whose work itself stands in a significant relation of influence to existentialist literature more narrowly conceived. This would seem to be true of specific works by Tolstoy and Hamsun, already considered briefly above, and there are a number of works by other writers to which this might be thought to apply also.

Within German literature the work of Herman Hesse (1877–1962) is particularly notable. Hesse was himself influenced by Hamsun, but perhaps less by any nascent existentialist elements in his work than by his romanticism and individualism. The influence of Dostoevsky is also evident in some of Hesse's writing, and the work that has perhaps the best claim to be viewed as standing in a close proximity to existentialist literature is Hesse's novel *Steppenwolf* (*Der Steppenwolf*, 1927), which itself echoes themes from the work of the great Russian writer. Hesse's work, and especially *Steppenwolf*, became extremely popular within the counter-culture of the 1960s (its popularity great enough to provide the name for the rock band whose music played a key part in the film *Easy Rider*). As with Sartre's *Nausea*, *Steppenwolf* is presented to the reader as made up of a set of papers found among the effects of the novel's main character, a writer by the name of Harry Haller. Like many existentialist figures, Haller is divided within himself in a way that threatens his sense of identity and his sanity. In Haller's case, he finds himself torn between two natures or modes of being – that of a man, an ordinary member of society, and that of a wolf of the steppes, beastly and antisocial. Containing a number of what appear to be hallucinatory scenes, as well as a series of encounters with a woman, Hermine, who also seems in some way to be a creation of or counterpart to Haller's own psyche, the novel explores themes of alienation, psychological disintegration, and discovery that draw on Dostoevsky, Nietzsche, and Kafka, although they are also influenced by the ideas of Carl Jung.

Within American literature, there are a number of essayists, novelists, poets, and playwrights who have produced individual works that have a strongly existentialist orientation or provenance or whose work otherwise stands in a close relation to the existentialist tradition. Sartre himself wrote about a number of American writers whom he saw as literary influences on his work and that of his contemporaries – Hemingway, Dos Passos, Faulkner – but while he acknowledges their importance, he does not view them as existentialists, nor should he have done so.[57] Nevertheless, one can find in these writers themes that certainly mirror those that appear in existentialist writing elsewhere, and the work of Ernest Hemingway (1899–1961), in particular, is often cited in discussions of existentialism as a literary form. Hemingway's "A Clean, Well-Lighted Place" (1926) can be read as providing a succinct statement of existential alienation, while Hemingway's repetition in the story of the Spanish word for "nothing" – *nada* – also has clear existentialist resonances.[58]

The work of writers such as Harlan Ellison (1934–) and Norman Mailer (1923–2007) provide obvious points of contact with existentialism as it appears in European literature, as do the plays of Arthur Miller (1915–2005). Existentialism provided a way of engaging with an emerging sense of alienation in American life, whether under the influence of consumer capitalism or the experience of social exclusion on the part of African-Americans. The Beat movement of the 1950s, exemplified in the work of writers such as Jack Kerouac (1922–69) and Alan Ginsberg (1926–97), clearly shows the influence of existentialist thought and writing – particularly the work of Camus, whose prose style has obvious affinities (as Sartre himself noted) with that of American writers such as Hemingway, themselves an influence on the Beats. In an early article on the "Beat Generation" in 1952, John Clellon Holmes characterized it in a way that was certainly suggestive of existentialist themes: "It involves a sort of nakedness of mind, and, ultimately, of soul; a feeling of being reduced to the bedrock of consciousness. In short, it means being undramatically pushed up against the wall of oneself."[59] Yet as Holmes himself noted, the Beats were a broad and ill-defined group, encompassing a wide range of ideas and approaches as well as an eclectic set of influences. In fact, the development of the Beats draws as much on Zen Buddhist thought as on the literary existentialism of Camus or Sartre, and it was undoubtedly even more strongly influenced, as was the work of such as Ellison and Mailer, by tendencies and movements already present within American culture.[60]

Among more recent European writing, *The Unbearable Lightness of Being* (*Nesnesitelná lehkost bytí*, 1984), by Czech writer Milan Kundera (1929–), stands in a close relationship to the existentialist literary tradition and seems to reflect ideas and themes present in a number of earlier writers from Dostoevsky to Camus. The novel begins with a reflection on Nietzsche's myth of the eternal recurrence, "the heaviest of all burdens," as Nietzsche characterizes it. If recurrence – the continual living of one's life again and again – is the heaviest of burdens, then the singular happening, the fact that one lives one's life but once, is surely the lightest. The novel deals with the intertwined lives and relationships of two couples, Tomáš and Tereza (as well as their dog, Karenin), and Franz and Sabina, in the period following the Prague Spring of 1968. As it explores the fragility and singularity of the lives and relationships of its main characters, so the novel explores and illuminates that which is also referred to in its title: the "unbearable lightness" of being.

While it may not be an "existentialist" work as such, Kundera's *The Unbearable Lightness of Being* nevertheless constitutes an excellent example of the literary exploration of existence that is also exemplified in, but not restricted to, existentialist works. Such explorations are characteristic of much modern (and postmodern) literature, so that modernity might itself be characterized in terms of the uncertainty that it gives to the human situation. In this respect, existentialist literature can be viewed as one expression of what is an essentially modern tendency – a tendency, it should be said, that is not dissipated by any move to the "postmodern." Moreover, as can be seen most clearly in the work of Sartre, Beauvoir, and Beckett, in the literary exploration of existence literature itself is also at issue. The question concerning the relation between existentialism and literature is thus not only an issue about the nature of existentialism, but also about the nature of literature.

NOTES

1. Throughout this essay, the year of first publication of a work is given in parentheses following the title of the work, and, in the case of foreign-language works, with the title as given in the original language in which the work first appeared.
2. Cooper, *Existentialism*, p. 8.
3. One might argue, as I think Cooper is inclined to do, that existentialism and existential phenomenology are co-extensive terms, but there seems to be good reason to distinguish between the two. Certainly, to assume a straightforward identity here is already to prejudice the case against the possibility that existentialism might also constitute itself as literature (unless, as Iris Murdoch suggests in the quotation in n. 5 below, one takes literature as itself a form of phenomenology), while one might also argue for the possibility of a mode of phenomenology that does indeed thematize the existential and yet is not existentialist.
4. Kundera, *The Art of the Novel*, p. 44.
5. Murdoch, *Sartre*, p. 9, writes that "The novelist proper is, in his way, a sort of phenomenologist."
6. While there have been attempts to enlist a range of thinkers from Augustine to Pascal within existentialist ranks, more serious argument over the *philosophical* scope of existentialism has generally focused on the extent to which the term applies beyond the small group clustered around Sartre and Beauvoir (or even whether it applies to anyone other than Sartre himself), and the extent to which it properly includes Kierkegaard (the figure most regularly seen as the founder of existentialism as it refers to a philosophical position that encompasses more than the Sartrean), and Nietzsche, Jaspers, and Heidegger.
7. That these terms are indeed distinct should be clear from even the most cursory consideration, but it is surprising how frequently the terms are conflated. Of course, given existentialism's concern with human existence, existentialist works will exhibit a concern with the existential, but the fact that *existential* concerns figure in a work cannot be sufficient for that work to be viewed as *existentialist*.
8. "[existential, adj.,] 1693 tr. *Barlow's Exercit.* i. Rem. 483 Enjoying the good of existence and the being deprived of that existential good," *Oxford English Dictionary*, vol. v, p. 543.

9. Although not discussed here, Gabriel Marcel (1889–1973) was as productive a playwright as a philosopher, viewing his dramatic works as just as important an expression of his ideas as his philosophical writing. In spite of receiving a number of literary prizes and awards during his lifetime, however, his work for the theater has never achieved the same international recognition as that of Sartre or Camus. Marcel's plays include *A Man of God* (*Un Homme de Dieu*, 1923), *The Broken World* (*Le Monde cassé*, 1932), and *Ariadne* (*Le Chemin de Crête* – "The Cretan Way" – 1936). Marcel is notable as an example of a writer who adopts a specifically religious version of existentialism (and is thus closer to Kierkegaard) in contrast to Sartre, in particular, who was quite explicit as to the atheistic presuppositions of his thinking.
10. Sartre himself situates Camus in direct relation to Voltaire. See Sartre, "Camus' *The Outsider*," p. 41.
11. One might argue that where there is an impetus towards literary expression in German philosophy, it is, in fact, an impetus that derives from and is associated with romanticism rather than existentialism.
12. Kaufmann, *Existentialism from Dostoyevsky to Sartre*, pp. 12, 14.
13. See Dostoevsky, *The Brothers Karamazov*, Book v, ch. 5.
14. "'Rebellion'? I don't like hearing such a word from you," Ivan said with feeling. "One can hardly live by rebellion, and I want to live. Tell me straight out, I call on you – answer me: imagine that you yourself are building the fabric of human destiny with the object of making people happy in the finale, of giving them peace and rest at last, but for that you must inevitably and unavoidably torture just one tiny creature, that same child who was beating her chest with her little fist, and raise your edifice on the foundation of her unrequited tears – would you agree to be the architect on those conditions? Tell me the truth." Dostoevsky, *The Brothers Karamazov*, p. 245.
15. For Camus, the circumstances were those of the Algerian War (1954–62) by which Algeria won its independence from France – a war characterized by terrorism and counter-terrorism, guerrilla warfare, and the use of torture. The same circumstances seem to be mirrored in our own time of "global terror."
16. A juxtaposition that is oddly present in the bibliography of Kafka's own writing, which includes, among his "Office Writings," such works as "The Scope of Compulsory Insurance for the Building Trades" (1908), and "Measures for Preventing Accidents from Wood-Planing Machines" (1910).

17. As well as being the translation, in the English edition, of the title of Camus's *L'Étranger*, *The Outsider* was also the title for a popular and notorious work of the 1950s by the writer Colin Wilson. Wilson presented the outsider as *the* figure of modernity, providing both fictional and real-life examples of this figure. Wilson drew heavily on existentialist writing, but also on a wide range of other sources, including figures as diverse as H. G. Wells, T. E. Lawrence, George Bernard Shaw, William Blake, and G. I. Gurdjieff.
18. "Keep a diary to see clearly – let none of the nuances or small happenings escape even though they might seem to mean nothing. And above all classify them. I must tell how I see this table, this street, the people." Sartre, *Nausea*, p. 1.
19. Sartre, *Nausea*, pp. 127–31.
20. *Roads to Freedom* comprises *The Age of Reason* (*L'Âge de raison*, 1945), *The Reprieve* (*Le Sursis*, 1947), and *Troubled Sleep* (*La Mort dans l'Âme*, literally "Death in the Soul", 1949), the fourth novel was to have been titled *A Strange Friendship* (*Drôle d'amitié*).
21. Sartre, *No Exit*, p. 45.
22. Sartre's other plays include: *The Respectful Prostitute* (*Le Putain respecteuse*, 1946); *Dirty Hands* (*Les Mains sales*; 1948); and *The Condemned of Altona* (*Les Séquestrés d'Altona*, 1959).
23. *When Things of the Spirit Come First* (*Quand prime le spirituel*, written in the 1930s, but not published until 1979), and *The Woman Destroyed* (*La Femme rompue*, 1967).
24. Including her four-part autobiography, *Memoirs of a Dutiful Daughter* (*Mémoirs d'une jeune fille rangée*, 1958), *The Prime of Life* (*La Force de l'âge*, 1960), *The Force of Circumstance* (*La Force des choses*, 2 vols., 1963), and *All Said and Done* (*Tout compte fait*, 1972), as well as *A Very Easy Death* (*Une Mort très douce*, 1964), concerning the death of her mother, and *Adieux: A Farewell to Sartre* (*La Cérémonie des adieux*, 1981).
25. See Beauvoir, "Literature and Metaphysics."
26. Maurois, *From Proust to Camus*, p. 330.
27. On this point, see Chapter 13 of this *Companion*.
28. Merleau-Ponty, "Metaphysics and the Novel" (1945).
29. Since the novel reveals Beauvoir's sympathies with the French Resistance, it was written in the knowledge that it could not be published until after the German Occupation had ended.
30. The issues of time, old age, and death become increasingly important in Beauvoir's writing, especially in her autobiographical works.
31. Even this *Companion* contains no extended discussion of Camus's work. His treatment here should thus be viewed as attempting to

provide a small corrective to Camus's relative *philosophical* neglect (not a neglect, it should be pointed out, mirrored in literature).

32. Sartre referred to *The Outsider* as itself a work that comes to the French reader from "outside." See Sartre, "Camus' *The Outsider*," p. 24.
33. Camus, "*La Nausée* by Jean-Paul Sartre," p. 145.
34. For the correspondence between Camus and Grenier, which provides some record of their relationship, see Rigaud, *Albert Camus and Jean Grenier: Correspondence*.
35. For more on Camus's life, see Todd, *Albert Camus*.
36. Sartre, "Camus' *The Outsider*," p. 41. *The Outsider* was foreshadowed in an earlier abandoned novel, *A Happy Death* (*La Mort heureuse*, 1971), written between 1936 and 1938, which also centers on a murder by a clerk named Meursault.
37. So that even in the 1980s it could be the inspiration for a hit pop song – "Killing an Arab" by The Cure – a song whose title (referring to the pivotal incident in the novel) led to it being banned by the BBC.
38. That the novel contains an apparently colonialist sub-text was first pointed out by O'Brien in "Camus, Algeria, and *The Fall*."
39. The sequence should probably also be taken to include the play written in 1943, *Cross Purpose* (*Le Malentendu*, 1944), whose plot is prefigured in a newspaper story mentioned by Meursault in *The Outsider*.
40. Camus himself charts out the movement in his thinking in terms of a shift from the question of suicide to that of murder (see Camus, *Carnets*, p. 97), as well as by reference to three figures from Greek mythology: Sisyphus, Prometheus, and Nemesis. The problem that Sisyphus exemplifies is that of the individual in an absurd situation (Sisyphus' task in Hades is to roll a huge rock to the top of a hill, but the rock is back at the bottom every morning); Prometheus exemplifies rebellion in the face of absurdity and evil (it is he who steals fire from the gods, and teaches human beings the arts of civilization); Nemesis is the symbol of our essential finitude, and so also of our concrete human situatedness, especially as that is evident in our relation to others (she is the goddess who punishes those who overstep the proper limits). See Camus, *Carnets*, p. 168.
41. See the passage from *The Brothers Karamazov* quoted in n. 14 above. It is notable that this passage appears in the chapter titled "Rebellion."
42. Camus, *The Plague*, p. 178.
43. See Isaac, *Arendt, Camus, and Modern Rebellion*, for a discussion of Camus's political thought alongside that of Hannah Arendt. Isaac sees both as holding to a similarly "rebellious politics."
44. Indeed, he has, he says, "accepted duplicity instead of being upset by it." Camus, *The Fall*, p. 103.

45. Clamence is "a false prophet for mediocre times." Camus, *Oeuvres complètes*, p. 1533.
46. For a discussion of the various readings at issue here, see Sprintzen, *Camus*, pp. 202–17.
47. Something that is clearly evident in the essays and other works that follow on from the writings of the absurd that characterize Camus's work in the early 1940s.
48. Camus, "Nuptials in Tipasa," p. 53.
49. Camus, *Carnets*, p. 9.
50. "Algeria ... is my true country." Camus, "Short Guide to Towns without a Past," p. 114. On the idea of the relation to place as a central issue for philosophical thinking (an idea that can be seen to be implicit in much existentialist writing, especially through its emphasis on human finitude and situatedness), see Malpas, *Place and Experience*, and Casey, *The Fate of Place*.
51. Eugène Ionesco (born Eugen Ionescu, 1909–94) is the next-best-known figure connected with absurdism after Beckett. His most celebrated plays include the short works *The Bald Soprano* (*La Cantatrice chauve*, 1950), *The Lesson* (*La Leçon*, 1951), *The Chairs* (*Les Chaises*, 1952), and *Jack, or The Submission* (*Jacques ou la Soumission*, 1955), as well as the full-length plays *The Killer* (*Tueur sans gages*, 1959), and *Rhinoceros* (*Rhinocéros*, 1959). Like Beckett, Ionesco also produced a number of novels and works of poetry.
52. Malraux, *The Temptation of the West*, p. 40.
53. "For [Camus] the absurd arises from the relation between man and the world, between man's rational demands and the world's irrationality. The themes which he derives from it are those of classical pessimism. I do not recognize the absurd in the sense of scandal and disillusionment that Camus attributes to it. What I call the absurd is something very different: it is the universal contingency of being which is, but which is not the basis of its being; the absurd is the given, unjustifiable, primordial quality of existence." Quoted in Cruickshank, *Albert Camus and the Literature of Revolt*, p. 45, from Grisoli, "Entretien avec Jean-Paul Sartre."
54. Esslin, *The Theatre of the Absurd*, pp. xix–xx.
55. Mercier, "The Uneventful Event," p. 6.
56. Beckett, *Proust*, p. 8.
57. See especially Sartre, "John Dos Passos and *1919*."
58. See Killinger, *Hemingway and the Dead Gods*, for an attempted, although unconvincing, portrayal of Hemingway's work, in general, as existentialist in character.
59. Holmes, "This Is the Beat Generation," p. 110.

60. See Cotkin, *Existential America,* for an excellent exploration of the impact of existentialism on American thought and culture. Cotkin shows how American writers were drawn into the conversation inaugurated by existentialists in Europe, but he also makes clear the way in which existentialism's impact in America connected with a strong tradition of existing existential concerns.

MEROLD WESTPHAL

15 Existentialism and religion

It is often said that existentialism has passed into the history of philosophy. But that is a problem only if we think of that history as a kind of museum in which we become antiquarians who observe animals no longer living or artifacts no longer useful. *It has nothing to do with us.* But if we have an existential spirit we will not read any of the history of philosophy that way. We will hear the texts of the great thinkers as voices that address us directly, offering interpretations of our being-in-the-world full of possibilities for our beliefs, our actions, and our affects or attitudes. *It has everything to do with us.*

No doubt this means that our title is less than perfect. "Religion" suggests an observable object or phenomenon. Thus we have Religious Studies departments where religion is what is studied. There's nothing very existential about being a scholarly observer. Existentialism is about the urgency of deciding what to do with our lives, more specifically, what to do with my own life. That is why in Plato's *Gorgias*, Socrates, perhaps the first existentialist philosopher, says to Callicles, "For you see, don't you, that our discussion's about ... *the way we're supposed to live.*"[1] Similarly, in a journal entry from the twenty-two-year-old Kierkegaard, we read:

> The thing is to understand myself, to see what God really wishes *me* to do; the thing is to find a truth which is true *for me*, to find *the idea for which I can live and die* ... what good would it do me to be able to explain the meaning of Christianity if it had *no* deeper significance *for me and for my life*; what good would it do me if truth stood before me, cold and naked, not caring whether I recognized her or not ... I certainly do not deny that I still recognize an *imperative of understanding* and that through it one can work upon men, *but it must be taken up into my life*, and *that is*, what I

now recognize as the most important thing ... What is truth but to live for an idea?[2]

"Faith" is perhaps a more existential term than "religion," signifying as it usually does the act of appropriation by which I (or we) commit ourselves to a particular set of religious beliefs and practices. We identify ourselves with them, even perhaps define our own identity in terms of these beliefs and practices. They are what we will live for and, perhaps, even die for. We have learned from Socrates, Jesus Christ, Mahatma Gandhi, and Martin Luther King, Jr. that the deepest existential question about how I should live my life asks not what, if anything, I am willing to kill for, but what I am willing to die for.

15.1 SØREN KIERKEGAARD (1813–1855)

So it should not surprise us that Kierkegaard, the founding father of modern existentialism, should speak more about faith than about religion. To be sure, he uses the latter term when distinguishing the three modes of being-in-the-world that he calls existence spheres, or stages on life's way: the aesthetic, the ethical, and the religious. These are best understood as the concrete embodiment of different criteria for successful living, different answers to the question, what makes the good life good?

For the aesthete (who may or may not be concerned with the arts), the criteria are pre-moral. Good and evil, right and wrong, if they function at all, do so in subordination to such criteria as the pleasant or the interesting. In the ethical sphere, moral criteria are at once the most basic and the highest. They do not preclude other goods, but they trump them. Thus, for example, wealth is good, but not if gained by theft or exploitation.

The difference between the ethical and the religious sphere concerns the highest source of these highest norms. For the ethical, which has a distinctly Hegelian character in Kierkegaard's presentation, one need not look beyond the laws and customs of one's people (*Sittlichkeit*). These are not ultimate until history reaches its climax, but we have no capacity to leap past our own socio-historical context, even in philosophical reflection. For "philosophy too is its own time apprehended in thoughts."[3] Absolute knowing and the highest good are available only to those fortunate enough to live at the culmination of history's long journey.

Kierkegaard[4] criticizes Hegel and an all-too-Hegelian Christendom for the arrogant complacency of thinking they have already arrived at that point, that their theories are absolute truth and their practices the ultimate good. For him the religious sphere of existence means not that we can escape our human horizons, but that God can explode their finality from a location at once immanent within and transcendent to them. "Revelation" is the theological term for this manifestation of God within our worlds in such a way as to challenge those worlds, to render them relative. Faith, the fundamental posture of the religious stage, is the response to such revelation. It is the acknowledgment that neither the individual nor the social order has arrived and is thus absolute.

In *Fear and Trembling,* Kierkegaard presents Abraham as the knight of faith. In this respect he echoes the three New Testament epistles in which Abraham is the paradigm of faith: Romans, Galatians, and Hebrews. Indeed, most of the time Kierkegaard interprets the religious sphere in terms of biblical faith.[5] In *Fear and Trembling* he retells the story of Genesis 22 in which, to test Abraham, God commands him to sacrifice his son Isaac. Readers should be familiar with the setting of this story in Genesis 12–22. It is the ongoing story of God's promises and commands to Abraham. At the heart of Genesis 22 is the command to sacrifice Isaac. But Kierkegaard knows that promise precedes command. "It was by his faith that Abraham could leave the land of his fathers to become a stranger in the land of promise ... It was faith that made Abraham accept the promise that all nations of the earth should be blessed in his seed."[6] And it was by faith that he was willing to sacrifice Isaac, though he was stopped from doing so at the last minute.

Three important corollaries follow in this account of biblical faith. First, it is more properly described as faith in ... rather than belief that ... Of course it presupposes various beliefs (that there is a God, that God had spoken to Abraham, etc.), but fundamentally is it a relation of a person to a person and not merely of an intellect to a proposition. It is trust in the promises of God and obedience to the commands of God. But this trust and this obedience presuppose that the God in whom Abraham puts his faith is a fully personal God, and this in a quite specific sense. God is personal as one who can perform speech acts, most especially promises and commands.[7] Faith does not have as its correlate some abstract principle or impersonal power.

Second, the discussion of the relation of faith and reason, a classical philosophical theme, is removed from the Platonic horizon in which it is all too frequently posed. In distinguishing the sensible/temporal world from the intelligible/eternal world, and in giving us two vivid images with which to express this dualism – namely the divided line and the cave allegory of the *Republic* – Plato gives a distinctively inferior status to *pistis* (usually translated "opinion"). While it is the upper half of the lower half of the divided line, its home remains the darkness of the cave rather than the sunshine of intelligibility outside. Its temporal, sensible objects are not fully real, and its mode of cognition is correspondingly inadequate. It is a failed attempt at genuine knowledge.

When the New Testament speaks about faith, including Abraham's, it uses the same term, *pistis*, but with a wholly different meaning. Here faith as trust and obedience – presupposing beliefs to be sure – is not simply a cognitive act of our sensible faculty but the act of a whole person in relation to a personal God. It is not an inferior mode of Subject–Object relation but a distinctive, even unique, mode of I–Thou relation. To treat it, as philosophers too often do, as if it were a failed attempt to be like mathematics and physics is to fail entirely to understand what it is.

The Platonic model contrasts the cognitive results of an inferior faculty in relation to inferior objects with the results of a superior faculty in relation to superior objects. For Kierkegaard, faith is a relation to a superior "object," but it is not the exercise of a faculty or power; it is more like the reception of a gift, a response to the initiative and agency of another person. It is a grateful response to revelation. It embodies a higher knowledge than either common sense or the sciences can provide. What is more, it concerns who we are at the deepest level and how we should live our lives.[8]

In *Philosophical Fragments*, Kierkegaard makes this abundantly clear. Reason signifies variations on the Platonic theme of knowledge as recollection. The truth is already within us and we have the ability to recognize it as such when (with or without external help) we find it before us. It is the product of our own faculties or powers. We are not essentially dependent on anyone else. Revelation, whose reception is faith, is not like that. The truth is not already in us and even when it is staring us in the face we do not have the power to recognize it as such. Only when the God who gives us the most important truth in the first place also gives us the capacity to recognize it as such does it become truth for us. It would seem clear that the knowledge that would arise in faith's reception of divine revelation would be superior to the knowledge that rests on human powers alone. So the assumption that faith is a failed attempt at the allegedly higher knowledge that reason provides begs the question whether revelation, in the sense just specified, actually occurs.

Third, on the assumption that revelation does not occur, faith's refusal to remain within the sphere of unaided human reason can only appear to be irrational. But instead of trying to prove that faith is, after all, reasonable – perhaps with an appeal to the time-honored formula that faith goes beyond reason but not against it – Kierkegaard concedes, or rather insists, that faith goes against reason.

Not that it does not have its own intelligibility; it does make sense when viewed from its own presuppositions. But the Enlightenment Project, which goes back to Plato but came to new flourishing in the modern period, claims full hegemony for (one of the many different versions of) reason independent of revelation. "Religion within the limits of reason alone" is not just the title of a book by Kant; it is the name of a project carried out in many ways by many different thinkers in the modern period. In relation to the traditions of biblical revelation, it either claims the right to pick and choose, to sort out the believable kernel from the unbelievable husk, or it claims the right to reinterpret the biblical materials so as to bring them into conformity with a philosophical system that doesn't depend on them. Spinoza, Kant, and Hegel are examples of the latter strategy, which ends up not being so very different from the former.

When some version of reason (Spinoza's, Kant's, or Hegel's, for example, being quite different from one another) either rejects revelation or reduces it to being an impure vehicle of its own pure rationality, Kierkegaard sees an inescapable conflict. In going *beyond* some philosophical theory that calls itself Reason, it goes *against* its claim to self-sufficiency and hegemony.

Accordingly, Kierkegaard speaks of faith as paradox, as absurd, as madness – not because it has no *logos* of its own, but because that is how it does and should look from the standpoint of the

Enlightenment Project's interpretation(s) of human cognitive powers. Later Kierkegaard will add the concept of offense to his account of faith's relation to autonomous human reason.[9] Faith's claim that reason is not sufficient and ultimate by itself is humbling to reason, so construed. If one sticks to reason's claim to primacy, one will be offended, and it is only by overcoming this offense that one can get to faith. "From the possibility of offense, one turns either to offense or to faith, but one never comes to faith except from the possibility of offense."[10]

Kierkegaard makes two observations about this conflict between faith as receptivity to revelation and reason as the claim to freedom from or hegemony over any purported revelation. First, that faith should seem unreasonable to reason, so understood, is perfectly natural, but it hardly settles the conflict. "It is just as you say [namely that the two are incompatible], and the amazing thing is that you think that it is an objection."[11] Perhaps, as Socrates suggested, the "heaven-sent madness" is superior to any "man-made sanity."[12] Second, conceding the honorific self-designation of Reason to autonomous human thought, Kierkegaard suggests that faith call itself the Paradox. Then he describes the "acoustic illusion" that arises when Reason purports to discover the opposition between itself and the Paradox. This is an illusion, according to Kierkegaard, because from the outset it has been the Paradox that has pointed to this opposition. It has insisted that what it takes to be the wisdom of God is at odds with the wisdom of the world.[13]

In *Fear and Trembling* Kierkegaard renders this conflict concrete by contrasting the knight of faith with two other characters, the knight of infinite resignation and the tragic hero. If asked to sacrifice his dearest for the highest, the knight of infinite resignation would do so, but without hope. He is reconciled to the fact that temporality and finitude must yield to the eternal and infinite. So, too, the knight of faith. But he makes one further move. Since Isaac is the son of promise and since with God all things are possible, he believes "by virtue of the absurd" that even if he has to go through with the sacrifice, he will get Isaac back *in this life*. This is "absurd" because he goes beyond any human calculation and the realm of finitude for which human understanding is the "stockbroker."[14]

Here God is personal not only as one who speaks but as one who acts. Moreover, the divine agency in question here – raising the dead – is supernatural. It is not the mediated agency by means of the normal operation of the created order, but the unmediated agency that suspends and transcends that order for some special purpose. Biblical faith believes in miracles, not because it is superstitious, but because it believes in the agency of a personal God.

There is a more troubling question than whether Abraham will get Isaac back. Is not his willingness to kill his son a willingness to murder, and, to make matters worse, if possible, to murder one to whom he has a special bond of love and responsibility? This is where Kierkegaard introduces the concept of the teleological suspension of the ethical. What he means by this phrase is what Hegel means by the concept of *Aufhebung*. In either case, something that is taken or that takes itself to be self-sufficient and absolute is rendered dependent and subordinate by being relocated as part of a larger whole of which it is not the organizing principle. It is not abolished but relativized in the claim that its *telos* or goal is beyond itself. It is given a supporting, ancillary role in relation to something higher.

It is important to remember that in this context the ethical does not signify what Plato or Kant would understand by it, the rational apprehension of eternal moral truth as in 2 + 2 = 4. In this sense the ethical would stand in judgment on the laws and customs of any particular society. One might speak of the teleological suspension of a society's laws and customs (convention) in the ethical (nature, in the moral and metaphysical sense of the term), which they are meant to serve. But for Kierkegaard, taking his cue from Hegel, the ethical signifies precisely those laws and customs. And their higher *telos* is not some moral philosophy but the will of God as given in divine revelation.

So the situation with Abraham is this: ethically speaking what he is willing to do is murder, but religiously speaking it is sacrifice.[15] As the knight of faith, Abraham can be a hero only if there is a teleological suspension of the ethical, or, as it is understood in this context, only if there is an absolute duty to God. In good Hegelian fashion, Kierkegaard speaks of the social order as the universal because its laws and customs transcend the particular individual both in their origin and their authority. So if we substitute "society" for "the universal" and "God" for "the absolute" in the following passage, we'll get Kierkegaard's meaning.

> Then faith's paradox is this, that the single individual is higher than the universal, that the single individual (to recall a theological distinction less in vogue these days) determines his relation to the universal through his relation to the absolute, not his relation to the absolute through his relation to the universal. The paradox can also be put by saying that there is an absolute duty to God; for in this tie of obligation the individual relates himself absolutely, as the single individual, to the absolute ... [T]he ethical is reduced to the relative. It doesn't follow, nevertheless, that [the ethical] is to be done away with.[16]

Abraham's faith that it is sacrifice and not murder that he is on his way to do is like his faith that God can and will raise Isaac from the dead, should that be necessary. In the one case God's agency is not limited to the ordinary course of nature; in the other case God's will is not limited to the conventional values into which one has been socialized. "Reason's" attempt to confine God within the natural order (as in Spinoza, for example), or within the social order (as in Hegel, for example), makes God disappear. One can retain God-talk for the sake of the many, but it is in principle eliminable, reducible to the other terms in which God has been defined. For Kierkegaard, faith is the conviction of and commitment to an irreplaceable God.

Of course, Abraham is a special case. Biblical faith in general does not involve the kind of test that Abraham underwent. Christian faith, which is Kierkegaard's major concern in the midst of a Christendom he sees as more pagan than Christian, has quite another focus. The paradox and point of possible offense is the claim that Jesus is God incarnate and our Savior from sin – an even more serious problem than mere finitude[17] – along with the practices that properly accompany such belief. He develops the nature of faith in this context in subsequent writings.[18] But the fundamental structure of biblical faith and its relation to the beliefs and practices whose only norm is autonomous human reason are already spelled out in *Fear and Trembling*. It is a crucial text not only because of its drama but also because of its decisive definition of the religious life in terms of faith.

But what, we may ask, is existential about this? Two interlocking features of faith as Kierkegaard understands it jump immediately to the fore: risk and passion. First, faith is risky. It involves commitment to beliefs, practices, and even to identity formation; but it comes without guarantees that it is not misplaced. Perhaps there is no God of the kind presupposed by biblical faith; or perhaps I (and we) have misunderstood who God is, what God wants of us, and what kind of life God has planned for our flourishing. Being religious doesn't make us infallible; nor does it keep distorted desire from deforming our beliefs, our practices, and even our identities. Modernity's quest, not merely for certainty but for guaranteed certainty, is the sustained failure to recognize the fragile and fallen nature of human existence.

Second, faith is a passion. It is not about cool and casual commitments. This does not mean that faith is in a constant state of psychic frenzy. When we say that someone has a passion for fly fishing or for opera, we do not attribute frenzied states to them. We mean to signify a love that is deep and lasting – a significant dimension of one's personal identity. Faith, Kierkegaard thinks, is like that except that it is the deepest passion of all.

These two features of faith are united in one classic definition.

> *The objective uncertainty maintained through appropriation in the most passionate inwardness is truth,* the highest truth there is for someone *existing* ... But the definition of truth stated above is another way of saying faith. Without risk, no faith. Faith is just this, the contradiction between the infinite passion of inwardness and objective uncertainty.[19]

A third existential dimension of Kierkegaardian faith is the emphasis on choice. The will, and not just the intellect, is deeply implicated in determining the existence-sphere in which I live and in whether I have faith or am offended by the claims of revelation. As with the emphasis on faith as a passion, we have a move away from modern philosophy's preoccupation with epistemology, as if the human person were first and foremost a cognitive relation to propositions of various sorts. Without denying the importance of beliefs, the self is portrayed more holistically as being its passions and its choices at least as much as it is its beliefs.[20] What is more, our beliefs may be functions of our passions and our choices at least as much as the other way around.

Linked to this third existential feature is a fourth: urgency. The choice whether to live in the aesthetic, the ethical, or the religious sphere is far more fundamental to my identity than the choice of clothes in the morning. The decision whether to cultivate the passion of faith or of offense in relation to the specific claims (theoretical and practical) of Christian revelation is weightier than the choice to cultivate a passion for fly fishing or opera. I can adopt or abandon fly fishing without becoming a deeply different person, but if I adopt or abandon faith I become just that, a deeply different person.

In sum Kierkegaard gives us an existential account of faith insofar as it is interpreted as a risky passion and an urgent choice. Borrowing a phrase from Nietzsche, we can say that what Kierkegaard found in Hegel and an all-too-Hegelian Christendom was simply "Wretched contentment!"[21] Though they thought of themselves as Christian, they fled from risky passion and urgent choice, reducing faith to systematic speculation and successful socialization.

15.2 FRIEDRICH NIETZSCHE (1844–1900)

Though Kierkegaard is by far the most important religious existentialist, others are important for our theme precisely by being anti-religious.[22] Nietzsche, the other "founding father" of modern existentialism, comes immediately to mind. Just as Kierkegaard doesn't try to prove the existence of God but operates in a hermeneutical circle that presupposes it, so Nietzsche doesn't try to prove the truth of atheism. He simply announces the death of God.[23] Both, we might say, are preaching to their (quite different) choirs, and each is arguing that being Christian or being secular, respectively, is much more strenuous than all too many assume. Away with "wretched contentment"!

Once again like Kierkegaard, Nietzsche recognizes that his claim will – indeed must –appear as madness to those who inhabit a different perspective.[24] So he allows a madman to announce the great event. "'Whither is God?' he cried; 'I will tell you. *We have killed him* – you and I. All of us are his murderers … Gods, too, decompose. God is dead. God remains dead. And we have killed him.'"[25]

There are several things to notice about this announcement, intended to shock – believers immediately and unbelievers eventually. First, it is a historical rather than a metaphysical event. It is not that once upon a time there was a God but this God got old and died. Rather, "We have killed him … All of us are his murderers … we have killed him." Two questions immediately arise. The first is, in what sense have we killed him? Answer: by ceasing to believe in him. "The greatest recent event – 'God is dead,' that the belief in the Christian god has become unbelievable – is already beginning to cast its first shadows over Europe."[26] The death of God signifies a great cultural revolution in the direction of atheistic secularism, a movement already begun but, as Nietzsche regularly insists, by no means completed.

This leads to the second question. Who are these "we" that have killed God by ceasing to believe in him. The question answers itself. They are "we" atheists, we who have stopped believing in God. This "we", of course, is not the whole of Europe, much less the whole human race. But Nietzsche is a kind of prophet, playing John the Baptist to his own version of Zarathustra's piety.[27] Just as John the Baptist and the New Testament writers present the crucified and risen Jesus as the Savior and Lord of all humanity, and just as many Western politicians, regardless of religion, present democracy and capitalism as the inevitable destiny of a fully globalized humanity, so Nietzsche prophesies the ultimate, universal kingdom of atheism. The New Testament writers claim that the long-promised messianic Kingdom of God has already been inaugurated in the death and resurrection of Jesus, though it has not yet been completed by the general resurrection, the final judgment, and the blessings of eternal life for the righteous; and on the basis of this event, in the middle of which we find ourselves, we should live in tune with the future that lies ahead thanks to what already lies behind. Similarly, Nietzsche announces the inbreaking of a kingdom free from God and urges his readers to live in the light of its ultimate but still awaited full realization.

Second, since, like Kierkegaard, Nietzsche views Europe as Christendom, the God of Jewish and Christian monotheism is his main target;[28] but he doesn't place any significance on the "o" that distinguishes the Platonic Good from the Christian God. As he sees it "Christianity is Platonism for 'the people.'"[29] He bemoans the fact that

> even we seekers after knowledge, we godless anti-metaphysicians still take our fire, too, from the flame lit by a faith that is thousands of years old, that Christian faith which was also the faith of Plato, that God is the truth, that truth is divine. – But what if this should become more and more incredible ... if God himself should prove to be our most enduring lie?[30]

What "God" signifies here is not just the personal God of the Jewish and Christian Bibles, but any eternal, transcendent, unconditioned reality to whose theoretical and practical norms everything temporal, worldly, and conditioned should conform.

Supporting and extending Nietzsche's analysis, Heidegger describes the death of God as the "deposing of the suprasensory ... The pronouncement 'God is dead' means: The suprasensory world is without effective power. It bestows no life."[31] But when God and the Church lose their authority (for "us"), secular modernity quickly finds replacements: conscience, reason, historical progress, the earthly happiness of the greatest number, creativity, and even business enterprise.[32] Heidegger is no Marxist, to be sure, but he sees the Market as one of the gods before whom secular modernity bows and to whom it builds temples. Before the Christian God there was Plato; and after the biblical Creator, Lawgiver, Judge, and Savior there are the many gods of secular modernity (served, it might be noted, by those who insist that God is still alive, who should see these gods as idols). The death of God for Nietzsche signifies the demise of all these stable, objectively given sources of normativity, grounds of the right and the good in human life.

As if anticipating Heidegger's list of new gods, Nietzsche calls attention to one of his own: scientific truth. Just before the passage cited above about how "we godless anti-metaphysicians" are still convinced that "truth is divine," Nietzsche says "that it is still a *metaphysical faith* upon which our faith in science rests."[33]

By science (*Wissenschaft*), Nietzsche does not mean just physics and chemistry. In his context all the academic disciplines are scientific. What he is challenging is epistemological objectivism in general, the view that "reason" can be free of particular presuppositions and thereby fully neutral and universal. Contrary to the hopes of the Enlightenment, our beliefs and practices cannot provide themselves with the guarantees they would like to have. Here we note an echo of Kierkegaard's "objective uncertainty" and the risk it involves. This puts Nietzsche and Kierkegaard in the company of those who, in the twentieth century, are sometimes called postmodern because they challenge the objectivism aspired to by philosophical modernity.

Third, Nietzsche notices the ambivalence the death of God is bound to generate, if and as it sinks in. On the one hand there will be a feeling of disorientation and homesickness, of darkness and gloom, and accordingly, a felt need for comfort. On the other hand there will be a new cheerfulness. The consequences "are not at all sad and gloomy but rather like a new and scarcely describable kind of light, happiness, relief, exhilaration, encouragement, dawn." The death of God represents "a new dawn ... at long last our ships may venture out again to face any danger ... the sea, *our* sea, lies open again; perhaps there has never yet been such an 'open sea'."[34] Just as Kierkegaardian faith has to pass through the possibility of offense to come into its own, so Nietzsche's atheism has to overcome the nostalgic need for the comfort and guidance provided by Plato's Good and the Christian God.

15.3 JEAN-PAUL SARTRE (1905–1980)

The death of God is as central to Sartre's thinking as it is to Nietzsche's. Like Kierkegaard and Nietzsche, he preaches to the choir. He does not so much try to prove God's unreality as he presupposes it and moves immediately to reflect on its significance. Also like Kierkegaard and Nietzsche, he thinks that his ontological commitments pose a much more urgent, personal challenge to those who share them than is usually realized. The issue, we might say, is fully existential.

Thus, his claim is not just that "God does not exist" but also "that we have to face all the consequences. The existentialist is strongly opposed to a certain kind of secular ethics [found among his choir members, no doubt – M. W.] which would like to abolish God with the least possible expense." So he opposes those secularists who discard God and then say:

> However, if we are to have a morality, a civil society, and a law-abiding world, it is essential that certain values be taken seriously; they must have an *a priori* existence ascribed to them. It must be considered mandatory *a priori* for people to be honest, not to lie, not to beat their wives ... [We must] show that such values exist all the same, and that they are inscribed in an intelligible heaven ... nothing will have changed if God does not exist; we will encounter the same standards.[35]

Over against this kind of thinking, Sartre writes:

> Existentialists, on the other hand, find it extremely disturbing that God no longer exists, for along with his disappearance goes the possibility of finding values in an intelligible heaven ... Dostoevsky once wrote: "If God does not exist, everything is permissible." This is the starting point of existentialism. Indeed, everything is permissible if God does not exist, and man is consequently abandoned, for he cannot find anything to rely on – neither within nor without. (*EH*, pp. 28–29)[36]

In speaking of this distress, it is as if Sartre is reminding us that when Nietzsche announced the death of God (through the madman and through Zarathustra), he called our attention to the darkness and disorientation this brought with it. He will articulate this distress in terms of anguish (*angoisse*; *Angst*), forlornness or abandonment, and despair (*EH*, pp. 25–38).

Sartre begins by noting that there are two kinds of existentialism, Christian and atheistic. Then he says that what they have in common is the belief that for human beings existence precedes essence. But it becomes immediately clear that the "they" who hold this in common are not these two kinds of existentialism but the atheistic existentialists. For what it would mean for essence to precede existence is for there to be a Creator who is guided in making us by an idea of who we are to be and how we are to live, just as an artisan who makes a paper-cutter is guided by an idea of what it is for. In each case the guiding idea is a normative essence. Knowing what the result *is* enables us to judge whether it is good or bad. A paper-cutter is good if it cuts paper well, not so good if it does so poorly, and an impostor posing as a paper-cutter if it doesn't do so at all. In the case of human beings created by God, the norms for our lives are already in the mind of God; our task is to *discover* them and to conform to them if we are to become who we already are.

But if God is dead in the comprehensive sense that Sartre shares with Nietzsche, then we have no normative essence that precedes our existence. Rather,

> man first of all exists: he materializes in the world, encounters himself, and only afterward defines himself ... He will not be anything until later, and then he will be what he makes of himself. Thus, there is no human nature since there is no God to conceive of it. Man is not only that which he conceives himself to be, but that which he wills himself to be. (*EH*, p. 22)

In other words, values and norms for human life are not "out there" to be *discovered*; they are to be *invented*, created by the choices in which we give ourselves an identity. Sartre is not denying that there are any universal features to human persons. Bodies, temporality, subjectivity, and intersubjectivity, for example, could be described in the language of human nature or essence. But in Sartrean language such features signify only the human condition and the limits inherent in it. Since Plato and Aristotle, the concepts of nature and essence have been inherently normative, and it is in this sense that Sartrean atheism insists that existence precedes essence.

This entails a radical freedom. It is not just that Sartre affirms freedom of the will over against scientific or metaphysical determinism, as Kierkegaard does and Nietzsche does not. His point is that we are free to exercise such freedom free of all normative constraints. There is no normative truth that we ought to discover and to which we ought to conform. The only values are those we choose. We are "condemned to be free" (*EH*, p. 29). Here we hear again the ambiguity to which Nietzsche points. On the darker side, this involves an enormous burden of responsibility without any guidance or guarantees; hence the anguish, forlornness, and despair of which Sartre speaks. On the brighter side, we are free from God and the Good and any Reason that would tell us who we are and how we should live prior to our choosing how to answer those questions.

Sartre makes two perplexing claims about these radically free choices. The first is that in choosing I not only make myself but also choose for all others and "create an image of man as [I] think he ought to be ... We always choose the good, and nothing can be good for us unless it is good for all" (*EH*, p. 24). But why is this? If there were some reason independent of my choice that I ought to make this choice rather than that one, my choice might implicate all the others. But in that case there would be an essence that precedes existence. If there is no such reason or ground, why should he think everyone should be like himself? His groundless choice for, say, left-wing politics would seem to leave me free, even in his own mind, to be a fascist or a capitalist, just as his preference for coffee ice cream, for which there is no antecedent reason, leaves me free to prefer chocolate. Is this moral universalism a residue of a Platonism, a Christianity, or a Kantianism he purports to have left behind?

The second puzzling claim Sartre makes is that our self-defining choices are not arbitrary and capricious. This is really the same issue in a different form. Of course it is not arbitrary *that* we choose. We are condemned to be free, and even the attempt to avoid choosing is a way of choosing. But the question concerns *what* we choose. Sartre says our choices are not arbitrary, because we do make moral judgments. But those judgments are grounded in our choices and cannot make those choices themselves non-arbitrary. He says that if someone asks him, "'What if I want to be in bad faith?' I'll answer, 'There's no reason why you should not be, but I declare that you are, and that a strictly consistent attitude alone demonstrates good faith'" (*EH*, p. 48). To which a seemingly Sartrean reply might well be, "Your saying that that's what I am has no force on your own grounds, for I *am* only what *I choose* to be, and I choose to be in bad faith. In any case, why should I be coherent? Are you Kant in disguise?" Here, as occasionally in Nietzsche, it looks as if honesty is the one value the two thinkers treat as a priori.

Though the Sartrean self does not exist, like Kierkegaard's, "before God," it is anything but alone. It is constantly exposed to the gaze of human others, and it experiences "the Look" in fear, pride, and shame – especially shame. The Look limits my freedom to define myself, for "the Other teaches me who I am."[37] God, as the infinite self, would be the greatest threat to my freedom, so I become the desire to be God myself, the absolute self who defines others before they can define me.

The desire to be God has dramatic import for my relations with human others. Sartre sees these as falling into two strategies for defending my freedom by neutralizing that of the Other: masochism and sadism. These strategies function not only as forms of sexual desire but beyond that as metaphors for all human intersubjectivity, which becomes the war of all against all. In masochistic relations I do not deny the subjectivity of the other outright but rather seek to possess, to own and control it for myself so that the Other's "freedom" becomes a means to my ends. *Sexual seduction* is the graphic image of many everyday modes of intersubjectivity. By contrast, sadistic relations are the attempt to deny – even to destroy – the subjectivity of the Other through various means of objectification. In this case it is *sexual violence* that becomes the graphic image of many everyday modes of intersubjectivity.[38]

Sartre does not speak here of sin, but he can be read as a secular theologian of original sin. For, on the one hand, he sees all human behavior as radically self-centered. On the other hand, despite the claim to radical freedom, he sees our desire to be God, the absolute self, as given, not as something we might or might not choose. In a haunting footnote he writes, "These considerations do not exclude the possibility of an ethics of deliverance and salvation. But this can be achieved only after a radical conversion which we cannot discuss here."[39]

15.4 GABRIEL MARCEL (1889–1973)

Marcel takes umbrage at this account. "I do not believe that in the whole history of human thought, grace, even in its most secularised forms, has ever been denied with such audacity and such impudence."[40] Not that the phenomena Sartre describes are fictions. Of Sartre's analysis of the Look Marcel writes, "There is perhaps nothing more remarkable in the whole of Sartre's work than his phenomenological study of the 'other' as looking and of himself as exposed," responding in fear, pride, or shame.[41] It is just that for Marcel there is more to the story.

Since he is a phenomenologist rather than a theologian, Marcel does not turn immediately to questions of salvation, conversion, and grace. He rather seeks to describe dimensions of human existence that Sartre has left out. Experience, he argues, is best understood as encounter and exposure. Sometimes we find that our response to encounter with others can be described as receptivity, welcome, hospitality, giving, active opening of ourselves, sympathy and sharing with thc other – and to sum it all up, as love. At the end of the essay in which he points to such phenomena, Marcel refers to God as the absolute thou whom we might invoke in prayer. This is not the conclusion of a logical inference but a hint, a hypothesis that in such moments of human intersubjectivity God may somehow be present.[42]

In another essay he explores three things we might say. "You belong to me" can mean that you are at my disposal and I can dispose of you at will. "I belong to myself" can be an act of defiant self-deification. Though he doesn't explicitly mention Sartre here, the reader will have no trouble recognizing these two modes of saying self and other as fitting easily into Sartre's account. But Marcel mentions a third possibility: "I belong to you." Here is a disposability of another kind. I am at your disposal. I can still make the first two statements, but if I place them in the context of the third, they will have a completely different meaning. Once again God is barely mentioned, but Marcel notes that we can genuinely admire others only if we have qualified the first two assertions by the third. If that other were God we would speak not of admiration but of adoration. So once again a hint: we do sometimes admire others, and perhaps this signifies an openness to a God whom we need not kill in order to be ourselves.[43]

Marcel's ethics is quite simple. "I must somehow make room for the other in myself."[44] It is a religious ethic insofar as God is the ultimate other for whom I must make room. But Marcel is not in a hurry to tie either this "must" to a divine command or this "somehow" to divine grace. He is content to "make room" for these possibilities and thereby offer a possible alternative to Sartrean despair.

Our four major existentialists form two pairs. Kierkegaard and Nietzsche on the one hand, and Sartre and Marcel on the other, can fruitfully be read as in dialogue and debate with each other about what it means to be most fully human.

NOTES

1. *Gorgias* 500c; emphasis added.
2. Kierkegaard, *The Journals of Kierkegaard*, pp. 44–45.
3. Hegel, *Philosophy of Right*, p. 11 (from the Preface).
4. Without going into the special problems raised by the fact that some of Kierkegaard's most important works are pseudonymous, I shall use "Kierkegaard" to signify the one who presents various interpretations of the religious stage to us for our consideration, sometimes pseudonymously and sometimes in his own name. For more on this issue, see Chapter 4 of this *Companion*.
5. Kierkegaard's account of religiousness A in *Concluding Unscientific Postscript* is an exception. It spells out the kind of religion available to, say, Socrates, without the benefit of biblical revelation. Another important exception comes in *Works of Love*, where Kierkegaard argues that genuine *faith*, which occurs in hidden inwardness, manifests itself outwardly in works of *love*.
6. Kierkegaard, *Fear and Trembling*, pp. 50–51.

7. For an illuminating account of God as speaker, with special reference to promises and commands (but not to Kierkegaard), see Wolterstorff, *Divine Discourse.*
8. Ferreira, *Love's Grateful Striving,* nicely translates the intertwining of trust and obedience in terms of grateful striving.
9. Especially in *Sickness unto Death, Philosophical Fragments, Practice in Christianity,* and *Works of Love.*
10. Kierkegaard, *Practice in Christianity,* p. 81. In a note Kierkegaard claims that the genuine opposites of faith are not doubt, but despair and offense, which are the responses of persons, not just of intellects. In *Sickness unto Death,* despair becomes the thematic focus.
11. Kierkegaard, *Philosophical Fragments,* p. 52. An example: if one side in the debate between pro-life and pro-choice views of abortion (1) noted the incompatibility of the two positions and (2) called its own position "Reason," that would hardly settle the debate between the two sides.
12. *Phaedrus* 244 d. Cf. Kierkegaard, *Fear and Trembling,* p. 56.
13. Kierkegaard, *Philosophical Fragments,* pp. 49–54. Cf. the first two chapters of 1 Corinthians.
14. Kierkegaard, *Fear and Trembling,* pp. 64–79. Kierkegaard shares with Kant and the British empiricists the view that human reason is finite in its powers. That Abraham would get Isaac back in this life is not part of the story in Genesis 22, but see Hebrews 11:17–19 in relation to vv. 8–12. The fallibility of stockbrokers is especially evident as this is being written, in the midst of the worst economic crisis since the Great Depression.
15. Whether the laws and customs of Abraham's (nomadic) society forbade or permitted child sacrifice is not the question here. Kierkegaard makes that assumption in order to make his point about the relation of biblical faith to any human social order.
16. Kierkegaard, *Fear and Trembling,* pp. 97–98.
17. Kierkegaard develops the significance of sin in the epistemic domain especially in *Philosophical Fragments,* while he develops the significance of sin in identity formation especially in *Sickness unto Death.*
18. Including but by no means limited to *Sickness unto Death, Philosophical Fragments, Practice in Christianity, Concluding Unscientific Postscript,* and *Works of Love.*
19. Kierkegaard, *Concluding Unscientific Postscript,* pp. 171–72; his italics.
20. This does not mean that we simply choose what to believe in the way we choose what clothes to wear in the morning. On the other hand, our choices make a difference in what we believe. See Evans, "Does Kierkegaard Think Beliefs Can Be Directly Willed?"

21. Nietzsche, *Thus Spoke Zarathustra*, pp. 13, 40, 287.
22. More specifically, anti-theistic and anti-Christian. For Nietzsche's alternative "piety," see Benson, *Pious Nietzsche.*
23. Alternatively, one might say that their comprehensive interpretations of human existence are their "arguments" for and against God's reality. But there is nothing syllogistic about such "proofs." As existentialists they think that kind of proof is neither possible nor appropriate in this domain.
24. On Nietzsche's perspectivist view of truth, see Nietzsche, *Philosophy and Truth*, and Clark, *Nietzsche on Truth and Philosophy.*
25. Nietzsche, *The Gay Science* III, section 125.
26. Nietzsche, *The Gay Science* V, section 343.
27. See Nietzsche, *Thus Spoke Zarathustra.*
28. Nietzsche seems at times to be playing up to Christian anti-Semites, but he is playing with them. After saying nasty things about the Jews, he calls attention (as do biblical scholars today) to the essential link between Christianity and Jewish monotheism. See, for example, *On the Genealogy of Morals*, First Essay.
29. Nietzsche, *Beyond Good and Evil*, Preface.
30. Nietzsche, *The Gay Science* V, section 344.
31. Heidegger, "The Word of Nietzsche," pp. 54, 61.
32. Heidegger, "The Word of Nietzsche," p. 64.
33. Nietzsche, *The Gay Science* V, section 344. Nietzsche develops this critique of secular modernity in greater detail in *On the Genealogy of Morals* III, sections 23–27.
34. Nietzsche, *The Gay Science* V, sections 124–25, 343.
35. Sartre, *Existentialism is a Humanism*, p. 28. Henceforth cited in the text as *EH*. The reference to a priori values and to a heaven of ideas suggests that along with the Creator God of the Bible, Kant's pure practical reason and Plato's Good are among the gods who have died.
36. Of course it was not Dostoevsky who said that. It was one of his characters, Ivan Karamazov.
37. Sartre, *Being and Nothingness*, p. 274
38. See Sartre, *Being and Nothingness*, pp. 361–412 ("Concrete Relations with Others").
39. Sartre, *Being and Nothingness*, p. 412.
40. Marcel, *The Philosophy of Existentialism*, p. 79.
41. Marcel, *The Philosophy of Existentialism*, p. 71.
42. Marcel, *Creative Fidelity*, ch. 1.
43. Marcel, *Creative Fidelity*, ch. 2.
44. Marcel, *Creative Fidelity*, p. 88.

ROBERT BERNASCONI

16 Racism is a system: how existentialism became dialectical in Fanon and Sartre

In the United States of America today, as in many other places, there is a tendency to locate racism primarily in the mind: one is racist only if one thinks racist thoughts. This means that because speech is thought to be the only clear proof of what someone is thinking, one can only be called a racist if one says something explicitly racist. The result is that the fight against racism has been largely reduced to the policing of racist language by the media. Meanwhile, less and less attention is given to addressing the question of whether the continuing massive differences in education, health, wealth, as well as educational and other opportunities – not just in the United States, but above all globally – are a perpetuation of past racisms in the present, a perpetuation which would call into question our commitment to the eradication of racism. We hear much less than we once did about institutional, structural, or systemic racism. For example, segregation in the schools, which was once unambiguously racist when sustained by laws, is tolerated when the segregation becomes merely de facto. Because the culture of the United States is dominated by individualism and legalism, the effects of past racisms that survive intact within the system are rendered virtually invisible because nobody is willing to own them or take responsibility for them: the problem is said to be non-imputable. This same culture appears to be spreading, so this is far from being a localized problem.

In this context there is still much to be learned from the analyses of Jean-Paul Sartre and Frantz Fanon, who both used the resources of existentialism in their struggle against colonialism to expose a systemic racism that transcends individual actions. What began in their work as phenomenological accounts of the experience of anti-Semitism and racism, became, as a result of what they learned in the course of their active attempts to combat racism, a critique of the racist structures of society that remains unsurpassed, albeit, relatively speaking, largely neglected. Their early phenomenological accounts showed how oppressed racial minorities find their identities in the experience of being seen as raced, and these are far from forgotten: they are central to the philosophical movement known today as critical philosophy of race. But the descriptions are largely understood as accounts of individual experience, with insufficient attention being given to the important role social structures play in shaping those experiences. Sartre's *Anti-Semite and Jew* and "Black Orpheus" did not neglect the societal dimension of racism, and that is even more true of Fanon's *Black Skin, White Masks,* but it has not been the focus of how these early works have been read. Furthermore, although Fanon's *Black Skin, White Masks* is now finally recognized as an existentialist classic, his later book, *The Wretched of the Earth,* is largely read only for its account of violence.

And yet it is only in those parts of *The Wretched of the Earth* that Fanon completed last that he fully addressed the problem already identified in *Black Skin, White Masks* and began to frame an adequate response to it. Similarly, many readers of *Anti-Semite and Jew* are unaware, for example, of the revision that the account given there undergoes in *Critique of Dialectical Reason* on precisely this point. Part of the explanation for the neglect of Sartre's account of racism and Fanon's response to it in *The Wretched of the Earth* lies simply in the sheer difficulty of the *Critique* as a whole. It is the aim of the present essay to make Sartre's mature account of racism more accessible and to show that it, together with *The Wretched of the Earth,* represents a continuation of existential philosophy, a philosophy rooted in experience, directed toward the concrete, and committed to freedom.

The idea that post-war existentialism can and should be seen as a political movement directed against the ills of society is foreign to many people, particularly in the English-speaking world, where existentialism is tied to the image of the self-obsessed adolescent ruminating over the question of the absurdity of existence. People tend to forget that *Being and Nothingness,* with its account of freedom as responsibility,[1] was conceived by Sartre in a prisoner-of-war camp and published while the Nazis were still occupying France.

And even more importantly in this context, people are also all too ready to ignore the way that existentialism in the 1950s was shaped not just by the Cold War, but also by wars of liberation fought by colonized peoples. In this essay I argue that the fight against racism and colonialism shaped the development of this central branch of existential philosophy in the 1950s. The importance of this context would not be news to philosophers in Africa and other parts of the so-called Third World, where Sartre never went out of fashion and where Fanon was early acknowledged as an important thinker, but this story has still not been fully integrated into the history of existentialism as it is told in Europe and North America.

After briefly rehearsing the better-known part of the story, where Fanon in *Black Skin, White Masks* takes up the tools supplied by Sartre only to turn them against the master, I will highlight their remarkable convergence toward the end of Fanon's life. Fanon's reservations about Sartre's "Black Orpheus" are much debated, as is Sartre's praise for Fanon's *The Wretched of the Earth* in his Preface to the book, but what happened in the intervening period is less well known, and parts of the story may always be unclear. We should certainly not exclude the possibility that Sartre was influenced by Fanon's *Black Skin, White Masks*, but as there is, so far as I am aware, no clear indication that Sartre ever read the book, let alone read it early, I have chosen not to assume that he must have done so, although it would not be surprising if he had.[2] However, as we do have evidence of Fanon's admiration for Sartre's *Critique of Dialectical Reason* I will explore that connection here, particularly as Fanon's relation to that book has received much less attention than it deserves. Apparently when already suffering from leukemia, he visited the Algerian–Tunisian border to meet with FLN combatants engaged in fighting the French colonists and spoke to them about, among other things, the importance of Sartre's book.[3] One goal of the present essay is to help clarify why Fanon might have responded to the *Critique of Dialectical Reason* so positively, as well as to investigate what reservations he might nevertheless have developed.

Fanon's early critique of Sartre is largely to be found in "The Lived Experience of the Black," which with minor changes became the fifth chapter of *Black Skin, White Masks*.[4] In *Being and Nothingness* Sartre had famously described how the gaze of another can strip me of my transcendence or subjectivity, as in the famous example of being caught looking through a keyhole.[5] Sartre employed this figure of the objectifying gaze in a number of works that followed, including his existential studies of Baudelaire and Genet.[6] In *Anti-Semite and Jew* he proposed that it was the anti-Semitic gaze which makes the Jew as such.[7] Sartre himself later acknowledged in response to critics that he was wrong to ignore how Jews received their self-understanding more from their own history and traditions than from anti-Semites.[8] But there was another troubling feature of the account: the fact that anti-Semitism had apparently left the Jews without any good options other than to await a classless society, which as such would have no place for anti-Semitism (*AS*, p. 149).

Fanon was impressed by Sartre's phenomenological description of anti-Semitism in *Anti-Semite and Jew*: it presented him with a rich philosophical framework within which to examine his own experiences when, arriving in France from Martinique, he found that he was always seen first and foremost as a Black man. With explicit reference to Sartre's account of anti-Semitism, Fanon declared: "It is the racist who creates the inferiorized."[9] To be sure, Fanon's primary concern at this point was neither with trying to develop a positive account of his racial identity, nor with offering a description of the lived experience of racism. The question was how to live authentically in such a society. It was the question that Sartre raised at the end of *Anti-Semite and Jew*, albeit without addressing it satisfactorily. Fanon's comment that Sartre's account of anti-Semitism in *Anti-Semite and Jew* was among the most powerful texts he had ever read, and that parts of it moved him to his core (*BSWM*, p. 158), did not relate to Sartre's proposed solution for the Jews but to their dilemma in a hostile society. These are among the lines about Jews that Fanon quoted from Sartre with admiration:

> His life is nothing but a long flight from others and from himself. He has been alienated even from his own body; his emotional life has been cut in two; he has been reduced to pursuing the impossible dream of universal brotherhood in a world that rejects him. (*AS*, p. 136; quoted *BSWM*, p. 159n.)

Fanon recognized himself in this description.

Fanon's problems with Sartre seem to have begun when he examined Sartre's attempt in "Black Orpheus" to develop an account of how Blacks should respond to this situation. "Black Orpheus" should not be read in isolation from the anthology of the so-called negritude poets to which it was the Preface.[10] In fact, Fanon's question of how to respond to the everyday racism suffered by a Black person living in France was addressed, not just to Sartre's Preface, but to the whole volume of poetry, especially the poems of Aimé Césaire and Leopold Sédar Senghor. Fanon was at least as critical of Senghor for being backward looking as he was critical of Sartre for closing off the future by determining it in advance, which was how Fanon saw Sartre's claim that negritude must renounce itself for the sake of a future universalism. Sartre argued that "Negritude is dialectical," by which he meant it was only a stage Blacks had to go through, and, in an unmistakable echo of the resolution offered at the end of *Anti-Semite and Jew*, that its surpassing was necessary to bring about a classless society.[11] He did not impose this idea dogmatically from outside the negritude movement. He was able to cite a line of the poetry included in the volume by a Black Communist, Jacques Roumain, which read: "I want to be only of your race / peasant workers of all countries."[12] But as Fanon pointed out there are many Black voices to choose from (*BSWM*, p. 115). The implication was that Sartre had to answer for his interpretation.

Fanon's main objection was that by placing the racial identity of Blacks within a dialectic, Sartre had already looked beyond the concrete moment in history in which they were living. The objection was not to dialectical reason as such, which neither of them seems to have had a good understanding of at this point, in spite of the frequency of references to dialectic in the works of both of them. Fanon's objection was that Sartre had used the dialectic to revert to a kind of Hegelianism that devalued and lost sight of concrete experience. His point was not that Sartre was wrong, but that he, Fanon, "needed not to know" (*BSWM*, p. 114): "Consciousness committed to experience knows nothing, has to know nothing, of the essence and determination of its being" (*BSWM*, p. 113). In effect, Fanon was complaining that Sartre had lost sight of existential philosophy. Fanon was presenting himself as a better existentialist than Sartre. And there was another point: Sartre, in the process of trying to appropriate the poetry of Césaire and Senghor for his political philosophy, had distorted the Black experience in a way that no Black person could. Fanon's famous line is that Sartre had forgotten how Blacks suffer in their bodies. Of course, in reality he could forget the experience only because he never truly knew it in the first place (*BSWM*, p. 117). In the course of criticizing Sartre, Fanon had identified with precision at least one aspect of what separates Blacks from Whites within a racist society: the fact that they experienced racism in their bodies in a way that those not targeted would never fully understand.[13]

Sartre's evocation of the dialectic in "Black Orpheus" was a fiasco because he did not yet have a clear understanding of its operation. Fanon was right to call him on this point. However, during the 1950s Sartre developed a notion of the dialectic that was not only compatible with existentialism, but also, he argued, necessary if existentialism was to fulfill its ambition of being a philosophy of the concrete. His starting point was an account of the limitations of analytic reason, which was already clearly articulated in *Anti-Semite and Jew* when he identified in bourgeois universalism an "analytic spirit" that "resolves all collectivities into individual elements" (*AS*, p. 55). He made a similar point at the beginning of *Search for a Method*, where he blamed the bourgeois analytic spirit of Cartesianism for its atomization of the Proletariat, even while acknowledging its role in undermining the *ancien régime*.[14] In other words, Sartre's view was that analysis had played a liberatory role but that that role was now played out and it had become reactionary. Similarly, on Sartre's account bourgeois universalism is not the corrective of racism but rather racism takes new forms to compensate for the universalism.[15] So, for example, it is only when the slaves are freed in the United States and thus become eligible for the rights that belong to citizens that certain racists decide that they are not human and write books with titles like Charles Carroll's *The Negro a Beast*. At another time and in other circumstances it might have been different, but then and there Sartre was against dissolving concrete collectivities within the category of the human. He objected that the analytic spirit "recognizes neither Jews, nor Arab, nor Negro, nor bourgeois, nor worker, but only man – man always the same in all times and all places" (*AS*, p. 55). Echoing Joseph de Maistre, Sartre wrote "*man* does not exist; there are Jews, Protestants, Catholics; there are Frenchmen, Englishmen, Germans; there are whites, blacks, yellows" (*AS*, pp. 144–45).[16]

Another feature of the analytic spirit that Sartre attacked in *Anti-Semite and Jew* was its tendency to see anti-Semitism – and thus also racism – as one idea among many. He believed that one should not try to separate the racist or anti-Semitic ideas of someone from their other opinions and indeed from other aspects of their character (*AS*, p. 8). Racism and anti-Semitism pervade every aspect of a person's life. The anti-Semitism of the anti-Semite belongs to a "syncretic totality" in the sense that it extends to all aspects of a person and to their conception of the world (*AS*, pp. 10, 17). Hence anti-Semitism was not one opinion among many: "I refuse to characterize as opinion a doctrine that is aimed directly at particular persons and that seeks to suppress their rights or to exterminate them" (*AS*, p. 9). This is important, because, as I will show, the denial that anti-Semitism and racism can be classified as opinions is the starting point for the account Sartre gives of them later in *Critique of Dialectical Reason*.

Already when he wrote *Anti-Semite and Jew* Sartre concluded that because anti-Semitism is not an opinion it is useless to combat it by education or legal interdictions (*AS*, pp. 10, 147). His account of the way forward relies heavily on the existentialist notion of the situation. Recalling the account of freedom in *Being and Nothingness*, Sartre wrote that anti-Semitism "is a total choice that a man in a situation makes of himself and of the meaning of the universe" (*AS*, p. 148). He concluded that the only way to battle anti-Semitism was to change the situation that produced the perspective from which someone chooses anti-Semitism: "Thus we do not attack freedom, but bring it about that freedom decides on other bases, and in terms of other structures" (*AS*, p. 148). The limitations of this account arc obvious, particularly if one broadens the focus to racism and understands the situation in terms of colonialism. One needs more than a will to change the situation when the racist not only has an ideology to support it but also an economic interest in maintaining it. This is why the struggle against colonialism was the occasion for existential philosophy to develop new philosophical tools.

Fanon took the first steps in *Black Skin, White Masks* at a time when Sartre, in discussions of the class struggle in France, still relied on the concept of situation at crucial moments in his argument.[17] The transformation of human existence that would be necessary to change the situation would need, as Fanon recognized, to be predicated on a "restructuring of the world" (*BSWM*, p. 63). The gaze was only a symptom. In the context of a discussion of Octave Mannoni's *Prospero and Caliban*, Fanon already argued that an understanding of "the colonial situation" (*BSWM*, p. 74) calls for a structural account of racism. He criticized Mannoni's attempt to think of racism as "the work of petty officials."[18] A place like South Africa has "a racist structure" (*BSWM*, p. 68). The same is true of France, which is a racist country where the racism is located in the collective unconscious (*BSWM*, p. 72). Furthermore, in the same place, again against Mannoni, Fanon insisted that colonial racism is the same as racism everywhere: "all forms of exploitation are the same" (*BSWM*, p. 69). The shift in focus away from the individual to society not only is important to Fanon in his argument concerning the limitations of Freudian psychoanalysis (*BSWM*, p. xv); it is also central to the very project of *Black Skin, White Masks* (*BSWM*, pp. 84–85). This is what forces the shift from situation to structure and his attempt to show that "the real source of the conflict" lies not in individuals as such but in social structures (*BSWM*, p. 80).

Although Fanon had already presented an account of colonization in terms of structure in 1952, it was not until 1956 that a similar depth of insight can be found in Sartre in a speech that was subsequently published under the title "Colonialism is a System." It is no longer the gaze of the Other that fabricates identities, but the rigor of the system introduced by the French Republic. It fabricates "the indigenous" and colonists through the functions and interests it imposes on them (*CN*, pp. 41, 44). Under these conditions, "the purest of intentions, if conceived within this infernal circle, is corrupted at once" (*CN*, p. 31), albeit Sartre exempts minor public officials and European workers who are "at the same time innocent victims and beneficiaries of the system" (*CN*, p. 32n.). Fanon was not so forgiving of Whites who, as he saw it, shirked their responsibility (*BSWM*, pp. 84–85), and he quoted Sartre in support of his view. Fanon included in the lengthy citation from *Anti-Semite and Jew* that I referred to earlier that "there is not one of us who is not totally guilty and even criminal; the Jewish blood that the Nazis shed falls on all our heads" (*AS*, p. 136). This is in keeping with Sartre's insistence in *Being and Nothingness* that the responsibility that derives from his existentialist conception of freedom means that I am responsible for everything except for the fact that I am responsible.[19]

In any event, Sartre took the decisive step not in "Colonialism is a System" but in a brief review of Albert Memmi's *The Colonizer and the Colonized* in the following year, 1957, insofar as it was there that Sartre thematized the shift in his view of racism.[20] Memmi's book provides a brilliant description of the colonial situation from the point of view of experience, specifically the experience of an Arab Jew in Tunisia. Memmi identified the privileges of the colonizer that accrue to them whether they want them or not. He highlighted their standard of living, which was better than they would have in their home countries. While all people in the so-called developed world benefit from low wages in the Third World, the benefits are even greater for those who have gone there. Nevertheless, these privileges which are not chosen and are simply lived give rise to attitudes that constitute "colonial racism." Memmi contrasted it with the doctrinal racism of Europeans who develop racist theories at a distance.[21] It is perhaps not surprising that Sartre latched onto its central idea that "colonization fabricates the colonized as it fabricates the colonizers,"[22] as it sounds so very Sartrean, but his response was revealing: "he [Memmi] sees a situation where I see a system" (*CN*, p. 51n.). Or, as Sartre put it in the *Critique of Dialectical Reason*, the colonized "was produced by the colonial system."[23] If one can say that Fanon had criticized Sartre for not being Sartrean enough, Sartre attacked Memmi for being too Sartrean, or, more precisely, Sartrean according to the old style. Sartre was announcing a development in his thinking in the context of the fight against colonialist racism as a system.

Sartrc fully recognized that the integration of a notion of system into a framework that was purportedly existentialist would present a challenge to some of his readers, particularly those whose idea of existentialism was shaped by Søren Kierkegaard, whose rejection of the Hegelian system was legendary. Sartre tried to address such qualms in *Search for a Method*, which proclaims the marriage of existentialism to Marxism.[24] More important here than any internal dispute among existentialists is Sartre's advocacy of dialectical reason, which can be seen as a consequence of the rejection of the analytic spirit that was already pervasive throughout *Anti-Semite and Jew*. This is not to be confused with the rejection of analytic reason.

Sartre was clear that analytic reason was an indispensable moment within dialectical reason, but insufficient on its own (*CDR*, p. 93).

Although the term "dialectical" sounds somewhat daunting and might even evoke ideas of mechanical necessity, Sartre used the word to refer to something familiar to everyone: the fact that the actions of individuals and groups receive their intelligibility from an objective, albeit one that is not usually set at the level of thought but of practice. In particular, as he put it toward the end of the *Critique*, the dialectic reveals itself in "the practical consciousness of an oppressed class struggling against its oppressor, is a reaction which is produced in the oppressed by the divisive tendency of oppression – but not at any arbitrary time or place" (*CDR*, p. 803). It is a reaction, but not just any reaction. It is a transformative reaction, a transcendence whose intelligibility derives from the fact that the pursuit of the objective takes place within an inherited system of relations which it modifies. This helps to explain why Sartre preferred the term "system" to "structure" and why we would do better to understand him as presenting an account of what I call "systemic racism" than of "structural racism," although it is also true that he employs the word "structure" with great frequency in the *Critique*. But he insisted there that "structure" lends itself to analytic rationality and tends to convey the sense of an external or even alien framework, whereas with the notion of "system" he wanted to direct us to the whole, a relational whole to which we belong and in which we participate, and which is only accessible to dialectical reason (*CDR*, pp. 498–504).

Sartre confronted the standard account of racism directly in a long footnote in *Critique of Dialectical Reason* from which Fanon quoted in *The Wretched of the Earth*.[25] His major claim was that "the essence of racism" is not a system of thought or even a thought at all (*CDR*, p. 300n.). Race laws, as well as racist doctrines and racist remarks, are mere symptoms of something deeper that is produced by the colonial system: "racism is a passive constitution in things before being an ideology" (*CDR*, p. 739). At first sight it might be hard to reconcile that formulation with Sartre's association of racism with the Idea, even though he alerts us that he is not returning to Hegel but rather to Marx's reworking of Hegel (*CDR*, p. 171n.). In fact his explanation of "the Idea" is based on his reading of Ferdinand Braudel's account of Spain's exploitation of the gold mines in Peru in his classic historical study *The Mediterranean and the Mediterranean World in the Age of Philip II*. Sartre learned from Braudel that gold as materiality "transforms human praxis into *antipraxis*, that is to say, into a *praxis without an author*" (*CDR*, p. 166).[26] The phrase needs some unpacking, but I introduce it to distance Sartre from the kind of social constructionism that is often attributed to him by some of the more prominent exponents of that position.[27] Sartre did not think of gold coins as "an invention of the mind," but as "a petrification of action," which he also called "the practico-inert." The point is that the gold produced its own Idea through the actions that it provoked, which actions subsequently came to reverberate through it (*CDR*, p. 171). Again, this does not mean that it has an existence only in thought. Sartre said of the Idea that it "has the materiality of a fact because no one thinks it" (*CDR*, p. 301n.).

Sartre presented colonization as a practico-inert field just like the world of gold coins: past actions have contributed to make the colony and its people appear to the colonizers as a land of opportunity. Hence he used the phrase "practico-inert system" (*CDR*, p. 720) to describe a system in which "the activity of others" is embedded "in so far as it is sustained and diverted by inorganic inertia" (*CDR*, p. 556). Even though the colonists are constantly competing against each other to see who can make the most of the opportunity, the success of any one of them depends on all of them recognizing that they have a common interest, which involves not only keeping the indigenous population down and maintaining their difference from them, but also seeing that population in a way that legitimates their exploitation. In other words, they must be seen as subhuman. It is in this way that colonialism takes on a life of its own and gives rise to a theoretical racism.

This helps us understand what Sartre meant when he wrote of colonialism that it produces its own Idea as Other, an idea that remains "an Idea of stone" whose "strength derives from its ubiquity of absence" (*CDR*, p. 300n.). The phrase "the Idea of stone" is best explained with reference to the review of Memmi's book, where Sartre explained that the racist dehumanization of the oppressed that is necessary for the persistence of the system leads inextricably to the dehumanization of the oppressor. Racism is an implicit affirmation of the humanity of the other because, as Sartre always insisted, to treat a man like a dog one must first consider him "as a man." It is only by being rigid and refusing humanity in oneself that one can continue to deny it to the oppressed: "as they deny it [humanity] to others, they find it everywhere like an enemy force. To escape from this, they must harden, give themselves an opaque consistency and impermeability of stone; in short they in turn must dehumanize themselves" (*CN*, pp. 52–53). This is the "pitiless reciprocity" of the colonial system. Fanon would have agreed. He also employed the notion of reciprocity, for example in an effort to explain the escalation of violence as colonizer and colonized respond to each other: "The violence of the colonized regime and the counterviolence of the colonized balance each other and respond to each other in an extraordinary reciprocal homogeneity" (*WE*, p. 46).

The violence that the colonized direct against each other in a "very real collective self-destruction" (*WE*, pp. 17–18) must also be understood dialectically, even though insight into a group's self-destruction had been prepared for earlier in *Black Skin, White Masks* under the label "a reactional phenomenon" (*BSWM*, p. 160). Fanon again generously attributed an understanding of this phenomenon to Sartre, although with a reference this time not to *Anti-Semite and Jew*, but to the novel *The Reprieve*, which Fanon understood to show that "in reaction against anti-Semitism, the Jew [in this case Birnenschatz] becomes an anti-Semite" (*BSWM*, p. 160).[28] According to Fanon, "the black man's first action is a reaction" (*BSWM*, p. 19). Reaction is a theme he returned to in the final paragraphs of the penultimate chapter when he attempted to point the way forward: "To induce man to be *actional*, by maintaining in his circularity the respect of the fundamental values that make the world human, that is the task of ultimate urgency for he who, after careful reflection, prepares to act" (*BSWM*, p. 197).

If one wants to locate a direct impact of Fanon on the writing of the *Critique of Dialectical Reason*, it might as well be located here, where Sartre's rich account of the internalization of racism seems to reflect Fanon's rich account of Black experience. Sartre had already introduced the idea of the inferiority complex into his account of freedom in *Being and Nothingness*,[29] and of the Jew in *Anti-Semite and Jew* (*AS*, p. 94), so he would have been receptive to Fanon's appropriation of the term throughout *Black Skin, White*

Masks, even if one can also understand Fanon's challenge to the suggestion that one makes oneself inferior. The suggestion that one is "inferiorized" (*BSWM*, p. 127) is perhaps intended, among other things, as a criticism of Sartre's conception of freedom. However, in the *Critique* Sartre abandoned his account of anti-Semitism in terms of the *idea* of the Jew (*AS*, p. 17) in order to present being-Jewish as what he called "a serial unity" (*CDR*, p. 267). That is to say, one's internalization of being-Jewish takes the form of a responsibility for all other Jews in such a way that there is a "perpetual being-outside-themselves-in-the-other" (*CDR*, p. 268). Sartre explained that this meant that if anti-Semites target Jews for getting all the best jobs, then every Jew with a good job comes to see the other Jews with good jobs as dispensable. So each Jew sees the other Jews as the problem getting in the way of his or her acceptance in society, much as, following Sartre's famous example of seriality, the people who arrive at a bus stop ahead of me are potentially an obstacle to my getting on the next bus (*CDR*, pp. 256–67). Sartre highlighted this analysis as one which helped to differentiate his approach from that of a standard Marxist analysis: there are no forces organizing this state of affairs that resist transformation but rather a resistance in matter itself that, since *Being and Nothingness*, Sartre, borrowing a phrase from Gaston Bachelard's critique of phenomenology, had called the coefficient of adversity in objects.[30] Whether Sartre knew it at this stage, Fanon had contributed a rich understanding of the experienc e of racism that illuminated this account because it highlights how society's racism makes one reactional.

Sartre's break with the standard account of racism is further marked by his statement that "racism is the colonial interest lived as a link of all thc colonialists of the colony through the serial flight of alterity" (*CDR*, p. 300n.). He understood colonialism as "the common interest of the colonists" (*CDR*, p. 300n.), by which he meant that there was no direct conspiracy, but rather a distribution of resources such that colonialists of all classes benefit from an arrangement which systemically exploits the colonized: "This interest common to all classes is manifested to all the colonialists in the simple fact that in Algeria the average income of the colonialists is ten times higher than that of the natives" (*CDR*, pp. 726–27n.). In society one tends to adopt one's role in a spirit of conformity: the colonist beats his servants because this is what colonists do, and the servants accept it, whether they are guilty of an offense or not, because they know the beating is not addressed to them personally but through them to the colonized in general (*CDR*, p. 731n.).

A racist does not necessarily own his or her racism or even have to proclaim it. It is enough simply to acquiesce in the racism of the others. To take a simple example, I only have to believe as a White person that other Whites will be reluctant to buy a house in the street in which I live if there are a number of Black families living there, for me to think about putting my house on the market after the first Black family has moved in, for fear that the prices will decline if other Black families follow suit. I might have nothing against Black people, in which case I would not suspect myself of racism. I would persuade myself it is the other Whites who would now refuse to buy on that street who are the racists. In trying to sell my house early I am simply acting rationally, trying to get the best price I can. But the point is that the effect – another step toward de facto segregation – is the same whether or not there are any White families who object to living near Black people. It is enough that some White people believe in the existence of some other White people who might object. It is in this sense that one can think even here of what Sartre called a "serial flight of alterity." The seriality of racism means that my racism is in fact the racism of the Other. This is why acquiescence in racism is already racism and how Sartre can present racism both as an Idea and as "a passive constitution in things before being an ideology" (*CDR*, p. 739). To say that racism is a system is to say that violent inequalities are inscribed in worked matter (which Sartre calls the practico-inert) in such a way that they are internalized by all parties and thus are constantly reproduced.

These ideas are reshaped in *The Wretched of the Earth*. Fanon began his essay "On Violence," which was expanded to become the famous first chapter of *The Wretched of the Earth*, with two gestures that signaled the book's continuity with Sartre. First, he endorsed the language of Sartre's response to Memmi when he wrote: "It is the colonist who fabricated and continues to fabricate the colonized subject. The colonist derives his validity, i.e., his wealth, from the colonized system" (*WE*, p. 2). To be sure, the basic idea was already in Fanon in 1952, but by embracing the language of system, where he had earlier written of structure, he indicated at the outset, as would become clear in what followed, a fully dialectical account. Parts of the book predate Sartre's *Critique of Dialectical Reason*, such as the chapter "On National Culture," which was a speech delivered to the Second Congress of Black Writers and Artists in Rome in 1959. But the preceding chapters, "The Trials and Tribulations of National Consciousness," which would be better rendered as "The Misadventures of National Consciousness" ("Mésaventures de la conscience nationale"), and the chapter on violence, both of which seem to have been written later, have numerous references to dialectic, "the dialectic which governs the development of an armed struggle for national liberation" (*WE*, p. 80). Second, Fanon highlighted, as Sartre had done in "Black Orpheus,"[31] the gaze that the colonized direct toward the colonizer, although in *Black Skin, White Masks* Fanon had been somewhat dismissive of this idea (*BSWM*, pp. 12–13). This changed when Fanon specifically identified the look as "a look of envy" whose basis lay in hunger and deprivation.

> Looking at the immediacies of the colonized context, it is clear that what divides this world is first and foremost what species, what race one belongs to. In the colonies the economic infrastructure is also a superstructure. The cause is effect: You are rich because you are white, you are white because you are rich. (*WE*, p. 5)

The terms on which Fanon appropriated the later Sartre are clear, and they were terms that he had already clearly set in *Black Skin, White Masks*: economic exploitation of one race by another (*BSWM*, p. 199). By the time of the *Critique* Sartre had come to share with Fanon a recognition of the importance of the mediation of materiality between oppressed and oppressor. In Sartre's *Critique* this insight was marked by the introduction of the critical notion of scarcity.

Fanon expressed a belief in humanity that went beyond anything one would find in Sartre at this time. The closing lines of *The Wretched of the Earth* read: "For Europe, for ourselves, and for humanity, comrades, we must cast the slough, develop a new way of thinking, and endeavor to create a new man" (*WE*, p. 239, trans. modified). Nor would Sartre have put his faith in nationhood to the extent that Fanon did, but the latter's participation in the decolonization movement led him to advocate the following proposal: "to embrace the nation as a whole, to embody the constantly dialectical truth of the nation, and to will here and now the triumph of man in his totality" (*WE*, p. 141). Just as Sartre employed dialectical reason to see beyond the abstract individual to the concrete totality, so did Fanon. He saw this happening through the nation: "Since individual experience is national, since it is a link in the national chain, it ceases to be individual, narrow and limited in scope, and can lead to the truth of the nation and the world" (*WE*, pp. 140–41). This is very far from the individualizing moment of anxiety that some people see as the quintessence of existentialism, but it was nevertheless conceived in terms of experience: "To politicize the masses is to make the nation in its totality a reality for every citizen. To make the experience of the nation the experience of every citizen" (*WE*, p. 140). Whereas Sartre's insight into the system arose in the context of a growing recognition of the constraints on freedom, Fanon's insights developed through the awareness that decolonization was leading to new opportunities for those who had previously been colonized.

For Fanon, the decisive category in the movement toward postcolonialism was not race, but nation. Already in an essay contemporaneous with *Black Skin, White Masks* Fanon wrote that racial histories were a superstructure, "an obscure ideological emanation concealing an economic reality."[32] And as he warned in "On National Culture": "This historical obligation to racialize their claims, to emphasize an African culture rather than a national culture leads the African intellectuals into a dead end" (*WE*, p. 152). Nevertheless he reaffirmed in texts written subsequently that during the process of decolonization race would remain a central issue. It would not simply be put to one side: "it is clear that what divides this world is first and foremost what species, what race one belongs to" (*WE*, p. 5). Hence he embraced a phrase introduced by Sartre in "Black Orpheus" that had proved controversial: "anti-racist racism" (*WE*, p. 89; "Black Orpheus," pp. 118, 137).[33] For both Sartre and Fanon it is the fight against racism rather than the promotion of an idea of race that provided the motivation for action, but neither of them in 1960 understand by "racism" the same thing that they had meant by it eight to ten years earlier.

One measure of this change that allows us to take stock of the distance they had traveled is the way in which Fanon adopted the phrase "anti-racist racism" only to go beyond it: "Racism, hatred, resentment, and 'the legitimate desire for revenge' alone cannot nurture a war of liberation" (*WE*, p. 89). Involvement in the struggle had taught Fanon that one must look beyond anti-racist racism. In the context of a discussion of the awakening of the people, he insisted that "people must know where they are going and why" (*WE*, p. 135), to which he added in the same place that "this lucidity must remain deeply dialectical." This discussion – particularly with the introduction of that last phrase – might sound like a concession to the Sartre of "Black Orpheus," but it is not. Not only did Fanon not go back on his rejection of negritude, but in promoting the idea that decolonization is dialectical and by insisting that the people cannot be preoccupied by the moment and must look beyond it to know where they are going, he also had not become Hegelian in the sense that he had accused Sartre of being ten years earlier. Along with a transformation of the notion of racism so that it is now thought of as a system, there is a deeper appreciation of what is meant by dialectical reason. It is true that there is a humanism here – "there must be a concept of man, a concept about the future of mankind" (*WE*, p. 143) – but at the end of the book Fanon united this creation of the nation with the creation of a new humanity in what he calls a "dialectical requirement" (trans. modified): "When the nation in its totality is set in motion, the new man is not an a posteriori creation of this nation, but coexists with it, matures with it, and triumphs with it" (*WE*, p. 233). In other words, Fanon was not talking about a stage in the dialectic that one could already look beyond, as Sartre had done in "Black Orpheus."

In sum, Sartre and Fanon still did not agree on everything, and not only because they did not fully understand each other. But it is fitting that in what were probably some of the last words of *The Wretched of the Earth* that Fanon dictated, he came back to his early disagreement with Sartre and modified his position. Where Fanon had earlier said that he needed not to know where he was going so he could inhabit the moment, he now identified it as what people must know – and it is not a determination of his being but a possibility for humanity. He could readily do this, because, whereas he believed that Sartre had attempted to determine his being from outside, he, Fanon, could now embrace a future which was both his own and a possibility for all of humanity. It was not the colonized but the colonizers who needed to learn renunciation. Nothing was going to be snatched away from him and his comrades, and perhaps this conviction and this commitment more than anything else separated Fanon from Sartre in 1960, leading one to suspect that he was still the better existentialist.

NOTES

1. Sartre, *Being and Nothingness*, pp. 707–11.
2. Ciccariello-Maher, "Internal Limits," p. 156, has argued that I have missed the influence of Fanon's *Black Skin, White Masks* on Sartre's *Critique of Dialectical Reason*. I have gone back and re-examined the evidence and am *not yet* convinced that Fanon led Sartre "by the hand until he was made to see" ("Internal Limits," p. 163). It seems to me that one does not need this hypothesis to explain Sartre's steep learning curve during the 1950s on the issue of colonialism. In any event, the truly important philosophical issues raised by the debate between Sartre and Fanon are not captured by the notion of "influence." Nor is there much at stake: Fanon might have been keen to get Sartre's endorsement in 1961; Fanon does not need it now. On Fanon's relation to Sartre by someone who knew him well, as well as Sartre's misunderstanding of Fanon, see Cherki, *Frantz Fanon*, pp. 160–64 and pp. 181–82, and Cohen-Solal's report of Claude Lanzmann's testimony that to Fanon Sartre was a god (*Sartre*, p. 431).
3. Cohen-Solal, *Sartre*, p. 431.
4. Fanon, "The Lived Experience of the Black." Originally published as "L'expérience vécue du Noir" (1951).
5. Sartre, *Being and Nothingness*, pp. 347–54.
6. See Sartre, *Baudelaire*, pp. 144–45; Sartre, *Saint Genet*, p. 17.
7. Sartre, *Anti-Semite and Jew*, p. 97; henceforth cited in the text as *AS*.
8. Judaken, *Jean-Paul Sartre*, pp. 241–44.
9. Fanon, *Black Skin, White Masks*, p. 73; henceforth cited in the text as *BSWM*.
10. Sartre, "Orphée noir," in Senghor, *Anthologie*, pp. xi–xliv.
11. Sartre, "Black Orpheus," p. 138.
12. Roumain, "Bois-d'Ébène," in Senghor, *Anthologie*, p. 116. Cited in Sartre, "Black Orpheus," p. 137.
13. This debate is more complex than need be shown here. For a fuller account, see Bernasconi, "The European Knows" and "On Needing Not to Know."
14. Sartre, *Search for a Method*, p. 5.
15. Sartre, *Colonialism and Neocolonialism*, p. 45; henceforth cited in the text as *CN*.
16. "In my lifetime I have seen Frenchmen, Italians, Russians, etc.; thanks to Montesquieu, I even know that *one can be Persian*. But as

for *man*, I declare that I have never in my life met him." De Maistre, *Considerations*, p. 97. Sartre was not underwriting a biological notion of race, but a notion of race as facticity, which he shared with Fanon. See Bernasconi, "Can Race Be Thought Of in Terms of Facticity?"

17. Sartre, *Communists and Peace*, pp. 97, 229, 273.
18. See Mannoni, *Prospero and Caliban*, p. 24.
19. Sartre, *Being and Nothingness*, pp. 555–56.
20. What is almost universally known as Sartre's Preface to Memmi's book was in fact only added later. It was first a book review in *Les Temps Modernes* 137–38 (1957), pp. 291–92.
21. Memmi, *Colonizer and Colonized*, pp. 69–70.
22. Memmi, *Colonizer and Colonized*, p. 56.
23. Sartre, *Critique of Dialectical Reason*, p. 739; henceforth cited in the text as *CDR*.
24. Sartre, *Search for a Method*, pp. 124–7.
25. Fanon, *The Wretched of the Earth*, p. 43n.; henceforth cited in the text as *WE*.
26. See Braudel, *The Mediterranean*, vol. 1, pp. 536–42.
27. For example, Hacking, *Social Construction*, pp. 14–17. For a critique, see Marcano, "Sartre and the Social Construction of Race."
28. Fanon probably had in mind the discussion in which Birnenschatz insists that he was French and was loyal to the French, not the German Jews. See Sartre, *Reprieve*, pp. 83–84.
29. See, for instance, Sartre, *Being and Nothingness*, pp. 459, 471.
30. Bachelard, *Water and Dreams*, p. 159.
31. Sartre, "Black Orpheus," p. 115.
32. Fanon, *Toward the African Revolution*, p. 18n. The essay from which this quotation is taken, "Antillais et Africains," first appeared in *Esprit*, February 1955.
33. "Anti-racist racism" corresponds to what is more frequently called today "affirmative action" or "positive discrimination."

MATTHEW RATCLIFFE AND MATTHEW BROOME

17 Existential phenomenology, psychiatric illness, and the death of possibilities

17.1 PSYCHIATRY AND EXISTENTIAL PHENOMENOLOGY

The aim of this chapter is to show how the insights of existential phenomenologists can help us to understand changes in the structure of experience that occur in psychiatric illness. We employ the term "existential phenomenology" to refer to a broad philosophical approach shared by various philosophers, including Jean-Paul Sartre, Maurice Merleau-Ponty, and Martin Heidegger. It is more specific than "existentialism," as one could be an existentialist without being a phenomenologist. It is also more specific than "phenomenology" and is often contrasted with the "transcendental phenomenology" of Edmund Husserl. However, it would be misleading to suggest that only existential, as opposed to transcendental, phenomenology makes a contribution here. Husserl's later phenomenology has also informed the interpretation of psychiatric illness and is often appealed to alongside largely complementary insights drawn from the works of Heidegger and others.[1] For current purposes though, we will be focusing upon philosophers such as Heidegger, Merleau-Ponty, and especially Sartre, who are generally recognized as "existential" philosophers.

Existential phenomenology encompasses a range of interrelated themes. A central concern of the current chapter, one that features in the work of Heidegger, Sartre and others, is the manner in which we find ourselves situated in a world that *matters* to us in a range

We would like to thank Steven Crowell for helpful comments on an earlier version of this chapter, and JB for agreeing to be interviewed for this chapter.

of ways, a world where things show up to us as valuable, functional, interesting, enticing, threatening, and so on. Inextricable from this is an emphasis upon how experience is structured by a sense of our possibilities. Associated with both these themes is an appreciation of the phenomenological role of the body.

Existential phenomenology and psychiatry have a long shared history, and many existential philosophers had close friendships with clinicians. For example, there was Heidegger's fluctuating friendship with the psychiatrist and philosopher Karl Jaspers and his long-term friendship with the psychiatrist Medard Boss. Heidegger participated in a series of seminars for trainee psychiatrists and psychotherapists, held at Boss's house in Zollikon, Switzerland, over a ten-year period (1959–69).[2] Several others have drawn on Heidegger's work in order to cast light on the phenomenology of schizophrenia and other conditions. For instance, Ludwig Binswanger, inspired by *Being and Time*, advocates what he calls *Daseinsanalyse*, a method of interpretation based upon Heidegger's analysis of human existence.[3] Binswanger resists objective, scientific conceptions of the human being, which split us into distinct psychological and physical components. He stresses instead how the whole human person is embedded in a significant world and oriented towards future possibilities. Certain forms of psychiatric illness, he suggests, can be analyzed in terms of alterations in the sense of belonging to a world and in the associated ability to pursue possibilities.[4]

Heidegger was far from alone in his interaction with psychiatry. In *Phenomenology of Perception* and elsewhere, Merleau-Ponty incorporates reflection upon anomalous experience into his phenomenological methods, and his work also serves as an interpretive framework through which to make sense of such experiences. And Sartre corresponded with R. D. Laing, whose analysis of schizophrenia in *The Divided Self* owes much to Sartre's study of interpersonal relations in Part III of *Being and Nothingness*.[5] Numerous others have contributed in important ways to the broad tradition of existential psychiatry and psychology, including Karl Jaspers, Kurt Schneider, Kurt Goldstein, Erwin Straus, Viktor von Weizsäcker, Viktor Frankl, Eugene Minkowski, Willy Mayer Gross, J. H. van den Berg, Rollo May, and Eugene Gendlin, and the tradition is still very much alive today. Some existential psychologists and psychiatrists have also either practiced or inspired forms of "existential psychotherapy," which seek not only to interpret psychiatric complaints in phenomenological terms and to inform therapy in the process but to explicitly integrate themes from existential philosophy into therapeutic practice.[6]

Hence there are three intermingled strands of interaction: (1) phenomenology has been employed as a framework through which to interpret the experiences associated with schizophrenia and other conditions; (2) reflection upon such experiences has been employed in order to inform phenomenological inquiry; (3) themes in existential philosophy have shaped therapy, an obvious example being existential therapy. Our focus in what follows will be on (1) and (2), on understanding rather than therapeutic application. However, we certainly do not wish to deny that existential phenomenology has a role to play in therapy. Rather than discussing the historical relationship between phenomenology and psychiatry in further detail, our aim here is to illustrate the continuing relevance of themes in existential philosophy to psychiatry and vice versa.[7] Insights from existential phenomenology can assist us in understanding a wide range of experiential changes that feature in psychiatric illness. These insights need not take the form of rigid interpretive frameworks that we impose upon the relevant experiences. We can *do* phenomenology by engaging with psychiatry, rather than just applying it in psychiatry. Reflection upon the descriptions offered by clinicians and psychiatric patients can contribute to phenomenological understanding, helping to further refine, elaborate, and revise our phenomenological descriptions.

The fact that we *can* interpret anomalous experiences by drawing on existential phenomenology does not imply that we *should*. However, such interpretations often appear extremely plausible. Indeed, the similarities between patients' reports and the descriptions offered by phenomenologists can be quite striking. Mary Warnock concludes that existentialism is a dead philosophical movement and that its demise is largely due to the fact that no arguments can be offered in support of the descriptions and assertions that its proponents offer:

> There is no real possibility of *argument* with the deliverances of the concrete imagination. If I see significance in some feature of the world around me, I am at liberty to say so. If I am a poet or a painter or a photographer or

film maker, then my vision of the world can be understood, perhaps shared, and may even be analysed, but argument need not come into the matter. But philosophy without arguments is not possible, in the long run.

She adds, referring specifically to Sartre, that we "cannot be expected to accept a whole theory of interpersonal relations" on the basis of an "image of the man listening at the keyhole and caught in the act," however compelling that image might seem.[8] We reject Warnock's assessment, on the basis that the illuminating application of existential phenomenology in psychiatry does amount to an argument in support of various claims made by existential philosophers. A substantial body of testimony from patients and clinicians can be cited in support of such claims. To illustrate this, we will focus upon R. D. Laing's Sartrean interpretation of changes in interpersonal experience that can occur in schizophrenia, especially paranoid schizophrenia. We will then generalize from this example, suggesting that existential thought can assist us in understanding a wide range of psychiatric illnesses.

Our aim is not to promote a specifically Sartrean account of interpersonal experience. As David Cooper's book *Existentialism: A Reconstruction* demonstrates (as does his chapter in this *Companion*), it is possible to offer a rough characterization of the generic existentialist, which incorporates themes that are common to the work of several philosophers, despite their many disagreements. In interpreting the experiences of psychiatric patients, we suggest that a fruitful approach is to focus upon some of these recurrent themes and thus draw on several philosophers, rather than restricting ourselves to the writings of one person. Amongst other things, existential approaches tend to emphasize the phenomenology of feeling, the primacy of practical involvement with the world over voyeuristic contemplation, the way in which the experienced world is imbued with significance and value, the poverty of an all-encompassing mechanistic view of the world, the phenomenology of the body and its inextricability from world-experience, the perceptual, affective and practical aspects of interpersonal understanding, and closely related themes such as freedom, temporality, and possibility. All of these are relevant to the interpretation of psychiatric illness. We will propose, more specifically, that the key to understanding many alterations in the overall structure of experience that occur in psychiatric illness is an appreciation that all experience incorporates a changeable sense of the *significance* of things and of one's own *possibilities*, which is tied up with our bodily phenomenology. We find just this appreciation in Sartre, amongst others.

17.2 THE DEATH OF POSSIBILITIES

In *Being and Nothingness*, Sartre begins his discussion of interpersonal experience or "Being-for-others" by considering the feeling of shame. Consider the example of spying on someone through a keyhole.[9] While attending to what is going on in the room, one's body does not appear as a salient object of attention but disappears into the background. One is not primarily conscious of oneself but of what is happening in the room. Now suppose that one then hears the unmistakable sound of a footstep. At this point, one feels shame. What form does this experience take? According to Sartre, our voyeur does not first infer that another person is present, then judge that it is wrong to spy on people or that it is not good to be caught spying on people, and finally feel ashamed. Instead, shame is a bodily feeling that follows perception of the footstep without any intervening thoughts. It is an immediate reaction to the perceived situation, a sudden, intense *bodily* shift in how one experiences oneself: "Shame is an immediate shudder which runs through me from head to foot without any discursive preparation" (*BN*, p. 302). This feeling is not just a change in how one perceives oneself. As one's body becomes conspicuous in shame, it ceases to be a transparent medium through which a scene is effortlessly perceived and instead becomes an object of experience. With this, perception of the scene changes markedly. When the body becomes a salient object of awareness, one ceases to be obliviously immersed in a situation, preoccupied principally with things in the world that are of interest or value.

However, shame is not merely a shift in experience of one's body and, with it, one's surroundings. It also incorporates the sense that another person is present. Bodily conspicuousness, of this kind at least, is inextricable from a sense of being perceived. Experience of one's body as an object is a sense of its being an object for someone else: "I am ashamed of myself as I *appear* to the Other" (*BN*, p. 302). Sartre generalizes from such experiences and argues that the capacity to undergo this kind of felt, bodily reorientation is central to our sense of others. He offers the famous example of walking in the park and seeing someone sitting on a bench (*BN*, pp. 341–43). The appreciation of being in the presence of another person consists, he says, in a gradual "regrouping" of objects around him. The world that was mine slips away and becomes a world for him, in which I appear as part of the scenery. As before, there is a shift from the experience of being immersed in some project to the awareness of one's body as an entity that appears to someone else in the context of her projects.

Shame thus constitutes the relation of "being-seen-by-another"; the "Look" of the "Other." Sartre stresses that this "Look" is not a matter of *actually* being seen. Rather, it is about having the *sense* of being seen. Thus, although the Look is often associated with perception of eyes pointing in one's direction, it could just as well arise as a result of a "rustling in the branches, or the sound of a footstep followed by silence" (*BN*, p. 346). We can of course be wrong about being seen. But Sartre's account does not claim certainty for every case. We can be mistaken when we think that someone is present and we can also doubt that someone is present even though we feel that she is. What we cannot do, though, is coherently doubt that there *are* other people. The disposition to experience the Look comprises our most fundamental sense of sharing a world with other people and, however many times one might utter "I doubt that there are any other people," the relevant experience cannot be switched off; it is sewn into the structure of our consciousness.

For Sartre, a bodily feeling just *is* at the same time a sense of oneself as an object before the gaze of another. In order to understand how this might be so and to further clarify what the look involves, it is important to appreciate the phenomenological role that Sartre assigns to the body. For Sartre, our consciousness, the for-itself, does not consist in an experience of being a kind of object with some fixed essence, rooted wholly in the present. Instead, it consists in the way our surroundings are revealed to us. Consciousness is an opening onto the world, rather than a thing in the world.[10] It is quite different in character from an entity that is revealed to consciousness, an "in-itself." But this should not be taken to imply that consciousness is distinct from the body. Indeed, Sartre says that the "for-itself" is not merely associated with a body; it must *be* a body: "the very nature of the for-itself demands that it be a body" (*BN*, p. 409).[11]

The world that consciousness reveals is not neutral, detached and indifferent but shaped by values, projects, and goals. Amongst other things, it is a world of potential activities, and the activities that things are perceived to offer reflect the contingent limitations of our bodies. Sartre points out that, without these limitations, we would not be able to make distinctions such as that between wanting something and getting it. For the unconstrained will, to want would be to get: "I could never distinguish within me desire from will, nor dream from act, nor the possible from the real" (*BN*, p. 431). Without the structure provided by a background sense of one's contingent bodily capacities, experience would lose all structure. Sartre goes so far as to say that it would simply disappear (*BN*, p. 432). The body, in playing this indispensable phenomenological role, is not an *object* of experience. Instead, it is experienced *as* the world we inhabit. The significance we perceive in things – their appearance as practically accessible, functional, useable, inaccessible, immovable, dangerous, threatening, or otherwise practically relevant – reflects our bodily capacities and vulnerabilities.[12] So a background awareness of the body just is an awareness of the significant world, a sense of the possibilities that it offers, which we might choose to take up or resist. We are our bodies and so we are our possibilities.

In shame, the way in which possibilities fall away is at the same time the feeling of being confronted by a source of possibility distinct from oneself. Experience of the Look incorporates "the solidification and alienation of my own possibilities"; "in the look the death of my possibilities causes me to experience the Other's freedom" (*BN*, pp. 352, 362). Hence tied up with our experience of others as people, as sources of possibility rather than mere things, is the effect that they have upon a sense of our own possibilities. We cannot perceive someone as a person or as the "other" (for current purposes, we treat the two terms as synonymous) without being somehow affected by them, without feeling to some extent the contingency and erosion of our significant world and thus our own possibilities. However, Sartre does not regard our experience of others as an unpleasant addition to our phenomenology, which we would be better off without. Rather, the experiential interplay between the for-itself (or experience of oneself as one's possibilities) and the in-itself (the object-self that appears to the other) is central to the structure of human experience. As Sartre says, "I need the mediation of the Other in order to be what I am" (*BN*, p. 384).

17.3 INTERPERSONAL EXPERIENCE IN SCHIZOPHRENIA

Sartre's view of interpersonal relations is rather bleak. Fundamental to a sense of other people is a feeling of threat, of being in danger of losing one's possibilities and thus one's freedom to them: "through him I am perpetually *in danger*" (*BN*, p. 367). It is arguable that he presents a somewhat one-sided view, which captures only some human relations and perhaps not those that are most fundamental to our sense of others. Merleau-Ponty, for instance, claims that Sartre's account accommodates only certain breakdowns of intersubjectivity, where "each of us feels his actions to be not taken up and understood, but observed as if they were an insect's."[13] Even assuming that some experiences do involve this erosion of possibilities, it is debatable how far the erosion actually goes. When encountering someone in a park, even if one does start to feel like an object before her gaze, many possibilities are preserved. It would be implausible to maintain that items of equipment dotted around the place all appear as "for him but not for me." The bin, the signs, the swings, and so on offer possibilities that are "there for me as well as him" or rather "there for us." Furthermore, although one's body might become uncomfortably conspicuous, it is still a far cry from a mere thing. It remains a locus of perception and action, able to actualize some of the numerous possibilities that remain.

There are also many instances where sharing an environment with someone else seems to enrich a scene rather than drain our possibilities out of it. As the phenomenologist and psychiatrist J. H. van den Berg observes:

> One who often shows the same town to different people will be struck by the ever new way in which the town appears in the conversation that is held about the sights during such a walk. These different ways are identical

with the people with whom one walks, they are forms of subjectivity. The subject shows itself in the things.[14]

However, although Sartre's account may not accommodate all kinds of interpersonal encounter, it does serve as a helpful interpretive framework through which to make sense of forms of interpersonal experience that can occur in psychiatric illness. The relevance of Sartre's phenomenology to psychiatry is most evident in the work of R. D. Laing, whose interpretation of schizophrenia in works such as *The Divided Self* is heavily influenced by Sartre.[15] Laing was a controversial figure, and we do not wish to endorse all or even most of what he said. Nevertheless, we think that his application of Sartrean phenomenology to experiential changes that occur in some cases of schizophrenia is very plausible. The kinds of experiences that Laing describes in Sartrean terms are frequently documented and well-established features of the condition, rather than artifacts of Laing's interpretations. To illustrate this, we include in what follows excerpts from an interview with JB, a young man diagnosed with schizophrenia, who was interviewed by one of us (Broome) in September 2008. As we will see, much of what JB says can be plausibly interpreted in terms of Laing's Sartrean phenomenological analysis.

Laing insists from the outset that, without the aid of an existential approach, it is not possible to understand the experience of schizophrenia: "The mad things said and done by the schizophrenic will remain essentially a closed book if one does not understand their existential context."[16] He stresses that we do not understand each other as minds that are hidden inside bodies, or indeed just as bodies, but as persons. We do so through a distinctive kind of implicit attitude, a felt, bodily receptiveness to each other. He criticizes the commonplace tendency to assume that a scientifically respectable approach to human beings must consist exclusively in a mechanistic account of how a certain kind of complicated object behaves. In place of such assumptions, he suggests that persons should be recognized as a basic ontological category and that a science of the personal is just as legitimate as a science of the impersonal (*DS*, p. 21).[17] Laing notes that an inability to recognize others as persons and to instead experience them as complicated mechanisms often features in psychiatric illness. A science that adopts the same approach is, he suggests, no less pathological.

According to Laing, we need to start off with an existential appreciation of persons and how they find themselves in a world. Unless we recognize the inextricability of our experience of body, other people, and surrounding world, and also the fact that the sense of belonging to a world can change quite dramatically in structure, we will not be able to interpret the predicaments of many psychiatric patients: "one has to be able to orientate oneself as a person in the other's scheme of things rather than only to see the other as an object in one's own world" (*DS*, p. 25). With his interpretive framework in place, he then turns to schizoid people and to those with full-blown schizophrenia, to offer an account that emphasizes changes in bodily phenomenology and the loss of possibilities. He notes that such people are unusually "exposed," "vulnerable," and "isolated." In effect, they are over-sensitized to the Look of the other, which in their case really is experienced as an eradication of possibilities that are integral to a sense of their being: "a schizophrenic may say that he is made of glass, of such transparency and fragility that a look directed at him splinters him to bits and penetrates straight through him" (*DS*, p. 38). The patient may quite literally *feel* the gaze of the other as something that invades him or her and threatens the sense of self: "in psychotic conditions the gaze or scrutiny of the other can be experienced as an actual penetration into the core of the 'inner' self" (*DS*, p. 113). Laing refers to this predicament as one of "ontological insecurity," where all interpersonal relations are perceived in terms of threat, that threat being the loss of one's identity, which is swamped by the other person's possibilities (*DS*, p. 45). Consider the following comments offered by JB, which convey a pronounced sense of vulnerability to others:

> I used to think my neighbours were watching me, [as] if they could see me through the walls, possibly a window a long way away they could see me from ... I didn't have any privacy anyway because I thought people wanted to play with my mind and different things, and I just felt very violated and I just felt lost like I was being used by people, I was being watched by other people and you felt very guilty, there was a very strong feeling of guilt.

JB later describes feeling that others were a threat to his very identity. He reports having been convinced that they could manipulate his thoughts, removing his moral attributes and replacing them with their own thought contents. He also refers to a conversation with the devil during which there was "a feeling that something was taken from me."

An extreme form of this vulnerability is what Laing calls "implosion," where the whole social world takes on the form of existential threat, offering only the possibility of one's own annihilation. The sufferer experiences "the full terror of the experience of the world as liable at any moment to crash in and obliterate all identity, as a gas will rush in and obliterate a vacuum. The individual feels that, like the vacuum, he is empty. But the emptiness is him" (*DS*, p. 47). The world as a whole becomes a threatening gaze from which there is no escape, before which all of one's own possibilities and thus the potential for any kind of purposive action are eradicated. The sufferer's response to this threat is either to surrender to it and become an object for others or to build defenses, retreating into a private realm that cannot be touched by them. These strategies are structurally similar to what Sartre calls "bad faith." For example, Sartre's café waiter tries to make his social role his essence; he becomes the object that he is in the eyes of the diners. In contrast, the woman whose hand is taken by a male dinner companion distances herself from her hand. She thus avoids having to acknowledge his amorous intentions and face up to the situation (*BN*, pp. 96–102).

Laing is clear that in schizophrenia the strategy of distancing oneself from the threat of the other is ultimately ineffective. He describes how a false self is constructed, a mask that is worn to shield oneself from others. Everyday conformity to situational norms of politeness can involve a degree of effort and attentiveness, but what Laing describes is much more extreme than this. The patient self-consciously performs all those acts that most of us unthinkingly and effortlessly carry out. She thus becomes hyperconscious of her own body, her behavior and even her thoughts, all of which are constantly monitored.[18] But this process of cutting herself off from a fake self fails, because altered bodily experience and associated detachment from other people also add up to a loss of possibilities and thus a diminishment of self and world. Laing quotes a patient as saying that

I've been sort of dead in a way. I cut myself off from other people and became shut up in myself. And I can see that you become dead in a way when you do this. You have to live in a world *with* other people. If you don't something dies inside. (*DS*, p. 145)

JB describes a slightly less severe version of this. He reports a kind of bodily rigidity or "coldness" that inhibited social activity, and explains how he attempted to compensate for a lack of natural social rapport by resorting to self-conscious "tricks" in place of spontaneous, unthinking social interaction:

[T]here was the stiffness of the body, there was a general feeling of coldness. I was very, very cold all the time and I know it was a cold winter but I was very, very cold and I had to learn how to make myself un-cold by using my mind. In a strange way, I remember I started using these tricks to talk to people and I started using them when I wasn't talking to people. I was just using them. It was like a conscious thing in my mind against this stuff ... I used to try and say things on the same level when people say things.

He adds that the sense of others as threatening and his consequent lack of emotional openness resulted in his feeling cut off from others, including his family. The relevant emotions were not altogether *gone*, but, having detached himself from any engagement with other people, he was unable to express emotion, to connect with them:

I couldn't interact with [my family] properly. I only really learned how to interact with people recently in the last sort of six months or so ... I couldn't even interact with my mum if she was crying next to me and telling me about how ill I was. I couldn't really connect with them, I didn't have the level of empathy that I would have had ... I felt sad but I didn't feel like I could express to her how sad I felt about it ... There was sort of a mental block, I couldn't really interact. I had so much stuff going on in my head – so much fear and paranoia – that I couldn't talk and I couldn't show people how I felt about them ... It was more of an anxious state of, I'd be sitting there and would probably be shaking a little bit or I would be very vacant. I wouldn't be able to connect with someone, I wouldn't be able to speak in a very, you know, people go, like, you know they have emotions and you can see it through their body language. I wouldn't be able to express myself very well.

Vulnerability to others and alienation from the social world are not the only problems that might be faced. Laing also suggests that the parts of the body that one ceases to experience the world *through*, ceases to fully inhabit, can then be experienced as possessions of the other. They can see through one's eyes, interfere with one's thoughts and activities, and play tricks. So the detachment is at the same time a disposition to develop certain kinds of delusion. Furthermore, social isolation in itself tends to make delusions and hallucinations – core symptoms of psychotic disorders such as schizophrenia – more intense and frequent.

Laing stresses that healthy interpersonal encounters need not take the form of threat. The loving gaze of a parent is essential to healthy development, and adults too have a need to be perceived. This, he says, is not just about being seen: "It extends to the general need to have one's presence endorsed or confirmed by the other, the need for one's total existence to be recognized; the need, in fact, to be loved" (*DS*, p. 125). So, unlike Sartre, he clearly distinguishes the phenomenology of healthy mutual perception from the death of possibilities. This is not to suggest that Sartre's view is applicable only to schizophrenia, however. Although it most probably does not encompass the full range of human social experience, less extreme variants of what Laing describes no doubt occur throughout our daily lives.

Sartre's analysis succeeds in accommodating aspects of interpersonal experience that orthodox approaches in philosophical psychology and cognitive science are ill-equipped to make sense of. Such approaches assume that the core achievement of everyday interpersonal understanding (or "folk psychology" as it is often called) is the attribution of internal mental states, principally beliefs and desires, to other people on the basis of behavioral observations, the primary goal being to predict and explain their behavior. The main issue with which debates are concerned is *how* we manage to do this. The current consensus is that we employ some combination of "simulating" others' mental states and deploying a largely tacit "theory" of other minds. A curious feature of the literature on folk psychology, theory of mind and simulation is that it concentrates on the perspective of a *detached* observer watching someone else's behavior, rather than the usual case of two or more people *interacting* with each other in a shared situation. Much of the literature also construes interpersonal understanding in a strangely impersonal way. The observed individual is seemingly presented as a kind of complicated object, the internal workings of which one attempts to figure out.[19] Sartre, in contrast, emphasizes that our sense of others *as* others is inextricable from how we are affected by them. It does not consist principally in an understanding of internal mental states, arrived at by theorizing, simulating, or some other cognitive process. It is a matter of affective, bodily, and perceptual relatedness. Most importantly, it involves a transformation in the experience of possibilities. His analysis thus serves as a plausible interpretive framework through which to approach kinds of interpersonal experiences that are intelligible in principle but not in terms of presuppositions that typify much current philosophical discourse. This, we think, significantly adds to its appeal.

17.4 THE STRUCTURE OF THE POSSIBLE

So far, we have suggested that Sartre's account of Being-for-others can help us to understand experiential changes that often feature in schizophrenia. Of course, not all psychiatric illnesses involve the same kinds of changes. In this section, we propose that a more generally applicable interpretive framework for understanding changes in how one *finds oneself in the world and with other people* can be drawn from existential phenomenology, which preserves Sartre's core insights. Central to it are the interrelated themes of significance, possibility, and bodily feeling. We begin by sketching this framework. Then we show how it can be applied to make sense of alterations in the overall shape of experience that are often reported in severe depression.

We noted, in discussing Sartre's view, that the possibilities offered by people and things reflect a background sense of one's bodily potentialities. For example, things might appear as graspable, manipulable, tangible or intangible, inaccessible or too cumbersome to manipulate effectively. Our bodies are equally implicated in our experiences of other people and the kinds of possibility that they offer, from communion to threat. JB describes a variety of anomalous bodily experiences, which seem to be closely linked to changes in his experience of self, others and world. For example:

> I had become very stiff and rigid and I couldn't, I felt very, because I was so anxious my body sort of felt very stiff, very lifeless ... I found it harder to do anything. There was a time when I couldn't even walk particularly well. I

had to keep stopping and starting when I was moving around and I couldn't really function well.[20]

Changes in our bodily phenomenology can also be changes in the perception of salient possibilities. For the person who is effortlessly situated in a context of activity and whose activities are regulated by a backdrop of goals and projects, the world is perceived as a realm of salient opportunities for action. But in the case of the seemingly lifeless, stiff, conspicuous body that is not comfortably immersed in a context of goal-directed activity, the world does not reflect the same kinds of possibility. The relevant changes do not simply involve expansions or contractions of some undifferentiated possibility space. Importantly, not all the possibilities we experience are of the same *kind*. There are a variety of different ways in which things and people can appear to us as significant. For instance, something can appear as enticing, dangerous, useable or not useable, accessible to others but not to me or vice versa, achievable with effort, easily done, and so on. People can be threatening, interesting, or boring, and one can feel practically and emotionally related to them in a range of different ways. To find oneself *in a world* is to inhabit a space of various different *kinds* of significant possibility, a space that is inseparable from our bodily phenomenology.

This general theme is common to the works of Merleau-Ponty, Sartre, and Heidegger. For instance, Merleau-Ponty indicates that the body is not just responsible for which concrete instances of possibility appear on which occasion (such as "that currently perceived cup is graspable"). It also constitutes the "universal horizon," "world horizon," or "horizon of horizons," meaning a space of possibilities that determines, amongst other things, the ways in which things can matter to us:

The natural world is the horizon of all horizons, the style of all possible styles, which guarantees for my experiences a given, not a willed, unity underlying all the disruptions of my personal and historical life. Its counterpart within me is the given, general and pre-personal existence of my sensory functions.[21]

Sartre makes a similar point in maintaining that the world is the "correlate of the possibilities which I am," taking the form of "the enormous skeletal outline of all my possible actions" (*BN*, p. 425). And Heidegger, although avoiding any explicit phenomenological engagement with the body, does maintain that the sense of belonging to a world involves inhabiting a space of possibilities where things can be encountered as mattering in a range of different ways. For instance, we might find a piece of equipment "unserviceable, resistant, or threatening." These kinds of significance, Heidegger says, are "ontologically possible only in so far as Being-in as such has been determined existentially beforehand in such a manner that what it encounters within-the-world can 'matter' to it."[22]

In order to understand the kinds of *existential change* (by which we mean a shift in the background sense of belonging to a world, which affects experience of self, others, world, and the relationship between them) that can occur in psychiatric illness and in other contexts, we suggest that it is fruitful to reflect upon what happens if certain *kinds* of possibility are overly salient, diminished, or unstructured. The experiences discussed by Laing involve one kind of possibility, threat, becoming a form that all experiences take on. A kind of bodily feeling is at the same time an altered space of possibilities, where possibilities for social and other activities drop out of the world. In their place, everyone and everything takes on the character of a danger before which one is passive, helpless, bereft of the potential for whatever action might have given one reprieve.

Various other conditions can also be understood in the same general way, as involving altered feeling and, with it, a change in the experience of what is possible. For example, people who are severely depressed often complain not of feeling threatened by others so much as feeling irrevocably disconnected, incapable of being moved by them and thus strangely, unpleasantly cut off from everyone and everything. It is not just that sufferers *happen to be* unaffected by people but that the *possibility* of being affected in this way is gone from experience. The possibility of objects appearing as practically significant in the usual way is similarly gone. The resultant transformation in the space of possibilities is often referred to in autobiographies and works of literature as a prison, glass wall, or container, from which escape is impossible. William James describes it as like being "sheathed in india-rubber." He adds, "nothing penetrates to the quick or draws blood, as it were. .... 'I see, I hear!' such patients say, 'but the objects do not reach me, it is as if there were a wall between me and the outer world!'"[23] Sylvia Plath's protagonist Esther, in her semi-autobiographical novel *The Bell Jar*, describes something very similar, when she says, "wherever I sat – on the deck of a ship or at a street café in Paris or Bangkok – I would be sitting under the same glass bell jar, stewing in my own sour air."[24] Almost everyone who describes an episode of major depression reports something along these lines.

What limits possibility in this kind of depression is the inability to be affected by others and a painful awareness of this inability, rather than being excessively vulnerable to others. Importantly, the sense that one might be affected by other people (and by impersonal events, too) in a range of significant ways is partly constitutive of the appreciation that one's current predicament, the way the world appears right now, is contingent, fragile, and changeable. Without it, experience would cease to incorporate the sense of there being significant alternatives to how one is now, alternatives that might be pursued and actualized. We thus arrive at another feature of severe depression that is reported in almost every case, the inconceivability of alternatives to how one currently finds oneself in the world and the conviction that recovery is thus impossible. For example, Lewis Wolpert recalls how, when his psychiatrist assured him that he would recover from his depression, he "did not believe a single word. It was inconceivable to me that I should ever recover. The idea that I might be well enough to work again was unimaginable."[25] The interplay between actuality and possibility that is presupposed by everyday thought, experience, and activity is thus altered.

With the experience of depression, we therefore have a seeming reversal of Sartre's claim that the other is the death of my possibilities, an experience that differs from the excessive vulnerability to others that Laing describes. However, the possibilities are not all gone from experience. Certain other kinds of possibility remain. For instance, many sufferers complain of an all-enveloping feeling of dread, anxiety, or impending doom. Hence, although the experience of depression can be contrasted with a Sartrean death of possibilities, it may well be that the two sometimes coexist. A sense of being cut off from others and unmoved by them could refer to only certain *kinds* of significant relations, such as emotional communion, effortless conversation, and so on. Other kinds of possibility involving people, such as that of being threatened, might remain. Even so, reflection upon depression illustrates that, just as other people may take away our possibilities, they also give us possibilities. Despite

Sartre's emphasis on others as threatening rather than enabling, he does recognize that they are also a source of possibility, as exemplified by his remark that "to die is to lose all possibility of revealing oneself as subject to an Other" (*BN*, p. 394). In fact, depressed people frequently describe the experience as akin to a living death. Without the possibilities of meaningful contact with other people and also of practical significance, of things "mattering" in the sense of being worth pursuing, the structure of experience is radically transformed.[26]

Depression thus involves a change in the constitution of the for-itself, in what Sartre calls freedom. Sartre claims that consciousness does not reside in the present but inhabits possibilities, always projecting ahead into potential futures. Thus, in a sense, we are what we are not, as our experience is directed towards and structured by the non-actual. To quote Sartre, the "for-itself" is always an "elsewhere in relation to itself." It is a being "which is not what it is and which is what it is not" (*BN*, p. 126). The sense that we do indeed have these different possibilities to choose from, that they are really there for us, is at the same time the sense that we are not deterministically constrained by the present or shackled by our past actions. If we were, we would not have any possibilities for action. But, in severe depression, the future no longer appears as a space of possibilities that are different from one's current predicament in any significant way. That predicament thus loses its sense of contingency, of changeability. So there is a profound alteration in the structure of consciousness. This includes a change in the experience of time. Without significant differences between past, present, and future, without a sense of possible activities transforming one's situation in a meaningful way, the phenomenological distinction between past, present, and future is eroded. There are various ways of describing this. People might complain of a torment without end, an eternity, timelessness, the absence of time, or of time slowing down.[27]

We could similarly interpret the relevant experiential changes in terms of the structure that Heidegger calls "thrown projection [*geworfenen Entwurf*]" (*BT*, p. 188). For Heidegger, as for Sartre, we do not experience ourselves or the worldly entities we encounter merely in terms of the present and the actual. Rather, all experience is structured by possibilities. We experience ourselves in terms of potential ways in which we might be, some of which we pursue through our projects. As Heidegger puts it, human existence or Dasein is "existentially" what it is "not yet"; it is always "*ahead* of itself," "beyond itself" (*BT*, pp. 185–86). But this "projection," this orientation towards the possible, is not unconstrained; we do not pluck our projects out of nowhere. The kinds of possibility that we are able to coherently pursue are determined by our "thrownness," by how we find ourselves situated in a realm where things matter to us in different ways, such as their being practically significant, enticing, inaccessible, available, pertinent to a project, threatening, terrifying, and so on. If all sense of practical significance were eradicated from experience, along with any sense of potential emotional connectedness with others, the structure of projection would be radically altered along with that of thrownness. One would no longer be able to take up certain kinds of possibility. Indeed, one could not pursue a project at all, seek to become something, or strive for significant change, as the kinds of mattering that such pursuits presuppose would be altogether absent. The entire structure of experience, the sense of Being-in-the-world, would shift.

Another kind of experiential change that can occur in psychiatric illness does not involve feeling cut off from others or threatened by them but instead the loss of something that both these experiential shifts continue to presuppose – the ability to experience others as people at all. Without some sense of people as a distinctive phenomenological category, there is nobody to feel vulnerable before or estranged from. A loss of personal experience is vividly described by an author known only as Renee in *Autobiography of a Schizophrenic Girl*. Everything, she says, looked strangely artificial and, with this, there was a loss of functionality and practical significance more generally. Eventually, this shift in the structure of experience came to encompass other people. She describes being confronted with something that "appeared strange, unreal, like a statue," "a statue by my side, a puppet, part of the pasteboard scenery," which became "more a statue than ever, a manikin moved by mechanism, talking like an automaton. It is horrible, inhuman, grotesque." She reports how her therapist became her last connection to an interpersonal world where things mattered – "the precious little oasis of reality in the desert world of my soul" – but eventually even this connection was lost.[28] Again, an alteration in the space of possibilities seems to be central here. In brief, the seeming artificiality of things and people consists in an absence of the possibilities that they usually offer, with the result that they look somehow different, not quite right, fake.[29]

Changes in the shape of interpersonal experience can therefore take quite different forms. Here, we have offered only a brief sketch of three of them (people as threat; disconnectedness from people; loss of a sense of others as people), so as to hint at the interpretive potential of an existential approach. What unites these experiences is an alteration in the sense of belonging to a world and being with other people, central to which are shifts in the experience of worldly significance, one's own possibilities, and one's body. More detailed analyses are of course required, and there are also many other forms of anomalous experience to explore. In the process of studying them, we can seek to refine our phenomenological analyses by drawing on psychiatry. Thus, what we have here is not a dead historical movement but an ongoing program of research in existential phenomenology.

NOTES

1. For example, Wolfgang Blankenburg draws on both Husserl and Heidegger to argue that schizophrenia involves a loss of "natural self evidence," an erosion of the habitual, practical orientation that ordinarily operates as a backdrop to experience and thought. See Sass, "Self and World in Schizophrenia," for a discussion. See also Ratcliffe, *Feelings of Being*, for a phenomenological approach to psychiatric illness that draws on complementary themes in Husserl, Heidegger, Merleau-Ponty, and Sartre.
2. There is an English translation of these seminars: Heidegger, *Zollikon Seminars*.
3. See, for example, Binswanger, *Being-in-the-world*. It was Binswanger who introduced Boss to Heidegger's work.
4. Heidegger liked the idea of a psychiatry grounded in his philosophy but disapproved of the specific way in which Binswanger appropriated his ideas. See Askay, "Heidegger's Philosophy and its Implications for Psychology," for further discussion.
5. Some of Laing's later works are similarly inspired by Sartre's later philosophy. See Raschid, *R. D. Laing*, especially the essays by Jenner, Poole, and Kirsner, for discussions of the relationship between Sartre and Laing.

6. For examples of existential psychotherapy, see Frankl, *Existentialism and Psychotherapy*; van Deurzen-Smith, *Everyday Mysteries*. See Spiegelberg, *Phenomenology in Psychology and Psychiatry*, and Halling and Nill, "A Brief History of Existential-Phenomenological Psychiatry and Psychotherapy," for historical surveys of the relationship between phenomenology, psychiatry, and psychotherapy. See Ratcliffe, *Feelings of Being*, for discussion of some current work in phenomenological psychiatry.
7. The fact that there remains considerable interest in phenomenological psychiatry is illustrated by the steady stream of publications in the area. See, for example, the 2007 special issue of *Schizophrenia Bulletin* (33:1) dedicated to "Phenomenology and Psychiatry for the 21st Century."
8. Warnock, *Existentialism*, p. 139.
9. Sartre, *Being and Nothingness*, p. 347; henceforth cited in the text as *BN*.
10. See also Sartre, *Transcendence of the Ego*.
11. Sartre's lengthy discussion of the body complements much of what Merleau-Ponty says in *Phenomenology of Perception*. Both insist that the body is experienced in terms of the possibilities that the world offers and that our bodily phenomenology cannot be adequately accounted for by any approach that treats the experienced body primarily as an object of perception.
12. Like Heidegger in Division One of *Being and Time*, Sartre discusses our experience of entities as items of equipment, embedded in wider systems of functions and purposes (Sartre, *BN*, pp. 423–26).
13. Merleau-Ponty, *Phenomenology of Perception*, p. 420.
14. Van den Berg, "The Human Body and the Significance of Human Movement," p. 166.
15. Laing is not the only psychiatrist to draw on Sartre. For instance, van den Berg, *A Different Existence*, adopts a Sartrean account of consciousness and the body in order to interpret what he refers to as the typical psychiatric patient.
16. Laing, *The Divided Self*, p. 15; henceforth cited in the text as *DS*.
17. Heidegger (*Zollikon Seminars*, p. 135), amongst others, similarly criticizes the project of modeling an account of human beings on impersonal, mechanistic science: "The unavoidable result of such a science of the human being would be the technical construction of the human being as machine."
18. Sass (e.g., *The Paradoxes of Delusion*) offers a largely complementary account of what he calls "hyperreflexivity," an involuntary excess of attention directed at one's own bodily activities, experiences, and

thoughts. This can involve, according to Sass, a loss of everyday practical significance and connectedness to others, leading to a quasi-solipsistic retreat into an impoverished, delusional, subjective realm.

19. For a summary and critique of recent work on folk psychology, theory of mind, and simulation, see Ratcliffe, *Rethinking Commonsense Psychology*.
20. This refers to a time before JB had received any medication. Hence the changes in bodily feeling that he reports are not attributable to the side-effects of medication.
21. Merleau-Ponty, *Phenomenology of Perception*, p. 385.
22. Heidegger, *Being and Time*, p. 176; henceforth cited in the text as *BT*.
23. James, *Principles of Psychology*, vol. II, p. 178.
24. Plath, *Bell Jar*, p. 178.
25. Wolpert, *Malignant Sadness*, p. 154.
26. See Ratcliffe, "Understanding Existential Changes in Psychiatric Illness," for a more detailed discussion of autobiographical accounts of depression and the phenomenological changes that are consistently described. See also Tellenbach, *Melancholy*; Stanghellini, *Disembodied Spirits and Deanimated Bodies*; and Fuchs, "Corporealized and Disembodied Minds," for recent work on the phenomenology of depression.
27. For recent discussions of altered time-consciousness in depression, see Wyllie, "Lived Time and Psychopathology," and Broome, "Suffering and Eternal Recurrence of the Same."
28. Sechehaye, *Autobiography of a Schizophrenic Girl*, pp. 36–38, 46. There are striking parallels between some of Renee's descriptions and the unpleasant revelation of contingency that Sartre calls "nausea" (see Sartre, *Nausea*).
29. See Ratcliffe, *Feelings of Being*, chs. 2, 4 and 5, for further discussion of this kind of experience.

BIBLIOGRAPHY

Agheanu, I. T. *The Prose of Jorge Luis Borges: Existentialism and the Dynamics of Surprise*. New York: Peter Lang, 1984.

Allen, J. and Young, I., eds. *The Thinking Muse: Feminism and Modern French Philosophy*. Bloomington: Indiana University Press, 1989.

Allison, D. *Reading the New Nietzsche*. Lanham, MD: Rowman & Littlefield, 2001.

Allison, H. E. "Christianity and Nonsense." *Review of Metaphysics* 20(3) (1967): 432–60; reprinted in J. Thompson, ed., *Kierkegaard: A Collection of Critical Essays*. Garden City, NY: Doubleday, 1972, pp. 289–323, and in D. W. Conway, ed., *Søren Kierkegaard: Critical Assessments of Leading Philosophers*, vol. III. London: Routledge, 2003, pp. 7–29.

Althusser, L., Ballibar, E., and Establet, R. *Lire le Capital*, 2 vols. Paris: François Maspero, 1965.

Anderson, T. *Sartre's Two Ethics: From Authenticity to Integral Humanity*. Chicago: Open Court, 1993.

Apel, K. O. "The Apriori of the Communication Community and the Foundation of Ethics: The Problem of a Rational Foundation of Ethics in the Scientific Age." In *Towards a Transformation of Philosophy*, trans. G. Adey and D. Frisby. London: Routledge and Kegan Paul, 1980, pp. 225–300.

Arendt, H. "French Existentialism." *The Nation* (February 23, 1946): 226–28; reprinted in McBride, ed., *Sartre's Life, Times, and vision du monde*, pp. 2–4.

Aron, R. *Marxism and the Existentialists*, trans. H. Weaver, R. Addis, and J. Weightman. New York: Harper & Row, 1969.

Aronson, R. *Camus and Sartre: The Story of a Friendship and the Quarrel that Ended It*. University of Chicago Press, 2004.

Sartre's Second Critique. University of Chicago Press, 1987.

Arp, K. "Beauvoir's Concept of Bodily Alienation." In Simons, *Feminist Interpretations of Simone de Beauvoir*, pp. 161–77.

The Bonds of Freedom: Simone de Beauvoir's Existentialist Ethics. Chicago: Open Court, 2001

Askay, R. "Heidegger's Philosophy and its Implications for Psychology, Freud, and Existential Psychoanalysis." In Heidegger, *Zollikon Seminars*, pp. 301–15.

Ayer, A. J. "Novelist-Philosophers. v – Jean-Paul Sartre." *Horizon* 12(67) (July 1945): 12–25 and 12(68) (August 1945): 101–10.

Bachelard, G. *Water and Dreams*, trans. E. R. Farrell. Dallas: Pegasus, 1983.

Bair, D. *Simone de Beauvoir: A Biography.* New York: Touchstone, 1990.

Baldwin, T., ed. *Reading Merleau-Ponty: On Phenomenology of Perception.* London: Routledge, 2007.

Barbaras, R. *The Being of the Phenomenon: Merleau-Ponty's Ontology*, trans. T. Toadvine and L. Lawlor. Bloomington: Indiana University Press, 2004.

Barnes, H. E. *The Literature of Possibility: A Study in Humanistic Existentialism.* Lincoln: University of Nebraska Press, 1959.

"Response to Margaret Simons." *Philosophy Today* 24 (1998): 29–34.

Barr, A. "Introduction." In *The New American Painting.* New York: Museum of Modern Art, 1959.

Barrett, W. "Talent and Career of Jean-Paul Sartre." *Partisan Review* 13(2) (Spring 1946): 237–46.

Bartky, S. *Sympathy and Solidarity, and Other Essays.* Lanham, MD: Rowman & Littlefield, 2002.

Beaufret, J. "À propos de l'existentialisme." *Confluences* 2–6; reprinted in Beaufret, *De l'existentialisme à Heidegger.* Paris: Vrin, 1986, pp. 11–54.

Beauvoir, S. de. *Adieux: A Farewell to Sartre* [1981], trans. P. O'Brian. New York: Pantheon Books, 1984.

All Men Are Mortal [1946], trans. L. M. Friedman. Cleveland: The World Publishing Company, 1955.

The Blood of Others [1945], trans. R. Senhouse and Y. Moyse. New York: Pantheon Books, 1983.

La Cérémonie des adieux, with *Entretiens avec Jean-Paul Sartre août–septembre, 1974.* Paris: Gallimard, 1981.

Le Deuxième Sexe, 2 vols. Paris: Gallimard, 1949.

The Ethics of Ambiguity [1947], trans. B. Frechtman. New York: Philosophical Library, 1976.

"Existentialism and Popular Wisdom." In *Philosophical Writings*, pp. 203–20.

"An Eye for an Eye." In *Philosophical Writings*, pp. 245–60.

The Force of Circumstance [1963], trans. R. Howard. London: Penguin Books, 1987.
Letters to Sartre [1990], trans. Q. Hoare. New York: Arcade Publishing, 1992.
"Literature and Metaphysics." In *Philosophical Writings*, pp. 269–77.
Les Mandarins. Paris: Gallimard, 1954.
"Moral Idealism and Political Realism." In *Philosophical Writings*, pp. 175–93.
The Prime of Life [1960], trans. P. Green. Cleveland: The World Publishing Company, 1962.
"Pyrrhus and Cineas." [1944] In *Philosophical Writings*, pp. 89–149.
"A Review of *The Phenomenology of Perception*." In *Philosophical Writings*, pp. 159–64.
The Second Sex, trans. Constance Borde and Sheila Malovany-Chevallier. New York: Alfred A. Knopf, 2009.
She Came to Stay [1943], trans. Y. Moyse and R. Senhouse. Cleveland: The World Publishing Company, 1954.
Simone de Beauvoir: Philosophical Writings, ed. and trans. M. Simons and S. Le Bon de Beauvoir. Chicago and Urbana: University of Illinois Press, 2004.
Wartime Diary, ed. M. Simons and S. Le Bon de Beauvoir. Urbana and Chicago: University of Illinois Press, 2009.
Beckett, S. *Proust*. London: Chatto & Windus, 1931.
Benson, B. E. *Pious Nietzsche: Decadence and Dionysian Faith*. Bloomington: Indiana University Press, 2008.
Berg, J. H. van den. *A Different Existence: Principles of Phenomenological Psychopathology*. Pittsburgh: Duquesne University Press, 1972.
"The Human Body and the Significance of Human Movement: A Phenomenological Study." *Philosophy and Phenomenological Research* 13 (1952): 159–83.
Bernasconi, R. "The Assumption of Negritude: Aimé Césaire, Frantz Fanon, and the Vicious Circle of Racial Politics." *Parallax* 23 (2002): 69–83.
"Can Race Be Thought Of in Terms of Facticity? A Reconsideration of Sartre's and Fanon's Existential Theories of Race." In F. Raffoul and E. S. Nelson, eds., *Rethinking Facticity*. Albany: SUNY Press, 2008, pp. 195–213.
"The European Knows and Does Not Know: Fanon's Response to Sartre." In M. Silverman, ed., *Frantz Fanon's Black Skin, White Masks*. Manchester University Press, 2005, pp. 100–11.
How to Read Sartre. New York: W. W. Norton, 2006.
"On Needing Not to Know and Forgetting What One Never Knew: The Epistemology of Ignorance in Fanon's Critique of Sartre." In S. Sullivan

and N. Tuana, eds., *Race and Epistemologies of Ignorance*. Albany: SUNY Press, 2007, pp. 231–39.

Binswanger, L. *Being-in-the-world: Selected Papers of Ludwig Binswanger*, trans. J. Needleman. London: Souvenir Books, 1975.

Birchall, I. *Sartre against Stalinism*. New York: Berghahn Books, 2004.

Blattner, W. "The Concept of Death in *Being and Time*." *Man and World* 27 (1994): 49–70.

Heidegger's "Being and Time": A Reader's Guide. London: Continuum Books, 2006.

"Transcendental Conscience." Paper presented at a conference on "Conditions of Experience," University of Aarhus, Denmark, 2009.

Braudel, F. *The Mediterranean and the Mediterranean World in the Age of Philip II* [1949], 2 vols., trans. S. Reynolds. New York: Harper and Row, 1972.

Broome, M. R. "Suffering and Eternal Recurrence of the Same: The Neuroscience, Psychopathology, and Philosophy of Time". *Philosophy, Psychiatry & Psychology* 12 (2005): 187–94.

Broome, M. R. and Bortolotti, L. eds. *Psychiatry as Cognitive Neuroscience*. Oxford University Press, 2009.

Broome, M. R., Harland, R., Owen, G., and Stringaris, A., eds. *The Maudsley Reader in Phenomenological Psychiatry*. Cambridge University Press, forthcoming.

Buber, M. *I and Thou* [1923], trans. R. Gregor Smith. Edinburgh: T. & T. Clark, 1937.

Busch, T. *The Power of Consciousness and the Force of Circumstances in Sartre's Philosophy*. Bloomington: Indiana University Press, 1990.

Butler, J. *Gender Trouble: Feminism and the Subversion of Identity*. New York: Routledge, 1990.

Cabestan, P. *L'Être et la conscience. Recherches sur la psychologie et l'ontophénoménologie sartriennes*. Brussels: Éditions Ousia, 2004.

Camus, A. *Carnets 1942–1951*, trans. P. Thody. London: Hamish Hamilton, 1966.

The Fall [1956], trans. J. O'Brien. Harmondsworth: Penguin Books, 1963.

Lyrical and Critical Essays, ed. and trans. P. Thody. London: Hamish Hamilton, 1967.

The Myth of Sisyphus, trans. J. O'Brien. London: Penguin Books, 1986.

Le Mythe de Sisyphe. Paris: Gallimard, 1942.

"*La Nausée* by Jean-Paul Sartre." In *Lyrical and Critical Essays*, pp. 145–47.

"Nuptials at Tipasa." In *Lyrical and Critical Essays*, pp. 51–56.

Oeuvres complètes I: Théâtre, récits, nouvelles, ed. R. Quilliot. Paris: Pléiade, 1962.

The Plague [1947], trans. S. Gilbert. Harmondsworth: Penguin Books, 1960.

"Short Guide to Towns without a Past." In *Lyrical and Critical Essays*, pp. 111–15.

Carman, T. *Heidegger's Analytic*. Cambridge University Press, 2003.

Merleau-Ponty. Abingdon: Routledge, 2008.

Carroll, C. *The Negro a Beast*. St. Louis: American Book and Bible House, 1900.

Casey, E. S. *The Fate of Place*. Berkeley: University of California Press, 1996.

Catalano, J. *A Commentary on Jean-Paul Sartre's Being and Nothingness*. University of Chicago Press, 1974.

Cerbone, D. R. *Understanding Phenomenology*. Stocksfield: Acumen, 2006.

Chatterji, R. "Existentialist Approach to Modern American Drama." In Chatterji, ed., *Existentialism in American Literature*. Atlantic Highlands: Humanities Press, 1983, pp. 80–98.

Cherki, A. *Frantz Fanon. A Portrait*, trans. N. Benabid. Ithaca: Cornell University Press, 2006.

Ciccariello-Maher, G. "The Internal Limits of the European Gaze." *Radical Philosophy Review* 9 (2006): 139–65.

Clark, M. *Nietzsche on Truth and Philosophy*. Cambridge University Press, 1990.

Cohen-Solal, A. *Jean-Paul Sartre. A Life*, trans. A. Cancogni. New York: The New Press, 2005.

Conant, J. "Kierkegaard, Wittgenstein, and Nonsense." In T. Cohen, P. Guyer, and H. Putnam, eds., *Pursuits of Reason*. Lubbock, TX: Texas Technical University Press, 1993, pp. 195–224.

"Putting Two and Two Together: Kierkegaard, Wittgenstein and the Point of View for their Work as Author." In T. Tessin and M. von der Ruhr, eds., *Philosophy and the Grammar of Religious Belief*. New York: St. Martin's Press, 1995, pp. 248–331.

Contat, M. and Rybalka, M., eds. *Les Écrits de Sartre*. Paris: Gallimard, 1970.

The Writings of Jean-Paul Sartre, 2 vols., trans. R. C. McCleary. Evanston: Northwestern University Press, 1974.

Conway, D. *Nietzsche's Dangerous Game*. Cambridge University Press, 1997.

Cooper, D. E. *Existentialism: A Reconstruction*, 2nd edn. Oxford: Blackwell, 1999.

Cotkin, G. *Existential America*. Baltimore: Johns Hopkins University Press, 2003.

Cox, C. *Nietzsche: Naturalism and Interpretation*. Berkeley: University of California Press, 1990.

Crowell, S. "A Conversation with Maurice Natanson." In S. Crowell, ed., *The Prism of the Self: Philosophical Essays in Honor of Maurice Natanson*. Dordrecht: Kluwer Academic Publishers, 1995, pp. 289–344.

"Existentialism." *The Stanford Encyclopedia of Philosophy* (Fall 2004 edn.). http://plato.stanford.edu/entries/existentialism.

Husserl, Heidegger, and the Space of Meaning: Paths toward Transcendental Phenomenology. Evanston: Northwestern University Press, 2001.

"*Sorge* or *Selbstbewußtsein*? Heidegger and Korsgaard on the Sources of Normativity." *European Journal of Philosophy* 15 (2007): 315–33.

"Subjectivity: Locating the First-Person in *Being and Time*." *Inquiry* 44 (2001): 433–54.

Cruickshank, J. *Albert Camus and the Literature of Revolt*. New York: Oxford University Press, 1960.

Cumming, R. "Existence and Communication." *Ethics* 65(2) (January 1955): 133–55; reprinted in McBride, *The Development and Meaning of Twentieth-Century Existentialism*, pp. 79–101.

Daigle, C. and Golomb, J., eds. *Beauvoir and Sartre: The Riddle of Influence*. Bloomington: Indiana University Press, 2009.

Danto, A. *Nietzsche as Philosopher*. New York: Columbia University Press, 1967.

Darwall, S. *The Second-Person Standpoint: Morality, Respect, and Accountability*. Cambridge, MA: Harvard University Press, 2006.

Derrida, J. "The Ends of Man." [1968] In *Margins of Philosophy*, trans. A. Bass. University of Chicago Press, 1982, pp. 109–36.

The Gift of Death [1992], trans. D. Wills. University of Chicago Press, 1995.

Descartes, R. *The Philosophical Writings of Descartes*, 3 vols., ed. J. Cottingham. Cambridge University Press, 1985.

Detmer, D. *Freedom as a Value: A Critique of the Ethical Theory of Jean-Paul Sartre*. Chicago: Open Court, 1986.

Dobrez, L. A. C. *The Existential and its Exits*. New York: St. Martin's Press, 1986.

Dostoevsky, F. *The Brothers Karamazov* [1880], trans. R. Pevear and L. Volokhonsky. San Francisco: North Point Press, 1990.

Drake, D. *Intellectuals and Politics in Postwar France*. New York: Palgrave, 2002.

Dreyfus, H. L. *Being-in-the-World: A Commentary on Heidegger's* Being and Time *Division I*. Cambridge, MA: MIT Press, 1991.

"Kierkegaard on the Self." In E. F. Mooney, ed., *Ethics, Love, and Faith in Kierkegaard*. Bloomington: Indiana University Press, 2008, pp. 11–23.

"Merleau-Ponty and Recent Cognitive Science." In T. Carman and M. B. N. Hansen, eds., *The Cambridge Companion to Merleau-Ponty*. Cambridge University Press, 2005, pp. 129–50.

Dreyfus, H. L. and Rubin, J. "Kierkegaard, Division II, and Later Heidegger." In Dreyfus, *Being-in-the-World*, pp. 283–340.

Dreyfus, H. L. and Wrathall, M., eds. *A Companion to Heidegger*. Oxford: Blackwell, 2005.

Dreyfus, H. L. and Wrathall, M., eds. *A Companion to Phenomenology and Existentialism*. Oxford: Blackwell, 2006.

Epistémon [Didier Anzieu]. *Ces idées qui ont ébranlé la France*. Paris: Feyard, 1968.

Esslin, M. *The Theatre of the Absurd*. New York: Anchor Books, 1961.

Evans, C. S. "Does Kierkegaard Think Beliefs Can Be Directly Willed?" In *Kierkegaard on Faith and the Self: Collected Essays*. Waco: Baylor University Press, 2006, pp. 301–12.

Passionate Reason: Making Sense of Kierkegaard's Philosophical Fragments. Bloomington: Indiana University Press, 1992.

Evernden, N. *The Natural Alien: Humankind and Environment*. University of Toronto Press, 1985.

Fallaize, E., ed. *Simone de Beauvoir: A Critical Reader*. London: Routledge, 1998.

Fanon, F. *Black Skin, White Masks* [1952], trans. R. Philcox. New York: Grove, 2008.

"L'expérience vécue du Noir." *Esprit* 19(179) (May 1951): 657–79.

"The Lived Experience of the Black," trans. V. Moulard. In R. Bernasconi, ed., *Race*. Oxford: Blackwell, 2001, pp. 184–201.

Studies in a Dying Colonialism [1959], trans. H. Chevalier. New York: Monthly Review, 1965.

Toward the African Revolution [1964], trans. H. Chevalier. New York: Monthly Review, 1967.

The Wretched of the Earth [1961], trans. R. Philcox. New York: Grove, 2004.

Fell, J. *Heidegger and Sartre: An Essay on Being and Place*. New York: Columbia University Press, 1979

Ferreira, M. J. *Love's Grateful Striving: A Commentary on Kierkegaard's* Works of Love. Oxford University Press, 2001.

Fichte, J. G. *Foundations of Natural Right* [1797], trans. M. Baur. Cambridge University Press, 2000.

Flynn, T. *Existentialism: A Very Short Introduction.* New York: Oxford University Press, 2006.

"L'Imagination au Pouvoir. The Evolution of Sartre's Political and Social Thought." *Political Theory* 7(2) (1979): 157–90.

Sartre and Marxist Existentialism: The Test Case of Collective Responsibility. University of Chicago Press, 1984.

"Sartre as Philosopher of the Imagination." *Philosophy Today* 50 (Supplement) (2006): 106–12.

Foucault, M. *The Archaeology of Knowledge* [1969], trans. A. M. Sheridan Smith. New York: Pantheon Books, 1972.

The Order of Things: An Archaeology of the Human Sciences [1966], trans. A. M. Sheridan Smith. New York: Random House, 1973.

"What is Enlightenment?" In P. Rabinow, ed., *The Foucault Reader.* New York: Pantheon, 1984, pp. 32–50.

Francis, C. and Gontier, F. *Simone de Beauvoir.* Paris: Perrin, 1985.

Frankfurt, H. *The Importance of What We Care About. Philosophical Essays.* Cambridge University Press, 1988.

Frankl, V. *Psychotherapy and Existentialism.* New York: Washington Square Press, 1967.

Fuchs, T. "Corporealized and Disembodied Minds: A Phenomenological View of the Body in Melancholia and Schizophrenia." *Philosophy, Psychiatry & Psychology* 12 (2005): 95–107.

Fullbrook, K. and Fullbrook, E., eds. *Simone de Beauvoir and Jean-Paul Sartre: The Remaking of a Twentieth-Century Legend.* New York: Basic Books, 1994.

Gadamer, H.-G. *Truth and Method* [1960], trans. J. Weinsheimer and D. G. Marshall. London: Continuum, 2004.

Gallagher, S. "Body Schema and Intentionality." In J. Bermúdez, A. Marcel, and N. Eilan, eds., *The Body and the Self.* Cambridge, MA: MIT Press, 1995, pp. 224–44.

Gardner, S. *Sartre's Being and Nothingness.* London: Continuum, 2009.

Garff, J. *Søren Kierkegaard: A Biography.* Princeton University Press, 2005.

Gavi, P., Sartre, J.-P., and Victor, P. *On a raison de se révolter.* Paris: Gallimard, 1947.

Gerassi, J. *Jean-Paul Sartre: Hated Conscience of his Century.* University of Chicago Press, 1989.

Gillespie, M. A. and Strong, T. B., eds. *Nietzsche's New Seas: Explorations in Philosophy, Aesthetics, and Politics.* University of Chicago Press, 1988.

Gilligan, C. *In a Different Voice: Psychological Theory and Women's Development*. Cambridge, MA: Harvard University Press, 1982.

Goodale, M. and Milner, D. *Sight Unseen*. Oxford University Press, 2005.

Gooding-Williams, R. *Zarathustra's Dionysian Modernism*. Stanford University Press, 2001.

Gordon, L. *Bad Faith and Anti-Black Racism*. Atlantic Highlands: Humanities Press, 1995.

Fanon and the Crisis of European Man. London: Routledge, 1995.

Gothlin, E. "Reading Simone de Beauvoir with Martin Heidegger." In C. Card, ed., *The Cambridge Companion to Simone de Beauvoir*. Cambridge University Press, 2003, pp. 45–65.

Grassi, E. *Heidegger and the Question of Renaissance Humanism. Four Studies*, trans. U. Hemel-John and M. Krois. Medieval and Renaissance Texts and Studies 21. Binghamton: State University of New York Press, 1983.

Il Problema della metafisica platonica. Bari: Laterza, 1932.

Grassi, E., Otto, W. F., and Reinhardt, K., eds. *Geistige Überlieferung. Das zweite Jahrbuch*. Berlin: Helmut Küpper, 1942.

Grisoli, C. "Entretien avec Jean-Paul Sartre." *Paru* (13 December 1945): 5–10.

Guignon, C. "Becoming a Self: The Role of Authenticity in *Being and Time*." In Guignon, ed., *The Existentialists: Critical Essays on Kierkegaard, Nietzsche, Heidegger, and Sartre*. Lanham, MD: Rowman & Littlefield, 2004, pp. 119–32.

"Existentialism." In E. Craig, ed., *The Routledge Encyclopedia of Philosophy*, vol. III. London: Routledge, 1998.

Haar, M. "Sartre and Heidegger." In H. Silverman and F. Elliston, eds., *Jean-Paul Sartre: Contemporary Approaches to His Philosophy*. Pittsburgh: Duquesne University Press, 1980, pp. 168–87.

Hacking, I. *The Social Construction of What?* Cambridge, MA: Harvard University Press, 1999.

Halling, S. and Nill, J. D. "A Brief History of Existential-Phenomenological Psychiatry and Psychotherapy." *Journal of Phenomenological Psychology* 26 (1995): 1–45.

Hannay, A. *Kierkegaard: A Biography*. Cambridge University Press, 2001.

"Kierkegaard en het einde van de religie" (Kierkegaard and the End of Religions). *Nexus* 50 (2008): 266–78.

Hannay, A. and Marino, G. D. eds. *The Cambridge Companion to Kierkegaard*. Cambridge University Press, 1998.

Hartmann, K. *Sartre's Ontology. A Study of Being and Nothingness in the Light of Hegel's Logic*. Evanston: Northwestern University Press, 1966.

Harvey, P., ed. *The Oxford Companion to French Literature.* Oxford University Press, 1959.

Hatab, L. *A Nietzschean Defense of Democracy: An Experiment in Postmodern Politics.* Chicago: Open Court, 1995.

Nietzsche's Life Sentence: Coming to Terms with Eternal Recurrence. New York: Routledge, 2005.

Haugeland, J. "Letting Be." In S. Crowell and J. Malpas, eds., *Transcendental Heidegger.* Stanford University Press, 2007, pp. 93–103.

"Toward a New Existentialism." In *Having Thought: Essays in the Metaphysics of Mind.* Cambridge, MA: Harvard University Press, 1998, pp. 1–6.

"Truth and Finitude: Heidegger's Transcendental Existentialism." In M. Wrathall and J. Malpas, eds., *Heidegger, Authenticity, and Modernity: Essays in Honor of Hubert L. Dreyfus*, vol. 1. Cambridge, MA: MIT Press, 2000, pp. 43–78.

"Truth and Rule Following." In *Having Thought: Essays in the Metaphysics of Mind.* Cambridge, MA: Harvard University Press, 1998, pp. 305–62.

Hegel, G. W. F. *Phenomenology of Spirit* [1807], trans. A. V. Miller. Oxford University Press, 1977.

Hegel's Philosophy of Right [1821], trans. T. M. Knox. Oxford: Clarendon Press, 1942.

Heidegger, M."The Age of the World Picture." In *The Question Concerning Technology and Other Essays.* W. Lovitt. New York: Harper & Row, 1977, pp. 115–154

Aus der Erfahrung des Denkens, ed. H. Heidegger. Gesamtausgabe 13. Frankfurt: Vittorio Klostermann, 1983. (Contains material originally published 1910–76.)

The Basic Problems of Phenomenology, trans. A. Hofstadter. Bloomington: Indiana University Press, 1982.

Being and Time [1927], trans. J. Macquarrie and E. Robinson. New York: Harper and Row, 1962.

History of the Concept of Time: Prolegomena, trans. T. Kisiel. Bloomington: Indiana University Press, 1985.

Holzwege, ed. F.-W. von Herrmann. Gesamtausgabe 5. Frankfurt: Vittorio Klostermann, 1977. (Contains essays originally published 1935–46.)

"Letter on Humanism" [1947]. In *Martin Heidegger: Basic Writings*, trans. D. F. Krell. San Francisco: HarperCollins, 1993, pp. 217–65.

"Plato's Doctrine of Truth." [1942] In *Pathmarks*, ed. W. McNeill. Cambridge University Press, 1998, pp. 155–82.

"The Question Concerning Technology." [1954] In *The Question Concerning Technology and Other Essays*, trans. W. Lovitt. New York: Harper & Row, 1977, pp. 3–35.

Reden und andere Zeugisse eines Lebensweges, ed. H. Heidegger. Gesamtausgabe 16. Frankfurt: Vittorio Klostermann, 2000.

Sein und Zeit, 15th edn. Tübingen: Max Niemeyer Verlag, 1979.

Sein und Zeit, ed. W. F. von Herrmann. Gesamtausgabe 2. Frankfurt: Vittorio Klostermann, 1977.

"Spiegel-Gespräch mit Martin Heidegger." In *Reden und andere Zeugisse eines Lebensweges*, pp. 652–83.

Vom Wesen der Wahrheit. Zu Platons Höhlengleichnis und Theätet, ed. H. Mörchen. Gesamtausgabe 34. Frankfurt: Vittorio Klostermann, 1988. (Texts originally published 1931–32.)

Wegmarken, ed. F.-W. von Herrmann. Gesamtausgabe 9. Frankfurt: Vittorio Klostermann, 1976. (Contains essays originally published 1919–58.)

"The Word of Nietzsche: 'God is Dead'" [1943]. In *The Question Concerning Technology and Other Essays*, trans. W. Lovitt. New York: Harper & Row, 1977, pp. 53–114.

Zollikon Seminars: Protocols – Conversations – Letters, ed. M. Boss, trans. F. Mayr and R. Askay. Evanston: Northwestern University Press, 2001.

Heinämaa, S. *Toward a Phenomenology of Sexual Difference: Husserl, Merleau-Ponty, Beauvoir*. New York: Rowman & Littlefield, 2003.

Holmes, J. C. "This Is the Beat Generation." *New York Times Magazine* (16 November 1952): 10; reprinted in Holmes, *Nothing More to Declare*. New York: Dutton, 1967, pp. 109–15.

Husserl, E. *Cartesian Meditations. An Introduction to Phenomenology* [1931], trans. D. Cairns. The Hague: Martinus Nijhoff, 1969.

Ideas: General Introduction to Pure Phenomenology [1913], trans. W. R. Boyce-Gibson. New York: Collier Macmillan, 1962.

Ideas Pertaining to a Pure Phenomenology and to a Phenomenological Philosophy. Second Book: Studies in the Phenomenology of Constitution, trans. R. Rocewicz and A. Schuwer. Dordrecht: Kluwer, 1989.

Ideen zu einer reinen Phänomenologie und phänomenologischen Philosophie. Zweites Buch: Phänomenologische Untersuchungen zur Konstitution, ed. W. Biemel. Husserliana IV. The Hague: Martinus Nijhoff, 1952.

Irigaray, L. *An Ethics of Sexual Difference* [1984], trans. C. Burke and G. C. Gill. Ithaca: Cornell University Press, 1993.

Isaac, J. C. *Arendt, Camus, and Modern Rebellion*. New Haven: Yale University Press, 1992.

Izard, G. "Jean-Paul Sartre o una nueva etapa de la fenomenología." *Sur* 14(130) (August 1945): 53–65.

Jachec, N. *The Philosophy and Politics of Abstract Expressionism*. Cambridge University Press, 2000.

James, W. "Pragmatism and Humanism." In *The Writings of William James: A Comprehensive Edition*, ed. J. J. McDermott. University of Chicago Press, 1977.

The Principles of Psychology, vol. II. New York: Holt, 1890.

Janaway, C. *Beyond Selflessness: Reading Nietzsche's Genealogy*. Oxford University Press, 2007.

Janicaud, D. "Heidegger und Jean-Paul Sartre. Anerkennung und Abweisung." In Thomä, *Heidegger Handbuch*, pp. 410–17.

Jaspers, K. "Introduction." In *Philosophy* [1932], vol. I, trans. E. Ashton. University of Chicago Press, 1969, pp. 43–98.

Nietzsche [1936], trans. C. F. Wallraff and F. J. Schmitz. Chicago: Henry Regnery, 1965.

"Philosophical Autobiography." In P. A. Schilpp, ed., *The Philosophy of Karl Jaspers*. LaSalle, IL: Open Court, 1957, pp. 3–94.

Philosophy [1932], vol. II, trans. E. Ashton. University of Chicago Press, 1970.

Jensen, F. *Sartre and the Problem of Morality*, trans. R. V. Stone. Bloomington: Indiana University Press, 1980.

Johnson, G. A. and Smith, M. B. eds. *The Merleau-Ponty Aesthetics Reader: Philosophy and Painting*. Evanston: Northwestern University Press, 1993.

Judaken, J. *Jean-Paul Sartre and the Jewish Question*. Lincoln: University of Nebraska Press, 2006.

Judaken, J. ed. *Race after Sartre*. Albany: SUNY Press, 2008.

Kafka, F. *The Office Writings*, eds. S. Corngold, J. Greenberg, and B. Wagner; trans. E. Patton with R. Hein. Princeton: Princeton University Press, 2009.

Kant, I. *Critique of Pure Reason* [1781], trans. N. K. Smith. New York: St Martin's Press, 1965.

Kaufmann, W. *Existentialism from Dostoyevsky to Sartre*. New York: Meridian, 1989.

Existentialism, Religion, and Death: Thirteen Essays. New York: New American Library, 1976.

Keefe, T. *French Existentialist Fiction: Changing Moral Perspectives*. London: Croom Helms, 1986.

Kelly, S. "Grasping at Straws: Motor Intentionality and the Cognitive Science of Skilled Behavior." In M. Wrathall and J. Malpas, eds., *Heidegger, Coping, and Cognitive Science*. Cambridge, MA: MIT Press, 2000, pp. 161–78.

Kendler, K. S. and Parnas, J. eds. *Philosophical Issues in Psychiatry*. Baltimore: Johns Hopkins University Press, 2008.

Kern, E. *Existential Thought and Fictional Technique: Kierkegaard, Sartre, Beckett*. New Haven: Yale University Press, 1970.

Kierkegaard, S. *The Concept of Anxiety* [1844], trans. R. Thomte. Princeton University Press, 1980.

The Concept of Irony [1841], trans. H. V. Hong and E. H. Hong. Kierkegaard's Writings 2. Princeton University Press, 1989.

Concluding Unscientific Postscript [1846], ed. and trans. A. Hannay. Cambridge University Press, 2009.

Eighteen Upbuilding Discourses [1843–45], trans. H. V. Hong and E. H. Hong. Kierkegaard's Writings 5. Princeton University Press, 1990.

Either/Or [1843], trans. A. Hannay. Harmondsworth: Penguin Books, 1992.

Fear and Trembling [1843], trans. A. Hannay. New York: Penguin Books, 2003.

From the Papers of One Still Living [1838], ed. and trans. J. Watkin. Kierkegaard's Writings 1. Princeton University Press, 1997.

The Journals of Kierkegaard, ed. A. Dru. New York: Harper and Row, 1958–59.

Kierkegaard's Journals and Papers, ed. N. J. Cappelørn *et al.* Princeton University Press, 2007–.

A Literary Review (Two Ages) [1846], trans. A. Hannay. Harmondsworth: Penguin Books, 2001.

Philosophical Fragments/Johannes Climacus [1844], trans. H. V. Hong and E. H. Hong. Princeton University Press, 1985.

The Point of View for My Work as an Author [1859], trans. H. V. Hong and E. H. Hong. Kierkegaard's Writings 22. Princeton University Press, 1998.

Practice in Christianity [1850], trans. H.V. Hong and E. H. Hong. Kierkegaard's Writings 20. Princeton University Press, 1991.

The Present Age [1846], trans. A. Dru. New York: Harper & Row, 1962.

The Sickness unto Death [1849], trans. A. Hannay. London: Penguin Books, 1989.

Søren Kierkegaards Papirer, 2nd enlarged edn., ed. N. Thulstrup. Copenhagen: Gyldendal, 1968–78.

Works of Love [1847], trans. H. V. Hong and E. H. Hong. Princeton University Press, 1995.

Killinger, J. *Hemingway and the Dead Gods: A Study in Existentialism*. Lexington: University of Kentucky Press, 1960.

Korsgaard, C. *Self-Constitution: Agency, Identity, and Integrity*. Oxford University Press, 2009.

The Sources of Normativity. Cambridge University Press, 1996.

Kritzman, L. D., Reilly, B. J., and DeBevoise, M. B., eds. *The Columbia History of Twentieth-Century French Thought*. New York: Columbia University Press, 2006.

Kruks, S. *Situation and Human Existence: Freedom, Subjectivity, and Society*. London: Unwin Hyman, 1990.

Kukla, R. "The Ontology and Temporality of Conscience." *Continental Philosophy Review* 35 (2002): 1–34.

Kundera, K. *The Art of the Novel*, trans. L. Asher. London: Faber & Faber, 1988.

Laing, R. D. *The Divided Self: A Study of Sanity and Madness*. London: Tavistock Publications, 1960.

Lefebvre, H. *L'Existentialisme*. Paris: Éditions du Sagittaire, 1946.

Light, S. *Shuzo Kuki and Jean-Paul Sartre: Influence and Counter-Influence in the Early History of Existential Phenomenology*. Carbondale: Southern Illinois University Press, 1987.

Locke, J. *An Essay Concerning Human Understanding* [1689]. Oxford University Press, 1979.

Lowrie, W. "Existence as Understood by Kierkegaard and/or Sartre." *Sewanee Review* (1950): 379–401.

"Translator's Introduction." In Kierkegaard, S., *Fear and Trembling and Sickness Unto Death*. Princeton University Press 1941: pp. 133–39.

Lukács, G. *Existentialisme ou Marxisme?*, trans. E. Kelemen. Paris: Nagel, 1948.

MacIntyre, A. *After Virtue: A Study in Moral Theory*. London: Duckworth, 1981.

Mackey, L. *Kierkegaard: A Kind of Poet*. Philadelphia: University of Pennsylvania Press, 1971.

Macquarrie, J. *Existentialism: An Introduction, Guide and Assessment*. London: Penguin Books, 1973.

Macy, D. *Frantz Fanon. A Biography*. New York: Picador, 2000.

Magny, C.-E. *Littérature et critique*. Paris: Payot, 1971.

Maistre, J. de. *Considerations on France* [1797], trans. R. A. Lebrun. Montreal: McGill-Queen's University Press, 1974.

Malpas, J. *Place and Experience*. Cambridge University Press, 1999.

Malraux, A. *The Temptation of the West* [1926], trans. R. Hollander. New York: Vintage, 1961.

The Voices of Silence [1951], trans. S. Gilbert. Princeton University Press, 1978.

Mannoni, O. *Prospero and Caliban* [1956], trans. P. Powlesland. London: Methuen, 1956.

Manser, A. *Sartre, a Philosophical Study*. New York: Oxford University Press, 1967.

Marcano, D. "Sartre and the Social Construction of Race." In R. Bernasconi, ed. with S. Cook, *Race and Racism in Continental Philosophy.* Bloomington: Indiana University Press, 2003, pp. 214–26.

Marcel, G. *Being and Having* [1928–33], trans. K. Farrar. London: Dacre, 1949.

Creative Fidelity [1940], trans. R. Rosthal. New York: Fordham University Press, 2002.

The Philosophy of Existence, trans. M. Harari. New York: Harvill, 1948.

The Philosophy of Existentialism, trans. R. Rosthal. New York: Philosophical Library, 1956.

Maurois, A. *From Proust to Camus. Profiles of Modern French Writers*, trans. C. Morse and R. Bruce. London: Weidenfeld and Nicolson, 1966.

May, R., Angel, E., and Ellenberger, H. F., eds. *Existence: A New Dimension in Psychiatry and Psychology.* New York: Simon & Schuster, 1958.

McBride, W. "Les premiers comptes rendus de *L'Être et le néant.*" In I. Galster, ed., *La Naissance du "phénomène Sartre": raisons d'un succès 1938–1945*. Paris: Éditions du Seuil, 2001, pp. 184–99.

Sartre's Political Theory. Bloomington: Indiana University Press, 1991.

McBride, W., ed. *The Development and Meaning of Twentieth-Century Existentialism.* Sartre and Existentialism 1. New York: Garland, 1997.

McBride, W., ed. *Sartre's Life, Times, and vision du monde.* Sartre and Existentialism 3. New York: Garland, 1997.

Mehring, R. and Thomä, D. "Eine Chronik. Leben und Werk Martin Heideggers im Kontext." In Thomä, *Heidegger Handbuch*, pp. 515–39.

Memmi, A. *The Colonizer and the Colonized* [1957], trans. H. Greenfield. Boston: Beacon Press, 1967.

Mercier, V. "The Uneventful Event." *Irish Times* (18 February 1956): 6.

Merleau-Ponty, M. "Le Doute de Cézanne." In *Sens et non-sens.* NRF collection Bibliothèque de philosophie. Paris: Gallimard, 1996, pp. 13–33; originally published in *Fontaine* 8 (December 1945). "Cézanne's Doubt." In *Sense and Non-Sense*, trans. H. L. Dreyfus and P. A. Dreyfus. Evanston: Northwestern University Press, 1964, pp. 9–25; and in *The Merleau-Ponty Aesthetics Reader*, ed. G. A. Johnson, trans. M. B. Smith. Evanston: Northwestern University Press, 1993, pp. 59–75.

L'Œil et l'esprit. Paris: Gallimard, 1964; originally published in *Art de France* 1(1) (January 1961). "Eye and Mind." In *The Primacy of Perception and Other Essays on Phenomenological Psychology, the Philosophy of Art, History and Politics*, ed. J. M. Edie. Evanston: Northwestern University Press, 1964, pp. 159–190; and in *The Merleau-Ponty Aesthetics Reader*, ed. G. A. Johnson, trans. M. B. Smith. Evanston: Northwestern University Press, 1993, pp. 121–50.

Humanism and Terror: An Essay on the Communist Problem, trans. J. O'Neill. Boston: Beacon Press, 1969.

Humanisme et terreur. Paris: Gallimard, 1947.

"Indirect Language and the Voices of Silence." [1952] In *Signes*. Paris: Gallimard, 1960; *Signs*, trans. R. McCleary. Evanston: Northwestern University Press, 1964, pp. 39–83.

"Metaphysics and the Novel." [1945] In *Sense and Non-Sense*, trans. H. L. Dreyfus and P. A. Dreyfus. Evanston: Northwestern University Press, 1964, pp. 26–40.

Phénoménologie de la perception. Paris: Gallimard, 1945.

Phenomenology of Perception, trans. C. Smith. London: Routledge, 2002.

The Visible and the Invisible, trans. A. Lingis. Evanston: Northwestern University Press, 1968.

Le Visible et l'invisible, ed. C. Lefort. Paris: Gallimard, 1964.

Montaigne, M. de. "Of the Inequality That Is among Us." In *The Complete Essays of Montaigne*, ed. and trans. D. M. Frame. Stanford University Press, 1998, pp. 189–95.

Moran, D. *Introduction to Phenomenology*. London: Routledge, 2000.

Moran, R. *Authority and Estrangement. An Essay on Self-Knowledge*. Princeton University Press, 2001.

Morin, A. "Possible Links between Self-Awareness and Inner Speech." *Journal of Consciousness Studies* 12.4–5 (2005): 115–34.

Morris, K. *Sartre*. Oxford: Blackwell, 2008

Mouille, J.-M., ed. *Sartre et la phénoménologie*. Paris: ENS Éditions, 2000.

Mulhall, S. *Heidegger and* Being and Time. London: Routledge, 1996.

Inheritance and Originality: Wittgenstein, Heidegger, Kierkegaard. Oxford University Press, 2001.

Murchland, B. *The Arrow That Flies by Day. Existential Images of the Human Condition from Socrates to Hannah Arendt: A Philosophy for Dark Times*. Lanham, MD: University Press of America, 2008.

Murdoch, I. *Sartre: Romantic Rationalist* [1953]. London: Fontana, 1967.

The Sovereignty of Good [1970]. London: Ark Paperbacks, 1986.

Natanson, M. *A Critique of Jean-Paul Sartre's Ontology*. New York: Haskell, 1972.

The Erotic Bird: Phenomenology in Literature. Princeton University Press, 1998.

Nehamas, A. *Nietzsche: Life as Literature*. Cambridge, MA: Harvard University Press, 1985.

Nietzsche, F. *The Antichrist* [1888]. In *The Portable Nietzsche*, pp. 565–656.

Beyond Good and Evil: Prelude to a Philosophy of the Future [1886], trans. W. Kaufmann. New York: Random House, 1966.
The Birth of Tragedy [1872], trans. W. Kaufmann. New York: Vintage, 1967.
The Case of Wagner [1888], trans. W. Kaufmann. New York: Vintage, 1967.
Daybreak [1881], trans. R. J. Hollingdale. Cambridge University Press, 1997.
Ecce Homo [1908], trans. W. Kaufmann. New York: Vintage, 1967.
The Gay Science: With a Prelude in Rhymes and an Appendix of Songs [1882–87], trans. W. Kaufmann. New York: Random House, 1974.
Human, All Too Human [1878], trans. R. J. Hollingdale. Cambridge University Press, 1996.
Nietzsche contra Wagner [1895]. In *The Portable Nietzsche*, pp. 661–83.
On the Genealogy of Morals [1887], ed. K. Ansell-Pearson, trans. C. Diethe. New York: Cambridge University Press, 2007.
On the Uses and Disadvantages of History for Life [1873]. In *Untimely Meditations*, trans. R. J. Hollingdale. Cambridge University Press, 1997.
"On Truth and Lie in a Nonmoral Sense." In *Philosophy and Truth*, pp. 79–97.
Philosophy and Truth: Selections from Nietzsche's Notebooks of the Early 1870s, ed. and trans. D. Breazeale. Atlantic Highlands: Humanities Press, 1979.
The Portable Nietzsche, ed. and trans. W. Kaufmann. New York: Viking, 1954.
Sämtliche Werke. Kritische Studienausgabe, 15 vols., ed. G. Colli and M. Montinari. Berlin: Walter de Gruyter, 1980–.
Schopenhauer as Educator [1874]. In *Untimely Meditations*, pp. 124–94.
Thus Spoke Zarathustra: A Book for All and None [1883–92]. In *The Portable Nietzsche*, pp. 103–439.
Twilight of the Idols [1888]. In *The Portable Nietzsche*, pp. 463–564.
Untimely Meditations [1873–76], trans. R. J. Hollingdale. Cambridge University Press, 1997.
The Will to Power, ed. W. Kaufmann, trans. R. J. Hollingdale. New York: Vintage, 1967.

Nivison, D. S. *The Ways of Confucianism*. LaSalle, IL: Open Court, 1996.

Noddings, N. *Caring: A Feminine Approach to Ethics and Moral Motivation*. Berkeley: University of California Press, 1984.

Nussbaum, M. *Cultivating Humanity: A Classical Defense of Reform in Liberal Education*. Cambridge University Press, 1997.

The Fragility of Goodness: Luck and Ethics in Greek Tragedy and Philosophy. Cambridge University Press, 1986.

Hiding from Humanity: Disgust, Shame, and the Law. Princeton University Press, 2004.

O'Brien, C. C. "Camus, Algeria, and *The Fall*." *New York Review of Books* (9 October 1969): 6, 8, 10–12.

O'Brien, W. and Embree, L., eds. *The Existential Phenomenology of Simone de Beauvoir*. Dordrecht: Kluwer Academic Publishers, 2001.

Olafson, F. *Heidegger and the Philosophy of Mind*. New Haven: Yale University Press, 1987.

Oliver, K., ed. *Ethics, Politics, and Difference in Julia Kristeva's Writings*. New York: Routledge, 1993.

Ortega y Gasset, J. "History as a System." [1935] In *History as a System and Other Essays toward a Philosophy of History*, trans. H. Weyl. New York: W. W. Norton, 1961, pp. 165–233.

"Man the Technician." In *History as a System and Other Essays toward a Philosophy of History*, trans. H. Weyl. New York: W. W. Norton, 1961, pp. 87–161.

Ott, H. *Martin Heidegger. Unterwegs zu seiner Biographie*. Frankfurt: Campus, 1988.

Oxford English Dictionary, 2nd edn., vol. v. Oxford: Clarendon Press, 1989.

Pascal, B. *Pascal's Pensées*, ed. and trans. W. F. Trotter. Introduction by T. S. Eliot. New York: Dutton, 1958.

Pascal's Pensées, trans. H. F. Stewart. New York: Modern Library, n.d.

Perrin, M. *Avec Sartre au Stalag XII D*. Paris: Delarge, 1980.

Philipse, H. "Heidegger and Ethics." *Inquiry* 42 (1999): 439–74.

Pippin, R. *Nietzsche, Psychology, and First Philosophy*. University of Chicago Press, 2010.

Plath, S. *The Bell Jar*. London: Faber & Faber, 1966.

Plato. *Gorgias*. In *The Collected Dialogues of Plato*, eds., E. Hamilton and H. Cairns. Princeton: Princeton University Press, 1969, pp. 229–307.

Phaedrus. In *The Collected Dialogues of Plato*, eds. E. Hamilton and H. Cairns. Princeton: Princeton University Press, 1969, pp. 475–525.

Poellner, P. *Nietzsche and Metaphysics*. New York: Oxford University Press, 1995.

Polt, R., ed. *Heidegger's Being and Time: Critical Essays*. Lanham, MD: Rowman & Littlefield, 2005.

Priest, S. *Merleau-Ponty*. London: Routledge, 1998.

The Subject in Question: Sartre's Critique of Husserl in The Transcendence of the Ego. London: Routledge, 2000.

"Question on Letter to Charles Morris on Heidegger & Sartre." http://newsgroups.derkeiler.com/Archive/Sci/sci.philosophy.meta/2005-12/msg00005.html.

Raffoul, F. *Heidegger and the Subject*, trans. D. Pettigrew and G. Recco. New Jersey: Humanities Press, 1998.

Raschid, S., ed. *R. D. Laing: Contemporary Perspectives*. London: Free Association Books, 2005.

Ratcliffe, M. *Feelings of Being: Phenomenology, Psychiatry, and the Sense of Reality*. Oxford University Press, 2008.

Rethinking Commonsense Psychology: A Critique of Folk Psychology, Theory of Mind and Simulation. Basingstoke: Palgrave Macmillan, 2007.

"Understanding Existential Changes in Psychiatric Illness: The Indispensability of Phenomenology." In Broome and Bortolotti, eds., *Psychiatry as Cognitive Neuroscience*, pp. 223–44.

Rée, J. and Chamberlain, J., eds. *Kierkegaard: A Critical Reader*. Oxford: Blackwell, 1998.

Reginster, B. *The Affirmation of Life: Nietzsche on Overcoming Nihilism*. Cambridge, MA: Harvard University Press, 2009.

Reisman, D. *Sartre's Phenomenology*. London: Continuum, 2007.

Reynolds, J. *Understanding Existentialism*. Chesham: Acumen, 2006.

Richardson, J. "Nietzsche's Power Ontology." In J. Richardson and B. Leiter, eds., *Nietzsche*. Oxford University Press, 2001, pp. 150–85.

Nietzsche's System. New York: Oxford University Press, 1996.

Ricoeur, P. "Philosophy after Kierkegaard." In J. Rée and J. Chamberlain, eds., *Kierkegaard: A Critical Reader*, 1998, pp. 9–25.

Rigaud, Jan F., ed. and trans. *Albert Camus and Jean Grenier: Correspondence, 1932–1960*. Lincoln: University of Nebraska Press, 2003.

Rizzolatti, G., Fogassi, L., and Gallese, V. "Mirrors of the Mind." *Scientific American* 295(5) (November 2006): 54–61.

Roberts, G. *Temas existenciales en la novela española de postguerra*. Madrid: Editorial Gredos, 1973.

Rorty, R. *Contingency, Irony, and Solidarity*. Cambridge University Press, 1989.

Roumain, J. "Bois-d'Ébène." In Senghor, L. S., ed. *Anthologie de la nouvelle poesie negre et malgache de langue francaise*. Paris: Presses Universitaires de France, 1948 pp. 113–118.

Rouse, J. *How Scientific Practices Matter: Reclaiming Philosophical Naturalism*. University of Chicago Press, 2002.

Rubini, R. "Philology as Philosophy: The Sources of Ernesto Grassi's Postmodern Humanism." *Annali d'italianistica* 26 (2008): 223–48.

Sallis, J. *Crossings: Nietzsche and the Space of Tragedy.* University of Chicago Press, 1991.

Sartre, J.-P. *Anti-Semite and Jew* [1946], trans. G. J. Becker. New York: Schocken, 1976.

Baudelaire [1947], trans. M. Turnell. London: Hamish Hamilton, 1964.

Being and Nothingness: An Essay on Phenomenological Ontology [1943], trans. H. Barnes. New York: Washington Square Press, 1992.

"Black Orpheus" [1948]. In R. Bernasconi, ed., *Race.* Oxford: Blackwell, 2001, pp. 115–42.

"Camus' *The Outsider.*" In *Literary Essays,* pp. 24–41.

Carnets de la drôle de guerre. Septembre 1939–mars 1940, new edn., enlarged. Paris: Gallimard, 1995.

Cahiers pour une morale. Paris: Gallimard, 1983.

Colonialism and Neocolonialism [1964], trans. A. Haddow, S. Brewer, and T. McWilliams. London: Routledge, 2001.

The Communists and Peace, with *A Reply to Claude Lefort* [1952–53], trans. M. H. Fletcher and P. R. Berk. New York: George Braziller, 1968.

Critique of Dialectical Reason [1960], 2 vols.: vol. I, *Theory of Practical Ensembles,* 2nd edn., rev., trans. A. Sheridan-Smith ; vol. II, 2nd edn., trans. Q. Hoare (London: Verso Books, 2004 and 2006 respectively).

"Les Damnés de la Terre." In *Situations v.* Paris: Gallimard, 1961, pp. 167–93.

The Devil and the Good Lord [1951], trans. K. Black. New York: Vintage Books, 1960.

L'Être et le néant. Paris: Gallimard, 1943.

Existentialism is a Humanism [1946], trans. C. Macomber. New Haven: Yale University Press, 2007.

Foreword to Paul Nizan, *Aden Arabie.* Boston: Beacon Press, 1970, pp. 9–56.

"I Discovered Jazz in America," trans. R. de Toledano. *Saturday Review of Literature* (November 29, 1947): 48–49.

L'Idiot de la famille, 3 vols. Paris: Gallimard, 1971–72; new edn. with appendix by Arlette Elkaïm Sartre, *Notes sur "Madame Bovary",* Paris: Gallimard, 1988; *The Family Idiot. Gustave Flaubert 1821–1857,* 5 vols., trans. C. Cosman. University of Chicago Press, 1981–93.

"The Itinerary of a Thought." In *Between Existentialism and Marxism,* trans. J. Matthews. New York: William Morrow, 1976, pp. 33–64.

"Jean-Paul Sartre Répond." *L'Arc* 30 (1966): 87–96.

"John Dos Passos and *1919.*" In *Literary Essays,* pp. 88–96.

Lettres au Castor et à Quelques Autres, 2 vols. Paris: Gallimard, 1983.

Life/Situations. Essays Written and Spoken. New York: Pantheon Books, 1977.

Literary Essays, trans. A. Michelson. New York: Philosophical Library, 1957.

"Materialism and Revolution." In *Literary and Philosophical Essays*, ed. and trans. A. Michelson. New York: Collier Books, 1962, pp. 189–256.

Nausea [1938], trans. L. Alexander. New York: New Directions, 1964.

No Exit and Three Other Plays [1944], trans. S. Gilbert. New York: Vintage International Edition, 1989.

Notebooks for an Ethics, trans. D. Pellauer. University of Chicago Press, 1992.

On Genocide, with a summary of the evidence and the judgments of the International War Crimes Tribunal by Arlette Elkaïm Sartre. Boston: Beacon Press, 1968.

"Orphée noir." In *Situations III*. Paris: Gallimard, 1949, pp. 249–86.

"Qu'est-ce que la littérature?" In *Situations II*. Paris: Gallimard, 1948, pp. 55–330.

"Réponse à Albert Camus." In *Situations IV*. Paris: Gallimard, 1964, pp. 90–129; originally published in *Les Temps Modernes* 82 (August 1952).

The Reprieve [1945], trans. E. Sutton. Harmondsworth: Penguin Books, 1968.

La Résponsibilité de l'écrivain. Paris: Éditions Verdier, 1998.

Saint Genet. Actor and Martyr [1952], trans. B. Frechtman. New York: New American Library, 1963.

Search for a Method [1957], trans. H. E. Barnes. New York: Vintage, 1968.

"The Singular Universal." In J. Thompson, ed., P. Goldberger, trans., *Kierkegaard: A Collection of Critical Essays*. New York: Doubleday, 1972, pp. 230–65.

Situations, 10 vols. Paris: Gallimard, 1947–76.

The Transcendence of the Ego [1936], trans. F. Williams and R. Kirkpatrick. New York: The Noonday Press, 1957.

War Diaries: Notebooks from a Phoney War, trans. Q. Hoare. London: Verso, 1984.

What is Literature? and Other Essays [1947]. Cambridge, MA: Harvard University Press, 1988.

Sartre, J.-P. and Lévy, B. *Hope Now*, trans. A. Van Den Hoven. University of Chicago Press, 1996.

Sartre, J.-P., Rousset, D., and Rosenthal, G. *Entretiens sur la politique*. Paris: Gallimard, 1949.

Sass, L. A. *Madness and Modernism: Insanity in the Light of Modern Art, Literature, and Thought*. New York: Basic Books, 1992.

The Paradoxes of Delusion: Wittgenstein, Schreber, and the Schizophrenic Mind. Ithaca: Cornell University Press, 1994.

"Self and World in Schizophrenia: Three Classic Approaches." *Philosophy, Psychiatry & Psychology* 8 (2001): 251–70.

Schacht, R. *Making Sense of Nietzsche*. Urbana: University of Illinois Press, 1995.

Nietzsche. London: Routledge and Kegan Paul, 1983.

"Philosophical Anthropology: What, Why and How." *Philosophy and Phenomenological Research* 50 (Supplement 1990): 155–76.

Schacht, R., ed. *Nietzsche: Selections*. New York: Macmillan, 1993.

Scheler, M. *On the Eternal in Man*, trans. B. Noble. London: SCM Press, 1960.

Schilpp, P. A., ed. *The Philosophy of Jean-Paul Sartre*. LaSalle, IL: Open Court, 1981.

Schönbaumsfeld, G. *A Confusion of the Spheres: Kierkegaard and Wittgenstein on Philosophy and Religion*. Oxford University Press, 2007.

Schrader, G. A. "Basic Problems of Philosophical Ethics. On Lewis White Beck: A Commentary on Kant's *Critique of Practical Reason*." *Archiv für Geschichte der Philosophie* 46 (1964): 102–17.

Schrift, A. "Judith Butler: une nouvelle existentialiste?" *Philosophy Today* (Spring 2001): 12–23.

Nietzsche and the Question of Interpretation: Between Hermeneutics and Deconstruction. New York: Routledge, 1990.

Schwarzer, A. *After The Second Sex*, trans. M. Howarth. New York: Pantheon Books, 1984.

Sechehaye, M., ed. *Autobiography of a Schizophrenic Girl*. New York: Signet, 1970.

Senghor, L.S., ed. *Anthologie de la nouvelle poésie nègre et malgache de langue française*. Paris: Presses Universitaires de France, 1948.

Sherman, D. *Camus*. Chichester: Wiley-Blackwell, 2009.

Simons, M. *Beauvoir and* The Second Sex. Lanham, MD: Rowman & Littlefield, 1999.

Simons, M. A., ed. *Feminist Interpretations of Simone de Beauvoir*. University Park: Pennsylvania State University Press, 1995.

Sluga, H. *Heidegger's Crisis. Philosophy and Politics in Nazi Germany*. Cambridge, MA: Harvard University Press, 1993.

Soll, I. "Attitudes toward Life: Nietzsche's Existentialist Project." *International Studies in Philosophy* 34(3) (2002): 69–81.

Solomon, R. *Dark Feelings, Grim Thoughts: Experience and Reflection in Camus and Sartre*. Oxford University Press, 2006.

Spiegelberg, H. *Phenomenology in Psychology and Psychiatry: A Historical Introduction*. Evanston: Northwestern University Press, 1972.

Sprintzen, D. *Camus: A Critical Examination*. Philadelphia: Temple University Press, 1988.

Stanghellini, G. *Disembodied Spirits and Deanimated Bodies: The Psychopathology of Common Sense*. Oxford University Press, 2004.

Stewart, J., ed., *The Debate between Sartre and Merleau-Ponty*. Evanston: Northwestern University Press, 1998.

Taylor, C. *The Ethics of Authenticity*. Cambridge, MA: Harvard University Press, 1992.

"Merleau-Ponty and the Epistemological Picture." In T. Carman and M. B. N. Hansen, eds., *The Cambridge Companion to Merleau-Ponty*. Cambridge University Press, 2005, pp. 26–49.

The Sources of the Self: The Making of the Modern Identity. Cambridge, MA: Harvard University Press, 1989.

Thomä, D., ed. *Heidegger Handbuch. Leben – Werk – Wirkung*. Stuttgart and Weimar: J. B. Metzler, 2003.

Thomson, I. *Heidegger on Ontotheology: Technology and the Politics of Education*. Cambridge University Press, 2005.

"Heidegger's Phenomenology of Death in *Being and Time*." In M. Wrathall, ed., *The Cambridge Companion to "Being and Time."* Cambridge University Press, in press.

Tellenbach, H. *Melancholy: History of the Problem, Endogeneity, Typology, Pathogenesis, Clinical Considerations*. Pittsburgh: Duquesne University Press, 1980.

Tillich, P. *The Courage to Be*. New Haven: Yale University Press, 1952.

Todd, O. *Albert Camus: A Life*. London: Chatto & Windus, 1997.

Towarnicki, F. de. *À la rencontre de Heidegger. Souvenirs d'un messager de la Forêt-Noire*. Paris: Gallimard, 1993.

Van Deurzen-Smith, E. *Everyday Mysteries: Existential Dimensions of Psychotherapy*. London: Routledge, 1996.

Wahl, J. *A Short History of Existentialism*, trans. F. Williams and S. Maron. New York: Philosophical Library, 1949.

Walsh, S. *Living Poetically: Kierkegaard's Existential Aesthetics*. University Park: Pennsylvania State University Press, 1994.

Warnock, M. *Existentialism*. Oxford University Press, 1970.

Wartenberg, T. E. *Existentialism: A Beginner's Guide*. Oxford: Oneworld, 2008.

Weiss, G. *Intertwinings: Interdisciplinary Encounters with Merleau-Ponty*. Albany: SUNY Press, 2008.

Westphal, M. *Becoming a Self: A Reading of Kierkegaard's* Concluding Unscientific Postscript. West Lafayette: Purdue University Press, 1996.

God, Guilt, and Death: An Existential Phenomenology of Religion. Bloomington: Indiana University Press, 1984.

Wider, K. *The Bodily Nature of Consciousness. Sartre and Contemporary Philosophy of Mind.* Ithaca: Cornell University Press, 1997.

Williams, B. *Ethics and the Limits of Philosophy.* Cambridge, MA: Harvard University Press, 1985.

Wilson, C. *The Outsider* [1956]. New York: Jeremy P. Tarcher, 1982.

Winsler, A., Diaz, R. M., and Montero, I. "The Role of Private Speech in the Transition from Collaborative to Independent Task Performance in Young Children." *Early Childhood Research Quarterly* 12 (1997): 57–79.

Withy, K. "Heidegger's Angst is Not (Only) a Mood." Paper presented at the 11th Annual Meeting of the International Society for Phenomenological Studies, Pacific Grove, CA, 2009.

Wittgenstein, L. *On Certainty*, ed. G. E. M. Anscombe and G. H. von Wright. New York: Harper & Row, 1972.

Philosophical Investigations, 2nd edn., trans. G. E. M. Anscombe. Oxford: Blackwell, 1958.

Wolpert, L. *Malignant Sadness: The Anatomy of Depression.* London: Faber & Faber, 1999.

Wolterstorff, N. *Divine Discourse: Philosophical Reflections on the Claim That God Speaks.* Cambridge University Press, 1995.

Wood, P. "A Revisionary Account of the Apotheosis and Demise of the Philosophy of the Subject: Hegel, Sartre, Heidegger, Structuralism and Postructuralism." In D. Minahen, ed., *Sartre Revisited.* New York: St. Martin's Press, 1997, pp. 165–95

Understanding Sartre. Columbia: University of South Carolina Press, 1990.

Wordsworth, W. *The Friend*, vol. III. London: Bell, 1884.

Wyllie, M. "Lived Time and Psychopathology." *Philosophy, Psychiatry & Psychology* 12 (2005): 173–85.

Zimmerman, M. *Heidegger's Confrontation with Modernity: Technology, Politics, Art.* Bloomington: Indiana University Press, 1990.

INDEX

OTHER VOLUMES IN THE SERIES OF CAMBRIDGE COMPANIONS

GADAMER *Edited by* ROBERT J. DOSTAL
GALEN *Edited by* R. J. HANKINSON
GALILEO *Edited by* PETER MACHAMER
GERMAN IDEALISM *Edited by* KARL AMERIKS
GREEK AND ROMAN PHILOSOPHY *Edited by* DAVID SEDLEY
HABERMAS *Edited by* STEPHEN K. WHITE
HAYEK *Edited by* EDWARD FESER
HEGEL *Edited by* FREDERICK C. BEISER
HEGEL AND NINETEENTH-CENTURY PHILOSOPHY *Edited by* FREDERICK C. BEISER
HEIDEGGER 2nd edition *Edited by* CHARLES GUIGNON
HOBBES *Edited by* TOM SORELL
HOBBE'S LEVIATHAN *Edited by* PATRICIA SPRINGBORG
HUME 2nd edition *Edited by* DAVID FATE NORTON and JACQUELINE TAYLOR
HUSSERL *Edited by* BARRY SMITH and DAVID WOODRUFF SMITH
WILLIAM JAMES *Edited by* RUTH ANNA PUTNAM
KANT *Edited by* PAUL GUYER
KANT AND MODERN PHILOSOPHY *Edited by* PAUL GUYER
KANT'S CRITIQUE OF PURE REASON *Edited by* PAUL GUYER KEYNES ROGER E. BACKHOUSE and BRADLEY W. BATEMAN
KIERKEGAARD *Edited by* ALASTAIR HANNAY and GORDON DANIEL MARINO
LEIBNIZ *Edited by* NICHOLAS JOLLEY
LEVINAS *Edited by* SIMON CRITCHLEY and ROBERT BERNASCONI
LOCKE *Edited by* VERE CHAPPELL
LOCKE'S 'ESSAY CONCERNING HUMAN UNDERSTANDING' *Edited by* LEX NEWMAN
LOGICAL EMPIRICISM *Edited by* ALAN RICHARDSON and T. UEBEL
MAIMONIDES *Edited by* KENNETH SEESKIN

MALEBRANCHE *Edited by* STEVEN NADLER
MARX *Edited by* TERRELL CARVER
MEDIEVAL JEWISH PHILOSOPHY *Edited by* DANIEL H. FRANK and OLIVER LEAMAN
MEDIEVAL PHILOSOPHY *Edited by* A. S. MCGRADE
MERLEAU-PONTY *Edited by* TAYLOR CARMAN and MARK B. N. HANSEN
MILL *Edited by* JOHN SKORUPSKI
MONTAIGNE *Edited by* ULLRICH LANGER
NEWTON *Edited by* I. BERNARD COHEN and GEORGE E. SMITH
NIETZSCHE *Edited by* BERND MAGNUS and KATHLEEN HIGGINS
NOZICK'S *ANARCHY, STATE AND UTOPIA* *Edited by* RALF BADER and JOHN MEADOWCROFT
OCKHAM *Edited by* PAUL VINCENT SPADE
THE 'ORIGIN OF SPECIES' *Edited by* MICHAEL RUSE and ROBERT J. RICHARDS
PASCAL *Edited by* NICHOLAS HAMMOND
PEIRCE *Edited by* CHERYL MISAK
PHILO *Edited by* ADAM KAMESAR
THE PHILOSOPHY OF BIOLOGY *Edited by* DAVID L. HULL and MICHAEL RUSE
PIAGET *Edited by* ULRICH MÜLLER, JEREMY I. M. CARPENDALE and LESLIE SMITH
PLATO *Edited by* RICHARD KRAUT
PLATO'S REPUBLIC *Edited by* G. R. F. FERRARI
PLOTINUS *Edited by* LLOYD P. GERSON
PICO DELLA MIRANDOLA: NEW ESSAYS *Edited by* M. V. DOUGHERTY
QUINE *Edited by* ROGER F. GIBSON JR.
RAWLS *Edited by* SAMUEL FREEMAN
THOMAS REID *Edited by* TERENCE CUNEO and RENÉ VAN WOUDENBERG
RENAISSANCE PHILOSOPHY *Edited by* JAMES HANKINS
ROUSSEAU *Edited by* PATRICK RILEY
BERTRAND RUSSELL *Edited by* NICHOLAS GRIFFIN
SARTRE *Edited by* CHRISTINA HOWELLS

SCHOPENHAUER *Edited by* CHRISTOPHER JANAWAY
THE SCOTTISH ENLIGHTENMENT *Edited by* ALEXANDER BROADIE
ADAM SMITH *Edited by* KNUD HAAKONSSEN
SOCRATES *Edited by* DONALD MORRISON
SPINOZA *Edited by* DON GARRETT
SPINOZA'S ETHICS *Edited by* OLLI KOISTINEN
THE STOICS *Edited by* BRAD INWOOD
LEO STRAUSS *Edited by* STEVEN B. SMITH
TOCQUEVILLE *Edited by* CHERYL B. WELCH
WITTGENSTEIN *Edited by* HANS SLUGA and DAVID STERN

Made in United States
North Haven, CT
04 February 2024